Contemporary Issues in Taxation Research

Volume 2

In memory of

Tim Vollans (1953 – 2013)

Contemporary Issues in Taxation Research

Volume 2

David Salter and Lynne Oats

Contemporary Issues in Taxation Research, Volume 2
Copyright © David Salter & Lynne Oats 2016

For more information, contact Fiscal Publications, Unit 100, The Guildhall Edgbaston Park Road, Birmingham, B15 2TU, UK or visit: http://www.fiscalpublications.com

All rights reserved by AccountingEducation.com Ltd 2008. The text of this publication, or any part thereof, may not be reproduced or transmitted in any form or by any means, electronic or mechanical, including photocopying, recording, storage in an information retrieval system, or otherwise, without prior permission of the publisher.

While the Publisher has taken all reasonable care in the preparation of this book the publishers make no representation, express or implied, with regard to the accuracy of the information contained in this book and cannot accept any legal responsibility or liability for any errors or omissions from the book or the consequences thereof.

Products and services that are referred to in this book may be either trademarks and/or registered trademarks of their respective owners. The publishers and authors make no claim to these trademarks.

ISBN 978-1906201296

 Typesetting by Mac Bride.

Cover design by Filter Design Ltd

Printed in Great Britain by Lightning Source, Milton Keynes, UK

Contents

	List of Contributors	viii
1	Contemporary Issues in Taxation Research: An Overview David Salter and Lynne Oats	1
2	Owner Occupied Housing Taxation: A Vertical Equity Evaluation of the UK and US Tax Systems Phyllis Alexander	5
3	Tax treatment of virtual money Aleksandra Bal	25
4	From Moral Duty to Legal Rule: A Blueprint for Reform of Taxpayer Rights to Fair Treatment in the UK and Australia John Bevacqua	37
5	Assessing the Legal Status of HMRC Guidance: Some first thoughts Lynda Burkinshaw and Jane Frecknall-Hughes	66
6	Power of Authorities and Trust in Authorities Determine the Interaction Climate and Tax Compliance Katharina Gangl, Eva Hofmann, Barbara Hartl and Erich Kirchler	87
7	Corporate Social Responsibility and Tax Planning: Rules and Principles Hans Gribnau	103
8	Tax risk management and tax compliance behaviour: Findings from a study of large Australian companies Catriona Lavermicocca and Margaret McKerchar	126
9	Taxation and Trade: Examining the Relationship Between SADC Trade Agreements and Tax Agreements Puseletso Letete	170
10	Developing a Customs Agents Compliance Behaviour Model in relation to Import Tax in Malaysia: A Study inspired by the Theory of Planned Behaviour Mirza Mohamed, Andrew Grainger and Jane Guinery	187

11 Alignment of Tax Planning Functions and Activities with
    Corporate Strategy in Multinational Corporations   215
    Emer Mulligan, James Gawley, and James Cunningham

12 An Evaluation of Two Alternative Approaches to Corporate-
    Shareholder Taxation of Inbound Investment for Australia   245
    C John Taylor

ACKNOWLEDGEMENT

The editors are grateful to the International Bureau of Fiscal Documentation (IBFD) which gave permission for the reproduction in this book of Chapter 3 'Tax Treatment of Virtual Money' by Aleksandra Bal which was published previously by the IBFD under the title 'Stateless Virtual Money in the Tax System' in *European Taxation* ((2013) 53 Eur. Taxn. 7, pp. 351-356).

List of Contributors

Phyllis Rea Alexander is a Senior Lecturer and Framework Leader in the Business School at Bournemouth University, United Kingdom. She joined the Business School in 2007 following a twenty year career as a US Certified Public Accountant. Her professional experience included general accounting and auditing services with a medium-sized accounting firm followed by international tax consultancy services with a Big4 accounting firm. She remains an active member of the American Institute of Certified Public Accountants and the New Jersey Society of CPAs. Her research interests include aspects of personal tax equity and efficiency, financial analysis, environmental reporting and taxation, corporate governance and fair access to higher education.

At the beginning of her academic career, Tim Vollans was a friend and mentor to Phyllis. Phyllis welcomes the opportunity to recognise her appreciation for Tim by contributing to this collection of essays.

Aleksandra Bal is a Tax Manager at the International Bureau for Fiscal Documentation (IBFD) in Amsterdam, The Netherlands. She is also the Managing Editor of the IBFD journal, The Bulletin for International Taxation. Aleksandra has two Masters degrees from Maastricht University (an LL.M in International and European Tax Law and an MSc in Fiscal Economics), and is finalising her PhD thesis on the taxation of virtual currency at Leiden University in The Netherlands. Prior to joining IBFD, Aleksandra worked as a tax consultant for Big4 firms in Germany, specialising in VAT. She publishes regularly on a wide variety of tax topics, especially on issues relating to the digital economy.

John Bevacqua is a lawyer admitted to practice in New South Wales, Victoria and Australian federal jurisdictions with almost twenty years of legal experience, including at top tier national commercial law firms specialising in tax litigation and taxation advisory roles. He commenced his full-time academic career in 2006, and, in 2010, completed his Doctorate in Tax Law at the University of New South Wales (UNSW), Sydney, Australia. His thesis examined the ability of taxpayers to claim compensation for operational errors by the Australian Tax Office. In 2011, John was awarded the CCH ATTA Australasian Doctoral Series Prize for this work. He joined La Trobe University as a Senior Lecturer in 2008, and he has taught Taxation Law and a range of Commercial Law subjects. He continues to publish in the field of taxpayer rights and remedies in Australia and elsewhere.

Lynda Burkinshaw is a Lecturer in Accounting and Finance at the University of Sheffield, United Kingdom. She has a degree in Accounting and Finance awarded by Leeds Metropolitan University and she is a Chartered Accountant and Chartered Tax Adviser Lynne spent her early career in practice with KPMG and, thereafter, worked in the tax department of a smaller firm. In 2007, she took up a lecturing post at Sheffield Hallam University before moving to her present post in 2012. Her research interests, which are closely allied to the experience she gained as a tax practitioner, are focused on the complexity of tax law and on the ways in which practitioners, within the context of tax law, extra-statutory material and guidance, provide advice to clients.

James Cunningham is the Director of the Whitaker Institute at the National University of Galway, Ireland. He is also a Senior Lecturer in Strategic Management at the J.E. Cairnes School of Business and Economics, National University of Ireland, Galway. His main research interests focus on strategy issues with respect to university research commercialisation, technology transfer, academic entrepreneurship and entrepreneurial universities. Awards for his research include three best paper awards at the Technology Transfer Society Annual Conference 2011, and a best paper award at the Irish Academy of Management Conference 2003. He has also co-authored strategy case studies that have won national and international case study competitions. His recent journal papers focus on entrepreneurial universities, scientists as principal investigators, university research and development collaborations and technology entrepreneurs' planning during new venture format.

Jane Frecknall-Hughes is Professor of Accounting and Taxation in the Business School at the University of Hull, United Kingdom. Following graduation from the University of Oxford, Jane qualified as a Chartered Accountant and Chartered Tax Consultant and worked for KPMG. In 1992, she joined the University of Leeds. Whilst at the University of Leeds, Jane gained postgraduate teaching qualifications and she was awarded a Doctorate in Revenue Law and Tax Practice. She was also awarded a Master's Degree (with distinction) in Commercial Law by the University of Northumbria in 2007. In 2008, Jane became Professor of Accounting at the Open University, and, thereafter, held, until taking up her current appointment in 2014 [this year], the post of Professor of Law and Head of Department of the Open University Law School. She is a Fellow of the Higher Education Academy.

Her research focuses on taxation from an interdisciplinary perspective. She has also been instrumental in leading tax research into the areas of strategic management (with particular reference to multinational enterprises and tax planning), international business, finance, history (including legal history), ethics, e-commerce and corporate governance. Jane has taught a wide range of subjects in the Accounting and Business Law areas (including

Taxation). Her textbook, *The Theory, Principles and Management of Taxation: An Introduction* was published by Routledge in 2014.

James Galway is International Operations Director at Aspect Software, Ireland. He is responsible for Aspect's international operations, but he has a specific focus on manufacturing, real estate and large project delivery. James has an MBA from the Open University, and, currently, he is undertaking a part-time Doctorate at the J.E. Cairnes School of Business and Economics, National University of Ireland, Galway. His research interests encompass an interdisciplinary examination of tax planning and its alignment and linkages with corporate strategy and organisational structure from the perspective of a multinational corporation.

Katharina Gangl holds a post-doctoral position in the Faculty of Psychology at the University of Vienna, Austria. She has a Doctorate and Master's degree from the University of Vienna. Her research interests focus on the impact of power and trust on tax compliance, problems of collective action and the psychology of crisis. She has published articles on tax psychology and the global financial crisis.

Andrew Grainger is a Lecturer in Logistics and Supply Chain Management in the Business School at the University of Nottingham, United Kingdom. He has a strong profile in the field of trade logistics and trade facilitation and, as a consultant, has advised international organisations and governments. His research interests include trade logistics and trade facilitation, trade and customs procedures, administration, law and regulation, port and border management, trade documents and standards, electronic trade and customs systems, and supply chain risk, security and resilience.

Hans Gribnau is Professor of Tax Law at Tilburg University in the Netherlands. He is also the Research Co-ordinator of the Fiscal Institute, Tilburg University and at Leiden University. Hans was awarded his Doctorate in 1998 by the Erasmus University, Rotterdam. He teaches Methodology of Tax Law, Procedural Tax Law and Legal Research Methodology. His current research is focused on the quality of tax regulation, the instrumental (regulatory) use of tax law, governance and tax ethics. He has published widely in these areas. In 2007, he was awarded the Giele-reward for his 'substantial [research] contribution to tax justice in The Netherlands'. In Spring 2013, Hans was a Visiting Professor at the University of Antwerp, Belgium.

Jane Guinery is a Lecturer in Operations Management in the Business School at the University of Nottingham, United Kingdom. Prior to working in academia, she gained extensive experience in industry acting as a production engineer, applications engineer, product support manager and special projects manager as well as fulfilling in line management and factory executive roles. She has managed the implementation of information and planning systems, lean systems, computer integrated manufacturing and quality programmes, and accreditations.

Her research interests include knowledge management, production planning and control systems, collaborative planning, lean systems, service evaluation, human factors and organisation design across industry and services (including healthcare).

Barbara Hartl is a Research Associate and Doctoral student in the Faculty of Psychology at the University of Vienna, Austria. Her research interests include tax compliance, co-operation in social dilemma, sustainable consumption and mental accounting. She is looking to publish articles on various topics, including the gender stereotypes of leaders.

Eva Hofmann is an Assistant Professor in the Faculty of Psychology at the University of Vienna, Austria. Her research focus is interdisciplinary and multi-methodological. It includes tax behaviour, sustainable consumption, creation of open source software, and the management of digital goods. She has published articles in journals, such as *The Journal of Business Ethics* and *The Journal of Psychology*.

Erich Kirchler is Professor of Applied Psychology in the Faculty of Psychology at the University of Vienna, Austria. He has been a Guest Professor at various universities in France, Germany, Italy and Switzerland and a Visiting Scholar at the University of Illinois, Urbana-Champaign, USA, and ANU, Canberra, Australia. His research focuses on money management in the household, expenditure and credit use, tax behaviour and the well-being of working people. He has published extensively in these fields. His books include *Wirtschaftspsycholoogie. Individuen, Gruppen, Märkte, Staat* (*Economic Psychology: Individuals, Groups, Markets, Nation-State*) 4th edition, 2011; *Arbeits- und Organisationspsychologie* (*Work and Organisational Psychology*), 3rd edition, 2011; *Conflict and Decision Making in Close Relationships*, 2001, and *The Economic Psychology of Tax Behaviour*, 2007.

Catriona Lavermicocca lectures in Taxation Law and is the Programme Director for the undergraduate and postgraduate Accounting programmes at Macquarie University, Sydney, Australia. Her research focuses on large company tax compliance behaviour, including the nature of tax decision making in a large company and the impact of reputational risk.

Puseletso Letete ia an Associate Professor in Tax Law at the University of South Africa (UNISA) where she lectures in tax law at undergraduate and postgraduate level and supervises postgraduate students. She holds a Doctorate (in Tax Law) awarded by the University of Edinburgh, a Masters degree in Commercial Law awarded by the University of Cape Town and an LL.B Honours Degree from the National University of Lesotho. Prior to joining the University of South Africa, Puseletso lectured in tax law and public international law at the National University of Lesotho. Her research interests focus on VAT and the taxation of cross-border transactions in the Southern African Development Community (SADC) and the Southern African Customs Union (SACU). She is registered as a Master practitioner by the South African Institute of Tax Practitioners.

Margaret McKerchar is Emeritus Professor of Taxation and former Head of the Australian School of Taxation (ATAX) at the University of New South Wales (UNSW), Sydney, Australia. Her main research interests are taxpayer compliance behaviour, tax policy, and research theory and its application (including mixed methodological designs).

Mirza Mohamed is a Doctoral Researcher in the Business School at the University of Nottingham, United Kingdom. Mirza is a Chartered Accountant. Prior to embarking on his postgraduate research, he was an Assistant Director of Customs in the Royal Malaysian Customs Department. His research is informed by the practical experience that he gained during his fifteen years with the Royal Malaysian Customs Department. His research interests include understanding business tax compliance, risk management, indirect tax compliance costs, trade and customs procedures and change management.

Emer Mulligan is Head of the J.E. Cairnes School of Business and Economics, National University of Ireland, Galway. She lectures on taxation and finance. Prior to joining academia, Emer was a tax manager with Pricewaterhouse Coopers in Dublin, Ireland. She completed her Doctorate on Tax Planning in Practice at the University of Warwick, and she is an International Fellow at the University of Exeter's Tax Administration Research Centre (TARC). In 2014, Emer was awarded a Fulbright-CRH Scholar Award to carry out tax research at the Harvard Kennedy School of Government. Her research interests include tax planning in practice, tax and strategy, performance measurement of the tax function, tax risk management, tax lobbying and tax administration.

C. John Taylor is a Professor and Head of the Australian School of Taxation and Business Law (ATAX) at the University of New South Wales (UNSW), Sydney, Australia. He received a B.A., an LL.B and LL.M (Hons) from the University of Sydney, and was awarded a Graduate Certificate in Higher Education by UNSW. His main areas of interest of research have been capital gains tax, corporate – shareholder taxation, taxation treaties and tax simplification. He has been a contributing author to each of the eight editions of *Understanding Taxation Law* (Lexis Nexis). The journals in which he has published include: *Melbourne University Law Review, British Tax Review,*

Canadian Tax Journal, Bulletin for International Fiscal Documentation, Australian Tax Forum, E-Journal of Tax Research and *Australian Tax Review*. John was the inaugural Honorary Research Fellow of the Taxation Institute of Australia, and in that capacity was the principal author of *Beyond 4100: A report on measures to combat rising compliance costs through reducing tax law complexity*, Taxation Institute of Australia, 2006. From 2006 to 2007, John conducted contract research for the Commonwealth Department of the Treasury on anti-avoidance provisions in income tax. He has been a Visiting Professor/Scholar at Harvard University, The University of Cambridge, Leiden University, The International Bureau of Documentation, The University of British Columbia, The University of Western Ontario and The Plunkett Centre for Co-operative Studies.

1 Contemporary Issues in Taxation Research: An Overview

David Salter and Lynne Oats

The chapters in this collection had their origins in the 22nd annual conference of the Tax Research Network (TRN), held at the University of Exeter in September 2013. The conference was sponsored by the Chartered Institute of Taxation, the Centre for Business Performance of the Institute of Chartered Accountants in England and Wales, and the Institute of Chartered Accountants in Scotland. Participants at the conference were invited to submit chapters for this special volume, which is dedicated to the memory of Tim Vollans, a former TRN secretary and a much loved and greatly missed member of our tax community.

The TRN is an interdisciplinary group of academics and practitioners from the UK and elsewhere with a shared commitment to pursuing and furthering academic research in taxation. The TRN held its first conference in 1991 and since then has gone from strength to strength, attracting scholars from all over the world and now incorporating a special workshop for early career academics as part of the commitment to capacity building.

Recent developments in the UK and elsewhere have raised the profile of tax issues significantly, and in the case of the UK this has brought to the surface concerns about underinvestment in tax as an area of academic research. This volume serves as a reminder that tax research is, in fact, alive and well, if unfortunately, often lacking in visibility. Indeed, the diversity of the topics covered in the ensuing chapters is testament to a vibrant community of scholarship with wide ranging interests and approaches to research.

This diversity has made the task of thematic grouping extremely difficult, and so they are presented alphabetically according to the last name of the first author. Although the editors of this volume have shied away from thematic grouping of the chapters, there are nonetheless topic overlaps and parallels that are worthy of mention:

- Several chapters deal with aspects of tax compliance for large corporate taxpayers (*Gribnau, Lavermicocca and McKerchar, Mulligan et al*), providing fascinating insights into the position in The Netherlands,

Australia and the USA respectively.

- The relationship between tax and trade is considered in two chapters, *Letete* at a broad, interregional agreement level, and *Mohamed et al* at the more micro level of individual agents involved in import taxes.

- The administration of tax systems features in chapters by *Bevacqua* (UK and Australia), *Burkinshaw and Frecknall-Hughes* (UK), and *Gangl et al* (Austria), dealing with the status of HMRC guidance, protection from administrative inequity and the relationship between power of revenue authorities and taxpayer trust in those authorities respectively.

- Tax policy choice also features, in relation to owner occupied housing (*Alexander*), virtual currencies (*Bal*) and inbound investment (*Taylor*).

The following overview gives a flavour of the content of each of the ensuing chapters.

Phyllis Alexander considers vertical equity with specific reference to the preferential treatment of owner occupied housing; comparing the UK and the USA tax systems in this regard. The analysis is underpinned by comprehensive micro simulations using consistent parameters to facilitate comparison, drawing on the Suits method to measure the progressivity of the two systems.

Aleksandra Bal provides a primer on digital money, explaining the operation of the two most prominent virtual currency schemes, bitcoin and virtual world money, before analysing the tax implications, by reference to Germany's schedular income tax and the United States' global system. As a relatively new phenomenon, digital money presents challenges for any tax system and its administration and it will no doubt take considerable time for consensus to be reached on appropriate treatment and regulation.

John Bevacqua presents a comparative study of the UK and Australia and the respective aspirations of both countries' tax authorities to treat taxpayers fairly. In neither jurisdiction, indeed in very few jurisdictions worldwide, is fair treatment of taxpayers codified, and proposed reforms are suggested to rectify this through formal monitoring and sanctions. The doctrine of legitimate expectation that applies in the UK has been rejected in Australia, leaving the likelihood of legislative protection of rights unlikely. There are three policy recommendations: express legislative pronouncement, compensation for taxpayers found to have been treated unfairly and, finally, independent oversight and sanctions.

Lynda Burkinshaw and Jane Frecknall-Hughes examine the legal status of tax authority guidance, with particular reference to Her Majesty's Revenue and Customs (HMRC). After observing that the proliferation of both forms and volume of guidance in the UK is linked to the complexity of the tax system, the authors consider how guidance fits with tax legislation, and the difficulties faced by taxpayers seeking to rely on such guidance.

Katharina Gangl, Eva Hofmann, Barbara Hartl and Erich Kirchler present the outcomes of an empirical test of the extended slippery slope framework that analyses the dynamics between power of the tax authority and trust in the tax authority in the presence of enforced compliance in an antagonistic environment, voluntary co-operation in a climate of confidence and committed cooperation in a service environment. Using an online survey to gather data about these interactions, the authors conclude that coercive power erodes trust, but that the additional costs of increasing services may nonetheless be beneficial in encouraging taxpayers to acknowledge taxpaying as a moral obligation.

Hans Gribnau raises the important issue of the relationship between corporate social responsibility and corporate tax planning using The Netherlands as a case study. Following a fascinating exploration of the nature of tax rules and their imperfections along with considerations of ethical conduct, he concludes that companies embracing corporate social responsibility should also embrace ethical obligations embodied within the law; the internal morality of the law that underpins the body of rules.

Catriona Lavermicocca and Margaret McKerchar present a detailed description of the method adopted in a study of identification and management of tax risk in large Australian companies and the impact of this on compliance behaviour. The authors present a review of the literature before discussing the findings from a series of in depth interviews conducted with tax managers together with a mail survey. The authors find comprehensive identification and management of tax risk leads to improved levels of compliance by large Australian companies.

Puseletso Letete introduces the Southern African Development Community (SADC), a free trade area formed in 2000, and examines the relationship between regional trade agreements and tax agreements entered into by SADC member states. She argues that taxation should form part of trade issues and agreements, particularly in developing countries; taxation should not be removed from scrutiny under trade agreements and the two issues need to be considered together, particularly in light of the shared principles of non-discrimination and national treatment.

Mirza Mohamed, Andrew Grainger and Jane Guinery use the theory of planned behaviour from social psychology to examine the compliance behaviour of customs agents. The authors develop a compliance behaviour model in relation to import taxes in Malaysia, where customs agents play an important role as intermediaries between importers and the customs department. They describe in some detail their mixed method design comprising an initial qualitative phase of interviews that then informed the second, quantitative phase using a survey questionnaire. Additional determinant factors that may serve as predictors of customs agents' compliance behaviour, specifically perception of quality of service, perception of fairness of tax contribution and complexity of procedures are also identified.

Emer Mulligan, James Gawley and James Cunningham bring important insights from the strategy literature to examine the various ways in which large multinationals organise and manage their internal tax function. The authors find that amongst the companies involved in the study, which are all based in Silicon Valley, there is significant variation in the organisation, location and focus of the tax function. Alignment of tax strategy with overall firm strategy was found to be weak, with variable practices in terms of formalisation of the tax strategy.

C John Taylor examines inbound investment for Australia and the prospects for two alternative approaches, an allowance for corporate equity (ACE) and an allowance for corporate capital (ACC) coupled with franked debt; the latter being preferable providing a more attractive environment at lower cost. This policy based study draws on a series of hypothetical examples to evaluate the alternatives. It is mooted that the ACC with franked debt alternative would facilitate removal of complex divisions such as debt/equity, which are problematic within the Australian tax code, as they are in other jurisdictions.

In addition to the rich coverage by topic area, and disciplinary background (law, policy, psychology, economics), the chapters also demonstrate considerable methodological diversity: microsimulation techniques (*Alexander and Taylor*), quantitative survey questionnaires (*Mohamed et al, Gangl et al, Lavermicocca and McKerchar*), in-depth interviews (*Lavermicocca and McKerchar, Mulligan et al*). The authors generously describe their methods, which will be invaluable for scholars interested, subsequently, in following similar paths. A final mention must be made of the geographical spread of the work presented here: Australia, Austria, Africa, The Netherlands Malaysia, the UK, and the USA, which underscores the value of the TRN in bringing together tax scholars from around the world.

We hope that these chapters will serve as inspiration for future research work. We must continue to celebrate, and make visible, the rich and diverse perspectives that can be brought to bear on tax issues, particularly in light of growing public interest in tax matters.

Finally, we would like to acknowledge and thank the contributors of these chapters for their commitment to this volume and for the patience they have shown in its preparation and publication.

2 Owner Occupied Housing Taxation: A Vertical Equity Evaluation of the UK and US Tax Systems

Phyllis Alexander

Abstract

Tax favouritism of homeowner occupiers continues to be discussed by academics and policymakers given its significant personal and fiscal importance. This research area has become even more topical in the last few years given the recent financial crisis. The multi-layered, comparative micro-simulation technique employed within this chapter provides a solid platform from which to appraise existing tax systems and proposals for future policy with regard to owner-occupied housing taxation.

This chapter presents the findings of evaluations on the vertical equity of specific US and UK tax policies affecting homeowner occupiers, as well as the impact on the overall tax systems. The evaluations include comparisons with investors in alternative capital assets within the two respective countries. Vertical equity is quantified using a combination of structural and distributional measurement techniques.

1 Introduction

Since World War 2, consecutive US and UK governments have promoted homeownership through fiscal policy. The recent global financial crisis brought on by the US subprime mortgage crisis leaves little doubt of the significant impact of misdirected and unregulated policy and practice in an economic super power. While mortgage-lending issues have been and continue to be addressed in both countries following the crisis, the US and UK governments' promotion of homeownership continues unabated.

The OECD condemns the fiscal favouritism of homeowner occupiers on grounds of neutrality and tax equity (OECD, 2001). The asserted optimal taxation of such individuals recognises an annual imputed rental income and the capital gain on transfer. The US and the UK are not unusual in their departure from such optimal taxation as very few countries tax either of these elements, let alone both. However, the US is becoming more unusual with its generous provision for mortgage interest and real estate tax relief as most other OECD countries have either eliminated or significantly restricted such allowances.

This chapter presents research findings on vertical tax equity evaluations of homeowner occupiers in the US and the UK. Comparisons are made with investors in alternative investments comprising either financial instruments or residential rental real estate in both countries to better understand the impact of the country-specific fiscal favouritisms to homeowner occupiers. The two-country comparison highlights the significant impact of specific tax subsidies on the respective overall tax systems.

2 Vertical Equity in Literature

Equity has a long history in law and public finance literature. The philosophical frameworks of distributive justice bear directly on various aspects of tax equity, particularly the vertical fairness of taxation (i.e. progressivity). The widely recognised primary criteria for determining distributive justice are libertarianism[1] (endowment-based), utilitarianism[2] (welfare economics), and egalitarianism[3]. In addition to these traditional philosophical platforms, feminism[4] also provides an alternative vision of distributive justice.

Vertical equity in taxation refers to a just or fair distribution of the tax burden. The distribution is with or without regard for the pre-tax distribution of wealth. With regard to the pre-tax situation, an equitable distribution considers correcting pre-existing inequities through the redistribution of wealth through taxation and benefit provision. When the pre-tax situation is not regarded, the tax burden is distributed equally, leaving any pre-existing inequities unchanged.

Adam Smith recognised the benefit principle and the ability-to-pay principle in his first canon[5] regarding tax equity (Smith, 1999/1776). The benefit principle calls for reflective taxation of persons with regard for

---

1   See Locke (1924/1690) for a discussion of "entitlement right" and Nozick (1974) for a discussion on the "principle of rectification"
2   See Mill (2001/1848) for a discussion of "equal sacrifices"
3   See Rawls (1971) for a discussion of the "the veil of ignorance" and the "original position" principle.
4   Kornhauser (1987) considered progressive taxation from an alternative perspective, feminism, in contrast to the perspectives of the neo-economists and neo-conservatives who are grounded in entitlement theory.
5   Smith's four canons of good tax design focused on equity, economic efficiency, simplicity and convenience (Smith, 1999/1776).

individual benefits derived from government expenditure. This approach is often criticised for the difficulty in tracing benefits to individual recipients, and it implies that the poor derive greater benefits and thus, should have a greater tax obligation.

According to the ability-to-pay principle, taxpayers should contribute to the required revenues of government according to their means. While the ability-to-pay principle is not without criticism, it is in comparison with the benefit principle a sounder platform on which to design or reform a tax-structure and from which to evaluate equity.

Tax equity can be evaluated from two perspectives with respect to the ability-to-pay principle: horizontal equity, requiring equal treatment of equals, and vertical equity requiring an appropriate differentiation among unequals (Musgrave 1959, p160). This chapter focuses on vertical equity.

Tax systems are deemed progressive when average tax rates rise with income and regressive when average tax rates fall as income rises. If average tax rates remain constant despite rising or falling income, then the system is deemed proportional. These basic definitions of progressivity, proportionality, and regressivity are found throughout the literature on vertical equity (Musgrave and Thin, 1948, Rosen, 2005, Norregaard, 1990, OECD, 1990, amongst others).

Progressivity within a tax structure may be achieved by three possible methods. Graduated tax rates are the most obvious method of producing a progressive tax structure. A flat tax rate with an exemption also achieves a level of progressivity; Blum and Kalven (1953), Kornhauser (1987) and Rothbard (2001) refer to this as a degressive tax. Finally, the withdrawal and/or removal of certain tax allowances (i.e. exemptions, deductions and/or credits) at higher levels of income will introduce or enhance progressivity in a tax system. This is sometimes referred to as "backdoor progression" (Byrne, 1995).

The principle of vertical equity suggests that the wealthy should pay more tax than the poor because they can afford to do so (i.e. they have a greater ability to pay). Given the pre-tax inequality inherent in a capitalist society, increasing tax rates applied to increasing tax bases ensures a more equal distribution of after-tax income. While the basic concept is generally agreed when one accepts that redistribution is a sound goal for taxation, the rate of progressivity is a matter for debate. The moral value of greater equality is not perceived as an absolute value (Head 1993, p.77). The very idea of progressive taxation has been and continues to be challenged in literature.[6]

---

6   The justification for progressive taxation was first examined by Blum and Kalven in their 1953 seminal work, *The Uneasy Case for Progressivity*, and has been widely debated ever since.

Arguably, a progressive income tax structure has been established as socially acceptable and politically desirable since the inception of income taxation in the US and the UK. The degree of progressivity has varied over time with regard to the number of tax bands and the associated marginal rates, but both countries have maintained nil-rate tax bands and graduated rate structures throughout their respective income tax histories.

The aim of this chapter is not to contribute to the on-going debate on progressive taxation but to establish how vertically equitable or inequitable owner-occupied housing tax policies are in the UK and the US. In addressing this research objective, vertical equity must be measurable. The degree of progressivity in a given tax system is the generally accepted proxy for establishing vertical equity. Whether a more progressive tax system is considered to be more vertically equitable is a matter of political and scholarly debate.

While comparisons of average tax rates to income are capable of classifying a tax system as progressive, proportional or regressive, these are simply qualitative characteristics and say nothing regarding the *degree of progression*. When progressivity is measured in degrees, the inequities may be quantified and cross-sectional and international comparisons may be made. Measurement techniques have varied over the decades. Kiefer (1984) provided an overview of the more common measures of progressivity (indices). He categorised them as structural (what affects their numerical value) and distributional (what they measure). This chapter applies both structural and distributive techniques to micro-simulated data in its evaluation of progressivity in US and UK tax systems.

Structural indices are point measures of progressivity based upon the tax paid at specific points of the income scale. This study employs Average Rate Progression to measure the degrees of progressivity at the incremental levels and over the established range of study. This structural index was established by Pigou (1928) and was discussed by Musgrave and Thin (1948).

2.1 Average Rate Progression (ARP)

As explained by Musgrave and Thin, 'the degree of progression may be measured by the rate of change in the average rate of tax' (Musgrave and Thin 1948, p 499):

$$ARP = \frac{\left(\dfrac{T_1}{Y_1} - \dfrac{T_0}{Y_0}\right)}{Y_1 - Y_0}$$

The above equation reflects the respective tax liabilities **(T)** for the corresponding incomes **(Y)** and Y_1 exceeds Y_0. In other words, the numerator represents the change in the average tax rate and the denominator represents the change in income.

If the average rate progression calculation yields a positive result, zero or a negative result, the tax system is progressive, proportional or regressive, respectively. What is effectively being measured is the slope of a curve obtained by plotting on an arithmetic scale the average tax rates against income (Musgrave and Thin 1948, pp.499 – 450).

Analysis involving a structural index is very detailed by nature in that it measures the degrees of progressivity at selected points on the income scale through applicable tax data. Therefore, the number of indices calculated for analyses are many. By contrast, distributional measures yield one index per annum and per period of study.

2.2 The Suits Index

Suits (1977) developed a distributional measure of tax progression which compares the concentration of the tax liability with that of pre-tax income where the cumulative tax liabilities are plotted on the vertical axis and the cumulative pre-tax incomes are plotted on the horizontal axis, yielding a single concentration index as the measure. A proportional tax is reflected in the 45-degree line (i.e. 10% of the income yields 10% of the tax burden, etc.). The progressivity index of such a tax would be nil. A progressive tax would sag below the diagonal and the corresponding index would be a positive fraction below +1, where +1 represents the extremely progressive tax falling on one taxpaying unit. A regressive tax would bow above the diagonal and the corresponding index would be a negative fraction above -1, where -1 represents the extremely regressive tax falling on one taxpaying unit. A graphical illustration of a Suits Curve is contained in Figure 2.1.

If the Suits curve is derived from five discrete values, the formula for the corresponding progressivity index according to Suits (1977) is as follows:

$$S_x = 1 - \left[\sum_{i=1}^{5} \frac{1}{2} [T_x(y_i) + T_x(y_{i-1})](y_i - y_{i-1}) \right] / K$$

The above formula first multiplies the accumulated percentage of tax burden (T) by the respective incremental differences in the accumulated percentage of income (Y). Then the sum of one-half these multiples is divided by the area of the triangle ABC (denoted by K) and then subtracted from one to yield the Suits (S) index.

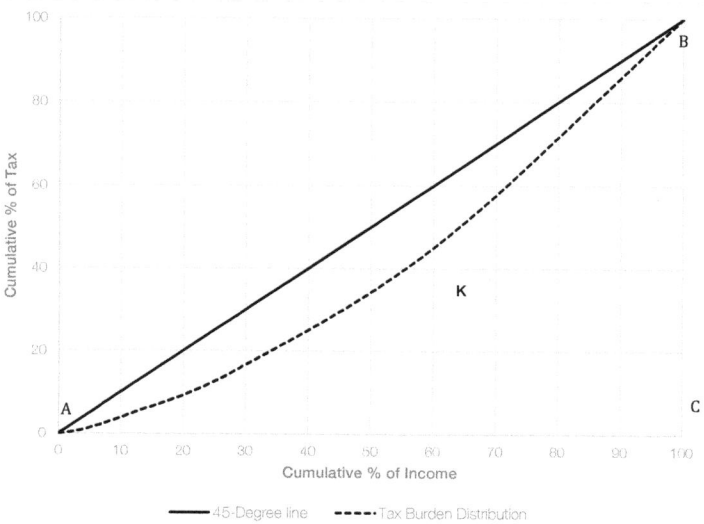

Figure 2.1: Suits curve illustration

The employment of the Suits methodology not only establishes the degrees of progressivity from the distributional perspective, more importantly it provides a measure of the progressivity of the overall tax system through the weighted average of the individual indices of which the system is comprised. This is a unique feature of this particular progressivity measure and is, therefore, employed in this chapter.

The superiority of one measure of progression has not emerged from the literature but Norregaard (1990) suggested the following with respect to the relative question:

> *If the emphasis is on the impact of taxes on the income distribution (i.e., post-tax compared to pre-tax distributions), Musgrave-type measures are preferable. If, however, progressivity is seen more of a question of how the percentage distribution of taxes across deciles compares to the percentage distribution of (pre-tax) income (disregarding the size of the average tax rate), Kakwani and Suits-types of measures should be used (Norregaard 1990, p.87).*

Different measures of progressivity may yield different results; therefore, it is advisable to utilise more than one measure. The structural indices are preferred when investigating the degree of progressivity on a given tax structure. The distribution indices are preferred when investigating the extent to which income is redistributed as a result of the tax system. This chapter considers both with regard to measuring the degrees of progressivity of the respective US and UK tax systems for respective investors in owner-occupied housing, financial instruments or residential rental real estate.

3 Methodology

In order to produce robust evaluations of tax equity, micro-simulations using consistent parameters and a representative agent technique[7] have been employed. The micro-simulations are spread sheet constructions underpinned by the respective tax systems of the two countries studied. Within each country-specific simulation fifteen hypothetical families are established, varying in two respects. First, the families reflect different levels of income earnings in that there are five multiples of the median incomes relative to the two countries in 1990. Secondly, the families vary in terms of their investment choice; five families of differing levels of income are invested in owner-occupied housing, five in residential rental real estate (e.g. tenant / landlords) and five in alternative (financial) investments (e.g. alternative investors). The specific taxes and associated subsidies considered in this research are the acquisition taxes, property taxes, the elements affecting income taxes and capital gains taxes. The tax equity of each of these four specific elements of the overall tax systems is evaluated separately and collectively. The analyses are first conducted within each country's study, and then comparatively on a cross-country basis. The time frames in which the studies are set are twenty-year periods, corresponding with each country's respective tax years.

Over the twenty-year period covered in this chapter (1990-2009), specific policy modifications and reforms occurred in both countries. These include the introduction of the Stamp Duty Land Tax and the Council Tax, the phase out and final abolition of Mortgage Interest Relief at Source (MIRAS) and several changes to the capital gains tax system in the UK. In the US, the capital gains taxation of the family home was significantly reformed. Modifications to the standard deduction, the alternative minimum tax and capital gains tax calculations indirectly but significantly impact the homeowners' tax benefits. Phase-out computational modifications of itemized deductions have a more direct effect.

The user cost framework[8] is well recognised in the literature regarding imputed rent taxation. It is with reference to this ideology that the incomes of the tenant / landlord families are established in the micro-simulations.

---

7 This is a technique used in simulations where a common reference point is established (i.e. an individual with median income) and additional points of reference are established in multiples. In this study, the median income families in the two respective countries in 1990 are the starting points for the simulations, and then multiples of ½, 2, 4 and 5 are derived.

8 This refers to the shifting of costs incurred by the landlord to the tenant through the rental charge.

The Average Rate Progression method of measuring progressivity is applied to the annual simulated data. The progressiveness for the transaction tax systems, the property tax systems and the income tax systems are analysed. The systems are measured between each successive multiple of income to give a comprehensive rate of progression and identify areas of greater, lesser or non-progression. In addition to determining the degree of progressivity at close intervals, the overall degree of progression is determined using the extreme data in each simulation. A comprehensive analysis is made to establish the winners and losers with regard to the specific and overall tax policies studied and a more general analysis is made for comparability within and across the subject countries.

In addition to the structural analysis, this research offers a distributional analysis with the application of the Suits methodology. The use of the Suits indices serves three purposes. First, it clearly depicts the temporal changes in progression, highlighting the effects of recent tax reforms. Secondly, the summation of simulation results into single measures facilitates the international comparison. Finally, this particular measure of progressivity is useful in that it is capable of yielding an overall estimation of the progressivity of an entire tax system through the weighted average of the specific indices which the system comprises, further facilitating cross-country analysis.

The progressivity of the tax systems affected by homeownership are compared and contrasted to the progressivity of the respective tax systems as experienced by the simulated families with alternative financial investments. By so doing, the effect on progressivity solely attributed to a country's owner-occupied housing tax policies can be quantified. The analysis is extended to a progressivity comparison between homeowner occupiers and investors in residential rental real estate (i.e. tenant / landlords) in order to highlight fully the effect occupied housing subsidies have on vertical equity.

4 Results

4.1 Acquisition Taxation

Progressivity is inherent in the UK acquisition tax system for property investment given the varying rates of taxation with respect to varying levels of investment. The introduction and subsequent modifications of higher tax thresholds improves the vertical equity given the ability-to-pay premise on which it is based. The Suits indices begin at 0.0040 in 1990/1991 and conclude at 0.2193 in 2005/2006, clearly indicating an improvement in progressivity as a result of reform.

The US acquisition tax system for property transactions varies among the states. The tendency is for proportional taxation, which is assumed within the simulation. The acquisition taxes in the UK are more vertically equitable than the US in that there is a level of non-taxation in the former and often not the latter. The rate of taxation, however, is greater in the UK than most US locales.

4.2 Property Taxation

The UK community charge was, and the council tax is, a regressive[9] form of property taxation. This is apparent in the rate structure and evident in the indices calculated within the simulations. The Suits indices calculated on the simulated data relevant to the years in which the community charge applies are -0.3840, whereas the results from the years in which the council tax applies are -0.1892. The significant fall in the negative results[10] affirm the council tax as a far less regressive property tax system in comparison with its predecessor, the community charge. Therefore, the vertical equity of the UK property tax system improves in 1993 with the adoption of the council tax. Because the community charge and the superseding council tax are assessed on the occupant of the property, the same liabilities are incurred whether the occupant is the homeowner or simply a tenant. Therefore, there is no variation in the vertical equity (or inequity) of the UK property tax system between homeowner occupiers and tenants of residential real estate.

The US property tax varies among municipalities and locales notably in terms of assessment, rate structure, and concessions. A particular state's policy is assumed within the simulation, with rates in line with the national averages as per the two relevant census' and administration policies that are deemed to be a reasonable representation. The rates applied are proportional with the exception of a slight concession for the lowest tiered homeowner in the first six years of the stated period. In conclusion, property taxation tends to be proportional with very little if any progressivity built in at the bottom of the income scale. Whether the analysis recognises the economical incidence of the property tax or simply the formal (legal) incidence, determines whether or not the tenant of a rental property realises the US property tax. As the simulations are set within the user-cost framework, the economic incidence is applicable. Therefore, the alternative investors and the tenant / landlords incur the same property tax obligations, which are proportional without concessions. Therefore, the US property tax system is slightly more vertically equitable for homeowner occupiers and tenants of residential real estate.

---

9   Certain concessions apply (i.e. full-time students, elderly, low income families) which positively affect the vertical distribution of the tax.

10   As previously indicated, the Suits indices range from -1 to +1, and the negative decimals are reflective of a regressive tax systems whereas positive decimals are indicative of progressive tax systems.

The UK property tax system is unquestionably regressive whereas the US locales tend towards proportionality with the possibility of mild progression at the lowest levels of income and investment. The average property tax rates for the two countries in the twenty-year period of study are 1.58% (UK) and 2.85% (US), based on the cumulative property tax obligations to the cumulative comprehensive income[11] as simulated.

4.3 Income Taxation

The UK income tax system is progressive with at least two rates of taxation and a personal allowance, which introduces a nil-rate band. Similarly, the US income tax system is progressive with at least three rates of taxation and standard allowances and personal exemptions introducing a nil-rate band. The focus in this chapter is on particular elements within the respective income tax systems that are related to housing (i.e. mortgage interest relief, real estate tax deductions in the US and rental property taxation).

Tables 2.1 and 2.2 set out the ARP indices and Suits indices for the homeowner occupiers against the other investors in both countries. The variations in these indices represent the degrees of progression (or regression) of the respective benefits. Subsidy (1) in Table 1 refers to the benefit of mortgage interest relief (and real estate tax deduction in the US). Subsidy (2) in Table 2 refers to the omission the imputed rental income as well as the mortgage interest relief (and real estate tax deduction). The negative differences reflect how much less progressive the other investors' tax systems are in comparison with homeowner occupiers. Positive differences are how much more progressive the systems are in comparison.

Table 2.1: Differences in ARP and S indices between homeowner occupiers and alternative investors in both countries: Subsidy (1)

	United Kingdom		United States	
	ARP Index	Suits Index	ARP Index	Suits Index
Homeowner	1.65739E-07	0.1270	5.15837E-08	0.1512
Alt Investor	1.58359E-07	0.1186	6.25914E-08	0.1626
Subsidy Index (1)	-7.38056E-09	-0.0084	1.10076E-08	0.0114

---

11 For the purposes of this chapter, comprehensive income is the cumulative, twenty years' income plus the capital gain realised on the final disposal of the capital investment at the end of this period (i.e. home, financial instruments or residential rental property).

Table 2.2: Differences in ARP and S indices between homeowner occupiers and tenant / landlords in both countries: Subsidy (2)

	United Kingdom		United States	
	ARP Index	Suits Index	ARP Index	Suits Index
Homeowner	1.65739E-07	0.1270	5.15837E-08	0.1512
Tenant / Landlord	1.47499E-07	0.1169	6.51215E-08	0.1687
Subsidy Index (2)	-1.82408E-08	-0.0101	1.35377E-08	0.0175

The UK allowed relief for mortgage interest through the Mortgage Interest Relief At Source (MIRAS) scheme until 1999/2000. The progressivity of the income tax system with respect to the homeowner occupiers benefiting from MIRAS decreases during the period in which MIRAS is being phased out and falls in line with the alternative investors for the remainder of the period covered in this chapter. Consequently, the abolition of MIRAS results in lower progressivity for the homeowner occupiers and the vertical equity of the UK income tax system is inadvertently hindered with this reform.

There has been an erosion of the benefits of the US mortgage interest and real estate tax deductions over the stated twenty-year period due to significant increases in the standard deductions. This coupled with significant changes to tax bands and income tax rates at around the same time affected the general progressivity of the income system for the better. However, the effect of restricting mortgage interest and real estate tax deductions to the higher levels of income result in a less progressive tax system when compared with the alternative investors and the tenant/landlords in the US simulations.

Both countries' income tax systems are progressive but the impacts of the owner occupied housing subsidies have very different effects. The UK homeowner occupiers experience more progression with regard to income taxation as a result of the two notable subsidies (i.e. the allowance of mortgage interest relief in the first half of the study and the omission of an imputed rental income from income taxation). The US homeowners experience less progression. The average tax rates based on the simulated cumulative income tax obligations in relation to cumulative income in the UK and the US are 24.8% and 14.4% respectively.

4.4 Capital Gains Taxation

The UK capital gains tax system fully exempts the gain on the disposal of the principal residence. For all other personal capital transactions, the system is progressive given the two rates of tax (i.e. 0% and 18%) in 2009/2010.

The progressivity of the UK capital gains tax system has been hindered with the introduction of a flat tax rate in April 2008. Prior to that date, there existed four rates of taxation. The system is still progressive in the sense that there is a nil rate band resulting from the annual exemption, but less progressive than it was prior to the introduction of the flat rate. With respect to the position of tenant / landlords, there is an improvement in that the higher tiered study families go from no taxation to progressive taxation with the abolition of the indexation allowance. Further, a slight drop in progressivity is noted with the abolition of taper relief[12] due to the fact that another study family is then exposed to CGT. In conclusion, the removal of inflationary relief exposing higher levels of gains to taxation improves the vertical equity of the system, while the introduction of a flat tax rate is a hindrance.

The US capital gains tax system is progressive given two levels of taxation (i.e. 0% and 15%). In addition to the pure capital tax, an ordinary tax on the accumulated depreciation of a capital asset (i.e. rental real estate) is levied on disposition. The tax on depreciation recapture (relevant for the tenant / landlords) is progressive up to a maximum rate of 25%. The effect of the change to capital gains taxation on the family home is not discernible in this study because the postponement of the tax in the early years (prior to the reform) means no immediate taxation and the exemption allowance available in the later years means no taxation. The modification in capital tax rates for other investors (i.e. alternative investors and tenant /landlords) significantly improves the progressivity of the tax system.

Both countries effectively exempt homeowner occupiers from capital gains taxation (the UK exempts entirely and the US study families do not breach the taxable threshold and are effectively exempt). Therefore, vertical equity cannot be considered with regard to capital gains taxation of homeowner occupiers, as it is not a factor in the overall tax scheme for families in either country.

4.5 Overall Taxation

The Suits indices measuring the degree of progressivity of overall tax systems for the UK homeowner occupiers, the tenant / landlords and alternative investors are 0.1071, 0.09976 and 0.09966, respectively. The homeowner occupiers bear the most progression in the overall tax system of the three investors.

The combined overall progressivity measure is a culmination (weighted average) of the specific progressivity measures as determined within the simulation. The progressivity of the UK specific taxes together with the

---

12 Taper relief was a method of eliminating the inflationary gain in the capital gains tax computation. Such relief was abolished with the introduction of the flat tax rate in April 2008.

progressivity of the overall tax systems as determined by the four specific taxes is reflected in the Suits curves of Figure 2.2.

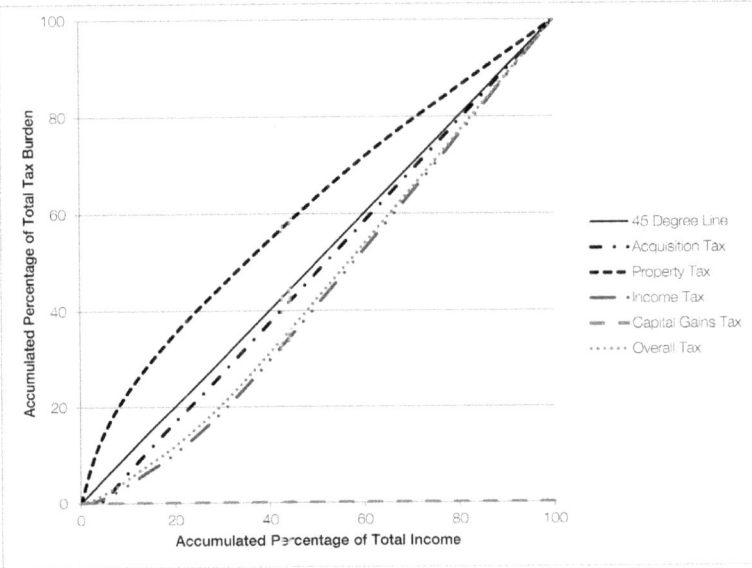

Figure 2.2: Suits curves depicting the progression of the UK specific and overall taxes for homeowner occupiers

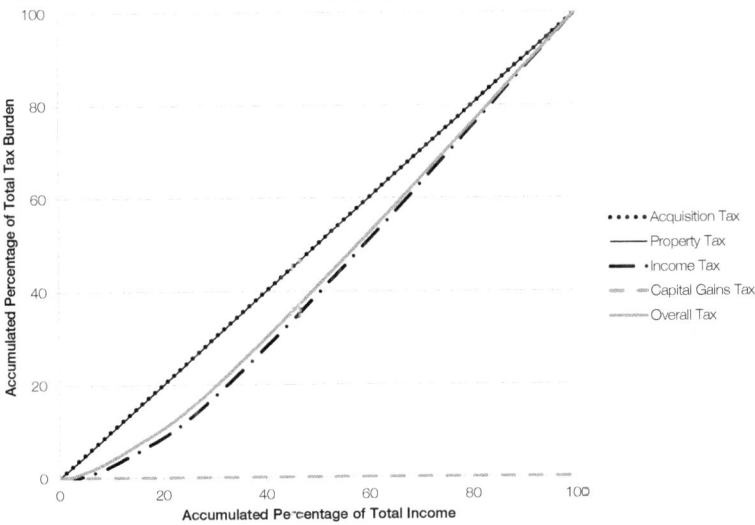

Figure 2.3: Suits curves depicting the progression of the US taxes for homeowner occupiers

The Suits curves reflecting the progressivity of the US specific and overall tax systems of the homeowner occupiers are depicted in Figure 2.3. The

Suits curve reflecting the progressivity of the acquisition taxes cannot be distinguished from the Suits curve of the property taxes as the acquisition taxes are completely proportional and the property taxes are nearly so. The Suits curve resting above the income tax Suits curve represents of the progressivity of the overall US tax system, which is the weighted average of the four taxes the system comprises.

The Suits indices measuring the degree of progressivity of overall tax systems for the US homeowner occupiers, tenant/landlords and alternative investors are 0.1260, 0.1326 and 0.1378, respectively. The homeowner occupiers bear the least progression in the overall tax system of the three investors.

When comparing the Suits indices measuring the progressivity of the countries' tax systems taken as a whole, besides the fact that the homeowner occupiers have opposing rankings in both countries, the variations between the three investors are notably greater in the US. With regard to the homeowner occupiers and alternative investors, this variation is partly due to the significant effect the US mortgage interest relief plays on progression in comparison with MIRAS and the fact that the MIRAS effect is limited to the first half of the study. The differences in rental real estate taxation in the two countries account for the variations between alternative investors and tenant / landlords.

The overall average tax rates calculated on the cumulative overall tax obligations to cumulative comprehensive income are 26.5% and 17.3% in the UK and the US, respectively. One final point on the comparisons of the two simulations is that while the UK imposes a far greater average overall percentage (mainly through the income tax system) on its taxpayers, the US tax system is notably more progressive. The degrees of overall tax progression are measured to be 0.1071 and 0.1260 for the homeowner occupiers of the UK and the US, respectively. The variation (i.e. a difference of 0.0189) is slight but discernible when the respective Suits curves are plotted together as in Figure 2.4.

The US/UK variations in progressivity for the other investors is even greater. The UK tenant/landlords measure at 0.09976 whereas the US tenant/landlords measure at 0.1326, a difference of 0.03284. The UK alternative investors' degree of progressivity measures at 0.09966 whereas the US alternative investors' progressivity measures at 0.1389, a difference of 0.03924.

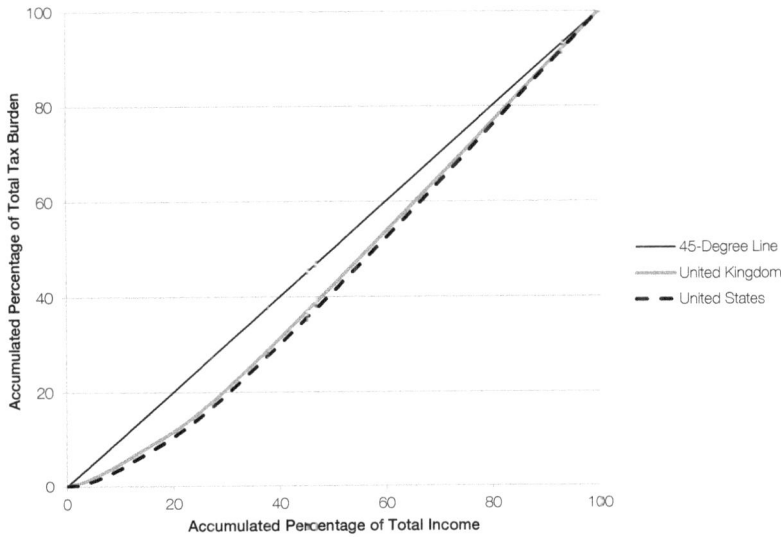

Figure 2.4: Suits curves depicting the progression of the UK and US overall tax systems for homeowner occupiers

5 Conclusion

This chapter focuses on the vertical equity aspect of the specific tax policies that affect homeowner occupiers as well as the overall tax impact in comparison with investors in alternative capital assets (i.e. residential rental real estate and financial securities). The methodology used within the study is a comparative micro-simulation using a combination of structural and distributive measures of progressivity. The use of the Suits method of analysis enables the measurement of the progressivity of overall tax systems, comprised of the specific tax systems studied.

Comparing the measures of progressivity determined for the homeowner occupiers with the measures determined for the other investors within the same country's tax system, the impact of the tax aspects specific to homeownership on progression become apparent. The general levels of progressivity and the respective influences of favourable tax policies are then compared with those of the other country to further inform.

Both countries' specific tax systems have varying inherent vertical inequities resulting from the differences in rate structures, allowances and exemptions. The UK homeowner occupiers experienced more progressivity in the acquisition tax system when compared with the US investors given the provision for a nil-rate band in the UK national tax system and no such provision in most US state systems. US homeowner occupiers experience more progressivity in a typical property tax system, which is either entirely proportional or mildly progressive given the possible provision of a low level concession. The two UK property tax systems considered in this chapter are regressive and therefore less progressive than even a proportional US property tax system. The US income tax system is more progressive than the UK income tax system, regardless of investment choice. In fact, the least progressively taxed US investors experience a greater degree of progressivity than the most progressively taxed UK investors. The homeowner occupiers are taxed more progressively in the UK as compared with the other UK investors, whereas the homeowner occupiers in the US are taxed less progressively than the other US investors. This leads one to conclude that the tax provisions specific to homeowner occupiers enhanced the progressivity of the UK income tax system and hinder the progressivity of the US income tax system. Finally, the US capital gains tax system with regard to the sale of the principal residence by the homeowner occupier is progressive whereas the UK tax system specifically excludes such property from capital gains taxation. While the US study families did not breach the taxing threshold, the system is nonetheless progressive.

Overall, the US investors experience a more progressive tax system when compared directly with the UK investors. In fact, the US homeowner occupiers, while experiencing the least progression from the US tax system, are taxed more progressively than the UK homeowner occupiers who are experiencing the most progression in the UK tax system relative to the other respective investors studied. The ranking of progression deduced in this study show that the elements considered within the overall taxation of homeowner occupiers enhance the progressive taxation of UK investors and hinder the progressive taxation of the US investors. It is evident that the different provision for mortgage interest relief is a significant contributing factor.

5.1   Discussion on the US mortgage interest deduction

The research analysed in this chapter also identifies and quantifies significant vertical inequities regarding the US mortgage interest allowance. Only those taxpayers able to itemize their deductions benefit from the mortgage interest and real estate tax reliefs. Elderly homeowners with little or no mortgage debt and low to middle income taxpayers with relatively modest debt may well not exceed the statutory standard deduction, and, therefore, will not benefit from these reliefs in the US tax code.

Academics have criticised the mortgage interest deduction for decades based on efficiency and equity grounds[13]. It is not an appropriate tool to

---

13   See Litzenberger and Sosin, 1978, Green and Vandell, 1999, Bourassa and Ming Yin, 2008, Toder *et al.*, 2010, Hilber and Turner, 2010 and Pozen, 2011.

encourage homeownership. The UK, Canada and Australia have similar homeownership percentages without the allowance. Further evidence suggests that while the benefits from mortgage and real estate tax relief have significantly eroded over the past two decades, homeownership in the US has steadily increased. However, this research suggests that the benefits are enjoyed only by a minority of homeowners at the upper end of the income scale. Quite simply, higher income households have a greater probability of itemizing their deductions. This may be for no other reason than the fact that they tend to have greater monetary investments in the home with correspondingly larger mortgage debt on which the interest is calculated. Further, as the deduction is allowed at the marginal rate of tax, which is greater at higher levels of income in a progressive tax system, it is worth more.

While the concept of vertical equity remains subject to social and political debate, it would be reasonable to postulate that larger housing subsidies ought to be targeted at lower income groups, particularly if the goal is to encourage homeownership at the margin. The failure of the current US income tax system in this regard ignores the basic principle of vertical equity as larger benefits accrue to those with greater wealth. The current mortgage interest and real estate tax deductions significantly reduce the progressivity of the US income tax system because of their inequitable distribution.

A proposal for mortgage interest credit as an alternative to the mortgage interest deduction has emerged in the literature (Litzenberger and Sosin, 1978, Green and Vandell, 1999, Bourassa and Ming Yin, 2008, Toder et al., 2010, Hilber and Turner, 2010 and Pozen, 2011). Tax credits are proportional and thereby more equitable than tax deductions, which tend to be regressive. If the goal is to provide assistance to all families financing their home purchase with debt, a non-refundable credit would ensure that lower and middle-income taxpayers actually receive the intended tax benefit.

President Obama has made several attempts to reform the current mortgage interest deduction. In the Final Report from the National Commission of Fiscal Responsibility and Reform (December 2010), it was proposed that the deduction be replaced with a 12% tax credit calculated on no more than $500,000 in mortgage indebtedness, eliminating the provision for second residences and home equity loans. The report failed by a few votes two days later. In the 2012 Budget, the President called for a 28% cap on the tax rate applicable to itemized deductions. This would affect taxpayers with $250,000 of taxable income and greater. While these measures seem reasonable to the academic considering tax equity, representatives from the National Association of Realtors and the National Association of Home Builders are very vocal in their opposition. These are particularly influential lobbyists, having spent a combined $65.8 million on Capitol Hill between 1989 and 2012 according to the Center for Responsive Politics (2012). Tax reform impacting housing has been and will continue to be a politically sensitive matter in the US.

This research establishes the effect that removing the mortgage interest deduction would have on the vertical equity of the existing US income tax system. More importantly, it establishes that the majority of US homeowners would not mourn the loss of this very expensive tax subsidy, as the majority of taxpayers do not benefit from it. However, the minority of taxpayers who would be affected by the removal of this deduction are the wealthy and often more influential US taxpayers.

6 Future research

The multi-layered, comparative micro-simulation methodology employed in this research has provided a sound platform from which to consider this and other policy issues and reform implications regarding the tax treatment of homeowner occupiers. The methodology in general and the simulation models in particular are adaptable to further tax equity considerations in either or both countries. Working models have been established from which future research can accurately identify and quantify vertical inequities. Current works in progress focus on the UK transaction taxes, and the US property tax systems.

Bibliography

Anderson, J. E., and Roy, A. G., 2001. Eliminating Housing Tax Preferences: A Distributional Analysis. *Journal of Housing Economics*, 10 (1), 41-58.

Atkinson, A. B., and Sandmo, A., 1980. Welfare Implications of the Taxation of Savings. *The Economic Journal*, 90 (359), 529-549.

Blum, W. J., and Kalven, J., Harry. 1953. *The Uneasy Case for Progressive Taxation*. London Cambridge University Press.

Bourassa, S., and Yin, M., 2008. Tax Deductions, Tax Credits and the Homeownership Rate of Young Urban Adults in the United States. *Urban Studies*, 45 (5-6), 1141-1161.

Burniaux, J.-M., Dang, T.-T., Fore, D., Forster, M., D'ercole, M., and Oxley, H., 1998. *Income Distribution and Poverty in Selected OECD Countries*. (OECD Working Paper 189).

Byrne, D. M., 1995. Progressive Taxation Revisited. *Arizona Law Review* 37 (739), 739-789.

Center For Responsive Politics: Heavy Hitters. Available from: http://www.opensecrets.org/orgs/list.php?order=A [Accessed 10/05/12].

Green, R. K., and Vandell, K. D., 1999. Giving Households Credit: How Changes in the US Tax code could Promote Homeownership. *Regional Science and Urban Economics*, 29 (4), 419-444.

Head, J., Osberg, L., Green, L., Cassin, A., and Panitch, L., 1993. *Fairness in Taxation, Exploring the Principles*. Toronto: University of Toronto Press.

Hilber, C., and Turner, T., 2010. *The Mortgage Interest Deduction and its Impact on Homeownership Decisions*. (SERC Discussion Paper).

Kiefer, D., 1984. Distributional Tax Progressivity Indexes. *National Tax Journal*, 37 (4), 497-513.

Kornhauser, M. E., 1987. The Rhetoric of the Anti-Progressive Income Tax Movement: A Typical Male Reaction. *Michigan Law Review*, 86, 465-523.

Ling, D., and Mcgill, G., 1992. Measuring the Size and Distributional Effects of Homeowner Tax Preferences. *Journal of Housing Research*, 3 (2), 273 - 303.

Litzenberger, R., and Sosin, H., 1978. Taxation and the Incidence of Homeownership Across Income Groups. *The Journal of finance*, 33(3), 947-961.

Locke, J., 1924. *Two Treatises of Government*. London: Dent.

Maylor, H., and Blackmon, K., 2005. *Researching Business and Management*. Basingstoke: Palgrave Macmillan.

Meng, R., and Gillespie, W. I., 1986. Horizontal Equity and Property Taxation in Canada. *National Tax Journal*, 39 (2), 221-228.

Mill, J. S., 2001/1848. *Principles of Political Economy*. Batoche Books. Available from: http://site.ebrary.com/lib/bournemouth/docDetail.action?docID=5000114. [Accessed 01/08/09]

Musgrave, R. A., 1959. *The Theory of Public Finance*. New York, Toronto and London: McGraw-Hill Book Company.

Musgrave, R. A., and Musgrave, P. B., 1989. *Public Finance in Theory and Practice*. Fifth ed. Singapore: McGraw-Hill Book Company.

Musgrave, R. A., and Thin, T., 1948. Income Tax Progression, 1929-48. *The Journal of Political Economy*, 56 (6), 498-514.

Netzer, D., 1966. *Economics of the property tax*. Washington DC: The Brookings Institute.

Norregaard, J., 1990. Progressivity of Income Tax Systems. *OECD Economics Studies*, 15, 83-110.

OECD. 1990. *The Personal Income Tax Base: A Comparative Survey*. Paris: OECD.

OECD. 2001. *Challenges for Tax Policy in OECD Countries, OECD Economic Outlook 69*. Paris: OECD.

Pigou, A. C., 1928. *A Study in Public Finance*. London: MacMillan.

Plotnick, R., 1981. A Measure of Horizontal Inequity. *Review of Economics & Statistics*, 63 (2), 283-288.

Plotnick, R., 1982. The Concept and Measurement of Horizontal Inequity. *Journal of Public Economics*, 17 (3), 373-391.

Pozen, R., 2011. *Toward a Three-Tiered Market for US Home Mortgages.* Cambridge, MA: Harvard University.

Rawls, J., 1971. *A theory of tax justice.* Cambridge: Harvard University Press, Belknap Press.

Rosen, H., 2005. *Public Finance.* 7 ed. New York: McGraw-Hill Companies.

Rothbard, M. N., 2001. The Uneasy Case for Degressive Taxation: A Critique of Blum and Kalven. *Quarterly Journal of Austrian Economics*, 4 (1), 43.

Simons, H. C., 1938. *Personal Income Taxation.* Chicago: The University of Chicago Press.

Slemrod, J., 1983. Do we know how Progressive the Income Tax System should be? *National Tax Journal*, 36 (3), 361-369.

Smith, A., 1999/1776. *Wealth of Nations.* Penguin Classics.

Suits, D. B., 1977. Measurement of Tax Progressivity. *The American Economic Review*, 67 (4), 747-752.

Toder, E., Turner, M., Lim, K., and Getsinger, L., 2010. *Reforming the Mortgage Interest Deduction.* Urban Institute and Brookings Institution.

3 Tax treatment of virtual money *

Aleksandra Bal

1   Introduction

Money is a social institution which has exhibited a great capacity to evolve and adapt to the character of the times. In early times, people used commodities as means of payment. Later on, those commodities were gradually replaced by paper money.[1] For a long time, private monies were commonplace – no government even thought to claim a formal monopoly over the issue and use of money within its political territory. The notion of absolute monetary sovereignty began to emerge in the nineteenth century with the formal consolidation of the powers of the nation-state in Europe and later elsewhere. Monetary instruments were standardized and the legal tender status was reserved to the national currency. The era of territorial money reached its zenith in the middle of the twentieth century with the invention of exchange and capital controls. However, the trend has clearly reversed in the recent years. Financial and monetary systems have become increasingly integrated, capital controls tend to disappear, and we see greater competition among currencies.[2]

In view of these events, it should not be surprising that money has been affected by the technological developments, especially by the widespread use of e-commerce and the emergence of virtual worlds. Stateless digital currencies have emerged and raised a series of legal questions, especially in the area of taxation.[3] For the tax administration, the challenge is how to

---

*   © 2013 IBFD. Originally published in 53 Eur. Taxn. 7, pp. 351-356, Journals IBFD. European Taxation is available online at www.ibfd.org. Reproduced with permission.

1   European Central Bank (ECB), Virtual Currency Schemes, October 2012, sec. 1.2. The ECB report considers whether virtual currencies might affect a central bank's tasks in the areas of payment systems, regulation, financial stability, monetary policy and price stability.

2   B.J. Cohen, Electronic Money: New Day or False Dawn? 8 *Review of International Political Economy* 2, p. 207 (2001).

3   Other legal questions that need to be considered are: who should be allowed to issue virtual money, and who will enact regulations for those issuers? How can it be ensured that payments made with digital money will be secure? How will consumers be protected? How will regulators prevent money laundering?

approach a system that is outside the traditional streams of commerce and finance. For users – to understand the tax consequences of their transactions in virtual currencies.

This article begins with a basic primer on the essential characteristics of digital money: what it is and how it operates. Section 3 discusses two prominent virtual currency schemes: Bitcoin and virtual world money. Section 4 outlines the most common income tax problems faced by virtual currency users and regulators. It aims to give an overview of the tax implications one should consider when exchanging virtual currencies. As those problems cannot be addressed in a one-fits-all manner, the focus is here on two exemplary countries: Germany and the United States. Finally, the article concludes with some remarks on the future developments.

2 Types of virtual money

2.1 Initial comments

Virtual money can be defined as a type of unregulated digital currency which is issued and often also controlled by its developers. There are typically two ways to obtain virtual currencies. One of them is to purchase it using real money. Second, users of virtual communities and online games can often increase their stock by performing specific activities; for instance, taking part in quests or engaging in in-world trade with other users.[4]

Virtual money must be distinguished from electronic money. According to article 2 of the Electronic Money Directive (2009/110), "electronic money" is monetary value as represented by a claim on the issuer, which is issued on receipt of funds for the purpose of making payment transactions and which is accepted by persons other than the issuer.[5] Although some of these criteria are also met by virtual currencies, there many significant differences. In electronic money schemes, the link between the electronic money and the traditional money format is preserved, as the stored funds are expressed in the same unit of account (e.g. US dollars, euro). In virtual currency schemes, the unit of account is changed into a virtual one (e.g. Linden Dollars, Bitcoins).[6] The link between virtual currency and currency with a legal tender status is not regulated by law, which might be problematic or costly when

---

4   ECB, *supra* n. 1, sec. 2.1.
5   EU Electronic Money Directive (2009): Directive 2009/110/EC of the European Parliament and of the Council of 16 September 2009 on the Taking Up, Pursuit and Prudential Supervision of the Business of Electronic Money Institutions Amending Directives 2005/60/EC And 2006/48/EC and Repealing Directive 2000/46/EC.
6   ECB, *supra* n. 1, sec. 2.2.

redeeming funds, if this is even permitted.[7] The issuer of virtual currency is usually a non-financial private company. Traditional financial institutions, including central banks, are not involved. This implies that typical financial sector regulation and supervision arrangements are not applicable.

There are many virtual currency schemes and it is not easy to classify them. This article suggests distinguishing between two main categories: community-related (e.g. Linden Dollar, Facebook Credit) and universal (e.g. Bitcoin) money. The former is accepted by the members of a specific virtual community, while the latter may be used by anyone to purchase various goods and services.[8]

2.2 Community-related virtual money

A virtual community is a place within cyberspace where individuals interact and follow mutual interests or goals by changing and observing the state of a common database. Chat rooms, blogs and networking sites, like Facebook and Twitter, are examples of virtual spaces. All information is stored in a common database, although not everyone can see all of it.[9] The most sophisticated virtual communities are virtual worlds, which are persistent computer-generated online environments that can be accessed remotely and simultaneously by a large number of people who interact with each other for social, entertainment or commercial purposes. Although there is much diversity among virtual worlds and each one is unique. two main categories of them can be distinguished: structured (massive multiplayer online role-playing games) and unstructured environments. Structured worlds (e.g. World of Warcraft) resemble traditional computer games - they have defined objectives and a significant amount of operator-developed content. Unstructured worlds (e.g. Second Life) lack pre-set challenges and utilize more user-generated content.[10]

The structure of both environments is designed to encourage transactions between participants through the use of an in-world medium of exchange. In World of Warcraft, the top unit of in-world currency is called Gold, and

---

7   Article 11 of the Electronic Money Directive (2009/110) explicitly says that "Member States shall ensure that, upon request by the electronic money holder, electronic money issuers redeem, at any moment and at par value, the monetary value of the electronic money held". This cannot be ensured in a virtual currency scheme.
8   A different classification is suggested in ECB, *supra* n. 1, sec. 2.1. The ECB report differentiates between: closed virtual currency schemes, virtual currency schemes with unidirectional flow and virtual currency schemes with bidirectional flow.
9   R.J. Bloomfield, *Worlds for Study: Invitation - Virtual Worlds for Studying Real-World Business (and Law, and Politics, and Sociology, and....)*, p. 17 (May 2007), available at: http://ssrn.com/abstract=988984.
10 For a more detailed description of structured and unstructured worlds, *see* A. Bal, Taxation of virtual earnings, 65 *Bull. Intl. Taxn.* 10, sec. 2 (2011), Journals IBFD.

is broken down into subunits called Silver and Copper. In Second Life, the sole unit of currency is the Linden Dollar, which can be purchased using US dollars and other currencies on the LindeX exchange provided by the world operator. There are several business reasons behind the establishment of virtual currency schemes. First, by implementing them, the world operator can generate additional revenue. Second, the use of virtual currencies can also help users by simplifying transactions and by preventing them from having to enter their personal payment details every time they want to make a purchase.

As the popularity of trade in virtual items is growing, virtual worlds are more and more likely to attract not only people interested in fantasy quests and socializing, but also those seeking new economic opportunities, seemingly less onerous than real world labor. Virtual worlds have already become an income producing venue.[11] Many people trade in virtual items solely for economic reasons. Gold farmers actually make a living by "farming" uncommon virtual objects and selling them to other players. In 2009, the gross revenues of third-party gaming services industry were approximately USD 3 billion. As a comparison, coffee growers in the developing world earned just USD 5.5 billion for their labour.[12]

Due to their growing popularity, virtual worlds have already captured the attention of government officials. The Chinese government has issued several regulations on virtual currency transactions.[13] In September 2008, it imposed a 20% tax on income generated from trade in virtual currencies. In June 2009, a circular addressing several key problem areas was issued. First, the circular prohibits one entity from providing both a virtual currency issuing service and an exchange market platform for virtual currency transactions among users. Second, the circular limits the use of virtual currency to trade in virtual goods and services only for the original issuer. The purpose of this restriction was to limit the possible impact of the rapidly growing online gaming market on China's real financial system. The circular also requires virtual currency exchanging platform providers to require a user who sells virtual currency to register with a real ID and use a real domestic bank account.[14]

---

11 For examples of successful virtual world entrepreneurs, see Bal, *supra* n. 10, sec. 2.4.4.
12 V. Lehdonvirta & M. Ernkvist, *Knowledge Map of the Virtual Economy*, 2011, p. XI, available at http://www.infodev.org/en/Publication.1056.html.
13 The example of China shows that governments are afraid of the impact of virtual money on the real financial system. A virtual currency Q-coin, introduced by a telecom company for the purchase of its goods and services, started being used on a larger scale. As the amount of traded Q-coins reached several billion yuan in one year, the Chinese authorities decided to ban this currency for trading in real goods in order to limit its possible impact on the real financial system. See ECB, *supra* n. 1, sec. 4.1.
14 T. Nakazaki, Real World Excessive Regulations Might Kill Economic Transactions in

In its 2008 Annual Report to Congress, the United States Taxpayer Advocate concluded that transactions involving virtual items should be subject to tax because "where there are economic profits, there is likely to be tax due from someone".[15] The report recommended that the Internal Revenue Service (IRS) issue guidelines addressing how taxpayers should report economic activities in virtual worlds.[16] However, to date, no such guidelines have been issued.

2.3 Universal virtual money

Bitcoin is a decentralized peer-to-peer currency that has recently gained enormous popularity and attention from the press. It is not the first example of decentralized digital money, but, undoubtedly, the most prominent so far.[17] The idea of stateless currency also has a long history. In 1976, the Nobel laureate Friedrich Hayek proposed a system of denationalized money shaped exclusively by market forces. In his opinion, macroeconomic performance would be improved if state control of money could be wholly erased, leaving currencies to be created solely by private financial institutions.[18]

The design of Bitcoin was first described in a paper published by Satoshi Nakamoto.[19] As the technical aspects of this system are complex and not easy to understand without a sound technical background, a comprehensive explanation of the technical mechanism of Bitcoin lies outside the scope of this article.[20] In simple terms, Bitcoin is transferred from computer to computer via a system of cryptographic hashes and kept secure through public-private key cryptography. Users can store their currency in a "wallet", which takes the form of either software installed on their computer or a web-based account. Each payment transaction is broadcast to the network and included in the block chain, so that the used Bitcoins cannot be spent twice. New Bitcoins are generated in a distributed fashion at a predictable rate. Computers called "bitcoin miners" solve complicated algorithms to generate new Bitcoins. The mathematics of the Bitcoin system was so set up that it becomes progressively more difficult to "mine". The upper limit of Bitcoins cannot exceed 21 million.

Virtual Worlds, *Journal of Internet Law* (June 2011), p. 5.
15 National Taxpayer Advocate, *2008 Annual Report to Congress*, p. 217, available at: http://www.irs.gov/pub/irs-utl/08_tas_arc_intro_toc_msp.pdf
16 National Taxpayer Advocate, *supra* n. 15, p. 213.
17 For an overview of academic papers on decentralized virtual currency schemes, *see* S. Barber, X. Boyen, E. Shi & E. Uzun, *Bitter to Better – How to Make Bitcoin a Better Currency*, in: *Financial Cryptography and Data Security* (Springer 2012), pp. 399-414.
18 F.A. Hayek, *Denationalization of Money: The Argument Refined*, 3rd ed. (IEA 1990).
19 S. Nakamoto, *Bitcoin: A Peer-to-Peer Electronic Cash System* (2009), available at: http://bitcoin.org/bitcoin.pdf
20 For detailed explanations, *see* Nakamoto, *supra* n. 19.

Bitcoin is distinct from community-related currencies as the popularity of the latter is linked to the use of the game and limited by their utility to other players. In contrast, Bitcoin can be used to make payments to anyone anywhere in the world. Currently, there are limited venues that accept payments in Bitcoin, but their number is increasing rapidly.[21]

One of the main benefits of using Bitcoin is that of privacy and anonymity in transactions. Unlike other electronic payments, Bitcoin transactions are not tied to identities (some think of Bitcoin as "personal offshore bank"). Another potential advantage is the lack of transaction fees associated with a fund transfer, as the transactions take place over a peer-to-peer network. However, the use of decentralized currency also carries a lot of risks. First, users can easily download the Bitcon application and start using virtual money although they do not fully understand how the system works and which risks they are taking. Second, the transactions are irrevocable. Third, as Bitcoin is not pegged to any real currency and its exchange rate is determined by supply and demand in the market, the whole system could collapse if people try to get rid of their Bitcoins and are not able to do so because of its illiquidity. Fourth, malware, system failures or human errors may cause the accidental loss of the wallet file, which stores the private keys needed to spend coins. If this happens, the person cannot use his Bitcoins any more and the coins turn into zombies.[22]

3 Nature of virtual currency

The first fundamental question is about the nature of virtual money. Some consider it an alternative form of currency, while others another type of software. To determine its nature, it is necessary to look at the general currency characteristics and examine whether digital money meets them. Regardless of the form, money is traditionally associated with three different functions:

- medium of exchange: money is used as an intermediary in trade to avoid the inconveniences of a barter system, i.e. the need for a coincidence of wants between the two parties involved in the transaction;
- unit of account: money acts as a standard numerical unit for the measurement of value and costs of goods, services, assets and liabilities;

---

21 A list of places that accept Bitcoins as means of payment is provided in: https://en.bitcoin.it/wiki/Trade.
22 Zombie coins are coins whose private key has been forgotten or destroyed. Such coins cannot be used any more, resulting in shrinkage of the money base. See Barber et al., supra n. 17, p. 5.

- store of value: money can be saved and retrieved in the future.[23]

In essence, virtual money acts as a medium of exchange and a unit of account within a particular virtual community (e.g. Linden Dollar) or among its users (e.g. Bitcoin). However, the mere fact that it looks and acts as real currency does not make it one. Community-related money does not store the value of all the goods and services in the marketplace, but merely the value of a set of goods or services in a closed system. As a virtual construct of limited scope, it is completely dependent on the private company issuing it. If a virtual world closes down, its virtual currency will become worthless. As for the Bitcoin, the question arises as to whether it fulfills the "store of value" function in terms of being reliable and safe. Given its enormous volatility, possible technical problems and lack of oversight, the answer must be in the negative. Thus, virtual money lacks the necessary monetary characteristics. It is properly classified as a digital commodity (software) and not as a currency.

4 Income tax aspects

4.1 Initial comments

From a structural viewpoint, two basic types of income tax systems can be distinguished: global and schedular. A schedular system distinguishes income categories (employment, investment and business income), and determines gross income and deductible expenses for each one of them. In a global system, all receipts and expenses are considered together in the calculation of net income.[24]

On account of the great variety in tax techniques, even among systems following the same model, the answer to the question whether virtual currency may constitute taxable income is likely to vary from country to country. The next sections examine whether, under the application of tax laws of some exemplary countries: the United States and Germany, the receipt of virtual currency may give rise to taxable income. In the United States, the income tax system has been of a global nature since its inception in 1913. Under the Internal Revenue Code (IRC), receipts from whatever source derived are subject to tax. The limits of the income concept are determined on a case-by-case basis by courts and administrators. In Germany, tax is levied on items belonging to particular income categories which are subsequently combined for the purpose of imposing a progressive tax rate and providing a personal tax relief.

---

23 ECB, *surpra* n.1, p. 10.
24 V. Thuronyi, *Tax law design and drafting: Volume 2*, p. 495 (IMF 1998); S. Plasschaert, The Definition of Gross Taxable Income in Schedular or Global Income Taxes, 31 *Bull. Intl. Fisc. Doc.* 12, p. 535 (1977).

Before considering tax issues in more detail, it is necessary to identify events that may generate taxable income. These might be: the creation of virtual money ("mining"), the receipt of virtual currency as gift (or reward for some achievements within the game), the receipt of virtual currency in exchange for (real or virtual) goods and services and the sale of digital money for real currency.

4.2 Schedular systems: Germany

German income definition is schedular in form. Tax is only levied on seven income categories, which are listed in section 2 (1) of the Individual Income Tax Act (*Einkommensteuergesetz*, EStG). In the context of virtual money, business income[25] and miscellaneous income[26] may be relevant. Those two categories are not of equal rank: business income must be considered first.[27]

If a taxpayer's income does not fall into any of the categories, it is not subject to income tax. Among benefits that are not covered by the income categories are: gifts, bequests, lottery winnings and prizes granted for personal achievements or a successful participation in an event.[28]

Business activity is defined as an independent repetitive activity that is undertaken with a profit motive and involves business relations with third parties. An activity is independent if the taxpayer acts in his own name and on his own account.[29] He must bear business risk and develop business initiative. Repetitive character requires an activity be performed regularly or at least with an intention to repeat it.[30] Profit intention is a desire to earn a favourable financial return on an activity.[31] As an inner component, it has to be determined on the basis of external circumstances.[32] Activities that are not undertaken for the purpose of making profits are considered a non-taxable hobby.[33] Finally, income must be earned through transactions with other market participants. The activity must be offered at the market against consideration, which does not have to be a fixed price but may be

---

25 Sec. 15 EStG.
26 Secs. 22 and 23 EStG.
27 G. Niemeier et al., *Einkommensteuer* (Erich Fleischer Verlag 2009), p. 50.
28 K. Tipke & J. Lang, *Steuerrecht* (Otto Schmidt 2010), sec. 9 mn. 123 and 129; H. Endriss at al., *Steuerkompendium, Band 1: Ertragsteuern* (NWB 2007), p. 40.
29 Niemeier, *supra* n. 27, p. 631; Tipke & Lang, *supra* n. 28, sec. 9 mn. 488.
30 Niemeier, *supra* n. 27, p. 632; Tipke & Lang, *supra* n. 28, sec. 9 mn. 488.
31 Niemeier, *supra* n. 27, p. 52.
32 S. Seeger, *Schmidt: Einkommensteuergesetz. Kommentar* (Beck 2012), sec. 2 mn. 22.
33 Thus, the painter van Gogh, who did not sell any of his paintings during his lifetime, or the novelist Franz Kafka, who wanted to burn his manuscripts, would not be considered as engaged in taxable activities. Their activities would be regarded as a non-taxable hobby.

performance-related.[34]

Based on the above-mentioned definition, "mining" activities do not result in taxable income. Virtual currency is created without participation of other people. Although the "miner" uses software developed by others, he does not pay any remuneration for the possibility to generate digital money. A different conclusion must be reached as regards the receipt of digital currency in exchange for goods and services or its sale for real currency. In such situations, a person who engages in trade on a regular basis, deciding independently about the time, place and character of his activity, may generate taxable income. The profit intention, which has to be determined on a case-by case basis, is the critical element. If the play ceases, taxation may begin. For a casual seller who occasionally receives Bitcoins as remuneration, the profit intention is likely to be denied. However, in the case of "power-sellers" who act like traders and not like individuals disposing of personal property, the profit motive may be confirmed.[35]

If the business profit criteria are not met, it is necessary to consider the miscellaneous income category, which includes gains derived from disposal of various assets. Those gains are only taxable if the time period between their purchase and sale does not exceed one year, and the assets do not constitute objects of everyday life.[36] The latter are personal assets whose value typically decreases through use but cannot increase at any time.[37] As virtual money is extremely volatile, increases in value cannot be excluded. Thus, profits from the disposition of virtual currency could be regarded as miscellaneous income.

To sum up, in a scheduler system, like Germany, it is first necessary to allocate an item to an appropriate category. Large-scale trade involving virtual currencies may give rise to business income. Gains from occasional transactions may fall under the other income article. The fact that virtual currency is treated as a commodity does not impact the evaluation. Benefits in kind resulting from barter transactions also form part of taxable income.

4.3 Global systems: United States

Section 61 of the IRC states that "except as otherwise provided in this subtitle, gross income means all income from whatever source derived".

---

34 DE: BFH, 11 Nov. 1993, XI R 48/91.
35 The German Federal Fiscal Court ruled that people that sell a lot of things on the internet platform "ebay" may be considered taxable persons for VAT purposes. *See* DE: BFH, 26 Apr. 2012, V R 2/11.
36 Secs. 22 (2) and 23 (1) No. 2 EStG.
37 H. Glenk, *Blümich: Einkommensteuergesetz. Loseblatt-Kommentar* (Beck 2012), sec. 23, mn. 62-63.

This provision emphasizes that taxpayers have gross income when they receive anything of economic value, whether in the form of cash, property, services or other benefits in kind. In the landmark case *Commissioner v. Glenshaw Glass Co.* (1955),[38] the Supreme Court laid down what has become the modern understanding of taxable income. It declared that income taxes could be levied on "accessions to wealth, clearly realized, and over which the taxpayers have complete dominion". If these requirements are met, any increase in wealth falls within the taxable income definition, unless Congress makes a specific exemption.

An accession to wealth means that taxpayers gain access to valuable resources. They are able to use more resources than before. Both Bitcoins and community-related currency have value, as they can be exchanged for real money on various internet platforms. Thus, they represent an accession to wealth.

The realization requirement intends to ensure that federal income taxes are always levied on flows.[39] For realization to take place, a transaction with another party must occur which changes the taxpayer's relationship to the asset.[40] The exchange of any combination of services or property for other services or property may constitute realization. The sale of virtual currency triggers a realization event, irrespective of whether it might be considered a taxpayer's property.[41] The taxpayer exchanges virtual money (which constitutes his property) or the right to use a particular amount of virtual money for real currency.

The Supreme Court shed more light on the term "complete dominion" in the case *CIR v. Indianapolis P & L*.[42] In determining whether a taxpayer enjoys "complete dominion" over a given sum, the crucial point is not whether his use of the funds is unconstrained during some interim period. The key issue is whether the taxpayer has some guarantee that he will be allowed to keep the money. If some other person can decide how, when, or whether the taxpayer can take actual possession, those funds are not realized income to the taxpayer. Following the reasoning of the Supreme Court, some community-related currencies cannot give rise to taxable income. Users of World of Warcraft or Second Life do not have a complete dominion over

---

38 US: SC, 28 Mar. 1955, *Commissioner v. Glenshaw Glass Co.*, 348 U.S. 426 (1955).
39 T. Seto, *When is a Game Only a Game?: The Taxation of Virtual Worlds*, Legal Studies Paper No. 2008-24 August 2008, p. 18.
40 T. Miano, *Virtual World Taxation: Theories of Income Taxation Applied to the Second Life Virtual Economy*, August 2007, p. 31, available at http://works.bepress.com/timothy_miano/1.
41 The terms of service of many virtual worlds state that the currency is exclusively own by the world operator, while users have only a license to use it.
42 US: SC, 9 Jan. 1990, *CIR v. Indianapolis P & L*, 493 U.S. 203 (1990).

their virtual money, as they have no guarantee that they will be able to retain it. By agreeing to the terms of service and user agreements, they have explicitly accepted that the world operator can terminate their accounts for no particular reason. Moreover, they can use their virtual resources only as long as they pay the subscription fee. Thus, taxable income can be generated only if community-related currency is exchanged for real money and not when it is credited to a user's account. Things look differently in the case of universal decentralized currencies, such as Bitcoin. The use of Bitcoin is not restricted by any contractual obligations. The person who buys them becomes their "owner" and can keep them in his wallet or spend them as he sees fit.

The conclusion is that community-related currency cannot be regarded as taxable income, while universal currencies can. This also seems to be correct and fair from a layman point of view: community-related currencies were invented to enhance game experience and not as an alternative means of payment. Bitcoin was designed to act as a currency, so it seems justified that it has the same consequences as transactions in real currencies have.

For the reasons of administrative convenience, the US tax law recognizes the concept of non-taxable imputed income. Imputed income comprises benefits derived from non-market transactions: value derived from self-benefiting activities, value from using self-owned property and benefits derived from utilization of leisure time. Virtual currency "mined" by the user is likely to within that category.[43] Another argument for non-taxation of self-created virtual currency is that it reflects mere investment; its acquisition is merely the middle step towards earning a profit and it should be excluded from the income concept until its owner disposes of it.

5 The future

For most people, money is something sanctioned by the sovereign state and used within a country's territory for all standard monetary purposes (medium of exchange, store of value, unit of account). However, what is often overlooked is how historically exceptional all this is. The rise of virtual money is no anomaly in historical terms and may be regarded as an entirely natural development in the context of today's rapidly globalizing world economy. The growth of virtual stateless currencies will most likely continue in the future. No doubt there will be much experimentation and thousands of forms of virtual currency might be tried. But after an inevitable sorting-

---

43 The administrative basis for excluding imputed income from the legal definition in section 61 of the IRC is explained each year in the *Joint Committee on Taxation's Report on Tax Expenditures. See*, for example, Joint Committee on Taxation, *Estimates of Federal Tax Expenditures for Fiscal Years 2011-2015*, p. 6 (2012).

out process, the number of monies that actually succeed in gaining some degree of general acceptability is sure to be much lower.

Although virtual money can have positive aspects in terms of financial innovation and the provision of additional payment alternatives for consumers, it is clear that it also entails significant risks. At no point in the process of purchasing Bitcoins is the user's identity verified beyond the requirement that he produce a valid e-mail address. It is not traced where the money is going, as users merely exchange cryptographic hashes. With no payment intermediaries involved, there is no third party that could provide any data on the taxpayer's identity. However, tax compliance can only be secured if there is a full disclosure of the parties involved in the transactions. Some believe that virtual currencies could be used to facilitate tax avoidance and money laundering, as they can be easily sent undetected in and out of a country. Tax evasion could become a matter of pushing a button. The Federal Bureau of Investigation (FBI) has issued a report on Bitcoin, in which it expressed its concerns about Bitcoin's popularity with criminals engaged in money laundering and other criminal activity.[44]

Usually law lags behind technological developments by some years. This is also the case in virtual currency schemes. Given their growth potential, governments and legislators should acknowledge their existence and provide some guidance for their users. They should also regularly monitor the developments in order to reassess the risks.

---

44 FBI, *Bitcoin Virtual Currency: Unique Features Present Distinct Challenges for Deterring Illicit Activity*, 24 April 2012.

4 From Moral Duty to Legal Rule: A Blueprint for Reform of Taxpayer Rights to Fair Treatment in the UK and Australia

John Bevacqua

Abstract

Tax authorities both in the UK and Australia aspire to treat taxpayers fairly. This article assesses the extent to which these aspirations have been recognised in formal legal rules in both countries. It shows that neither jurisdiction has imposed on the Revenue any broad express legal obligation to treat taxpayers fairly. The legislatures in both jurisdictions have largely left the matter to the judiciary. As a consequence, neither country is far advanced along the path to translating the moral duty of tax officials to treat taxpayers fairly into a clear and certain legal right. This chapter proposes a number of reforms which, taken together, set out a blueprint for addressing this situation. The proposed reforms comprise legislative clarification of taxpayer rights to fair treatment, taxpayer rights to compensation for serious failures to treat taxpayers fairly and formal monitoring and sanctions to ensure compliance with Revenue commitments to treat taxpayers fairly.

1   Introduction

Tax authorities in the UK and Australia share a common aspiration to treat taxpayers fairly. The Australian Commissioner of Taxation refers to fairness in his preamble to the Australian *Taxpayers' Charter*, pointing to an aspiration to be "professional, responsive and fair"[1]. The Australian *Charter* itself contains a commitment by the Australian Taxation Office (ATO) to

---

1   Australian Taxation Office, "Taxpayers' Charter: What You Need to Know" available at http://www.ato.gov.au/content/downloads/cor63133_n2548.pdf [Accessed 20 April 2012], foreword.

treat taxpayers "fairly and reasonably"[2]. In the UK, Her Majesty's Revenue and Customs (HMRC) have also recently adopted a new Charter which incorporates an aspiration to provide "even-handed" treatment, tantamount to a commitment to treat taxpayers fairly.[3] In that document HMRC further expressly refer to their desire to provide "a service that is even-handed, accurate and based on mutual trust and respect."[4]

These revenue authority aspirations to treat taxpayers fairly are, in part, motivated by self interest. Judges have recognised that fair treatment of taxpayers is in the "interests not only of all individual taxpayers...but also in the interests of the Revenue."[5] The OECD Centre for Tax Policy and Administration explains why, noting that "[t]axpayers who are aware of their rights and expect, and in fact receive, a fair and efficient treatment are more willing to comply."[6] Research into compliance behaviour is rapidly extending to examination and confirmation of various aspects of the link between fair treatment and tax compliance.[7]

---

2   Australian Taxation Office, "Taxpayers' Charter: What You Need to Know", above fn. 1, 2. This includes the following specific commitments under that heading: "We will:
    • treat you with courtesy, consideration and respect
    • behave with integrity and honesty
    • act impartially
    • respect and be sensitive to the diversity of the Australian community
    • make fair and equitable decisions in accordance with the law
    • resolve your concerns, problems or complaints fairly and as quickly as possible."
3   Many of the commitments captured under the heading of the right to be treated fairly set out above at fn. 2 are also contained in the HMRC Charter, albeit under different headings.
4   Her Majesty's Revenue and Customs, "Your Charter" available at http://www.hmrc.gov.uk/charter/charter.pdf [Accessed 12 April 2012].
5   Vestey v Inland Revenue Commissioners [1977] STC 414, 439 per Walton J.
6   OECD, Centre for Tax Policy and Administration, Principles of Good Tax Administration (2001), OECD, Practice Note GAP0013, 154. The UK Treasury also recently acknowledged that "the service standards provided by HMRC cannot be treated as a separate issue from the collection of tax revenues and the level of tax compliance." House of Commons. Treasury Committee, Administration and Effectiveness of HM Revenue and Customs - Sixteenth Report of Session 2010-12 (2011), (Session 2010-11), Vol. 1, 47.
7   See, for example, Robert Mason and Lyle Calvin, "Public Confidence and Admitted Tax Evasion" (1984) 37 *National Tax Journal* 489; Michael Roberts and Peggy Hite, "Progressive Taxation, Fairness and Compliance" (1994) 16 *Law and Policy* 27; Steven Sheffrin and Robert Triest, "Can Brute Deterrence Backfire? Perceptions and Attitudes in Tax Compliance" in Joel Slemrod (ed), *Who Pays Taxes and Why? Tax Compliance and Enforcement* (1992) 193; Josef Falkinger, "Tax Evasion, Consumption of Public Goods and Fairness" (1995) 16 *Journal of Economic Psychology* 63; and Frank Cowell, "Tax Evasion and Inequity" (1992) 13 *Journal of Economic Psychology* 521. Typically, such studies focus on the positive compliance effects of fostering a relationship of trust and confidence between taxpayer and tax authority. For a good Australian example of such a study see Jenny Job and Monika Reinhart, "Trusting the Tax Office: Does

Given this accepted link between tax compliance and fair treatment, it is pertinent to assess the extent to which aspirations to treat taxpayers fairly have been legally recognised in Australia and the UK as legally enforceable rules.[8] This chapter makes this assessment and draws on it to propose a blueprint for effectively dealing with the common challenges and obstacles in the way of translating a moral commitment to treat taxpayers fairly into enforceable legal requirements.

Part 2 discusses the recognition of the right to fair treatment in the UK. It focuses predominantly on the cases which have developed the UK doctrine of legitimate expectations. That doctrine has its roots in a requirement that taxpayers are treated fairly. The discussion extends to consideration of the potential extension of taxpayer rights to fair treatment facilitated by the application within the UK of law emanating from the Human Rights Act 1998 and European Union law.

Part 3 discusses the Australian position. The emphasis is on demonstrating how Australian courts, while recognising the desirability of treating taxpayers fairly, have avoided setting precedents imposing on the Commissioner a legal duty to treat taxpayers fairly. This judicial trend extends to the rejection of the UK doctrine of legitimate expectations in Australia, and an overriding concern to ensure duties to individual taxpayers do not impinge on Revenue duties to the Crown.

Part 4 sets out guidelines for both countries in translating the right to fair treatment from a mere moral duty into an enforceable legal right. Specifically, it makes three recommendations which, taken together, could be used as a blueprint for effectively dealing with the common challenges inherent in striking the appropriate balance between taxpayer rights to fair treatment and tax official public law duties. These recommendations are: (1) legislative clarification of taxpayer rights to fair treatment; (2) rights to compensation for serious failures to treat taxpayers fairly; and (3) formal and independent avenues for enforcement and oversight of Revenue commitments to treat taxpayers fairly.

Putnam's Thesis relate to Tax?" (2003) 38 *Australian Journal of Social Issues* 307. See also Kristina Murphy, "The Role of Trust in Nurturing Compliance: A Study of Accused Tax Avoiders" (2004) 28 *Law and Human Behaviour* 187. There has also been significant international focus on the relationship between treatment of taxpayers and compliance behaviour. See, for example, John Scholz, "Trust, Taxes and Compliance" in Valerie Braithwaite and Margaret Levi (eds), *Trust and Governance* (1998), 135.

8   This mirrors the question posed by UK judge Lord Scarman in *Inland Revenue Commissioners v National Federation of Self-Employed and Small Business Ltd* (Fleet Street Casuals) [1981] UKHL 2, 18; [1981] STC 260, 280: "Is it [fairness] a mere moral duty, a matter for policy but not a rule of law?"

2 Fairness in the UK

There is no express statutory recognition of taxpayer rights to fair treatment in the UK. There has, however, been judicial recognition of limited legally enforceable taxpayer rights to fair treatment, particularly in cases where HMRC has sought to resile from conduct or representations reasonably relied upon by taxpayers. The focus in this Part is on explaining these judicial developments. The examination also extends to consideration of further enhancements of taxpayer rights to fair treatment due to the increasing influence of European Union law in the UK.

2.1 Judicial recognition of UK taxpayer rights to fair treatment

The right to fair treatment has been discussed in the UK in a number of relatively recent cases which have recognised and developed a doctrine of legitimate expectations in judicial review proceedings against the Revenue. This doctrine, which recognises a right to substantive as well as procedural justice, has been judicially described as "rooted in fairness".[9] In this context, in 1982, Lord Scarman in *Inland Revenue Commissioners v National Federation of Self-Employed and Small Business Ltd*[10] (*Fleet Street Casuals*) stated that "modern case law recognises a legal duty owed by the revenue to the general body of the taxpayers to treat taxpayers fairly."[11]

His Lordship pointed out that this duty is more than simply a matter of "desirable policy or moral obligation"[12] and that the duty extends to ensuring HMRC officials:

> "...use their discretionary powers so that, subject to the requirements of good management, discrimination between one group of taxpayers and another does not arise; to ensure that there are no favourites and no sacrificial victims."[13]

---

9 Bingham LJ in *R. v Inland Revenue Commissioners Ex p. MFK Underwriting Agencies Ltd* (MFK Underwriting) [1990] 1 WLR 1545, 1569-1570; [1989] STC 873, 892-893.
10 Fleet Street Casuals, above fn. 8, [1981] STC 260. This case involved a special arrangement under which the Revenue agreed not to collect back taxes owed by certain casual workers. The Federation respondent alleged this arrangement unfairly discriminated against the Federation's members who were typically vigorously pursued by the Commissioner for non-payment of taxes. The case has become popularly known as the "Fleet Street Casuals" case.
11 Fleet Street Casuals, above fn. 8, [1981] STC 260, 280. His Lordship cites a number of authorities in support of this proposition including *Latilla v Inland Revenue Commissioners* (1943) 25 TC 107 (CA); *Vestey v Inland Revenue Commissioners* (No. 2) [1978] STC 567 (HC); and *Congreve v Inland Revenue Commissioners* (1948) 30 TC 163 (HL).
12 Fleet Street Casuals, above fn. 8, [1981] STC 260, 280.
13 Fleet Street Casuals, above fn. 8, [1981] STC 260, 280.

Subsequently, in *R. v Inland Revenue Commissioners Ex p. Preston*[14] (*Preston*) Lord Scarman, while falling short of suggesting that fairness, on its own, could constitute a basis for judicial review, confirmed that fairness is a key consideration in determining whether a statutory power has been abused or exceeded by the Revenue.[15] In *Preston* Lord Templeman also further elaborated on the link between unfairness and abuse of power:

> "...[A] taxpayer cannot complain of unfairness merely because the commissioners decide to perform their statutory duties... The court can only intervene by judicial review to direct the commissioners to abstain from performing their statutory duties or from exercising their statutory powers if the court is satisfied that 'the unfairness' of which the applicant complains renders the insistence by the commissioners on performing their duties or exercising their powers an abuse of power by the commissioners."[16]

Lord Templeman also made it clear that unfairness could form the basis for successful judicial review proceedings against HMRC by a taxpayer where HMRC conduct is equivalent to a breach of contract or breach of representation capable of sustaining a common law estoppel action. Such circumstances could also be considered so unfair as to constitute an abuse of power.[17]

However, UK courts have also been quick to point out the practical factual limitations of the doctrine. For instance, taxpayers cannot complain of unfairness if they have not themselves acted in a transparent and open manner. Nor can they complain of unfairness if they rely on qualified or indefinite representations made and ultimately resiled from by HMRC. Bingham LJ in *R. v Inland Revenue Commissioners Ex p. MFK Underwriting Agencies Ltd*[18] pointed out that:

> "...fairness is not a one-way street. It imports the notion of equitableness, of fair and open dealing, to which the authority is as much entitled as the citizen. The Revenue's discretion, while it exists, is limited. Fairness requires that its exercise should be on a basis of full disclosure... Nor, I think...would it be fair to hold the Revenue bound by anything less than a clear, unambiguous and unqualified representation."[19]

As a consequence of factual limitations such as these, no taxpayer

---

14 *R. v Inland Revenue Commissioners Ex p. Preston* [1984] UKHL 5; [1985] STC 282.
15 Preston, above fn. 14, [1985] STC 282, 298.
16 Preston, above fn. 14, [1985] STC 282, 293.
17 Preston, above fn. 14, [1985] STC 282, 294.
18 MFK Underwriting, above fn. 9. [1989] STC 873.
19 MFK Underwriting, above fn. 9. [1989] STC 873, 892-892.

succeeded in any substantive legitimate expectations claim against HMRC until *R. v Inland Revenue Commissioners Ex p. Unilever plc*[20] (*Unilever*). In *Unilever* the taxpayer had lodged claims taking advantage of loss relief provisions contained in the *Income Incorporation Taxes Act 1988* outside of the statutory time limit - as it had done for over 20 years. HMRC's past practice had been to allow the claims, despite being out of time. However, HMRC now sought to resile from that practice and enforce the statutory time limit. In finding for the taxpayer, the Court of Appeal concluded that to reject the taxpayer's claim in this instance was so unfair as to amount to an abuse of power.[21]

The finding in *Unilever* was also significant in that it established that in appropriate cases, fairness demands that the Revenue be bound by previous practices or conduct falling short of express and unqualified statements made to, and relied upon by, particular taxpayers - even where the relevant practice is evidenced only by passive acquiescence. The Court of Appeal in *Unilever* also pointed out that the potential categories of unfair treatment capable of sustaining a taxpayer claim against the Revenue remain open, with precedent acting "as a guide not a cage"[22] requiring each case to be judged on its own facts.

In recent years, numerous attempts have been made to expand the categories of recovery, including attempts to hold HMRC to erroneous oral advice. While none of these cases have succeeded, the possibility of success remains open. However, in *Bourne v HMRC*[23] it was noted that "it will usually be difficult or impossible to prove such a claim unless the guidance given by HMRC is recorded in writing."[24]

In addition to these practical challenges, numerous commentators have called for a clearer account of the general standards and role of fairness in judicial review proceedings. The observations of Bamforth are typical:

"No real attempt has been made...to clarify what – as a general matter – counts as 'fair' or 'unfair', or the role which fairness plays in the overall scheme of judicial review."[25]

---

20 *R. v Inland Revenue Commissioner Ex p. Unilever plc* [1996] STC 681 (CA).
21 Simon-Browne LJ, in Unilever, above fn. 20, [1996] STC 681 at 695, elaborated on the link between unfairness and abuse of power, observing that "it is illogical or immoral or both for the public authority to act with conspicuous unfairness and in that sense abuse its power."
22 Unilever, above fn. 20, [1996] STC 681, 690.
23 *Bourne v HMRC* (Bourne) [2010] UKFTT 294 (TC).
24 Bourne, above fn. 23, [2010] UKFTT 294 (TC) at [27]. For similar reasoning see also *Watson v HM Customs and Excise* (2004) (VAT18675) and *Corkteck Ltd v HMRC* [2009] EWHC 785 (Admin).
25 Nicholas Bamforth, "Fairness and Legitimate Expectation in Judicial Review" (1997)

Despite the practical challenges and continuing uncertainty as to the precise role of fairness in judicial review proceedings, it is clear that the right to fair treatment remains an important consideration in weighing up public and private interests to determine whether a taxpayer can succeed in judicial review proceedings against HMRC.[26]

2.2 European influences on UK taxpayer rights to fair treatment

As already noted, there is no direct statutory recognition of a taxpayer right to fair treatment in the UK. However, arguably, statutory recognition of human rights via enactment of the *Human Rights Act 1998* (HRA) "has caused fundamental changes to the Constitutional structure of England and the relationship between the courts and government"[27] which have facilitated judicial dynamism allowing the development of the doctrine of legitimate expectations described above.

The HRA brings into law the provisions of the European Convention for Protection of Human Rights and Fundamental Freedoms (Convention).[28] Section 6(1) of the HRA provides that "[i]t is unlawful for a public authority to act in a way which is incompatible with a Convention right."[29]

There have been numerous attempts to apply the provisions of the HRA in cases of alleged unfair treatment of taxpayers. For instance, arguments concerning the potential infringement of the right to a fair hearing in Article

---

56 *Cambridge Law Journal* 1, 1. See also Richard Clayton, "Legitimate Expectations, Policy and the Principle of Consistency" (2003) 62 *Cambridge Law Journal* 93: and Cameron Stewart, "Substantive Unfairness: A New Species of Abuse of Power?" (2000) 28 *Federal Law Review* 617.

26 This weighing up process was explained by Lord Woolfe MR in *R. v North and East Devon Health Authority Ex p. Coughlan* [1999] EWCA Civ 1871, at [57]: "Where the court considers that a lawful promise or practice has induced a legitimate expectation of a benefit which is substantive, not simply procedural, authority now establishes that … the court will in a proper case decide whether to frustrate the expectation is so unfair that to take a new and different course will amount to an abuse of power. Here, once the legitimacy of the expectation is established, the court will have the task of weighing the requirements of fairness against any overriding interest relied upon for the change of policy."

27 Matthew Groves, "Substantive Legitimate Expectations in Australian Administrative Law" [2008] 32 *Melbourne University Law Review* 470, 492.

28 The HRA came into force on 2 October 2000.

29 Section 6(2) qualifies this general principle: "Subsection (1) does not apply to an act if— (a) as the result of one or more provisions of primary legislation, the authority could not have acted differently; or (b) in the case of one or more provisions of, or made under, primary legislation which cannot be read or given effect in a way which is compatible with the Convention rights, the authority was acting so as to give effect to or enforce those provisions."

6 of the Convention[30] have been raised in a number of cases where HMRC have sought to use coercive powers against taxpayers accused of tax evasion.[31] In one of these cases - *R. v Allen*[32] - the Court acknowledged that HMRC's coercive powers to compel the disclosure of information must be exercised in a manner which does not violate the right against self-incrimination.[33]

Allegations of unfair treatment have also been central to numerous cases in which allegations of breaches of the Convention Article 14 right to non-discrimination on grounds of sex have been levelled against HMRC.[34] For example, in *R. v Commissioners of Inland Revenue Ex p. Wilkinson*[35] the taxpayer alleged discrimination through being denied a tax deduction known as a "widow's bereavement allowance" simply because he was a widower rather than a widow.[36] The taxpayer's claim was ultimately unsuccessful.[37] However, subsequent successful challenges by widowers on grounds of discrimination have been made direct to the European Court of Human Rights.[38] These taxpayer successes demonstrate that unfairness amounting

---

30 Article 6(1) provides (among other things) that: "In the determination of his civil rights and obligations or of any criminal charge against him, everyone is entitled to a fair and public hearing within a reasonable time by an independent and impartial tribunal established by law."

31 See, for example *R. v Allen* (Allen) [2001] UKHL 45; [2001] STC 1537 and *R. v Dimsey* [2001] UKHL 46; [2001] STC 1520. For discussion of these cases see Graham Virgo, "Cheating the Public Revenue" (2000) 59 *Cambridge Law Journal* 42 and Graham Virgo, "Cheating the Public Revenue: Fictions and Human rights" (2002) 61 *Cambridge Law Journal* 47.

32 Allen, above fn. 31, [2001] STC 1537.

33 The taxpayer did not succeed on factual grounds in this case. The taxpayer had been compelled to supply certain ultimately self-incriminatory information pursuant to the Commissioners' exercise of power pursuant to section 20(1) of the Taxes Management Act 1970 (UK).

34 Article 14 provides: "The enjoyment of the rights and freedoms set forth in this Convention shall be secured without discrimination on any ground such as sex, race, colour, language, religion, political or other opinion, national or social origin, association with a national minority, property, birth or other status."

35 *R. v Commissioners of Inland Revenue Ex p. Wilkinson* [2005] UKHL 30; [2006] STC 270.

36 The widows' allowance was set out in section 262 of the Income and Corporation Taxes Act 1988 (UK). In challenges taken to the European Court of Human Rights prior to enactment of the HRA the Commissioner had settled similar claims. These included two separate similar claims by widowers Crossland and Fielding in 1997.

37 The court held that the case fell within the exception to the general requirement to comply with the Convention (contained in section 6(2)(b) of the HRA) because HMRC were acting so as to give effect to a statutory provision which could not reasonably be read or given effect so as to make it compatible with the Convention rights. Section 6(2) is set out in full above at fn. 29.

38 In 2006, in *Hobbs, Richard, Walsh and Geen v United Kingdom* [2006] ECHR 63684/00, four widowers took their cases to the European Court of Human Rights. The court found that the denial of the widows' allowance to widowers was discriminatory and violated the Convention.

to discrimination by the Revenue is now clearly actionable in the UK by virtue of the influence of the HRA and related jurisprudence of the European Court of Human Rights.

The influence of EU law in the UK is also likely to further specifically aid taxpayers in cases alleging unfairness constituting a breach of the doctrine of legitimate expectations. The protection of legitimate expectations is recognised in EU law.[39] In *Mavridis v Parliament*[40] the European Court of Justice has observed that "...the right to rely on the principle of the protection of legitimate expectation ...extends to any individual who is in a situation in which it appears that the administration's conduct has led him to entertain reasonable expectations."[41]

However, the approach under EU law is more expansive than the UK doctrine. For example, a plaintiff may recover even in some cases where upholding a legitimate expectation would result in a breach of a statutory duty imposed on the relevant offending authority.[42] Such an approach is yet to be applied in the UK. It is conceivable that this approach could influence and embolden UK judges to eventually expand the circumstances in which taxpayer rights to fair treatment are recognised as legally enforceable.

3 Fairness in Australia

There are a number of informal acknowledgements of a right to fair treatment of Australian taxpayers but, similar to the UK, none of these have legislative backing, the breach of which is enforceable against the Australian Commissioner of Taxation.[43] Given this absence of any legislative recognition

---

39 The principles of legitimate expectation were applied by the European Court of Justice in the tax context in a case involving Dutch VAT: Gemeente Leusden v Staatssecretaris van Financien (C-487/01 and C-7/02) [2004] ECR I-5337; [2007] STC 776.
40 *Mavridis v Parliament* (Mavridis) (C-289/81) [1983] ECR 1733.
41 Mavridis, above fn. 40, [1983] ECR 1733 at [21].
42 The European doctrine is derived from the German concept of Vertrauenschutz. In the development of that concept in German law it has been recognised that requiring an administrator to act illegally is not necessarily a bar to legal protection of a citizen's substantive legitimate expectations that the administrator will so act. Legality needs to be weighed against the expectation of certainty in determining whether a legitimate expectation should be remedied in these circumstances. Forsyth describes this weighing up process as follows: "There had to be a weighing of the principles to determine whether the public interest in the legality of the administration outweighed the need to protect the trust placed by the citizen in the validity of the administrative act. Only in that event was an unlawful administrative act revocable." Christopher Forsyth, "The Provenance and Protection of Legitimate Expectations in Administrative Law" (1988) 47 *Cambridge Law Journal* 238, 244.
43 As noted in the Introduction of this article, Australia has a Taxpayers' Charter which recognises a taxpayer right to fair treatment. However, the Charter remains

of a right to fair treatment of Australian taxpayers, the focus of this Part is on judicial attitudes to the recognition and legal enforceability of such a right.

In Australia, the concept of a duty to treat taxpayers fairly was first judicially flagged by Isaacs J in his 1926 judgment in *Moreau v FCT*[44] (*Moreau*). His Honour stated in that case that the Commissioner's function "is to administer the Act with solicitude for the Public Treasury *and with fairness to the taxpayers*"[45] (emphasis added). While these views have been positively received in a number of subsequent Australian tax cases, there has been no express confirmation of their correctness. Generally, the effect of subsequent cases has been to qualify the general right to fair treatment recognised by Isaacs J.

For example, in *David Jones Finance & Investments Pty Ltd v FCT*[46] (*David Jones*), the Commissioner resiled from his usual practice of allowing intercorporate dividend rebates, contrary to a decision of the Australian High Court in *FCT v Patcorp Investments Ltd*.[47] The taxpayer unsuccessfully argued that this was unfair and constituted an abuse of process by the Commissioner. O'Loughlin J, in the first instance hearing of the case, distinguished the remarks of Isaacs J in *Moreau*, by confining them to the specific statutory provision in question in *Moreau*.[48]

His Honour was, however, prepared to concede that the mandate given to the Commissioner under s8 of the *Income Tax Assessment Act 1936* (Cth)[49]

---

a document without any legislative force and which does not purport to create any new legal rights. This is contrary to the recommendations of the Australian Joint Committee of Parliamentary Accounts, Report 326 - An Assessment of Tax (1993); and OECD, Committee of Fiscal Affairs Working Party, "Taxpayers Rights and Obligations - A Survey of the Legal Situation in OECD Countries" (Paper Number 8, OECD, 1990). The legal enforceability of the Charter was keenly debated prior to its adoption in 1997, with many commentators critical of the non-binding nature of the Charter and most commentators at the time calling for legislative entrenchment of the Charter rights. See, for example, Karen Wheelright, "Taxpayers' Rights in Australia" in Duncan Bentley (ed), Taxpayers' Rights: An International Perspective (*Gold Coast: Revenue Law Journal*, 1998), 57; and Duncan Bentley, "A Taxpayers Charter: Opportunity or Token Gesture" (1995) 12 *Australian Tax Forum* 1.

44   Moreau v FCT (1926) 39 CLR 65.
45   Moreau, above fn. 44, (1926) 39 CLR 65, 67.
46   *David Jones Finance & Investments Pty Ltd v FCT* (1991) 21 ATR 1506.
47   FCT v Patcorp Investments Ltd (1976) 6 ATR 420.
48   His Honour observed (David Jones, above fn. 46, (1990) 21 ATR 718, 722) that in "In assessing the significance of these remarks and the introduction of the concept of 'fairness' it is, in my opinion, relevant to note that Isaacs J, was discussing a provision of the legislation which was dealing with the Commissioner having 'reason to believe' that the taxpayer had defrauded or attempted to evade the revenue law. Hence the obligation to act fairly related to the activities of the Commissioner and his officers in determining whether there was 'reason to believe.'"
49   This section provides that "[t]he Commissioner shall have the general administration

(ITAA36) "requires him to exercise his statutory powers with 'procedural fairness'"[50].

Similarly, in *Bellinz v Federal Commissioner of Taxation*[51] (*Bellinz*) Hill, Sundberg and Goldberg JJ recognised a taxpayer right to fair treatment in principle, but similarly imposed clear boundaries on this right, observing that:

> [t]here is little difficulty in accepting that, where a decision-maker, including the Commissioner of Taxation, has a discretion, a principle of fairness will require that that discretion be exercised in a way that does not discriminate against taxpayers… But … it is difficult to see how the Commissioner can properly be said to have acted unfairly, even if there is an element of discrimination, where he has acted in accordance with the law itself.[52]

However, the key limitation on the development of any recognition of rights to fair treatment in Australian Courts either in judicial review proceedings or in common law proceedings has been the judicial interpretation of the various express or implicit statutory protections of the Australian Commissioner of Taxation.

In judicial review proceedings the key limitations are the privative clauses contained in sections 175 and 177 of the ITAA36. These were acknowledged in *David Jones* as the main obstacles barring the possibility of the taxpayer succeeding in its claim against the Commissioner. According to section 175, an assessment is not invalid merely because the Commissioner has not complied with any provision of the ITAA36. Further, section 177(1) provides that where the Commissioner produces a notice of assessment, that assessment will be conclusive evidence of the due making of the assessment and that the amount and details of that assessment are correct.[53] These provisions have been interpreted as prohibiting judicial review except in cases where the complaint is either not directly related to a tax assessment

---

of this Act."
50 David Jones, above fn. 46, (1990) 21 ATR 718, 723.
51 *Bellinz v Federal Commissioner of Taxation* (1998) 155 ALR 220.
52 Bellinz, above fn. 51, (1998) 155 ALR 220, 233-234. There is a striking contrast between this reasoning and the European approach to application of the doctrine of legitimate expectations which expressly recognises the potential for recognising taxpayer rights even where that would result in the administrative official being required to act outside the law, as discussed in Part 2.
53 The section does preserve the rights of taxpayers to seek a review or appeal against the assessment using the procedures contained in Part IVC of the Taxation Administration Act 1953 (Cth) (ADJR). These procedures too, however, make no allowance for unfairness as a sufficient ground for appeal.

or there is evidence of bad faith, illegality or improper purpose.[54] Mere unfairness is not enough.

Express statutory restrictions on reviewability of tax assessment decisions in the *Administrative* Decisions *(Judicial Review) Act 1977* (Cth)[55] and the restrictive interpretation by courts of the availability of judicial review pursuant to section 39B of the *Judiciary Act 1903* (Cth)[56] have further hindered the possibility of development of any principle of any enforceable taxpayer entitlement to fair treatment – either procedural or substantive.

Consequently, the only instances in which taxpayers have succeeded in administrative law proceedings against the Commissioner on grounds of unfairness have been cases in which the facts of the case allowed a finding for the taxpayer without breaching these statutory limitations. For instance, in *Darrell Lea Chocolate Shops Pty Ltd v Commissioner of Taxation*[57] (*Darrell*

---

54 Walpole more fully expands on the circumstances in which judicial review might be available to a taxpayer generally: "The major ground on which an action for review might be based would be: that the Commissioner did not have jurisdiction to make the decision; that the decision was not authorized by the Act; that the making of the decision was an improper exercise of the power conferred by the Act, because the Commissioner failed to take a relevant consideration into account or exercised the power in a way that constitutes an abuse of power; or that the decision was otherwise contrary to the law." See Michael Walpole, "Taxpayer Rights and Remedies - Australia, New Zealand and China" in Second World Tax Conference (Dublin: Institute of Taxation, 2001).

55 Paragraph (e) of Schedule 1 of the Administrative Decisions (Judicial Review) Act 1977 (Cth) excludes from review decisions forming part of the process of making of, leading up to the making of, or refusing to amend, an assessment of tax. The exclusions in paragraph (e) of Schedule 1 have been interpreted as clearly prohibiting review of decisions dealing with the calculation of tax, irrespective of whether the decisions are unfair. See the comments of Beaumont J in *Constable Holdings Pty Ltd v Federal Commissioner of Taxation* (1987) 72 ALR 265 at 268-269; Ellicott J in *Tooheys Ltd v Minister for Business & Consumer Affairs* (1981) 36 ALR 64 at 78; and Smithers J in *Intervest Corporation Pty Ltd v FCT* (1984) 3 FCR 591 at 595–596.

56 Section 39B of the Judiciary Act 1903 (Cth) provides the Federal Court of Australia with original jurisdiction in respect of any matter in which a writ of mandamus or prohibition or an injunction is sought against an officer of the Commonwealth. The Federal Court generally allows applications under both section 39B and the ADJR to be made and heard concurrently. In tax proceedings, the section 39B jurisdiction may be preferred given the absence of any express tax-specific limitations on review similar to those contained in paragraph (e) of Schedule 1 of the ADJR. However courts have broadly interpreted sections 175 and 177 of the ITAA36 to restrict their jurisdiction to review tax cases under section 39B. Aside from Moreau, above fn. 44, (1926) 39 CLR 65, all of the cases discussed above in this Part concerned applications for judicial review under section 39B.

57 *Darrell Lea Chocolate Shops Pty Ltd v Commissioner of Taxatio*n (1996) 141 ALR 713. In this case the Commissioner issued four separate assessment for sales tax of the same taxpayer in respect of the same transactions in the same goods made under a four different assessment Acts – and all without making any genuine attempt to assess

Lea), Spender Burchett and Hill JJ had no difficulty confirming that "the extensive powers conferred upon the Commissioner in connection with the assessment and collection of sales tax, or for that matter any other tax, must be so exercised as to deal fairly with each taxpayer."[58] The Court freed itself of the constraints of the privative clause in the sales tax legislation in question (which protected from review decisions concerning ascertainment or calculation of tax) by holding that there was no genuine assessment in this case as the Commissioner had made his "assessment" on facts known by him to be untrue. Hence, the taxpayer was able to succeed in its claim of unfair treatment by the Commissioner.[59] However, as most taxpayer complaints concern bona fide tax assessment activities such successes are likely to remain exceedingly rare.

There has also been no judicial recognition in Australia of any legal right to fair treatment in the equally rare cases involving taxpayer attempts to invoke the common law to enforce their rights. Australian judges have refused to impose any common law duties alongside the Commissioner's duties to the Crown for fear of contradicting an implicit legislative intent that the Australian Commissioner of Taxation owes duties only to the Crown. For example, in *Lucas v O'Reilly*[60] a case involving allegations of tortious breach of statutory duty by the Commissioner of Taxation,[61] Young CJ, in comprehensively rejecting the taxpayer's submissions, stated:

> "If the cause of action relied upon by the plaintiff is based upon a breach of statutory duty, the plaintiff must show...that the statute creating the duty confers upon him a right of action in respect of any breach...However, it is, I think, clear that the defendant owes the plaintiff no such duty. The duty of the Commissioner is owed to the Crown."[62]

---

the sale value of particular goods under each Act and on a factual basis which the Commissioner knew was wrong.

58 Darrell Lea, above fn. 57, (1996) 141 ALR 713, 726. For similar comments, made in the context of discussing the line of UK legitimate expectation cases discussed in Part 2 of this article see *Pickering v Deputy Commissioner of Taxation* (1997) 37 ATR 41; *Ando Minerals NL v Deputy Federal Commissioner of Taxation* (1994) 94 ATC 4163; and *Federal Commissioner of Taxation v Biga Nominees Pty Ltd* (1988) 88 ATC 4270.

59 The High Court recently re-examined the issue in *Commissioner of Taxation v Futuris Corporation Ltd* (2008) 237 CLR 146, with the Court confirming that judicial review is only available in cases involving a tax assessment decision where the assessment is tentative or provisional or there has been conscious maladministration by the Commissioner. Again, no room was allowed for mere unfairness as a sufficient ground for review of an assessment.

60 *Lucas v O'Reilly* (Lucas) (1979) 79 ATC 4081.

61 Breach of statutory duty was also separately unsuccessfully pleaded by the taxpayer in *Harris v Deputy Commissioner of Taxation* (Harris) (2001) 47 ATR 406.

62 Lucas, above fn. 60, (1979) 79 ATC 4081, 4085. This is very similar to the stance taken in

This confinement of the Commissioner's duties to the Crown is a recurring theme in Australian tax cases and extends to equitable as well as common law taxpayer claims against the Commissioner.[63] This prevailing judicial attitude allows little scope for recognition of any private law taxpayer right to fair treatment in Australia in the foreseeable future.

Australian judges have also rejected the UK doctrine of legitimate expectations. While cases such as *Bellinz*, *Darrell Lea* and *David Jones* discuss the UK legitimate expectation cases, the doctrine has clearly been rejected in Australia.[64] Further, as former High Court Chief Justice Sir Anthony Mason has extra-judicially observed; "[i]t would require a revolution in Australian judicial thinking to bring about an adoption of the English approach to substantive protection of legitimate expectations."[65]

This suggests that, in the absence of legislative intervention, any significant legal recognition of Australian taxpayer rights to fair treatment in the foreseeable future is highly unlikely.

Harris v Deputy Commissioner of Taxation, above fn. 61, (2001) 47 ATR 406. In that case, Grove J asserted, at 408, that "[t]here is no basis upon which to conclude that there is a tort liability in the Australian Taxation Office or its named officers towards a taxpayer arising out of the lawful exercise of functions under the Income Tax Assessment Act."

63 For example, similar views, strongly suggestive of the extreme judicial sensitivity to encroaching on statutorily imposed duties of the Commissioner, were plainly stated by Hill J in the equitable estoppel context in *AGC (Investments) Ltd v Federal Commissioner of Taxation* (1991) 91 ATC 4180, at 4195: "[T]here is no room for the doctrine of estoppel operating to preclude the Commissioner from pursuing his statutory duty to assess tax in accordance with law. The Income Tax Assessment Act imposes obligations on the Commissioner and creates public rights and duties, which the application of the doctrine of estoppel would thwart."

64 In accordance with the approach taken by the *High Court in Re Minister for Immigration & Multicultural & Indigenous Affairs: Ex parte Lam* (2003) 214 CLR 1. Gummow and McHugh JJ stated in that case, at 21, that "...nothing in this judgment should be taken as ... adoption of recent developments in English law with respect to substantive benefits or outcomes." The approach of Gummow and McHugh JJ is consistent with earlier High Court authority such as *Attorney-General (NSW) v Quin* (1990) 170 CLR 1.

65 Sir Anthony Mason, "Procedural Fairness: Its Development and the Continuing Role of Legitimate Expectations" (2005) 12 Australian Journal of Administrative Law 103, 108. Another former High Court Chief Justice, Sir Michael Kirby has recently written a paper outlining the increasing influence of human rights law in Australia, but there is no evidence of such reasoning being applied in Australian tax cases to indicate that the revolution alluded to by Sir Anthony Mason has begun. See Sir Michael Kirby, "Australia's Growing Debt to the European Court of Human Rights" (2008) 34 *Monash University Law Review* 239.

4 Fair treatment of taxpayers as a legal rule – A blueprint for reform

The preceding analysis reveals a number of common challenges inherent in translating the moral duty to treat taxpayers fairly into an enforceable legal right which does not unduly impinge on the Revenue's tax administration duties to the Crown. This Part proposes a blueprint in the form of three recommendations for addressing these challenges. These recommendations are:

1   An express legislative pronouncement on the issue;

2   Extending the availability of compensation as a remedy for taxpayers treated unfairly; and

3   Establishing mechanisms for independent oversight to monitor and sanction tax officials for unfair treatment of taxpayers.

Each of these recommendations is discussed in turn below:

4.1   Legislative pronouncement

It is evident from the analysis in the preceding Part that one of the primary impediments in the way of entrenching the moral duty to treat taxpayers fairly in enforceable legal rules is a judicial concern with interfering with the legislature and executive by imposing duties to taxpayers on the Revenue which are inconsistent with legislatively-imposed primary public duties to administer and collect taxes. The preceding analysis reveals that this concern is particularly prominent in Australia. This concern is evident both in Australian administrative law cases and private law cases involving claims of unfair treatment of taxpayers by tax officials.

However, this judicial concern with justiciability and offending the doctrine of separation of powers by imposing private law duties to individual taxpayers which might conflict with Revenue duties to the Crown is also evident in the reasoning of UK judges in considering claims of unfair treatment of taxpayers.[66] For example, in the UK, some judges have conceded that the duties of HMRC are owed exclusively to the Crown, hence judicial recognition of duties to individual taxpayers might be considered "subversive to the whole system"[67].

---

66   For discussion about the prevalence of such concerns in tax cases see John Bevacqua, 'Public Policy Concerns in Taxpayer Claims against the Commissioner of Taxation – Myths and Realities' (2011) 40 *Australian Tax Review* 10.

67   Lord Wilberforce in Fleet Street Casuals, above fn. 8, [1981] STC 260, 266. Cf the comments of Lord Scarman who, in the same case, at 280, directly rejected the suggestion that "the duty to collect 'every part of inland revenue' is a duty owed exclusively to the Crown."

This is very similar reasoning to that often used by Australian judges to deny relief to taxpayers complaining of unfair treatment.[68] Further, the development of the doctrine of legitimate expectations in the UK requires judges to specifically weigh up private duties to taxpayers against the public responsibilities of the Revenue.[69] Inherent in such a weighing up are questions of justiciability and separation of powers which have deeply troubled many Australian judges.

Despite these common threads of judicial concern, direct comparisons are difficult as the different constitutional frameworks and conventions in each country underpin the various judicial approaches. For example, in explaining the rejection of any administrative law recognition of a right to substantive fairness in Australia, it has been observed that:

> "...notions of 'good administration' and 'fairness' inform English administrative law. Australian administrative law reflects more of a separation of powers approach, perhaps influenced by the character of the Australian Constitution as a delineation of government powers rather than as a charter of citizen's rights."[70]

Similarly, the specific legislative frameworks establishing and regulating the ATO and HMRC also significantly influence the willingness and ability of courts to recognise legally enforceable rights to fair treatment of taxpayers. This fact also makes generalisations difficult. For example, UK judges are guided by the "care and management" provisions contained in section 5(1) of the *Commissioner for Revenue and Customs Act 2005*.[71] Australian judges have less legislative guidance but, as discussed in Part 3, must be mindful of

---

[68] See, for example, the comments of Young CJ in Lucas, above fn. 60, (1979) 79 ATC 4081, reproduced above in the text accompanying fn. 62.

[69] As explained by Lord Woolfe MR in *R. v North and East Devon Health Authority Ex p. Coughlan* [1999] EWCA Civ 1871, at [57]. This explanation is reproduced above at fn. 26.

[70] Sir Anthony Mason, "Procedural Fairness: Its Development and Continuing Role of Legitimate Expectations" (2005) 12 *Australian Journal of Administrative Law* 103, 109. These comments echo the sentiments expressed by Gummow J in Re Minister for Immigration and Multicultural Affairs ex parte Lam, above fn. 65 at 24 where His Honour, in rejecting the recognition of the UK doctrine of legitimate expectations in Australia, observed that "a written federal constitution, with separation of the judicial power, necessarily presents a frame of reference which differs both from the English and other European systems ..."

[71] This subsection requires the Commissioners for Revenue and Customs to be responsible for the "collection and management of revenue". The Act imputes the same meaning on this phrase as in the express references to "care and management" contained in the Taxes Management Act 1970 (UK) which was repealed in 2005 and replaced with the Commissioner for Revenue and Customs Act 2005 (UK). This care and management requirement was a focus of significant judicial consideration in cases such as Fleet Street Casuals, above fn. 8, [1981] STC 260.

provisions such as the privative clauses protecting tax assessment decisions contained in sections 175 and 177 of the ITAA36.

Nevertheless, there is a clear lesson which can be extrapolated from the preceding analysis: the desirability of express and clear legislative guidance to assist courts to reconcile taxpayer rights to fair treatment with the Revenue's primary public tax administration and collection duties. A detailed and comprehensive legislative statement setting out when (if at all) taxpayers have a legal right to take action for unfair treatment by tax officials would enable judges to proceed with greater confidence as to the intent of the legislature than presently possible for judges in either the UK or Australia.

In Australia, the absence of express legislative guidance on these issues has seen judges consistently err on the side of caution by denying the existence of any enforceable taxpayer rights to fair treatment in almost every case in deference to unstated legislative intent to confine the duties of the Commissioner to the Crown.[72] This may at first seem counter-intuitive as it could be argued that a legislative vacuum such as that in Australia leaves scope for judges to fill that vacuum by confirming rather than denying taxpayers legal rights to fair treatment. However, this result depends on the prevailing judicial culture and the various degrees of judicial deference to the legislative law-making function. Most Australian judges have not been willing to adopt the expansive approach to judicial activism advocated by Lord Scarman in *Fleet Street Casuals*:

> "Are we in the twilight world of "maladministration" where only Parliament and the Ombudsman may enter, or upon the commanding heights of the law? The courts have a role, long established, in the public law ... I would not be a party to the retreat of the courts from this field of public law merely because the duties imposed upon the Revenue are complex and call for management decisions in which discretion must play a significant role."[73]

Of course, the legitimate expectations cases in the UK show that many UK judges also do not share Lord Scarman's permissive attitude to judicial activism.[74]

This variability in judicial attitudes is natural. It also illustrates that the development of judicially recognised rights to fair treatment of

---

72　See for example, the cases discussed above at fn. 60 to fn. 62.
73　Fleet Street Casuals, above fn. 8, [1981] STC 260, 280.
74　The various judicial approaches have resulted in the uncertainty as to the role of unfairness in judicial review proceedings in the UK, as discussed in the articles cited in fn. 25.

taxpayers will necessarily be slower, more uncertain and more piecemeal than considered legislative action. Neither taxpayers nor the Revenue are likely to benefit from the uncertainty and cost associated with this type of incremental judicial development. Given the recognised link between voluntary taxpayer compliance and fair treatment, delay and uncertainty are especially insidious. Consequently, this fact also advances the case for clear and express legislative guidance on the question of taxpayer rights to fair treatment by tax officials. Judges in both Australia and UK would benefit from such guidance, as would Revenue officials, taxpayers and other tax administration system stakeholders.

4.2 A right to compensation for unfair treatment

A second recommendation for addressing the challenges in recognising taxpayer rights to fair treatment evident from the preceding analysis is the desirability of a taxpayer right to compensation for unfair treatment by the Revenue. There are a number of reasons for considering compensation as a particularly effective tool for striking an appropriate balance between ensuring fair and proper treatment of taxpayers and the public duties of revenue officials.

The primary reason is that an express right to damages would provide a more nuanced approach to dealing with the continuing separation of powers and other public policy concerns expressed by judges in taxpayer claims asserting unfair treatment at the hands of tax officials.

For example, there has been much debate in the UK and in Australia centred on the desirability of recognising a right to *substantive* fairness as distinct from a right to procedural fairness alone. The concern judges express in many such cases is that allowing substantive relief comes dangerously close to engaging courts in matters which offend the longstanding administrative law principle in both of those countries that judges do not engage in merits review.[75]

A more nuanced approach to such cases is possible if a right to damages for substantive unfairness is conceded.[76] Presently, courts in such cases typically respect any separation of powers and other administrative law policy concerns by not overturning the substantive discretionary decision of the Revenue in such a case even where the result would be patently unfair on the taxpayer. However, the same result could be achieved through leaving the Revenue's substantive decision unchanged but recognising resulting

---

75 For detailed discussion see Groves (2008), above fn. 27.
76 Forsyth suggests that the availability of damages has been one of the reasons for the more expansive European approach to recognising substantive legitimate expectations. See Forsyth (1988), above fn. 42.

unfairness to taxpayers through an award of damages. Such an award could be considered a "price" for upholding the Revenue's stance. Fordham provides an example of how such a system might operate:

"Take, for example, the situation of a 'substantive legitimate expectation', but where it is said to the Court that there is some 'overriding public interest' by virtue of which the State should be able to interfere with the expectation. It may very well be that, in such a case, the Court could ... reconcile (a) the need to vindicate the claimant's expectation and (b) the public interest in the State defeating it, by ensuring reparation, as the 'price' for upholding the state action, whether offered to or exacted by the Court."[77]

Monetary compensation awards used in this way serve a dual purpose in that they can act as a "powerful incentive to improve service"[78] and treat taxpayers fairly without, strictly speaking, being directive in the sense of imposing changes in decisions or behaviour on the Revenue. The relevance of this distinction can be appreciated with an example utilising the facts in *David Jones*.[79] It will be recalled from Part II that in this case, the Australian Commissioner resiled from his usual practice of allowing inter-corporate dividend rebates. The taxpayer unsuccessfully argued that this was unfair and constituted an abuse of process by the Commissioner.[80]

Despite the apparent unfairness to the taxpayer, the Australian Court's decision has a logical appeal. For the court to have directed the Commissioner to revert to his previous practice would have been tantamount to restricting or fettering the Commissioner's legislatively sanctioned discretion in applying the tax laws.[81] The Court would have potentially faced the criticism

---

77 Michael Fordham, "Reparation for Maladministration: Public Law's Final Frontier" (2003) 8 *Judicial Review* 104, 107.
78 Office of the Commonwealth Ombudsman, Commonwealth of Australia, To Compensate or Not to Compensate? Own Motion Investigation of Commonwealth Arrangements for Providing Financial Redress for Maladministration (1999), 11.
79 David Jones, above fn. 46, (1991) 21 ATR 1506.
80 The factual similarity with the UK case of Unilever, above fn. 20, [1996] STC 681, is striking. It will be recalled from the discussion in Part 2 that the taxpayer succeeded in that case.
81 Similar reasoning is applied in both Australia and the UK to generally deny the availability of an estoppel action against the Revenue. In Australia, the traditional position has been bluntly and concisely stated by Kitto J in FCT v Wade (1951) 84 CLR 105: "No conduct on the part of the Commissioner could operate as an estoppel against the operation of the Act." See also the comments of Wade J in *AGC (Investments) Ltd v FCT* (1991) 91 ATC 4180. The broader principle underlying this restrictive approach is known as the "non-fetter" principle that "government should not be shackled in exercising its power to make decisions in the public interest in the future." See Margaret Allars, "Tort and Equity Claims Against the State" in Paul Finn (ed), *Essays on Law and Government* (North Ryde: Law Book Company, 1996) Vol. 2, 49, 86. For further discussion of the non-fetter principle see Chris Hilson, "Policies, the Non-

of having overstepped its role and infringed the principles of justiciability and the underlying doctrine of separation of powers. Accordingly, it is understandable that the Court left the taxpayer with no remedy.

However, if the option of an award of damages was open to the Court in *David Jones*, the result could have been very different. An award of damages in such a case could not be seen as a substitution of the Court's decision for that of the Commissioner. It would, however, place a "price" on the Commissioner changing his long-standing practices where such changes would unfairly cause loss to taxpayers. While the public expectation that a tax authority should be free to change its position in the public interest is respected, an award of damages recognises that the public may be best placed to bear the losses flowing from that freedom, rather than adversely affected individual taxpayers.[82]

Additionally, in a broader sense, the operation of compensation as a signalling mechanism for the boundaries of acceptable tax administration behaviour in such cases could be valuable for maintaining tax administration legitimacy.[83] A monetary remedy sends an unambiguous signal of disapproval of unfair tax administration activity.[84] This signal potentially plays an important role in taxpayers having confidence that the system of tax administration will operate within reasonable boundaries. This, in turn, will aid in fostering a climate of voluntary tax compliance.[85] Again, therefore, legislative reform aimed at recognising taxpayer rights to compensation for specific forms of unfair treatment by tax officials is worthy of serious consideration.[86]

Fetter Principle and the Principle of Substantive Legitimate Expectations: Between a Rock and a Hard Place?" (2006) 11 *Judicial Review* 289; and Chris Hilson, "Judicial Review, Policies and the Fettering of Discretion" [2002] *Public Law* 111.

82 The utilitarian argument is that levying everyone to compensate for losses suffered by particular individuals increases the total good. Cohen discusses this argument at length. See David Cohen, "Suing the State" (1990) 40 *University of Toronto Law Journal* 630, 644-645.

83 The legitimacy argument has long been recognised in the US – see, for example, Bernard Schwartz, *An Introduction to American Administrative Law* (New York: Oceana Publishing, 1962), 218.

84 Writers such as McBride, Roots and Fordham make this point in calling for the availability of damages awards in administrative review proceedings – see Jeremy McBride, "Damages as a Remedy for Unlawful Administrative Action" (1979) 38 *Cambridge Law Journal* 323; Lachlan Roots, "A Tort of Maladministration: Government Stuff-Ups" (1993) 18 *Alternative Law Journal* 67, 71; and Michael Fordham (2003), above fn. 75.

85 As confirmed in numerous studies including those noted above at fn. 7.

86 It is beyond the scope of this article to formulate a specific statutory damages remedy. However, an example of a general monetary compensation remedy for loss caused by tax official wrongs is formulated and presented in John Bevacqua, Taxpayer Rights to Compensation for Tax Office Mistakes (Sydney: CCH, 2011).

4.3 Independent oversight and sanctions for unfair treatment

There is no lack of aspirational statements and informal, often self-administered systems, standards and guidelines aimed at ensuring fair treatment of taxpayers in the UK and Australia. As already noted, in both jurisdictions, Charter entitlements to fair treatment are recorded.[87] Further, service standards and other measures exist to measure compliance with these commitments to taxpayers.[88] These guidelines and standards are an important cog in ensuring fair treatment of taxpayers and should not all be enshrined in legislation enforceable by taxpayers against the Revenue. It is undesirable to allow taxpayers to recover compensation in every conceivable instance of unfair treatment.[89] As Lord Wilberforce observed in *Fleet Street Casuals*, "the income tax legislation contains a large number of anomalies which are naturally not thought to be fair by those disadvantaged."[90] Further, in practical terms it would be impossible to objectively judge every instance of fair treatment encapsulated in value-laden concepts such as "courtesy" and "politeness" which are often referred to in Revenue service charters and guidelines.[91]

---

87 See for example, the commitments referred to above at fn. 2 – fn. 4.

88 For example, the Australian Taxation Office has shown an increasing concern with responsiveness benchmarks which strongly indicate a taxpayer service-oriented attitude. See Australian Taxation Office, "Our Service Standards" available at http://www.ato.gov.au/corporate/distributor.aspx?menuid=0&doc=/content/25940.htm&page=2#P24_2573 [Accessed 1 Feb 2013]; and Australian Taxation Office, Annual Report 2010-11 (2011). Further, it has close to 50 consultative forums with taxpayers, professionals and other stakeholders. See Australian Taxation Office, "Stakeholder Consultation Overview" available at http://www.ato.gov.au/corporate/content.asp?doc=/content/00131220.htm&mnu=430198mfp=001 [Accessed 1 Feb 2013]. This is also a strong indicator of the perceived importance of providing good and fair service to taxpayers. Similarly, in the UK, HMRC are currently producing a performance management system. It has produced a business plan as part of its performance management system which describes its vision as including making taxpayers "feel that the tax system is...even-handed..." HM Revenue & Customs, "Business Plan 2011-2015" available at http://www.number10.gov.uk/wp-content/uploads/2011/01/HMRC-Business-Plan.pdf [Accessed 21 April 2012], 1. Similar commitments are made in HM Revenue & Customs, "HMRC Service Standards for Excise, Customs, Stamp Taxes and Money Services Customers" available at http://www.hmrc.gov.uk/customs/ecsm-service-standards.pdf [Accessed 1 Feb 2013].

89 The filing of frivolous lawsuits may well ensue. Such a concern led one judge in the US to observe that "filing of frivolous lawsuits merely to protest the assessment of federal income tax has become a new and unpleasant indoor sport" (*McKirney v Regan* 599 F.Supp. 126, 129-30 (M.D. La. 1984)); similarly, the filing of such suits has been judicially described as a vampire requiring a sharpened stake to kill it (*United States v Craig*, 73 A.F.T.R.2d 1099 (D.N.D. 1994)).

90 Fleet Street Casuals, above fn. 8, [1981] STC 260, 266.

91 See, for example many of the commitments contained in the list of commitments under the heading of fairness and reasonableness contained in the Australian Taxpayers' Charter and reproduced above at fn. 2.

However, it is possible to devise legal rules which make revenue authorities accountable and incentivise revenue authorities to treat taxpayers fairly which do not create any commensurate taxpayer avenues of relief for unfair treatment. Such laws are an essential third limb of any attempt to translate taxpayer moral rights to fair treatment into legal rules. Precedents for devising such laws already exist. For example, the US Congress has enacted a number of provisions which might serve as a useful template for Australian and UK lawmakers.

The US Congress has enacted legislative provisions expressly requiring tax official performance of Internal Revenue Service (IRS) employees to be measured by reference to fair and equitable treatment of taxpayers.[92] Further provisions charge the US Treasury Inspector General for Tax Administration with the task of annually evaluating IRS compliance with this obligation, ensuring a high level of accountability.[93] Congress has also enacted a list of "ten deadly sins"[94] which requires the IRS Commissioner to terminate the employment of any employee on misconduct grounds in cases of proven commission of one or more of these "sins". This also provides further specific and real incentives for tax officials to treat taxpayers fairly.[95]

---

[92] Specifically, section 1204(b) of the Internal Revenue Service Restructuring and Reform Act of 1998, Pub L No 105-206, 112 Stat 685 (1998) directly requires IRS managers to "use the fair and equitable treatment of taxpayers by employees as one of the standards for evaluating employee performance."

[93] Section 7803(d)(1)(2000) of the US Internal Revenue Code requires the Treasury Inspector General for Tax Administration to annually evaluate whether the IRS has complied with section 1204(b) of the Revenue Service Restructuring and Reform Act of 1998, Pub L No 105-206, 112 Stat 685 (1998).

[94] Section 1203 of the Revenue Service Restructuring and Reform Act of 1998, Pub L No 105-206, 112 Stat 685 (1998) requires the Commissioner of Internal Revenue to terminate the employment of any employee on misconduct grounds if there is a final administrative or judicial determination that the employee committed one or more of a range of ten infringements of taxpayer rights including infringement of a taxpayer's Constitutional rights and a range of other civil rights, violations of tax laws and IRS policies in order to harass a taxpayer and a range of other wilful or personally motivated activities adversely affecting taxpayers. These have become known as the "ten deadly sins."

[95] The Australian regulation of tax official fair treatment of taxpayer provides a stark contrast to the US approach. In *Commissioner of Taxation v Futuris Corporation Ltd* above fn. 59, (2008) 237 CLR 146, the High Court made reference to the requirement that tax officials, as members of the Australian Public Service act with care and diligence, honesty and integrity in accordance with the Public Service Act 1999 (Cth). Australian tax officers, as members of the Australian Public Service are, indeed, required to act in accordance with Australian Public Service values and standards of conduct. These are set out in the Public Service Act 1999 (Cth) and Public Service Regulations 1999 (Cth). Further, section 13 of the Public Service Act 1999 (Cth) contains the Australian Public Service Code of Conduct which emphasises the need to deliver "services fairly, effectively, impartially and courteously to the Australian public." (See Australian

These enactments provide a particularly pertinent starting point for formulating similar rules in the UK and Australia given the judicial concern in both jurisdictions that entrenching a right to fair treatment through providing taxpayers with avenues of relief against the Revenue might create inconsistencies with the public duties the Revenue. This is because provisions such as these focus on incentivising tax officials to treat taxpayers fairly without directly disturbing any specific Revenue decision concerning any particular taxpayer.

5 Conclusions

This chapter has not sought to pass judgment on the effectiveness of laws for ensuring fair treatment of taxpayers in either Australia or the UK. However, it is clear that in each jurisdiction the current approach is neither perfect nor complete. This is unsurprising because taxpayer rights to fair treatment at the hands of tax officials will always be the subject of a delicate balancing exercise between the private interests of individual taxpayers and the public interest in ensuring that the vital tax administration function is not unduly obstructed or fettered. Consequently, assessments as to the adequacy of protection of taxpayer rights to fair treatment necessarily involve value-laden judgments of how to resolve the trade-off between these competing interests. These judgments will evolve and shift over time.[96] Further, final determinations must be considered in the context of the constitutional and political framework in which the relevant decision-makers operate.

None of these facts, however, are sufficient reasons for law-makers to shy away from the issue entirely. Legislators and judges are regularly faced with having to make difficult trade-offs between public and private interests.[97]

Public Service Commission, "APS Code of Conduct" available at http://www.apsc.gov.au/aps-employment-policy-and-advice/aps-values-and-code-of-conduct/code-of-conduct [Accessed 1 February 2013]. However, the only sanction for breach of the Code is contained in section 15 which provides for a number of possible employee sanctions including possible termination of employment, reprimand, demotion or reduction in salary. In contrast with the US system, there is nothing in this legislation which requires independent oversight of public official compliance with these requirements or which compels managers to terminate the employment of officials for particular breaches of the Code.

96 As Bentley has noted "[e]ssentially taxation can be seen as a barometer of the developing balance between State and individual rights." (emphasis added). See Duncan Bentley, *Taxpayers' Rights: Theory, Origin and Implementation* (Alphen aan den Rijn: Kluwer, 2007), 15.

97 As one author has generally noted: "If all such political 'hot potatoes' were to be deemed unsuitable for judicial scrutiny the administrative law casebooks would be slim volumes indeed." Chris Finn, "The Justiciability of Administrative Decisions: A Redundant Concept?" (2002) 30 *Federal Law Review* 239, 249.

The preceding analysis demonstrates that both in the UK and Australia legislators have not taken up the challenge of weighing up these competing interests. The result in both countries has been that the judiciary has been left with this responsibility.

UK judges, by developing the doctrine of legitimate expectations, have shown a greater willingness to accept this responsibility than Australian judges. Arguably, the increasing influence of the HRA and the recognition of the doctrine of legitimate expectations under European Union law has aided in fostering this judicial receptiveness in the UK. By comparison, Australian judges have been less willing to set precedents which recognise taxpayer fair treatment as more than a mere moral duty on tax officials. The difference in judicial approaches is at least in part explained by the differing constitutional and legislative frameworks of the two countries. However, neither country is far advanced along the path to translating the moral duty of tax officials to treat taxpayers fairly into a clear and certain legal right.

This chapter has set out three recommendations for effectively translating the moral duty to treat taxpayers fairly into enforceable legal rules and injecting a degree of clarity and certainty in both jurisdictions. Only one of these recommendations directly centres on providing taxpayers with enhanced formal avenues of relief for unfair treatment – the recognition of a limited right to compensation for unfair treatment. Of the remaining two recommendations, one calls for a statutory pronouncement of taxpayer rights to fair treatment. The second calls for legal rules aimed at providing independent oversight and real incentives for tax officers to treat taxpayers fairly, akin to those in countries such as the US.

The aim of these recommendations is not a *per se* increase in taxpayer ability to successfully sue tax officials in cases of unfair treatment – the desirability or otherwise of such an increase is a matter for the UK and Australian legislatures. Instead, the primary objective is to break the legislative silence in order to assist judges to resolve many of the public policy difficulties which have troubled judges in considering cases concerning claims of unfair treatment by tax officials.

While the challenge of striking the appropriate trade-off between taxpayer rights to fair treatment and the public duties of tax officials will always be a difficult one, these three recommendations provide a useful starting point for proactively and directly addressing the issue. By acting directly and proactively in this way we can at least start the search for an answer to the question posed by Lord Scarman about the obligation to treat taxpayers fairly: "Is it a mere moral duty, a matter for policy but not a rule of law?"[98]

---

98 Fleet Street Casuals, above fn. 8, [1981] STC 260, 280.

4   Bibliography

Articles & Books

Allars, Margaret, (1996) "Tort and Equity Claims Against the State" in Paul Finn (ed), *Essays on Law and Government* (North Ryde: Law Book Company, Vol. 2, 49.

Bamforth, Nicholas, (1997) "Fairness and Legitimate Expectation in Judicial Review" *Cambridge Law Journal* 56, 1.

Bentley, Duncan, (1995) "A Taxpayers Charter: Opportunity or Token Gesture" *Australian Tax Forum* 12,1.

Bentley, Duncan, (2007) *Taxpayers' Rights: Theory, Origin and Implementation* (Alphen aan den Rijn: Kluwer,).

Bevacqua, John, (2011) 'Public Policy Concerns in Taxpayer Claims against the Commissioner of Taxation – Myths and Realities' *Australian Tax Review* 40, 10.

Bevacqua, John, 92011) *Taxpayer Rights to Compensation for Tax Office Mistakes* (Sydney: CCH,).

Clayton, Richard, (2003) "Legitimate Expectations, Policy and the Principle of Consistency" *Cambridge Law Journal* 62, 93.

Cohen, David, (1990) "Suing the State" *University of Toronto Law Journal* 40 ,630.

Cowell, Frank, (1992) "Tax Evasion and Inequity" *Journal of Economic Psychology* 13,521.

Falkinger, Josef, (1995) "Tax Evasion, Consumption of Public Goods and Fairness" *Journal of Economic Psychology* 16, 63.

Finn, Chris, (2002) "The Justiciability of Administrative Decisions: A Redundant Concept?" *Federal Law Review* 30, 239.

Fordham, Michael, (2003) "Reparation for Maladministration: Public Law's Final Frontier" *Judicial Review* 8, 104.

Forsyth, Christopher, (1988) "The Provenance and Protection of Legitimate Expectations in Administrative Law" *Cambridge Law Journal* 47, 238.

Groves, Matthew, (2008) "Substantive Legitimate Expectations in Australian Administrative Law" *Melbourne University Law Review* 32, 470.

Hilson, Chris, (2002])"Judicial Review, Policies and the Fettering of Discretion" *Public Law* 111.

Hilson, Chris, (2006) "Policies, the Non-Fetter Principle and the Principle of Substantive Legitimate Expectations: Between a Rock and a Hard Place?" *Judicial Review* 11, 289.

Job, Jenny, and Reinhart, Monika, (2003) "Trusting the Tax Office: Does Putnam's Thesis relate to Tax?" *Australian Journal of Social Issues* 38, 307.

Kirby, Sir Michael, (2008) "Australia's Growing Debt to the European Court of Human Rights" *Monash University Law Review* 34, 239.

Mason, Robert, and Calvin, Lyle, (1984) "Public Confidence and Admitted Tax Evasion" *National Tax Journal* 37 , 489.

Mason, Sir Anthony, (2005) "Procedural Fairness: Its Development and the Continuing Role of Legitimate Expectations" *Australian Journal of Administrative Law* 12, 103.

McBride, Jeremy, (1979) "Damages as a Remedy for Unlawful Administrative Action" *Cambridge Law Journal* 38, 323.

Murphy, Kristina, (2004) "The Role of Trust in Nurturing Compliance: A Study of Accused Tax Avoiders" *Law and Human Behaviour* 28 , 187.

Roberts, Michael, and Hite, Peggy, (1994) "Progressive Taxation, Fairness and Compliance" *Law and Policy* 16, 27.

Roots, Lachlan, (1993) "A Tort of Maladministration: Government Stuff-Ups" *Alternative Law Journal* 18, 67.

Scholz, John, (1998) "Trust, Taxes and Compliance" in Valerie Braithwaite and Margaret Levi (eds), *Trust and Governance*, 135.

Schwartz, Bernard, (1962) *An Introduction to American Administrative Law* (New York: Oceana Publishing,).

Sheffrin, Steven, and Triest, Robert, (1992) "Can Brute Deterrence Backfire? Perceptions and Attitudes in Tax Compliance" in Joel Slemrod (ed), *Who Pays Taxes and Why? Tax Compliance and Enforcement* 193.

Stewart, Cameron, (2000) "Substantive Unfairness: A New Species of Abuse of Power?" (2000) *Federal Law Review* 28 , 617.

Virgo, Graham, (2000) "Cheating the Public Revenue" *Cambridge Law Journal* 59, 42.

Virgo, Graham, (2002) "Cheating the Public Revenue: Fictions and Human rights" *Cambridge Law Journal* 61, 47.

Walpole, Michael, (2001) "Taxpayer Rights and Remedies - Australia, New Zealand and China" in *Second World Tax Conference* (Dublin: Institute of Taxation,).

Wheelright, Karen, (1998) "Taxpayers' Rights in Australia" in Duncan Bentley (ed), *Taxpayers' Rights: An International Perspective* (Gold Coast: Revenue Law Journal), 57.

Case Law

AGC (Investments) Ltd v Federal Commissioner of Taxation (1991) 91 ATC 4180.

Ando Minerals NL v Deputy Federal commissioner of Taxation (1994) 94 ATC 4163.

Attorney-General (NSW) v Quin (1990) 170 CLR 1.

Bellinz v Federal Commissioner of Taxation (1998) 155 ALR 220.

Bourne v HMRC (Bourne) [2010] UKFTT 294 (TC).

Commissioner of Taxation v Futuris Corporation Ltd (2008) 237 CLR 146.

Congreve v Inland Revenue Commissioners (1948) 30 TC 163 (HL).

Constable Holdings Pty Ltd v Federal Commissioner of Taxation (1987) 72 ALR 265.
Corkteck Ltd v HMRC [2009] EWHC 785 (Admin).
Darrell Lea Chocolate Shops Pty Ltd v Commissioner of Taxation (1996) 141 ALR 713.
David Jones Finance & Investments Pty Ltd v FCT (1991) 21 ATR 1506.
FCT v Patcorp Investments Ltd (1976) 6 ATR 420.
FCT v Wade (1951) 84 CLR 105.
Federal Commissioner of Taxation v Biga Nominees Pty Ltd (1988) 88 ATC 4270.
Gemeente Leusden v Staatssecretaris van Financien (C-487/01 and C-7/02) [2004] ECR I-5337; [2007] STC 776.
Harris v Deputy Commissioner of Taxation (Harris) (2001) 47 ATR 406.
Hobbs, Richard, Walsh and Geen v United Kingdom [2006] ECHR 63684/00.
Inland Revenue Commissioners v National Federation of Self-Employed and Small Business Ltd [1981] UKHL 2, 18; [1981] STC 260.
Intervest Corporation Pty Ltd v FCT (1984) 3 FCR 591.
Latilla v Inland Revenue Commissioners (1943) 25 TC 107 (CA.
Lucas v O'Reilly (1979) 79 ATC 4081.
Mavridis v Parliament (Mavridis) (C-289/81) [1983] ECR 1733.
McKinney v Regan 599 F.Supp. 126, 129-30 (M.D. La. 1984).
Moreau v FCT (1926) 39 CLR 65.
Pickering v Deputy Commissioner of Taxation (1997) 37 ATR 41.
R. v Allen [2001] UKHL 45; [2001] STC 1537.
R. v Commissioners of Inland Revenue Ex p. Wilkinson [2005] UKHL 30; [2006] STC 270.
R. v Dimsey [2001] UKHL 46; [2001] STC 1520.
R. v North and East Devon Health Authority Ex p. Coughlan [1999] EWCA Civ 1871.
R. v Inland Revenue Commissioners Ex p. MFK Underwriting Agencies Ltd (MFK Underwriting) [1990] 1 WLR 1545, 1569-1570; [1989] STC 873.
R. v Inland Revenue Commissioners Ex p. Preston [1984] UKHL 5; [1985] STC 282.
R. v Inland Revenue Commissioner Ex p. Unilever plc [1996] STC 681 (CA).
Re Minister for Immigration & Multicultural & Indigenous Affairs: Ex parte Lam (2003) 214 CLR 1.
Tooheys Ltd v Minister for Business & Consumer Affairs (1981) 36 ALR 64.
United States v Craig, 73 A.F.T.R.2d 1099 (D.N.D. 1994).
Vestey v Inland Revenue Commissioners [1977] STC 414.
Vestey v Inland Revenue Commissioners (No. 2) [1978] STC 567 (HC).
Watson v HM Customs and Excise (2004) (VAT18675).

Legislation

Administrative Decisions (Judicial Review) Act 1977 (Cth).
Commissioner for Revenue and Customs Act 2005 (UK).
Human Rights Act 1998 (UK).
Income and Corporation Taxes Act 1988 (UK).
Income Tax Assessment Act 1936 (Cth).
Internal Revenue Service Restructuring and Reform Act of 1998, Pub L No 105-206, 112 Stat 685 (1998).
Judiciary Act 1903 (Cth).
Public Service Act 1999 (Cth).
Public Service Regulations 1999 (Cth).
Taxation Administration Act 1953 (Cth).
Taxes Management Act 1970 (UK).

Papers, Reports and Other Sources

Australian Joint Committee of Parliamentary Accounts, *Report 326 - An Assessment of Tax* (1993).

Australian Public Service Commission, "APS Code of Conduct" available at http://www.apsc.gov.au/aps-employment-policy-and-advice/aps-values-and-code-of-conduct/code-of-conduct [Accessed 1 February 2013].

Australian Taxation Office, "Our Service Standards" available at http://www.ato.gov.au/corporate/distributor.aspx?menuid=0&doc=/content/25940.htm&page=2#P24_2573 [Accessed 1 February 2013].

Australian Taxation Office, *Annual Report 2010-11* (2011).

Australian Taxation Office, "Stakeholder Consultation Overview" available at http://www.ato.gov.au/corporate/content.asp?doc=/content/00131220.htm&mnu=430198mfp=001 [Accessed 1 February 2013].

Australian Taxation Office, "Taxpayers' Charter: What You Need to Know" available at http://www.ato.gov.au/content/downloads/cor63133_n2548.pdf [Accessed 20 April 2012], foreword.

Her Majesty's Revenue and Customs, "Your Charter" available at http://www.hmrc.gov.uk/charter/charter.pdf [Accessed 12 April 2012].

HM Revenue & Customs, "Business Plan 2011-2015" available at http://www.number10.gov.uk/wp-content/uploads/2011/01/HMRC-Business-Plan.pdf [Accessed 21 April 2012].

HM Revenue & Customs, "HMRC Service Standards for Excise, Customs, Stamp Taxes and Money Services Customers" available at http://www.hmrc.gov.uk/customs/ecsm-service-standards.pdf> [Accessed 1 February 2013].

House of Commons. Treasury Committee, *Administration and Effectiveness of HM Revenue and Customs - Sixteenth Report of Session 2010-12* (2011), (Session 2010-11), Vol. 1.

OECD, Centre for Tax Policy and Administration, *Principles of Good Tax Administration* (2001), OECD, Practice Note GAP0013.

OECD, Committee of Fiscal Affairs Working Party, "Taxpayers Rights and Obligations - A Survey of the Legal Situation in OECD Countries' (Paper Number 8, OECD, 1990).

Office of the Commonwealth Ombudsman, Commonwealth of Australia, *To Compensate or Not to Compensate? Own Motion Investigation of Commonwealth Arrangements for Providing Financial Redress for Maladministration* (1999).

5 Assessing the Legal Status of HMRC Guidance: Some first thoughts

Lynda Burkinshaw and Jane Frecknall-Hughes

Abstract

This chapter reviews the literature about tax guidance. Tax guidance and its use are topical subjects for a number of reasons. The chapter looks at why this is, discusses what tax guidance is, the reason for it, its possible legal status and legal redress for the taxpayer where guidance is not followed, along with a consideration of the relevance and use of soft law in the EU and elsewhere.

1 Introduction

To a tax practitioner, referring to, interpreting and trying to follow taxation legislation is a common daily battle. The relevant section of the law may (sometimes) appear to be clear on first reading, but does it apply to the transaction in hand? If so, how? What pitfalls and 'traps' may there be? Inevitably, 'guidance' is sought – that is, the footnotes at the bottom of the relevant page of legislation, the professional guidance books, the plethora of HM Revenue and Customs (HMRC) guidance, professional body opinions, relevant case law and so on. It is generally acknowledged that HMRC guidance, which is the focus of this chapter, is based upon the interpretation of the law as perceived by HMRC and that practitioners need not apply it in that way should they not agree. Little thought may be given to what would happen should there be a disagreement, if the decision had been made to rely upon the published guidance. This, however, came into the spotlight with the *Gaines-Cooper* case[1] – where a taxpayer had relied upon guidance regarding his residency status and it appeared (see later) that this guidance was not followed by HMRC. This appears to have been one of several well publicised instances where HMRC seem to have changed their stance, subsequent to earlier published guidance.

---

1 R *(on the application of Davies) v Revenue and Customs Commissioners; R (on the application of Gaines-Cooper) v Commissioners for Her Majesty's Revenue and Customs* [2011] UKSC 47.

Taxpayer guidance is topical for several reasons. In cases of apparent changes to issued guidelines, obtaining legal redress is problematic for the taxpayer. As guidance is seemingly outside the statutory framework, available redress may be via judicial review (which, per Eden (2005, p. 6), is an increasingly frequent mechanism used by the taxpayer, although not altogether successfully), and through claiming legitimate expectation that the taxpayer had relied upon the guidance and therefore that such reliance should be valid in dealing with HMRC. Bullock and Gillham (2010, p. 19) noted (at the time of writing) that legitimate expectation is a relatively new doctrine in administrative law (approximately 20 years old) but one which is increasingly being applied in the area of taxation law – hence this is a developing area to consider. Additionally, there is a wider debate about the increasingly common use of non-legal instruments and the reason for their issue. This is of interest in academic literature in relation to guidelines, recommendations, codes of conduct, etc., issued in the EU and elsewhere, under the guise of 'soft law'. Christians (2011, p. 41) and Goldmann (2012, p. 366) both note this as an under-researched area, although legal scholars have only recently been concerned with these type of instruments. Whilst the application of soft law does not appear to operate in the same way as the taxation guidance issued in the UK – as will be highlighted – the instruments in question are similar.

The objective of this chapter is to consider some of the literature in this area, and to highlight future areas for research, given the issues which will be identified surrounding the use of and reliance upon tax guidance. The chapter is arranged as follows: section 2 looks at the type of guidance issued in the UK, along with possible reasons why so much guidance exists; section 3 considers where guidance 'fits' in the legal system; section 4 discusses the potential issues for the taxpayer should he/she rely on guidance; section 5 considers potential resolutions for the taxpayer in case of dispute; section 6 discusses guidance in the EU arena and the differences between, and links to, guidance in the UK system. The final section offers conclusions and suggestions for further research.

2 Types of guidance and why guidance is needed

2.1 Types of guidance

Many sorts of documents may be classed as guidance. The following types appear on HMRC's website:[2]

- Tax information and impact notes

---

2   www.hmrc.gov.uk, as at 2 July 2013.

- Notices, information sheets and other reference material
- Revenue and Customs briefs (bulletins)
- Leaflets, factsheets and booklets (23 areas of taxation mentioned)
- Budget and pre-budget reports
- Specialist publications (technical guides, reports)
- Statements of Practice and Extra-statutory concessions (ESCs) (numerous)
- Banking code of practice
- HMRC Manuals

Similar guidance may exist in an EU and international context and this is considered later.

Why is there so much guidance?

2.2 Complexity of taxation law

It is well recognised that the UK has a complex and voluminous tax code and guidance is needed as regards its operation.

Davidson (1996, p. 105) suggests that "explanatory memoranda" be produced to help with the understanding and workings of the law, which he noted when reviewing the work of the Tax Law Rewrite Committee (TLRC) – a project set up in order to rewrite tax law in simpler language. He notes that the TLRC itself acknowledged that it is "unreasonable" for the law to be clearly written in all cases, given its complexity – hence the need for guidance/explanation. After the end of the TLRC project, Salter (2010, p. 686) reviewed its work and echoed comments made by the Law Society in its paper, *Tax: Good Governance and Better Law Making – A Manifesto for Improving Tax Law* (2010) that the rewrite seems to have emphasised the "volume, frequency of change and sheer complexity" of the law. Salter (2010, p. 684) also refers to Kerridge (2003), who notes that the rewrite has made the law harder to follow as the "history" of the relevant sections cannot be easily tracked: the legislation has been rewritten into different acts and different section numbers. This may also have an effect on interpreting and applying the law. James and Wallschutzky (1997, p. 458) also suggest that there is more to simplifying the tax law than amending the language.

Ideally, as Rowland (1995, p. 115) suggests, clearer and more precise legislation is desirable. There is extensive literature on the desirable characteristics of laws, reflecting diverse views, which could be applied to tax legislation. For example, Freedman and Vella (2011, p. 94), referring to Raz (2009), suggest that a law should (amongst other requirements) be "capable of guiding the behaviour of its subjects", while Rowland (1995, p. 115) notes that it would be preferable if the law were clear, "with limits as to its application" (acknowledged as unlikely, since laws thought too specific or precise, are often 'widened' by subsequent laws which may then bring within their scope unintended transactions and circumstances). Gribnau (2013, p. 54) suggests that "legal certainty" is valued, as this enables future planning of transactions, that is, one has prior knowledge of the tax effect. Edwardsson and Wockelberg (2013, p. 365), in their analysis of European legal method, refer to Frändberg's (1996) three conditions for legal certainty, namely laws which are clear and precise, easily accessible and upheld. However, they note that laws are often not "clear and precise", leaving the "constant need for interpretation". Many would agree, and this need for interpretation may have led, in part, to the wealth of guidance that is issued.

Complexity is not easily resolved and the government acknowledged this in 2010 by setting up the Office of Tax Simplification (OTS). The OTS is charged with giving independent advice to the government on simplifying the tax system – with the aim being to reduce compliance burdens on both business and individual tax payers: perhaps not an easy task. The OTS has to date produced a number of publications.[3]

2.3 The language and drafting of the law

The work of the Inland Revenue, now HMRC, entitled *The Path to Tax Simplification*, is discussed by Salter (2010, p. 673) in reference to the many problems arising in the drafting of law – issues of wording and syntax, for example, which can add to the problems of understanding, certainty, meaning, application and interpretation. Lamb (2003, p. 186) notes that tax policy has its own discourse and vocabulary and additionally (1997, p. 116) that tax has its own "jargon, concepts and principles". Hence, as tax assessments are based on the words of legislation (Lamb, 1997, p. 392), interpretation can be difficult. Problems with drafting are also considered by Thuronyi (1996, p. 2) who notes that laws are not clear or well written and that a well drafted law needs "understandability", "organisation", "effectiveness" and "integration".

In addition to problems with the language of the law, there may be no law that deals adequately with a particular issue, which itself causes problems. A recent example of this relates to the concept of residency for the UK, as no statutory test for residency has existed until recently. This was at the root of the *Gaines-Cooper* case, cited earlier. Other areas of the law may be problematic for other reasons, again leading to doubt, uncertainty and the

---

3 For more information and for details of the work undertaken, see: https://www.gov.uk/government/organisations/office-of-tax-simplification

need for additional guidance. For example, 'trade' is defined as including "any venture in the nature of trade" (Income Tax Act 2007, s. 989), but what is a "venture"?[4] There is no further statutory guidance.

2.4 General observations about the UK tax system

Many commentators observe that the UK tax system is used for more than just raising income (Freedman, 2003; James and Wallschutzky, 1997; Kay, 1990). It is used to achieve a multitude of objectives which can only add to the complexity of the system. The approach to tax policy, according to Bowler (2010, p. 2) is "disjointed", owing to the gap between those creating policy and those who use it. Steinmo (1989, p. 523) suggests that the UK tax system lacks "coherence".

UK tax law is a rules-based system – and some suggest that such a system itself causes complexity as gaps have to be plugged (Chittenden and Foster, 2009; James and Wallschutzky, 1997; Thuronyi, 1996), leading others to discuss the need for a principles-based system (as considered, for example, by Freedman, 2010) – although Freedman and Vella (2010, p. 2) suggest that more guidance, not less, may be required if the UK moves towards a principles-based system, referring to the recent introduction of the General Anti-Abuse Rule and in relation to which provision for HMRC guidance is made.

There are many issues and complexities in relation to UK tax law, the language and the system generally, which undoubtedly contribute to the need for taxpayer guidance. The above is only a brief review of many articles that have been written about these issues.

2.5 The desire to influence behaviour

In addition to the need for guidance as a result of complexities, various authors suggest that 'guidance' may be issued to influence taxpayer behaviour. Several examples, some from the professional press, illustrate HMRC's apparent attempt to influence changes in practice and in the behaviour of taxpayers. Some attempts appear to be based on nothing other than HMRC's viewpoint, but this is not often apparent to the taxpayer – and the implication is that taxpayers are being encouraged to behave in the way that HMRC would prefer.

For example, Macleod (2013) suggests that HMRC may provide "incomplete" impressions regarding the current state of deliberations in the on-going debate about the tax issues concerning employee benefit trusts, in

---

4   Prior to the rewrite, the word used was "adventure", which perhaps conveys a sense of risk taking associated with a business undertaking.

that some, but not all, aspects are mentioned in letters sent to the taxpayer in order to discourage tax planning. Macleod (2013) uses words such as "misleading" and "exaggeration". He suggests that this could be intended to "unsettle" taxpayers in the hope that they pay over any tax which *may* be perceived as due.

Harris (2012) provides a further example, in questioning the wording in the HMRC manuals, to which many will turn for guidance. Referring to a section described in the *Employment Income Manual* (EIM 11341) which looks at the benefit in kind in respect of accommodation, Harris (2012) concludes that the narrative "considerably overstates HMRC's case" and suggests that the information provided in the manuals should be treated cautiously. Could this perhaps be another means of indirectly influencing taxpayer behaviour?

The above two examples consider guidance first in the form of the information provided by letter directly to the taxpayer and, in the latter case, via HMRC published material. A further example of guidance which could be said to influence behaviour is the *Code of Practice on Taxation for Banks* (2009) whereby HMRC appeal to taxpayers to comply with the 'spirit' of the law.

If taxpayers do conform with HMRC's point of view, Freedman and Vella (2010, p. 17) suggest that this may avoid potentially costly negotiation with HMRC and (2011, p. 97) that this would also be favourable for the taxpayer's risk profile – which HMRC may utilise when considering a taxpayer's affairs. Is this an acceptable position? This may not perhaps garner trust with the taxpayer – as considered by Bober (2012), de Cogan (2011, p. 11) and Gribnau (2007a) – see below, section 4.

The above gives rise to significant issues, not least because guidance issued may not be based upon a correct interpretation of the law, as noted by Freedman and Vella (2010, p. 17) – and it is the law that should be considered when arranging one's tax affairs. If HMRC's interpretation of the law is incorrect, Freedman and Vella (2010, p. 17) question how this can then be used to influence behaviour. Clearly, the language used in the professional press, as indicated above by Macleod (2013), also indicates a lack of trust. It is worth noting at this point that a desire to change behaviour by issuing guidance, like the *Code of Practice on Taxation for Banks* (2009), is similar to the operation of the 'soft law' guidelines issued via the EU or elsewhere (see below, section 3.2).

2.6   HMRC discretion

Some elements of guidance involve HMRC using its discretion, as opposed to relying on the strict letter of the law, most commonly by means of ESCs.

Several commentators question the legality of ESCs and HMRC's ability to issue them (e.g., Booth, 2000; de Cogan, 2011; Freedman and Vella, 2010; and Nolan, 1981, citing Williams, 1979). Application of ESCs can result in certain groups of taxpayers being favoured above others, which may be questionable practice, although the original intention might have been to prevent the law having an unduly harsh impact. Following the case of *Wilkinson v IRC*,[5] a review of ESCs has been taking place, and some have now been included within statute while others have been withdrawn. This has not, however, been without controversy, as there are instances where HMRC have taken the opportunity to amend the way in which the ESCs have previously operated, which in itself has attracted criticism.[6]

The paragraph above assumes that the application of ESCs comes within the boundaries of discretionary decisions by HMRC, although others would question this, considering that discretion amounts to "delegated authority" which differs from "activities such as interpretation or extra-statutory concession" (de Cogan, 2011, p. 3).

Discretion is itself a wide topic and draws many aspects of guidance generally within its net – not just ESCs referred to above, which are but one element (see Freedman and Vella (2011) for detailed consideration).

3 The place of guidance within the current legal system

Freedman and Vella (2011, p. 113) note that

"[a]t present this guidance is completely outside the legislative system as it is not contained in secondary legislation but is simply issued by HMRC".

However, does it have any legal traits? It may be useful to look briefly at some of the characteristics of 'real' or 'hard' law. This then may help ascertain whether guidance contains any elements of these characteristics when trying to assess its legal status.

---

5 *R (on the application of Wilkinson) v Inland Revenue Commissioners* [2005] UKHL 30.
6 For example, legislative effect has now been given to ESC C16. This concession allowed certain distributions on the winding up of a company to be treated as a capital distribution, which ordinarily, without a formal liquidation, would not be possible. Prior to the concession being given legislative effect, there was no upper limit to the amount of distribution which could be treated as capital. However, a cap of £25,000 has now been imposed (if a company has more than this to distribute, all funds will be classified as dividends unless a formal liquidation takes place) to deal with a perceived abuse of the concession – for further consideration of this, see Miller (2012).

3.1 Characteristics of the law

Laws usually need the consent of a sovereign state's governing body (such as the UK Parliament), meaning that there has been a formal, transparent process prior to the law being enacted, or, as Gribnau (2013, p. 52) notes "democratic legitimacy". This latter point is important when considering the legal status of guidance and particularly the nature of 'soft law' and its effects, as discussed in later sections of this chapter. Goldmann (2012, p. 361) notes that if a 'rule' is not legally binding it may only have "political ends" – an interesting comment that perhaps ties into the debate about influencing behaviour. Additionally, Goldmann (2012, p. 361) and Dourado (2011, p. 17) cite the work of Fuller (1969 and 1964 respectively), who refers to the generality and the legality of the law. There need to be principles of legality otherwise the law is not binding, and this issue needs to be considered when looking at the legal status of guidance. Goldman (2012, p. 361) notes that Fuller (1969) refers to "eight criteria of legality, which any rule needs to meet to be considered law".[7]

The process by which something (an act, transaction, process, substance, material, item, document, etc.) becomes legal, often referred to as 'legalisation',[8] is discussed at length by Abbott et al. (2000) and Abbott and Snidal (2000). Characteristics of legalisation are (per Abbott et al. (2000), pp. 401–401):

- Obligation (i.e., one is legally bound by the provision);
- Precision (there is clarity about the conduct that one must adopt to follow the law); and
- Delegation (i.e., the rules can be delegated to a third party).

The problem with the types of guidance noted above is that they do not have these characteristics. The first characteristic is clearly lacking, as the guidance itself is not the law, but HMRC's interpretation of it, which may, or may not be, correct. Abbott et al. (2000, p. 402) acknowledge that there are various levels of legalisation – ranging from the ideal (where all three characteristics are maximised), to hard legalisation (which may have high levels of the three characteristics), to soft (with different combinations of attributes), to complete absence of legalisation. These debates raise issues concerning the legal basis on which HMRC may, for example, seek to influence taxpayer behaviour and can be explored further.

---

7   These eight criteria are generality, promulgation, limited retroactivity, clarity, absence of contradictions, not requiring the impossible, constancy through time, and congruence between official action and declared rule.

8   This term is also often used in the context of making something legal which has been previously illegal (e.g., often drug use) but it also applies in the sense of giving legal status (of some kind) to an act (etc.) which has hitherto had no legal status whatever.

3.2 Categorisation of guidance in terms of the law

Various terms have been coined which could be used to describe guidance, including 'quasi-legislation' (see Ganz, 1987; and Gribnau, 2007a, p. 303), and, as already suggested, 'soft law'. The terms 'secondary legislation' and 'subsidiary legislation' are also sometimes found, but these may be misleading as these are used (in the UK, at least) to denote, for example, legislation put in place by statutory instruments and with authority given by an over-arching Act of Parliament.

Ganz (1987, p. 1) notes that the term 'quasi-legislation' was first used in 1944 to describe "law-which-is-not-a-law such as tax concessions and 'Practice Notes' ..... and administrative arrangements...." also "Codes of Practice, guidance, guidance notes, guidelines, circulars, White Papers, development control policy notes, development briefs, practice statements, tax concessions, Health Service Notices, Family Practitioner Notices, codes of conduct, codes of ethics and conventions......". Gribnau (2007a, p. 303), however, describes quasi-legislation as "policy rules", referring to rules "laid down by an administrative body as a form of self-regulation over the exercise of its administrative powers". There is no clear or agreed definition of 'quasi-legislation', possibly because it covers many different types of instrument which serve different functions.

The term 'soft law' appears to relate to instruments which have no legal force, but which nevertheless have legal effect (Stefan, 2012, p. 879), and seems most commonly used in reference to instruments issued in an international context, which then lead to sovereign states incorporating such instruments into their own statutes or legal codes. The term does not appear to be used in relation to UK tax guidance. There are various definitions for soft law (e.g., Gersen and Posner, 2008; Klabbers, 1998; Senden, 2005; and Stefan, 2012, p. 880, referring to Snyder, 1995 and 1993), but it commonly encapsulates guidelines, codes of conduct and recommendations, so is not dissimilar in concept to UK tax guidance.

Various views are held about the levels of authority possessed by rules and regulations that may not be 'law' in the traditional sense. Some authors (e.g. Klabbers, 1998, p. 382) believe that rules must either be "law" or "non law", that is, the regulation is either law, or it is not. Klabbers (1998) believes that there cannot be an 'in between': such rules either end up becoming hard law, or remain outside the law altogether.

On the other hand, Christians (2007, p. 331) suggests that there may be a type of continuum between actual "hard law" and no law, namely "soft law". This would tie in with Abbott and Snidal's (2000, p. 421) characteristics of obligation, precision and delegation, as they suggest that laws may become "soft" when "legal arrangements are weakened along one or more" of these "dimensions" – which can result in different varieties of softer law.

Rose and Page (2001) suggest that there are different categories of law and regulation, suggesting classification into: hard laws, hard regulations, pseudo-laws, soft resolutions (" 'law-like rules'.....lacking the enforcement mechanisms of hard law" (p. 11)), official advice (which "lacks the authority of laws and regulations" and can be thought of as "quasi voluntary compliance", p. 12) and unofficial standards (described, for example, as "best practice" – such as those issued by organisations, p. 13).

Senden (2005, pp. 23–24) indicates a potential threefold framework for categorisation of soft law:

1 Preparatory and informative instruments (such as Green Papers, informative communications, etc.) which are used in a "pre-law" manner, that is, prior to new law being issued (although she questions whether these instruments could actually be described as soft law).

2 Interpretative and decisional instruments (including guidance and interpretation of case law and community law, notices, guidelines, frameworks, for example). These she describes as having a "post law" function, that is, one which supports the law.

3 Steering instruments which give formal effect to objectives and policies (the *Code of Conduct for Business Taxation*[9] would fall within this category – also mentioned below in section 6), which are described as having a "para-law function". (Senden (2005, p. 24) refers to Thürer (1990), suggesting this means structured "in a comparable way to legal rules" and that "various principles of law can be applied to them by analogy".)

Aspects of the UK tax guidance may possibly fit into one of these categories – perhaps "soft resolutions" or "official advice", per Rose and Page (2001) or there may be links, in some respects, to Senden's (2005) and Abbott et al.'s (2000) frameworks above.

Clearly, opinions and ideas differ about the legal status of items which are not technically seen as law, and the term 'soft law' can encapsulate many types of instrument which fall outside the normal legal system. 'Soft law' is discussed further in section 6.

---

9 As set out in the conclusions of the Council of Economics and Finance Ministers (ECOFIN) of 1 December 1997.

4 Potential issues for the taxpayer

As suggested in the Introduction, several cases about HMRC guidance and taxpayer reliance thereon have recently been in the headlines, for example: the *Gaines-Cooper*[10] case (reliance on IR 20); an apparent change in the 'width of the goal posts' regarding ESC A19; a reversal of guidance previously issued regarding the *Mansworth v Jelley*[11] share option case; the *Hanover*[12] case, regarding reliance on guidance in HMRC manuals; HMRC writing to taxpayers about employee benefit trusts; and the fact that guidance on using form R85 (a form that individuals may complete to prevent tax being deducted at source from interest, typically used by non-taxpayers) is not clear enough (acknowledged by HMRC, although they suggest it is too complicated to change it, as discussed by Service (2013, p. 55)).

Considering some of these examples further, the ESC A19 changes appear to be a change in policy without prior consultation, resulting in claims being refused that would have previously have been settled unchallenged (McKay, 2012). With regard to *Mansworth v Jelley*, guidance previously issued in 2003 (queried at the time by the professional bodies, as it appeared to be incorrect (see ICAEW, *TAXGUIDE* 1/10, point 20)) has, years later, been overturned (and the question of legitimate expectation (see below, section 5) is being widely debated in the professional press in respect of this matter). The issue here, per *TAXGUIDE* 3/13, is that HMRC are trying to disallow losses realised prior to the change in guidance. Comments in *TAXGUIDE* 3/13 note that the "view set down in HMRC guidance was so novel that no taxpayer would have come up with it......so all claims were in accordance with and in reliance on the HMRC guidance". The suggestion is that HMRC have simply changed their mind with respect to the guidance previously issued. This is contrasted with the case of Mr Gaines-Cooper, who, HMRC felt, had misinterpreted the guidance in IR 20 (*TAXGUIDE* 3/13). Mr Gaines-Cooper believed that, as he met the conditions in IR20, he would be treated as non-resident. HMRC disagreed, and suggested that IR20 did not apply to Mr Gaines-Cooper as he had never left the UK in the first place (feeling that his continued significant ties with the UK indicated uninterrupted UK residency), although this did not appear to be included in the guidance as a condition (Bullock and Gillham, 2010, p. 19).

Guidance, as discussed, is based on HMRC's own view of the law which may encourage the taxpayer to pay tax according to HMRC's preferred

---

10 *R (on the application of Davies) v Revenue and Customs Commissioners; R (on the application of Gaines-Cooper) v Commissioners for Her Majesty's Revenue and Customs* [2011] UKSC 47.
11 *Mansworth (Inspector of Taxes) v Jelley* [2002] EWCA Civ 1829.
12 *Hanover Company Services Ltd v Revenue and Customs Commissioners* [2010] UKFTT 256 (TC).

interpretation. Leaving aside debates about whether HMRC have the correct interpretation of the law, how can this situation be workable if HMRC subsequently amend their position? Taxpayers should be able to rely on guidance to obtain certainty about the legal consequences of their transactions. If the aim of guidance is to increase, not decrease, certainty about how the law should be applied, any amendment of interpretation by HMRC would have the opposite effect. As Bober (2012, p. 8) notes, for the tax system to function fairly there should be an element of trust between HMRC and the taxpayer. Some would argue that, if guidance cannot be relied upon, then this trust is lost. De Cogan (2011, p. 10) raises similar issues.

Gribnau (2007a, p. 292) comments that the trust of the taxpayer is seen as an important issue in The Netherlands, where, for example, the tax system encourages participation in the setting of tax law, and guidelines, which were previously only used internally by the tax authorities, have been made public in an attempt to help to improve relationships with the taxpayer and to make the system more democratic. This contrasts somewhat with the position in the UK, and Freedman (2007, p. 658) points to the fact that what businesses say and need is often not considered prior to the drafting of tax law – and if changes are subsequently made as a result of lobbying, this makes the law even more complex. Therefore, this is not indicative of a participative system, which, *prima facie*, appears different from the system in The Netherlands.

Much HMRC guidance is accompanied by a caveat that the taxpayer should not necessarily rely on guidance (Freedman and Vella, 2011, p. 105 and p. 114). As guidance is outside the law, this perhaps is understandable, but it does beg the question as to the purpose of guidance in the first place. Further difficulties for the taxpayer arise when changes take place: old guidance is removed from HMRC websites and previous versions of HMRC manuals disappear, making it impossible to track the changes made (Freedman and Vella (2011, p. 105 and p. 113)). De Cogan (2011, p. 13) notes that guidance is often issued "piecemeal" and is regularly altered. Comments arising in *TAXGUIDE* 3/13 suggest that better management of the changes to HMRC guidance is needed. All these issues pose challenges for the taxpayer in both using and relying on issued guidance.

5 Potential resolutions for the taxpayer who has relied on guidance

Should HMRC appear to change its position in respect of published guidance, there are problems for taxpayers in defending their position if they have relied on such guidance. As guidance has no statutory authority, its wording and meaning cannot be looked at closely. Thus the taxpayer cannot rely upon the literal wording of the guidance. Freedman and Vella (2010, p. 23) note that the language of guidance is often "loose" and that examples provided to show the intended operation of the law are "too simple". The inherent nature of guidance means that it cannot address all circumstances that might possibly be envisaged, and in many instances, it is not at all clear how the guidance should actually operate (e.g., the guidance on substantial non-trading activities in respect of Entrepreneurs' Relief would be a case in point[13]).

As the taxpayer cannot lodge an appeal in the traditional manner, the option open to the taxpayer, when relying on guidance, is to seek a judicial review. The judicial review process is complex and taxpayers need to be aware of the constraints (especially the various time limits), to protect their position. The judicial review process is designed to protect citizens from the abuse of power of public bodies, of which HMRC is one. Freedman and Vella (2011, p. 101) note that a judicial review can be sought in the case of illegality, irrationality (or unreasonableness) or procedural impropriety. Bullock and Gillham (2010, p. 18) add a fourth, namely, "legitimate expectation".

Put simply, Bullock and Gillham (2010, p. 18) note that legitimate expectation:

> "….concerns the fact that a public body such as HMRC may, by its own statements or conduct, be required to act in a certain way, even if it subsequently changes its mind, where there is a legitimate expectation on the part of those affected that the public body will act in a certain way".

Freedman and Vella (2011, p. 102) discuss the doctrine of legitimate expectation, observing that this has developed in the context of judicial review and that there should be a balance between "certainty and fairness" for the individual and "flexibility and public interest". A further issue raised by Freedman and Vella (2011, p. 113) is that, if HMRC exceed their authority (i.e., if they act *ultra vires*), there is no protection for the taxpayer – with the additional problem that the line between acting within, or outside, authority is rather finely drawn. A further question is then to ask what the position is when HMRC act on a concessionary basis, perhaps using their discretion in applying an ESC for certain taxpayers: would the taxpayer be protected?

---

13 HMRC guidance indicates that Entrepreneurs' Relief may not be available if 20% of activities relate to non-trading activities, for example, the receipt of rental income (when compared with total income), or the value of investment assets as compared to trading assets, etc. The 20% is HMRC's own figure: it is not included in the legislation. Examples are given in the guidance as to how it may be used.

In a tax context Eden (2005, p. 16) comments that legitimate expectation may arise in various circumstances, though the main circumstance is generally reliance on a statement made by HMRC which may have been in respect of clearance, settling a dispute, a published document or previous established action by HMRC. She considers a number of tax cases brought under the legitimate expectation doctrine, although few have been successful. One such case is *R v IRC ex parte Unilever* (1996)[14] (a successful claim based on the previous established practice of the then Inland Revenue accepting loss relief claims after the official time limit). Another is *R (on the application of Greenwich Property Ltd) v Customs and Excise Commissioners*[15] (a 2001 VAT case based on reliance on a concession relating to zero rated items). A more recent success is *Cameron & others v Revenue and Customs* (2012)[16] in which taxpayers had sought to rely on a published concession. HMRC attempted to deny the claim based on their contrary view about the operation of the concession (the view about which had been published, but not in the main documentation to which the taxpayer referred). It was held that, once a legitimate expectation has been created, the taxpayer can rely upon this, until there is revocation of the concession which must be communicated to the whole class of taxpayers.

Part of the reason for the limited success of cases brought under this doctrine is that various principles have been derived from the cases heard (see Eden, 2005; Fordham, 2000; Freedman and Vella 2011; and Wilson, 2013), one of which is that the taxpayer is expected to be totally honest and give disclosure to HMRC prior to acting or relying on the guidance or their advice.[17]

There are other general legal principles which may also apply to ensure success under a legitimate expectation claim. Fordham (2000) lists six "principles" relating to legitimate expectation – including "Rule 2: Basic ingredients" (p. 188) of legitimate expectation, of which there are four, although he notes that all need not be present at the same time. These are: "(1) prior disclosure by the applicant; (2) a clear and unqualified representation; (3) communication to the applicant (or that 'class'); and (4) a detrimental reliance". *TAXGUIDE* 3/13 indicates that the taxpayer must demonstrate that reliance on guidance has resulted in suffering a "financial detriment". Detriment is noted as important in determining whether a change of view by HMRC amounts to an "abuse of power".

---

14 [1996] STC 681 (CA).
15 [2001] EWHC 230.
16 *R (on the application of Cameron) v Revenue and Customs Commissioners; R (on the application of Palmer) v Revenue and Customs Commissioners* [2012] EWHC 1174 (Admin).
17 See, for example, *R v IRC ex parte MFK Underwriting Agents* [1990] 1 All ER 91 (QBD) and *R v IRC ex parte Matrix-Securities Ltd* [1993] STC 774 (QBD) (CA).

In determining whether legitimate expectation exists, Steyn (2001, p. 245) considers the "nature of the commitment" by the authority, as commitments differ and consequently may have a different impact upon whether a legitimate expectation claim can be made. Commitments could be "promises, practices....policies". Steyn (2001, p. 245) suggests that a "promise" relates to a reliance on future conduct, a "practice" relates to "implied representation about future conduct" (and refers to the *Unilever* case as an example) and that a "policy" would suggest that changes can occur as needed in fulfilment of public duty. This would imply that the nature of the commitment needs to be considered to ascertain whether a legitimate expectation case would be possible.

The difficulty, however, for the taxpayer, lies not just in addressing all the apparent requirements, but also in the authorities acting within their powers, as protection could be lacking if they do not.

6 EU and international aspects: guidance in the EU arena

Interestingly, EU and international soft law instruments (such as guidance, recommendations, etc.) do not appear to operate in the same way as similar UK instruments. They appear to have a supporting role, with the underlying idea being to gain the co-operation of states in implementing law, that is, to provide a framework as to how law within specific jurisdictions can be implemented. This helps take account of the national sovereignties of member nations, as it would be impossible to legislate in the traditional sense. Stefan (2012, p. 890) suggests that such instruments are used to enhance the consistency of EU law and that they act as guidance and clarification and should help enhance legal certainty. Good examples are the OECD transfer pricing rules and the *Code of Conduct for Business Taxation*. No penalties attach to non-compliance, but instead it is suggested that compliance is the result of peer pressure generating a feeling of an obligation (Christians, 2007, p. 331) to implement the guidelines. Brodzka (2012, p. 400) highlights the principle of peer pressure in getting states to conform with regulations and notes the use of "blacklists" in certain circumstances for non-compliance. Gribnau (2007b, p. 30) refers to soft law as a "gentleman's agreement". From a UK perspective, one example that may have these characteristics is, perhaps, the *Code of Practice on Taxation for Banks* (2009) – which, although voluntary, involved the publication of the names of the banks which had signed up to the *Code*.

The link to the effect on behaviour is implicit. For example, Gribnau (2007a, p. 292) describes a change in stance by the revenue authorities in The Netherlands, which moved from a penalty and punishment regime towards one of trust, to encourage compliance and change the relationship between the state and the taxpayer. He notes however, in this context, that soft law is "generally considered to be an important instrument to enhance the legitimacy and responsiveness of regulation".

Furthermore, Senden (2005, p. 1) notes that soft law can be seen as either an alternative or complement to the more traditional 'command and control' type of legislation. This clearly contrasts with the operation of UK guidance (subject to the comments re the *Code of Practice on Taxation for Banks* (2009) above), although Senden (2013, p. 61) suggests that soft law "mirrors" certain aspects of national legal systems, as many are "familiar with some form of soft interpretative and decisional rules or policy guidelines".

In addition to having a role with regard to 'behaviour', Christians (2011, p. 41) observes that soft law, in a tax context, "mediates between the need for more legal certainty… and the desire for confidentiality in tax matters…".

Gribnau (2007b, p. 30) notes that the use of soft law ties in with the aims of EU legislative policy which is to issue "less and better legislation" and to use "more diversified European governance mechanisms" (which would include the use of soft law).

Soft law does have its critics. Klabbers (1998) believes that it creates more uncertainty, not less, and he deplores (p. 390) the growth in the number of guidelines issued (considering the period 1986–1997). Rose and Page (2001, p. 2) describe soft law as "pseudo law", which has been "promulgated outside the normal process of legislative enactment", highlighting (p. 19) the problem of "judicial creep", when "… judges invoke soft laws …. to arrive at decisions that differ from what would be produced by applying hard laws". This highlights another issue regarding the use of soft law: the danger that soft law can become hard law through the 'back door', if referred to in legal judgments which are then used in deciding later cases. Gribnau (2007b, p. 39) notes that public administrative rules can, in some cases, be considered law and suggests this is illustrative of the hardening of soft law. Could the intention to formalise the *Code of Practice on Taxation for Banks* (2009) in the UK be an illustration of this too?[18]

There is a considerable amount of literature on this issue and it is clear that different authors have many different perspectives on both the usefulness of soft law and its legal position.

---

18 See Dalton (2013) for more details.

7 Conclusions and suggestions for further research

The above review shows that there is extensive literature in the area of tax guidance – what it is, reasons for it, how it can be classified, where it 'sits' within the law, problems for the taxpayer and legal redress. Any one of the sections above could be developed and researched in much more depth. An additional area for research could be an examination of the effects of tax guidance on both taxpayers and their advisers, as clearly there are difficulties in using and relying upon guidance in certain circumstances. The following areas may be usefully explored further in this context.

- Guidance is outside the statutory framework, but what characteristics of 'law' does the guidance have in the light of the various frameworks which are offered by a number of authors?

- The principles of legitimate expectation and judicial review are clearly a growing phenomenon in the tax arena, but many cases appear unsuccessful when action is brought: is this because the ingredients of a successful case are missing, or has the authority acted ultra vires?

- Soft law is clearly used in the EU in a different manner from that in the UK, if comparing similar instruments and the effect on taxpayer behaviour is a large part of the reason for issuing this material. There are signs that various elements of this are creeping into the UK – as with the Code of Practice on Taxation for Banks (2009) – and it would be interesting to explore this further and, perhaps, consider the experience in The Netherlands for a comparative study, particularly looking at the relationship between the taxpayer and the tax authorities.

- The type of solutions to the problems that can be offered – perhaps, a better system would be beneficial for both the taxpayer and tax authorities. This has not been touched upon above, but it is an important question.

Table of cases

Hanover Company Services Ltd v Revenue and Customs Commissioners [2010] UKFTT 256 (TC).

Mansworth (Inspector of Taxes) v Jelley [2002] EWCA Civ 1829.

R (on the application of Cameron) v Revenue and Customs Commissioners; R (on the application of Palmer) v Revenue and Customs Commissioners [2012] EWHC 1174 (Admin).

R (on the application of Davies) v Revenue and Customs Commissioners; R (on the application of Gaines-Cooper) v Commissioners for Her Majesty's Revenue and Customs [2011] UKSC 47.

R *(on the application of Wilkinson) v Inland Revenue Commissioners* [2005] UKHL 30.

R *(on the application of Greenwich Property Ltd) v Customs and Excise Commissioners* [2001] EWHC 230.

R v IRC ex parte Matrix-Securities Ltd [1993] STC 774 (QBD) (CA).

R v IRC ex parte MFK Underwriting Agents [1990] 1 All ER 91 (QBD).

R v IRC ex parte Unilever plc [1996] STC 681 (CA).

Table of statutes

Great Britain. *Income Tax Act. Elizabeth II. Chapter 3* (2007) London: The Stationery Office.

Bibliography

Abbott, K., O'Keohane, R., Moravcsik, A., Slaughter, A-M., Snidal, D. (2000). The concept of legalization. *International Organization*, 54(3): 401–419.

Abbott, K. and Snidal, D. (2000). Hard and soft law in international governance. *International Organization*, 54(3): 421–456.

Bober, L. (2012). When can you rely on HMRC guidance? *TAXline*, June, 6: 8–9.

Booth, J. (2000). Taxation Inland Revenue concessions: convenience or just illegal? *Journal of the Institute of Advanced Legal Studies, Amicus Curiae*, 27: 23–28.

Bowler, T. (2010). Tax policy making in the UK. *Institute for Fiscal Studies, Tax Law Review Committee*, Paper No 8.

Brodzka, A. (2012). The era of exchange information and fiscal transparency: The use of soft law instruments and the enhancement of good governance in tax matters. *European Taxation*, 82(8): 394–408.

Bullock, J and Gillham, G. (2010). What can you expect from HMRC? *Tax Adviser*, July: 18–20.

Chittenden, F. and Foster, H. (2009). Is there a way out of the tax labyrinth? *ACCA discussion paper*. [Online] Available at http://www.accaglobal.com/content/dam/acca/global/PDF-technical/tax-publications/tech-tp-tl.pdf [accessed 8 July 2013]

Christians, A. (2007). Hard law, soft law and international taxation. *Wisconsin International Law Journal*, 25(2) 325–333.

Christians, A. (2011). Hard law, soft law and no law: the world of international tax dispute resolutions. Wisconsin Law School, New York University School of Law, Colloquium on Tax Policy and Public Finance, Spring, draft. [Online] Available at https://www.law.nyu.edu/academics/.../taxpolicy/ECM_PRO_068030. [Accessed 10 February 2013]

Code of Conduct for Business Taxation (1997). [Online]. Available at http://ec.europa.eu/taxation_customs/taxation/company_tax/harmful_tax_practices/index_en.htm#code_conduct. [Accessed 22 February 2013]

Dalton, S. (2013). Code of Practice on Taxation for Banks. *Tax Adviser*, October: 19.

Davidson, C. (1996). An update on the work of the tax law review committee. *Fiscal Studies*, 17(2): 103–110.

de Cogan, D. (2011). Tax, discretion and the rule of law. In *The Delicate Balance Tax, Discretion and the Rule of Law*, Evans, C., Freedman, J. and Krever, R. (eds)., The Netherlands. IBFD, pp. 1–14.

Dourado, A. (2011). Revenue authority discretions and the rule of law – some thoughts in a legal theory and comparative perspective. In *The Delicate Balance Tax, Discretion and the Rule of Law*, Evans, C., Freedman, J. and Krever, R. (eds)., The Netherlands. IBFD, pp. 15–38.

Eden, S. (2005). Judicial control of tax negotiation. *ejournal of Tax Research*. 3(1): 5–27 [Online]. Available at http://www.asb.unsw.edu.au/research/publications/ejournaloftaxresearch/Documents/paper1_v3n1.pdf [Accessed 2 July 2013]

Edwardsson, E. and Wockelberg, H. (2013). European legal method in Denmark and Sweden – using social science theory and methodology to describe the implementation of EU law. *European Law Journal*, 19(3): 364–381.

Employment Income Manual (EIM 11341). Living accommodation exemption: necessary for proper performance of the duties. [Online]. Available at http://www.hmrc.gov.uk/manuals/eimanual/EIM11341.htm. [Accessed 29 July 2013]

ESC (Extra-Statutory Concession) A19. Arrears of tax arising through official error. [Online]. Available at http://www.hmrc.gov.uk/specialist/esc.pdf. [Accessed 22 February 2013]

ESC (Extra- Statutory Concession) C16. Dissolution of companies under Section 652, Companies Act 1985: distributions to shareholders. [Online]. Available at http://www.hmrc.gov.uk/specialist/esc.pdf. [Accessed 19 December 2013]

Fordham, M. (2000). Legitimate expectation: domestic principles. *Judicial Review*, 5: 188–192.

Freedman, J. (2003). Tax and corporate responsibility. *Tax Journal*, 695 (2) [Online, via Lexislibrary, accessed 15 July 2013]

Freedman, J (2007). Tax: a political issue, editorial. *British Tax Review*, 6: 657–659.

Freedman, J (2010). Improving (not perfecting) tax legislation: Rules and principles revisited. *British Tax Review*, 6: 717–736.

Freedman, J. and Vella, J. (2010). HMRC's management of the UK tax system: The boundaries of legitimate discretion. Oxford University Centre for Business Taxation. WP 10/22 (2010), draft 8 October. [Online] Available at denning.law.ox.ac.uk/tax/documents/WP1022.pdf. [Accessed 3 January 2013]

Freedman, J and Vella. J (2011). HMRC's management of the UK tax system: the boundaries of legitimate discretion. In *The Delicate Balance Tax, Discretion and the Rule of Law*, Evans, C., Freedman, J. and Krever, R. (eds). The Netherlands. IBFD, pp. 79–119.

Ganz, G. (1987). *Quasi-legislation: Recent Developments in Secondary Legislation*. London: Sweet and Maxwell.

Gersen, J.E. and Posner, E.A. (2008). Soft law – lessons from congressional practice. *Stanford Law Review*, 61(3): 573–627.

Goldmann, M. (2012). We need to cut off the head of the king: past, present and future approaches to international soft law. *Leiden Journal of International Law*, 25(2): 335–368.

Gribnau, H. (2007a). Soft law and taxation: the case of the Netherlands. *Legisprudence*, 1(3): 291–326.

Gribnau, H. (2007b), Improving the legitimacy of soft law in EU tax law. *Intertax: European Tax Review*, 35(1): 30–44.

Gribnau, H. (2013). Equality, legal certainty and tax legislation in the Netherlands fundamental legal principles as checks on legislative power: A case study. *Utrecht Law Review*, 9(2): 52–74.

Harris, D. (2012). Manual transmission. *Taxation*, 170(4362): 9 [Online, via Lexislibrary, accessed 20 May 2013]

HM Revenue and Customs (2009). *Code of Practice on Taxation for Banks* [Online]. Available at http://www.hmrc.gov.uk/thelibrary/code-practice.htm. [Accessed 20 February 2013]

Inland Revenue (1995). *The Path to Tax Simplification*. London: HMSO.

Institute of Chartered Accountants in England and Wales (ICAEW) (2010). Mansworth v Jelley revisited. *TAXGUIDE 1/10*. [Online]. Available at http://www.icaew.com/~/media/Files/Technical/Tax/Tax%20news/TaxGuides/TAXGUIDE-1-10-Mansworth-v-Jelley-revisited.pdf [Accessed 9 July 2013]

Institute of Chartered Accountants in England and Wales (ICAEW) (2013). Legitimate expectation and reliance on HMRC guidance. *TAXGUIDE 3/13*. [Online]. Available at http://www.ion.icaew.com/TaxFaculty/27324 (members' only link). [Accessed 19 December 2013]

IR 20 Residents and non-residents: Liability to tax in the United Kingdom. [Online]. Available at http://www.hmrc.gov.uk/pdfs/ir20.pdf. [Accessed 22 February 2013]

James, S. and Wallschutzky, I. (1997). Tax law improvement in Australia and the UK: the need for a strategy for simplification. *Fiscal Studies*, 18(4): 445–460.

Kay, J. (1990). Tax policy: a survey. *Economic Journal*, 100(399): 18–75.

Klabbers, J. (1998). The undesirability of soft law. *Nordic Journal of International Law*, 67: 381–391.

Lamb, M. (1997). *Tax Practice in the United Kingdom and the Emergence of Interrelationships between Accounting and the Taxation of Business Profits*. Unpublished PhD Thesis, The University of Reading.

Lamb, M (2003). Questions of taxation framed as accounting historical research: a suggested approach. *Accounting Historians Journal*, 30(2): 175–196.

Macleod, I. (2013). Nudge, nudge! *Taxation*. 171(4395): 10 [Online, via Lexislibrary, accessed 15 May 2013]

McKay, P. (2012). Jumping the gun. *Taxation*, 170(4368): 7 [Online, via Lexislibrary, accessed 20 May 2013]

Miller, H. (2012). Danse Macabre. *Taxation*, 170 (4377): 9 [Online, via Lexislibrary, accessed 11 November 2012]

Nolan, M. (1981). The unsatisfactory state of the current tax law. *Statute Law Review*, 3: 148–153.

OECD (2010). *Transfer Pricing Guidelines for Multinational Enterprises and Tax Administrations*. The Netherlands: OECD.

Rose, R. and Page, E. (2001). *Lawmaking Through the Back Door*. London: European Policy Forum.

Rowland, A.K. (1995). Is the Revenue being fair? Revenue statements and judicial review. *British Tax Review*, 2: 115–121.

Salter, D. (2010). The tax law rewrite in the United Kingdom: plus ça change plus c'est la meme chose? *British Tax Review*, 6: 671–687.

Senden, L. (2005). Soft law, self-regulation and co-regulation in European law: Where do they meet? *Electronic Journal of Comparative Law*, 9.1. [Online] Available at http://www.ejcl.org/. [Accessed 19 December 2012]

Senden, L. (2013). Soft post-legislative rulemaking: A time for more stringent control. *European Law Journal*, 19(1): 57–75.

Service, R. (2013). Receiving interest gross – the misunderstood form R85. *Tax Adviser*, June: 55

Stefan, O. (2012). European soft law: New developments concerning the divide between legally binding force and legal effects. *Modern Law Review*, 75(5): 865–893.

Steinmo, S. (1989). Political institutions and tax policy in the United States, Sweden and Britain. *World Politics*, 41(4): 500–533.

Steyn, K. (2001). Substantive legitimate expectations. *Judicial Review*, 6: 244–249.

Thuronyi, V. (1996). Drafting tax legislation, tax law design and drafting, Volume 1, Chapter 3. *International Monetary Fund*. [Online] Available at http://www.imf.org/external/pubs/nft/1998/tlaw/eng/ch3.pdf [accessed 9 July 2013]

Wilson, R. (2013). Legitimate expectation: trust law principle or public law distraction. *Journal of International Tax and Corporate Planning*, 20(1): 94–102.

6 Power of Authorities and Trust in Authorities Determine the Interaction Climate and Tax Compliance

*Katharina Gangl, Eva Hofmann, Barbara Hartl and Erich Kirchler**

> **Abstract**
>
> Taxpayers differ in their tax compliance depending on the interaction climate between tax authorities and taxpayers. The present study investigates mechanisms underlying the interaction climate – such as power of authorities and taxpayers' trust in authorities – resulting in enforced compliance, voluntary co-operation or committed co-operation. Results show that enforced compliance depends on coercive power whereas voluntary co-operation depends on legitimate power of tax authorities. Committed co-operation was found to originate in a confidence climate which is characterized by mutual implicit trust and a moral obligation to co-operate. Concluding theoretical and practical implications are presented, on how to strengthen taxpayers' voluntary and committed co-operation.

1 Introduction

Tax authorities influence tax compliance of citizens in various ways. According to the Slippery Slope Framework, tax authorities applying power measures enforce tax compliance whereas tax authorities who are trusted by the taxpayers gain voluntary co-operation (Kirchler, 2007; Kirchler, Hoelzl and Wahl, 2008). Power deals with pressure through audit probabilities and fines (Allingham and Sandmo, 1972; Blackwell, 2010), whereas trust originates in perceived benevolence of the authorities, transparency and fairness of tax law, tax collection procedures, and tax burden (Braithwaite, 2003b; Wenzel, 2002, 2004). The Slippery Slope Framework treats power and trust as independent dimensions determining taxpayers' behavior. The extended Slippery Slope Framework, however, takes into account

---

* Acknowledgement – The authors thank Stefanie Lietze and Lauri Metz for their assistance with data collection. This study was partly financed by the Austrian Science Fund (FWF), project number P24863-G16.

the dynamics between power and trust that result in different interaction climates between tax authorities and taxpayers and different forms of tax compliance (Gangl, Hofmann, Pollai and Kirchler, 2012). This chapter empirically tests the extended Slippery Slope Framework by analyzing the dynamics between power and trust underlying the interaction climates and enforced compliance, voluntary and committed co-operation.

The extended Slippery Slope Framework differentiates between different qualities of power and different qualities of trust (Gangl et al., 2012). Departing from the theory of bases of social power (French and Raven, 1959; Pierro, Raven, Amato and Bélanger, 2012; Raven, Schwarzwald and Koslowsky, 1998)[1] the framework distinguishes between coercive power and legitimate power. While coercive power is manifested through severe controls and punishment of tax evaders and rewarding of cooperative tax behavior, legitimate power means that authorities are accepted as legitimized to give orders and are perceived as holding expertise and behaving professionally when providing information and establishing rules of conduct. Trust is defined in the context of socio-cognitive trust theory and differentiated into reason-based trust and implicit trust (Castelfranchi and Falcone, 2010). Reason-based trust means that the tax authorities are trusted because they pursue relevant goals, because taxpayers depend on the authorities, because the authorities appear competent and benevolent, and because the authorities are supported but not hindered in reaching their goal. In contrast, implicit trust is defined as an automatic and unconscious trust reaction to the perception that the tax authorities are part of one's own community, sharing one's own values.

The dynamics between coercive and legitimate power and reason-based and implicit trust lead to three types of interaction climates. Coercive power results in an antagonistic interaction climate and erodes implicit trust. The tax authorities treat taxpayers as potential criminals who must be forced to comply with the law. In turn, taxpayers feel prosecuted and feel the need to hide from the tax authorities (Braithwaite, 2003a; Feld and Frey, 2002). Overall, willingness to co-operate is low and taxpayers only pay taxes if they cannot avoid it, thus, their compliance is enforced (see, Figure 6.1).

Legitimate power and reason-based trust are two sides of the same coin. Supportive and transparent procedures of authorities offer taxpayers reasons to trust in tax authorities. Together, legitimate power and reason-based trust lead to a service climate between tax authorities and taxpayers. In a service climate, tax authorities are perceived as a professional, rule-based institution

---

1 Raven, Schwarzwald and Koslowsky (1998) call coercive power "harsh power" and legitimate power is called "soft power". We stick to the terminology of regulation theory and use the terms coercive power and legitimate power (Tyler, 2006).

which provides services to its clients, the taxpayers (Alm and Torgler, 2011; Braithwaite, 2003b). The tax authorities are not focused on detecting potential evaders but try to assist honest taxpayers in complying with the law (Braithwaite, 2003a). In turn, taxpayers are convinced that the authorities are benevolent as long as taxpayers co-operate. As a consequence, taxpayers are voluntarily motivated to follow the rules of the law (see, Figure 6.1).

Implicit trust is assumed to lead to a confidence climate where taxpayers are committed to co-operate and coercive power is unnecessary. Tax authorities and taxpayers have a common purpose and common values and interact with empathy. Tax authorities trust taxpayers as responsible citizens and avoid coercive measures. Taxpayers perceive the tax authorities as a partner as well as a high social norm of tax honesty among their fellow citizens (Alm and Torgler, 2011). They not only follow the letter of the law but the spirit of the law and see tax paying as a moral obligation (Braithwaite, 2003a). In a confidence climate, taxpayers are committed to co-operate (see, Figure 6.1 below).

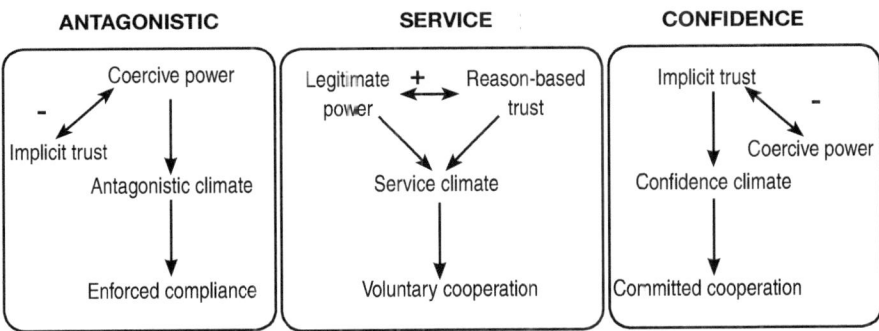

Figure 6.1: Dynamics between power and trust and resulting interaction climate and tax compliance according to the extended Slippery Slope Framework

The dynamics between qualities of power and qualities of trust allow conclusions on the transformation from one interaction climate to another (Gangl et al., 2012). An increase of legitimate power by the tax authorities is assumed to foster reason-based trust and to be a precondition for the perception of a service climate and voluntary cooperation. Positive long term experience and routine with the legitimated and trusted authorities are likely to transform a service climate into a confidence climate. However, the confidence climate based on implicit trust might be destroyed by the introduction of coercive power measures (Feld and Frey, 2002; Gangl et al., 2012).

The assumptions of the Slippery Slope Framework about the effect of power of tax authorities and trust in tax authorities on tax compliance has received empirical support (Kogler et al., 2013; Muehlbacher, Kirchler and

Schwarzenberger, 2011; Wahl, Kastlunger and Kirchler, 2010). Empirical findings on the extended Slippery Slope Framework, however, are rare (Hofmann, Gangl, Kirchler and Stark, 2013). Insights into the dynamic between power and trust may enhance the understanding of enforced compliance, voluntary co-operation, and committed cooperation. In the following part of this chapter, the method and results of the present study are presented.

2 Method

2.1 Sample

The sample consisted of 132 taxpayers (60% male; on average 39.26 [SD = 17.60] years old). The majority of the sample was employed (68.2%), 14.4% were self-employed, 7.6% were in education, 6.8% were retired, 2.3% were unemployed, and 0.8% were on maternity leave. About two thirds of participants reported a monthly net income of 1,001 to 2,000 Euro (35.6%); 22.7% reported an income of 2,001 to 3,000 Euro, and 25% an income higher than 3,000 Euro; 16.7% reported an income below 1,000 Euro. About half of the participants had a university degree (49.2%); 28.0% had a high school degree, 9.8% a degree from a vocational school, 9.8% a vocational training certificate, 0.8% had a secondary degree, and 2.3% indicated other degrees. Participants were mostly from Austria (81.1%) and Germany (15.2%). About 60% employed no tax practitioner; 22% used a practitioner occasionally, and 17.4% employed a tax practitioner regularly. Participants indicated having some experience with the tax authorities (M = 2.51, SD = 0.69; scale ranging from 1=no experience to 4=high experience).

2.2 Material

In an online questionnaire 10 concepts and socio-demographic characteristics were assessed. The concepts were (a) *perceived coercive power* with two sub-dimensions (punishment and reward power; six items), (b) *perceived legitimate* power with four sub-dimensions (legitimate power, expert power, information power and referent power; 13 items), (c) *reason-based trust* with four sub-dimensions (shared goals, dependency, internal factors [competence, motivation, and benevolence], external factors [external opportunities and dangers] 14 items), and (d) *implicit trust* with one dimension (three items). The scales (e) *perceived antagonistic climate* (three items), (f) *perceived service climate* (three items), (g) *perceived confidence climate* (three items), (h) *enforced compliance* (four items), (i) *voluntary co-operation* (four items), and (j) *committed co-operation* (four items) were assessed by one sub-dimension each. As socio-demographics, sex, age, occupation, income, country of residence, use of tax practitioners, and experience with tax authorities were assessed. All items, factor loadings, and scale reliabilities as well as inter-correlations can be found in the Appendix.

2.3 Procedure

The questionnaire was presented online. A link to the online questionnaire was posted in discussion forums of Austrian newspapers asking readers to fill out a questionnaire on the perception of tax authorities. The first item in the questionnaire was a filter item in order to ascertain whether they had paid taxes in the past. Only those participants who indicated that they had experiences with tax paying were allowed to continue with the questionnaire, all others were thanked and debriefed without filling out the questionnaire.

Table 6.1: Inter-correlations of scales

	2	3	4	5	6	7	8	9	10	11
1. Coercive power	-.19*	-.11	-.28**	-.29**	.35***	-.24**	-.23**	.39***	-.11	-.21*
2. Reward power		.49***	.49***	.17	-.17	.31***	.43***	-.13	.40***	.18*
3. Legitimate power		1	.61***	.27**	-.26**	.52***	.57***	-.15	.44***	.37***
4. Reason based trust				.45***	-.38***	.57***	.70***	-.13	.49***	.50***
5. Implicit trust					-.29**	.27**	.39***	-.27**	.24**	.30***
6. Antagonistic climate						-.23**	-.39***	.48***	-.07	-.44***
7. Service climate							.68***	-.04	.48***	.28**
8. Confidence climate								-.16	.46***	.45***
9. Enforced compliance									.03	-.36***
10. Voluntary compliance										.29**
11. Committed co-operation										

Note: %, Pearson correlations. *, **, *** represent statistical significance at the $p < .05$, $p < .01$, $p < .001$ levels, respectively. Coercive power includes only items on punishment

3 Results

To test the dynamics between power and trust and the resulting interaction climates, structural equation modeling was conducted (SEM analysis, Byrne, 2001). We tested the three models displayed in Figure 6.1, which we call antagonistic model, service model, and confidence model. For each of these models adjusted versions were estimated as well to identify the model which best fits the data.

To test the antagonistic model, we analyzed whether a negative relationship between coercive power and implicit trust exists which leads to an antagonistic climate that, in turn, induces enforced compliance. As the scale coercive power consists of two sub-dimensions (punishment power and reward power) the items belonging to each dimension were averaged to use the two dimensions as parcel scores in place of item scores in the analysis (Bandalos, 2002). The estimated Model A, displayed in Table 6.2 and in Figure 6.2 below, has good fit indices, indicating that the model is matching the data. About 42% of variance of the antagonistic climate and about 27% of variance of enforced compliance can be explained by the model. However, the two dimensions of coercive power, punishment and reward, have different impacts. Whereas coercive power is increased by punishment power (β = .58, p < .01), it is diminished by reward power (β = -.34, p < .01). This indicates that reward power assesses a different concept than punishment power. As a consequence, we adjusted the model estimations by omitting the reward power dimension and estimate coercive power only through three items measuring perceived punishment of the tax authorities. The resulting Model B (see, Table 6.2 and Figure 6.2 below) has also good fit indices and matches the data well (antagonistic climate: R^2 = .19; enforced compliance: R^2 = .27). Additionally, we estimated another adjusted Model C, in which we added direct relations between implicit trust and the antagonistic climate and coercive power and enforced compliance (see, Figure 2 below). Model C captures the theoretical assumption that there is no implicit trust in the antagonistic climate and also shows that the direct relationship between coercive power and enforced compliance (β = .47, p < .01) is not totally mediated through the perception of an antagonistic climate. Model C has good fit indices indicating that this model matches the data well (antagonistic climate: R^2 = .21; enforced compliance: R^2 = .35). Comparing all estimated models, Model C seems to have the best fit to explain the mechanism behind the antagonistic climate and enforced tax compliance (see, Table 6.2).

Table 6.2: Model fit indices of the antagonistic model

Antagonistic model	χ^2	df	p	χ^2/df	CFI	RMSEA
A	71.61	51	.03	1.40	.98	.06
B (without reward power items)	95.18	62	.004	1.54	.97	.06
C (with direct relations)	77.69	60	.06	1.30	.98	.05

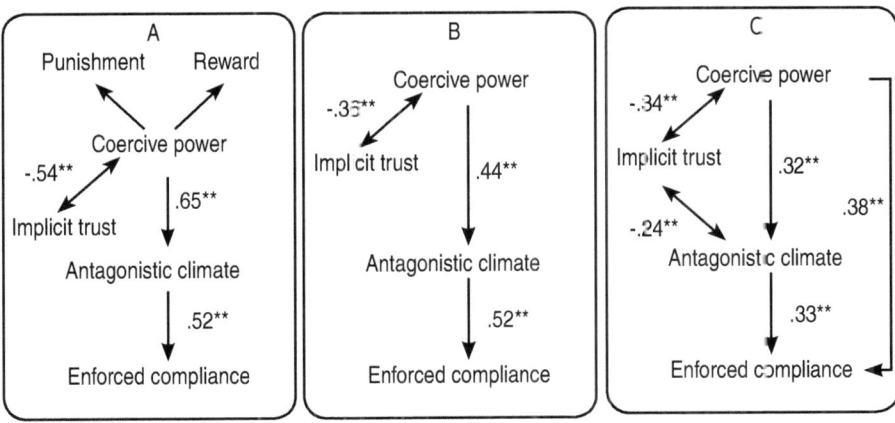

Figure 6.2: Structural equation models of the antagonistic model

To test the service model we analyzed whether a positive relationship between legitimate power and reason-based trust leads to a service climate and in turn to voluntary co-operation. As the scales legitimate power and reason-based trust consist of four sub-dimensions each, the items of each sub-dimension were averaged to use these sub-dimensions as parcel scores in place of item scores in the SEM analysis (Bandalos, 2002). Based on theory, we additionally allowed a correlation of the errors between expert power and information power for the scale legitimate power. In the Model A displayed below in Figure 6.3, legitimate power and reason-based trust correlate with β = .90, in turn, the path between legitimate power and service climate excels 1 and the path between reason-based trust and service climate becomes negative indicating a specification error and, thus, implies a modification of the model (Dillon, Kumar and Mulani, 1987). Although this model explains 81% of variance of service climate and 47% of variance of voluntary co-operation, the model fit indices indicate a bad fit of the model to the data (Table 6.3). Assuming multicollinearity between legitimate power and reason-based trust, a model was estimated in which only legitimate power or reason-based trust is estimated as a predictor. Whereas the model with legitimate power (Model B) explains 81% of variance of service climate and 45% of variance of voluntary cooperation with a good fit (see, Table 6.3 below), the model with reason-based trust (Model C) explains only 57% of variance of service climate and 45% of variance of voluntary cooperation. Comparing Models A, B, and C indicates that legitimate power as well as reason-based trust explain the service climate and voluntarily cooperation. However, Model B with legitimate power has the overall highest explanatory power. If we additionally add a direct relation between legitimate power and voluntary co-operation, as depicted in Model B.1 again a specification error occurs (probably due to multicollinearity, the path between legitimate power and voluntary co-operation excels 1). Model B.1 has a good fit as well and explains 74% of variance of service climate and 75% of variance of voluntary co-operation. Additionally, this model indicates that the mechanism through which legitimate power impacts voluntary co-operation is direct ($\beta = .84, p < .01$) via the mediation through the perception of a service climate. Comparing all models and weighing the different statistical values, Model B seems to explain the service climate and voluntary co-operation more accurately than the other models (see, Table 6.3).

Table 6.3: Model fit indices of the service model

Service model	χ^2	df	p	χ^2/df	CFI	RMSEA
A (original)	190.38	85	< .001	2.24	.88	.10
B (legitimate power)	68.50	41	.005	1.67	.95	.07
B.1 (legitimate power plus direct relation)[a]	55.11	40	.06	1.38	.97	.05
C (reason-based trust)[b]	91.59	42	< .001	2.18	.93	.10

Note: [a] For exploratory reasons, in another adjusted Model B.2, we included reward power as a sub-dimension of legitimate power to the analysis. The model has a marginally good fit ($\chi^2(50) = 81.71$, $\chi^2/df = 1.38$, $CFI = .94$, $RMSEA = .07$) and explains 58% of the variance of the service climate and 61% of the variance of voluntary co-operation.

[b] For exploratory reasons, in another adjusted Model C.1, we included a direct relation between reason-based trust and voluntary co-operation. The model has a slightly better fit ($\chi^2(41) = 81.89$, $\chi^2/df = 2.00$, $CFI = .94$, $RMSEA = .09$) and explains 52% of the variance of the service climate and 49% of the variance of voluntary co-operation.

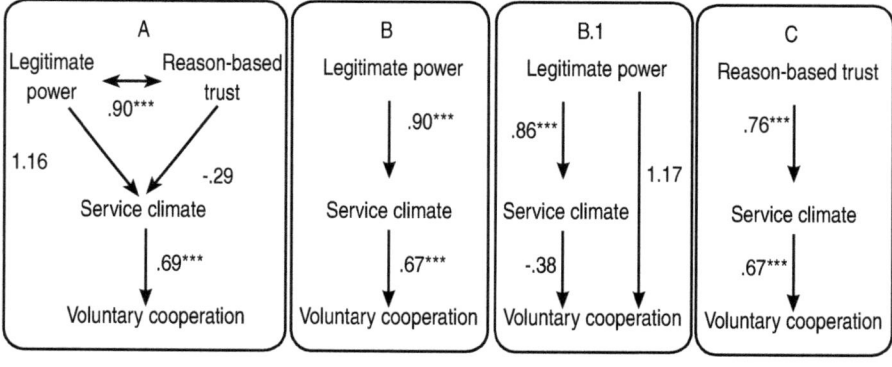

Figure 6.3: Structural equation models of the service model

To test the confidence model we analyzed whether the negative relationship between implicit trust and coercive power exists and leads to a confidence climate that in turn, induces committed co-operation. As shown in the analyses of the antagonistic climate model, the sub-dimension reward power correlates negatively with the scale coercive power ($\beta = -.35, p < .01$) thus, does not fit with the scale coercive power. However, Model A (see,

Table 6.4 and Figure 6.4 below) has a good model fit (confidence climate: $R^2 = .19$; committed cooperation: $R^2 = .25$). In the adjusted Model B, coercive power only composes punishment items leading to a good fit (confidence climate: $R^2 = .19$; committed cooperation: $R^2 = .25$). Also Model C, in which a direct relation between implicit trust and committed co-operation and between coercive power and the confidence climate is added, has a good fit (confidence climate: $R^2 = .19$; committed co-operation: $R^2 = .25$). Model C indicates that the direct relation between implicit trust and committed co-operation ($\beta = .33$, $p < .001$) is totally mediated by the perception of a confidence climate. Comparing all models indicates that Model B and C likewise overall describe the mechanism behind the confidence climate and committed co-operation best (see Table 6.4).

Table 6.4: Model fit indices of the confidence model

Confidence model	χ^2	df	p	χ^2/df	CFI	RMSEA
A (original)	81.00	51	.005	1.59	.97	.07
B (without reward items)	74.91	62	.13	1.21	.99	.04
C (with direct relations)	70.86	60	.16	1.18	.99	.04

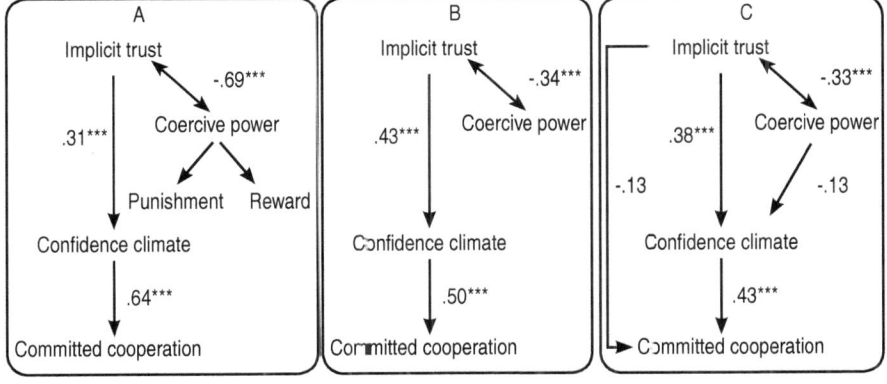

Figure 6.4: Structural equation models of the confidence model

4 Discussion

Taxpayers differ concerning their compliance to pay taxes. Understanding how these differences emerge allows us to determine how tax authorities' may increase voluntary and committed co-operation. The present study confirms the assumptions of the extended Slippery Slope Framework and, empirically, shows how the dynamic between coercive and legitimate power and implicit, namely reason-based trust determines three distinct interaction climates and enforced compliance, voluntary and committed co-operation (Gangl et al., 2012).

Results show that coercive power of tax authorities erodes implicit trust of taxpayers, a dynamic, which is associated with an antagonistic interaction climate and enforced compliance. Although the perception of coercion is a determining factor of the antagonistic climate, enforced compliance is a direct consequence of perceived tax authorities' coercive measures and not mediated via the antagonistic relationship between authorities and taxpayers.

The positive dynamic between legitimate power and reason-based trust is related to a service climate and voluntary co-operation. Interestingly, results indicate that legitimate power of tax authorities, rather than reason-based trust, is the characterizing factor in the service model. Reason-based trust explains the service climate as well, but not as well as legitimate power. Analysis shows that legitimated authorities directly impact voluntary co-operation of taxpayers as well as trust in the authorities and the perception of a service climate.

As expected, the negative dynamics between implicit trust and coercive power are the prevailing mechanism behind the confidence climate which, in turn, is determining committed tax co-operation. In contrast to enforced compliance and voluntary co-operation, committed co-operation is based on the mediation via the interaction climate, thus the relation between tax authorities and taxpayers. Hence, the current study shows, that enforced compliance and voluntary co-operation result from the tax authorities' direct characteristics perceived as deterring or professional, whereas committed co-operation results from the interaction climate between the tax authorities and the taxpayers stemming from implicit trust.

The inter-correlations among all present scales illustrate the opposition between mechanisms determining the antagonistic model and the confidence model and, on the other hand, how the mechanisms of the service model are compound with those of the confidence model. Hence, the transformation to a confidence climate and committed co-operation seems to depend on the presence of a service climate and voluntary co-operation (Gangl et al., 2012). In the service climate, interactions are initially based on legitimate power and careful consideration about the others' trustworthiness. However, they might become automated with routine and repeated interaction (Castelfranchi and Falcone, 2010; Nooteboom, 2002). Thus, the transformation from an antagonistic climate to a service climate implies a reduction of tax authorities' perceived deterrence measures and an increase of tax authorities' assistance activities. A transformation from a service climate to a confidence climate, however, depends on time and a relationship of mutual trust based on positive experience and familiarization of the taxpayers with the legitimated authorities (Gangl et al., 2012). To test these assumptions on the transformation from one climate of interaction to another climate of interaction, further longitudinal studies would be necessary.

Unexpectedly, results show that reward power is not part of the scale coercive power (Raven et al., 1998). Thus, that coercive power of authorities is based on punishments and not rewards. However, as explorative analyses indicate, reward power also does not fit with legitimate power explaining a service climate and voluntary co-operation (see, Table 6.3). It can be concluded that reward power might define an own entity leading to a distinct quality of tax compliance. Existing literature on motivation suggests that rewards similar to punishments have the potential to crowd out the intrinsic motivation to co-operate (Frey and Jegen, 2001; Raven et al., 1998). However, it might be that the crowding out effect of rewards only occurs among taxpayers who paid taxes voluntarily beforehand but that taxpayers who feel enforced to comply, react positively to rewards offered for compliant behavior (Deci. Koester and Ryan, 1999). Further theoretical and empirical analyses are necessary to determine the differential effects of rewards on tax compliance.

The current study allows some practical conclusions. Tax authorities should avoid being perceived as coercive because this might lead to an antagonistic climate and enforced compliance. Coercive power erodes trust and voluntary or committed co-operation which makes more costly the coercive measures necessary to maintain at least a certain level of tax compliance (Kirchler et al., 2008). Trying to be perceived as a legitimated tax authority is advantageous concerning the interaction with taxpayers and a voluntary co-operation. However, whereas costs of audits might be reduced, the administrative costs of services increase (Gangl et al., 2012). Nonetheless, positive experiences in the service climate and a trustful interaction might make taxpayers take on responsibility. An example for such an interaction between tax authorities and taxpayers is the horizontal monitoring initiative applied in some OECD countries (Stevens, Pheijffer, van den Broek, JKeijzer and van der Hel - van Dijk, 2012). The current results indicate that a co-operative interaction might cause taxpayers to perceive taxpaying as their moral obligation. Thus, in the confidence climate costly audits, but also costly administrative procedures, could be avoided.

The current study is the first empirical test of the assumptions of the extended Slippery Slope Framework, and, hence, on the impact of the dynamic between power and trust on the interaction climate and tax compliance. Although the current study allows some theoretical and practical conclusions, replications and extension of the current findings are needed with behavioral data. Further insights into the dynamic between power and trust may be utilized to improve the interaction between tax authorities and taxpayers and hence, increase voluntary and committed tax compliance.

Bibliography

Allingham, M. G., & Sandmo, A. (1972). Income tax evasion: A theoretical analysis. *Journal of Public Economics, 1,* 323-338.

Alm, J., & Torgler, B. (2011). Do ethics matter? Tax compliance and morality. *Journal of Business Ethics, 101,* 635-651. doi: 10.1007/s10551-011-0761-9

Bandalos, D. L. (2002). The effects of item parceling on goodness-of-fit and parameter estimate bias in structureal equation modeling. *Structural Equation Modeling: A Multidisciplinary Journal, 9,* 78-102.

Blackwell, C. (2010). A meta-analysis of incentive effects in tax compliance experiments. In J. Alm, J. Martinez-Vazquesz & B. Torgler (Eds.), *Developing alternative frameworks for explaining tax compliance* (pp. 97-112). London, UK: Routhledge.

Braithwaite, V. (2003a). Dancing with tax authorities: Motivational postures and non-compliance actors. In V. Braithwaite (Ed.), *Taxing Democracy* (pp. 1-11). Aldershot, UK: Ashgate.

Braithwaite, V. (2003b). A new approach to tax compliance. In V. Braithwaite (Ed.), *Taxing Democracy . Understanding tax avoidance and tax evasion.* Aldershot, UK: Ashgate.

Byrne, B. M. (2001). *Structural equation modeling with AMOS. Basic concepts, applications, and programming.* Mahwah, NJ: Lawrence Erlbaum.

Castelfranchi, C., & Falcone, R. (2010). *Trust theory: A socio-cognitive and computational model.* West Sussex: Wiley.

Deci, E. L., Koester, R., & Ryan, R. M. (1999). A meta-analytic review of experiments examining the effects of extrinsic rewards on intrinisc motivation. *Psychological Bulletin, 125*(627-668).

Dillon, W. R., Kumar, A., & Mulani, N. (1987). Offending estimates in covariance structure analysis: Comments on the cause of and solutions to Heywood cases. *Psychological Bulletin, 101,* 126-135.

Feld, L. P., & Frey, B. S. (2002). Trust breeds trust: How taxpayers are treated. *Economics of Governance, 3*(2), 87-99. doi: 10.1007/s101010100032

French, J. R., & Raven, B. (1959). The bases of social power. In D. Cartwright (Ed.), *Studies in social power* (pp. 150-167). Ann Arbor: University of Michigan.

Frey, B. S., & Jegen, R. (2001). Motivation crowding theory. *Journal of Economic Surveys, 15*(5), 589-611. doi: 10.1111/1467-6419.00150

Gangl, K., Hofmann, E., Pollai, M., & Kirchler, E. (2012). The dynamics of power and trust in the Slippery Slope Framework. *SSRN Working Paper 2024946.*

Hofmann, E., Gangl, K., Kirchler, E., & Stark, J. (2013). Enhancing tax compliance through coercive and legitimate power of authorities. *WU International Taxation Research Paper Series No. 2013-01*.

Kirchler, E. (2007). *The economic psychology of tax behaviour*. Cambridge: University Press.

Kirchler, E., Hoelzl, E., & Wahl, I. (2008). Enforced versus voluntary tax compliance: The "slippery slope" framework. *Journal of Economic Psychology, 29*, 210-225. doi: 10.1016/j.joep.2007.05.004

Kogler, C., Batrancea, L., Nichita, A., Pantya, J., Belianin, A., & Kirchler, E. (2013). Trust and power as determinants of tax compliance: Testing the assumptions of the slippery slope framework in Austria, Hungary, Romania and Russia. *Journal of Economic Psychology, 34*(0). doi: 10.1016/j.joep.2012.09.010

Muehlbacher, S., Kirchler, E., & Schwarzenberger, H. (2011). Voluntary versus enforced tax compliance: Empirical evidence for the "slippery slope" framework. *European Journal of Law and Economics, 32*(1), 89-97. doi: 10.1007/s10657-011-9236-9

Nooteboom, B. (2002). *Trust: Forms, foundations, functions, failures and figures*. Cheltenham: Edward Elgar.

Pierro, A., Raven, B. H., Amato, C., & Bélanger, J. J. (2012). Bases of social power, leadership styles, and organizational commitment. *International Journal of Psychology*, 1-13.

Raven, B. H., Schwarzwald, J., & Koslowsky, M. (1998). Conceptualizing and measuring a power/interaction model of interpersonal influence. *Journal of Applied Social Psychology, 28*, 307-332. doi: 10.1111/j.1559-1816.1998.tb01708.x

Stevens, L. G. M., Pheijffer, M., van den Broek, J. G. A., Keijzer, T. J., & van der Hel - van Dijk, E. C. J. M. (2012). Tax supervision - Made to measure. From Committe Horizontal Monitoring Tax and Customs Administration, Ministry of Finance, The Netherlands http://www.ifa.nl/Document/Publicaties/Enhanced%20Relationship%20Project/tax_supervision_made_to_measure_tz0151z1fdeng.pdf

Tyler, T. R. (2006). Psychological perspectives on legitimacy and legitimation. *Annual Review of Psychology, 57*, 375-400.

Wahl, I., Kastlunger, B., & Kirchler, E. (2010). Trust in authorities and power to enforce tax compliance: An empirical analysis of the "Slippery Slope Framework". *Law & Policy, 32*, 383-406. doi: 10.1111/j.1467-9930.2010.00327.x

Wenzel, M. (2002). The impact of outcome orientation and justice concerns on tax compliance: The role of taxpayers' identity. *Journal of Applied Psychology, 87*, 629-645. doi: 10.1037/0021-9010.87.4.629

Wenzel, M. (2004). Motivation or rationalisation? Causal relations between ethics, norms and tax compliance. *Journal of Economic Psychology, 26*(4), 491-508. doi: 10.1016/j.joep.2004.03.003

Appendix

Scales and items to assess power, trust, interaction climate, and tax compliance

Scales and Items	Factor-loadings	Reliability
Coercive Power		α = .77
The tax authority punishes severely.	.77	
The tax authority enforces its demands through audits and fines.	.83	
The tax authority prosecutes taxpayers mainly with audits and fines.	.88	
Reward power		α = .80
The tax authority grants tax reliefs to taxpayers.	.84	
The tax authority grants concessions to taxpayers in a number of ways.	.85	
The tax authority rewards taxpayers in many ways.	.86	
Legitimate Power		α = .75
The tax authority has the right to levy taxes from taxpayers because of its significance in the state.	.04	
The tax authority is an institution taxpayers feel obliged to co-operate with, because of the good services in the past.	.57	
The tax authority depends on taxpayers who fill out their tax forms correctly in order to work efficiently.	.54	
The tax authority should especially receive diligently filled out tax returns from taxpayers whose past tax returns were too often completed incorrectly.	.42	
The tax authority makes all taxpayers understand, which taxes they have to pay and to what extent they have to pay them.	.65	
The tax authority informs taxpayers of possible errors occurring when completing their tax return.	.57	
The tax authority does share understandable information.	.60	
The tax authority knows how a correct tax return of each taxpayer has to look like.	.41	
The tax authority knows how a correctly filled in tax return should look like.	.36	
The tax authority is an expert on tax regulations and their practice.	.45	
The tax authority is regarded for their work by the taxpayers.	.71	
The tax authority is appreciated for their services by taxpayers.	.46	
The tax authority is acknowledged for their work by taxpayers.	.57	
Reason Based Trust		α = .92
I trust the tax authority because I agree with its main objectives.	.80	
I trust the tax authority because its goals seem plausible.	.75	
I trust the tax authority because I have no choice.	.22	
I trust the tax authority because there is no alternative.	.30	
I trust the tax authority because of its highly motivated employees.	.73	

I trust in the tax authority because it has committed employees.	.74
I trust the tax authority because it provides competent work.	.75
I trust the tax authority because it is fulfilling its tasks well.	.80
I trust the tax authority because it behaves benevolently toward taxpayers.	.79
I trust the tax authority because it solely wants the best for taxpayers.	.72
I trust the TA because its decisions are politically supported.	.77
I trust in the tax authority because politics ensure that sufficient resources are available, so it can work.	.76
I trust the tax authority because the political situation ensures that the tax authority can work.	.81
I trust the tax authority because the economic stability guarantees that the tax authority can work.	.79
Implicit Trust	$\alpha = .92$
I trust the tax authority usually without thinking about it.	.93
I trust the tax authority usually without dealing with it deeply.	.93
I trust the tax authority most of the time automatically.	.91
Antagonistic Climate	$\alpha = .88$
Between the tax authority and taxpayers there exists a climate of inconsiderateness.	.91
Between the tax authority and taxpayers there exists a climate of ruthlessness.	.92
Between the tax authority and taxpayers there exists a climate of 'cops and robbers'.	.87
Service Climate	$\alpha = .87$
Between the tax authority and the taxpayers there exists a climate that is characterized by the fact that the TA treats the taxpayer as their customer.	.90
The relationship between the tax authority and the taxpayers is similar to an enterprise and their customers.	.89
The relationship between the tax authority and taxpayers is service-oriented in nature.	.87
Confidence Climate	$\alpha = .91$
The relationship between the tax authority and taxpayers is characterized by mutual trust.	.92
The relationship between the tax authority and taxpayers is characterized by joint responsibility.	.93
Between the tax authority and taxpayers there exists a climate of that is characterized by cooperation.	.91
Enforced Compliance	$\alpha = .84$
When I pay taxes, I do so because a great many tax audits are carried out.	.88
When I pay taxes, I do so because I know I will be audited.	.89
When I pay taxes, I do so because the TA often carries out audits.	.91
When I pay taxes, I do so because I feel forced to pay my taxes.	.59

Voluntary Co-operation		α= .74
When I pay taxes, I do so because the tax authority will probably reciprocate my cooperation.	.84	
When I pay taxes, I do so because the tax authority treats me correctly as long as I admit mistakes.	.83	
When I pay taxes, I do so because the tax authority supports taxpayers who make unintentional mistakes.	.83	
When I am paying my taxes correctly, I do so, because it is easier than to deceive the tax authority.	.52	
Committed Co-operation		α = .92
When I pay taxes, I do so because it is the right thing to do.	.91	
When I pay taxes, I do so because it is ultimately in everyone's interest.	.89	
When I pay taxes, I do so because I feel a moral obligation to pay taxes.	.90	
When I am paying my taxes correctly, I do so, because it is an important civic duty.	.89	

7 Corporate Social Responsibility and Tax Planning: Rules and Principles

Hans Gribnau[1]

Abstract

Taxpayers have to organise their tax affairs to plan their life or develop their business strategy. Often tax planning is encouraged and intended by tax legislation. Tax incentives may be used to steer (corporate) citizens' behaviour to achieve all kind of policy goals. In this way, the tax legislator stimulates taxpayers to adopt a calculating attitude towards the tax system, breeding a rule-based mindset focused on tax planning. This rule-focus crowds out ethics.

Companies endorsing corporate social responsibility accept ethical obligations beyond compliance with the law. It is argued that these companies should agree that the interpretation and use of tax rules is based on a moral choice; all the more because the tax system is a moral phenomenon because it regards the provision of public goods and the distribution of tax burden. However, they should take one more step in endorsing the view that tax is a body of rules which itself is grounded in principles which make up the internal morality of law. Therefore, they should take these principles seriously when engaging in tax planning.

1 Introduction

Taxation is key to the character and functioning of the state, economy and society. Tax revenues enable government to provide the public with all kinds of public goods and services. Government provides a framework for the functioning of society and economy supported by taxes, e.g., enforcing contracts supports markets. The state fosters innovation, encourages investment, boosts worker productivity, and stimulates the efficient use of scarce resources. Often, tax incentives are used to affect behaviour. Through

---

[1] The author wishes to thank Rem Hamers for his valuable comments on a previous draft of this chapter and David Salter for patient editorial work. ˚ For a more elaborated version of this chapter, see H Gribnau (2015) Corporate Social Responsibility and Tax Planning: Not by Rules Alone. 24 *Social & Legal Studies* 2: 225–250.

a wide range of activities, the social welfare state tries to create substantive freedom and equality for its citizens. Thus, taxation has an enormous impact on all kinds of activities and situations of the members of society, citizens as well as enterprises. In order to keep in control of their finances people have to know the impact of taxation and atune their behaviour to this impact. Thus, they may engage in tax planning. In an international context tax planning is often used to avoid double taxation.

Tax planning, tax avoidance and tax evasion are different ways in which businesses respond to tax legislation. In one way or another, businesses, like all taxpayers, make use of tax legislation – be it domestic legislation or international tax rules, such as tax treaties. In this chapter, I will first deal with the relationship between the tax legislature and taxpayers, tax planning being an essentially rule-based affair shared by the two of them. In the framework of this chapter the Dutch (corporate) income tax system is used as a case study. Reference is also made to literature concerning other jurisdictions, cautiously suggesting that some arguments may be generalised. Dutch tax legislation is nowadays a continuously growing, very complex, and often muddled, inconsistent body of rules which sometimes violates important legal principles. Taxpayers, in turn, seem to focus on rules, paying little attention to underlying principles. This rule-focus crowds out ethics. Subsequently, I will have a closer look at the consequences of these rule-based reciprocal tax planning activities from the perspective of tax compliance.

In recent debates on aggressive tax planning, corporations like Google, Starbucks and Facebook argued that they acted legally, i.e. in conformity with the prevailing legal rules. Rules are an important regulatory instrument and as a generalization they guarantee a measure of certainty and equality. However, rules have a drawback and that is why the rule focus becomes increasingly problematic. Rules are imperfect; it is just not possible to perfectly 'translate' in a rule the goal sought to be served. Imperfectly drafted rules account for traditional legal issues such as the interpretation of rules and gaps in the law.

So the question is whether taxpayers, and more specifically, companies ought to include ethical considerations in their tax decision-making framework. Here, I will focus on companies which engage in Corporate Social Responsibility (CSR), so this chapter is subject to a limitation. In what way should companies that accept this kind of responsibility comply with the tax rules? Where can they find guidance when faced with a less than perfect body of rules? A subsequent question is whether the legal system contains specific guidelines for ethical conduct which go beyond the (letter of the) law.

I will tackle the issue of the use of the inherent imperfection of rules from a legal philosophical perspective on rules. In this approach, legal principles make up the internal morality of law, underlying the body of legal rules (see, Dworkin (1977 and 1986), Fuller (1977)). In my view, in particular companies endorsing CSR should take these principles to heart because they encompass ethical obligations beyond compliance with the law.

2 Tax Legislation

2.1 Complexity of tax law and its causes

Modern society is complex. Tax law cannot but reflect the complexity of societies, having to attach legal consequences to all kinds of facts and actions. Dutch tax legislation exhibits a tantalizing complexity due to its ongoing proliferation (this not only goes for The Netherlands). No wonder, since taxation not only is an important instrument to collect money for the Treasury, but it is also used to implement redistributive policies, and all kinds of other government policies.[2] The primary function of taxation is to raise revenue for necessary governmental functions, such as the provision of public goods, and the redistributive function, which is aimed at reducing the unequal distribution of income and wealth seems to be overshadowed by the instrumental or regulatory function. The regulatory function may even be favoured at the expense of the redistributive function.[3] Thus, taxation is seen as an important regulatory instrument of wide-scale social and economic planning.

The Dutch government advocates the view that the use of tax legislation for non-fiscal goals is an integral part of government policy. It is an instrument to micromanage choices of taxpayers. Dutch tax law, therefore, contains all kinds of incentives mostly in the form of tax reductions, e.g., for commuting by bike, employee's training, day-care centres, production of Dutch movies, research and development, ecologically sound investments or the letting of rooms by private persons.[4] Of course, tax legislation to support CSR is

---

2 Avi-Yonah R S (2006-2007) The Three Goals of Taxation. *Tax Law Review* 60: 3; Gribnau J L M (2013) Legislative Instrumentalism vs. Legal Principles in Tax Law. 18 *Coventry Law Journal* (special issue): 89-109.
3 Campbell A L (2012) America the Undertaxed: U.S. Fiscal Policy in Perspective. *Foreign Affairs* 91: 106.
4 Gribnau J L M (2003) Equality, Consistency, and Impartiality in Tax Legislation. in H Gribnau (ed.), *Legal Protection against Discriminatory Tax Legislation*. The Hague, London, Boston: Kluwer Law International: 7-32. For the U.S.A, see Goldberg D S (2013) *The Death of the Income Tax: A Progressive Consumption Tax and the Path to Fiscal Reform*. New York: Oxford University Press: 63: 'Important public initiatives such as subsidized housing, welfare, health and energy cannot be understood without looking at the tax code.'

another option.⁵

States use tax legislation to attract businesses. This instrumental use of taxation also has an international component. As a result there is a fierce tax competition among states, which capitalizes on and reinforces businesses' leaning towards tax planning. In an age of increasing mobility of undertakings and especially capital investments, companies and entrepreneurs consider low tax costs an important factor in deciding where to set up undertakings and invest capital. States are aware of this, of course, and they will try to compete with their tax system in order to attract economic activities from other states.⁶ States see corporation tax as an important instrument in this bid for economic activity, for example, lower corporate taxes might induce multinational corporations not to allocate their economic activities and profits to other countries.⁷ The political dimension of corporation tax issues, therefore, should not be neglected.⁸

This overuse of taxation to achieve disparate goals and objectives is one of the main causes of an ever growing body of very detailed rules, but also an increasing number of vague provisions in tax legislation.⁹ In short, tax law has become excessively complex at the expense of legal certainty¹⁰. The quality of tax legislation is also often impaired by reasons of political opportunity and the need to reconcile disparate interests. This is partly due to the interference of pressure groups in the legislative process. Pressure groups

---

5   Perrini F, Pogutz S & Tencati A (2006) *Developing Corporate Social Responsibility: A European Perspective*. Cheltenham: Edward Elgar : 38. Cf. Greider W (2006) The Future is Now. *The Nation* 26th June. <http://www.thenation.com/article/future-now >: 23-6, where it is proposed that 'corporation taxation could be refashioned, so that tax liabilities might be reduced for those that adhere to higher social or environmental standards.'
6   For an analysis of the concept, methodology, and economic aspects of tax competition, see Pinto C (2003) *Tax Competition and EU Law*. The Hague/London/New York: Kluwer Law International.
7   Cf. Peters C (2014) *On the Legitimacy of International Tax Law*. Amsterdam: IBFD: 56 conceptualises the 'pressure' asserted by markets and tax competition as pressure asserted by the 'tax law market' – referring to Schön, W (2005) Playing Different Games? Regulatory Competition in Tax and Company Law Compared. 42 *Common Market Law Review* 2: 331–365.
8   Snape J (2007) Corporation Tax Reform – Politics and Public Law. 103 *British Tax Review* 4: 382-389.
9   Vague norms are frequently introduced in tax law, leaving the tax administration a considerable latitude to determine the law and, thereby, diminishing the predictability of tax statutes by establishing administrative rules. These vague concepts are deliberately indeterminate to deter taxpayers from bending the rules, at the expense of legal certainty ('chilling effect').
10 Gribnau H (2013) Legal Certainty: A matter of principle. In Gribnau H and Pauwels M (eds), *Retroactivity of Tax Legislation* (2010) EATLP Congress, Leuven, Amsterdam: EATLP, 69-93.

seek to create and preserve expenditures in the form of tax exemptions and attempt to shift the burden of taxation in their own favour. Tax expenditures result in lower tax payments by taxpayers than would be due under the normal tax rules.[11] They also may try to obtain tax privileges at the cost of the principle of equality. Moreover, often the fair share principle is not easy to identify in tax legislation.[12] In short, tax rules frequently lack quality by violating important legal principles. It is important to comply with these principles because they constitute the internal morality of law.

2.2 Complexity implies tax planning

Here, I employ the term 'tax planning' in a broad way including very different forms of taxpayer behaviour. For the purposes of this chapter, tax planning should be understood in a neutral ethical way, as opposed to e.g. tax evasion and tax avoidance, which often have a negative – unethical – overtone. Hasseldine and Morris (2013) suggest two necessary conditions be met for behaviour to qualify as tax evasion, in contradistinction with 'every other type of tax-related behavior' - failure to satisfy a tax liability that has crystallized and intent, based on an event that has occurred, to be deceitful, fraudulent and/or corrupt with respect to that event.[13] The term 'aggressive tax planning' in a way moves away from this legal distinction between tax evasion and tax avoidance. Aggressive tax planning or tax aggressiveness, according to Lanis and Richardson (2012), can be broadly defined as 'the downward management of taxable income through tax planning activities. It thus encompasses tax planning activities that are legal or that may fall into the gray area, as well as activities that are illegal. Moreover, they argue that the term can be used 'interchangeably with tax avoidance and tax management'.[14]

Due to the excessive complexity of tax law, taxpayers are almost forced to engage in tax planning; otherwise they would be insecure with regard to a large part of their financial affairs. For some taxpayers the complexity of tax law offers opportunities to deploy tax minimisation techniques to shift their burden of taxation to others; for these taxpayers complexity is not problematic, but rather provides opportunities for (aggressive) tax planning.[15] They often

---

11 Cf. Vording H (2013) The Concept of Instrumentalism in Tax Law. 18 *Coventry Law Journal* (special issue): 41-60.
12 Bundesministerium der Finanzen (2010) Die gefühlte Steuerbelastung. In: Idem, *Monatsbericht Februar* 2010: 70.
13 Hasseldine J & Morris G (2013) Corporate social responsibility and tax avoidance: A comment and reflection. *Accounting Forum* 37: 5.
14 Lanis R & Richardson G (2012) Corporate Social Responsibility and Tax Aggressiveness: An Empirical Analysis. *Journal of Accounting and Public Policy* Jan/Feb 2012: 1.
15 Cf. Goldberg (2013): 28: thus 'the income tax fails to treat similarly situated taxpayers equally.'

do so by financial engineering exploiting the complexity of the body of rules by contriving complexity themselves. For example, as the European Commission, recently stated: 'some taxpayers may use complex, sometimes artificial, arrangements which have the effect of relocating their tax base to other jurisdictions within or outside the European Union.'[16]

The instrumentalist, i.e. extremely policy-oriented, attitude of the legislator adds greatly to this complexity. At the same time, the legislator shows a calculating behaviour with regards to taxes, seducing businesses to tax planning. Looking for optimisation of the use of the tax instrument the legislator calculates benefits and costs, and consciously designs and redesigns rules to influence taxpayer's behaviour. Incentives are introduced to stimulate or discourage taxpayers to act in a way which actually means paying less (or not more) taxes. This way, the tax legislator leads taxpayers to behave according to his ends and thus creates a good deal of tax planning. As shown above, this use of taxes as a policy instrument is not limited to a national context; at the international level, states compete with their tax system in order to attract economic activities from other states. Furthermore, the tax legislator breeds a rule-based mindset focused on tax planning – as will be shown (see, section 3.2).

3 Taxpayers

3.1 Tax planning: a common affair

Partly due to the instrumentalist use of tax legislation, taxation affects almost every aspect of human life. As a result, tax often has a major and long-term financial impact on taxpayers' decisions and actions, such as where to live, when to retire and where to carry on an enterprise. Citizens simply have to take into account the tax consequences of their actions and decisions, as taxes function as a budget constraint. In one way or another, taxpayers have to plan their tax affairs to plan their life or develop their business strategy. Often tax planning is encouraged and intended by tax legislation, but sometimes it is not. I shall now take a closer look at how taxpayers may use – whether or not intended by the legislator – tax rules to lower their tax bill. To show that tax planning is indeed a common affair for all taxpayers and calls for a nuanced approach, I shall give an example of both personal and corporate tax planning.

In The Netherlands the decision where to live is affected by the fact that mortgage interest is deductible from gross taxable income, while rent is not. The tax allowance is nowadays considered to stimulate home-

---

16 European Commission (2012) *Action Plan to Strengthen the Fight Against Tax Fraud and Tax Evasion*. COM (2012) 722 final. 6 December 2012: 6.

ownership, and works as an incentive for debt-financed home-ownership. The tax deduction makes borrowing relatively cheaper, thereby creating an incentive to use funds for other purposes.[17] Financial institutions created complex 'products' making optimal use of the tax deductibility of mortgage interest (most of them approved by the tax authorities). Examples are endowment and investment mortgage loan arrangements, whereby debtors are obliged to save or invest part of their income – thereby securing the bank's loan – but actual repayment of the loan is deferred as long as possible to maximize interest deduction. Besides these more institutionalized tax structures, taxpayers may, of course, also optimize and customize their own tax position. An example would be someone borrowing from his parents to buy a house, and having the parents use (part of) the (deductible) interest for making a tax exempt gift to their child/borrower. Two tax incentives, tax deduction of mortgage interest and tax exemption for certain gifts, are thus combined to optimize the tax position.

As with most corporate income tax laws worldwide, The Netherlands corporate income tax law treats interest and dividend payments differently, by allowing interest expenses as a taxable deduction whilst disallowing dividend payments. Usually businesses, including all multinational enterprises, are organised as a group of legal entities, with a parent company/head office and subsidiaries. This legal structure makes it possible to finance each subsidiary company with as much debt or equity as the group may deem appropriate. From a group perspective, the tax factor is often decisive in this financing decision, as the overall leverage at a group level is not affected by the intra-group financing structure.[18] Tax-wise, a benefit can be obtained by financing high-taxed subsidiaries with debt and low-taxed subsidiaries with equity. It is this mechanism that has led most jurisdictions, in any case the high-tax jurisdictions, to put some limitation on interest deductions to protect the domestic corporate tax base.

A not too complicated rule, tax deductibility of interest, thus creates a good deal of tax planning. It can be concluded that it is fair to say that all taxpayers are to some extent tax planners, as everybody takes into account tax rules in their decisions, whether or not the rules are fully grasped and whether or not taxpayers are aware that they are engaging in tax planning. In short, tax legislation and tax planning are dynamic and reciprocal.

---

17 Assuming a marginal tax rate of 50%, it would be beneficial to borrow instead of using one's own funds if savings yield a return of at least half the mortgage interest.
18 Of course, there may be commercial reasons influencing the debt-to-equity ratio as well, such as currency restrictions, or external financing at sub-group level.

3.2 Rule-focus: crowding out ethics

Being aware of taxpayers' responsiveness to tax rules, tax legislators may use tax legislation to steer taxpayer behaviour by creating a command and control environment. Incentives should be considered, along with coercion and persuasion, as an alternative means of exerting power and influence over taxpayers' behaviour.[19] The use of incentives reflects an economic view which rests on the principle of rational choice which is related to the fundamental assumption of the homo economicus, 'the primary concept of economic anthropology'.[20] Interestingly, legislative regulatory measures assume taxpayers behave as economic-rational people, although there are many more circumstances and factors affecting actual taxpayer behaviour, besides purely economic reasons, as, for example, the economic-psychological research on tax compliance shows.[21] Individual behaviour and the willingness to change one's behaviour according to government's wishes are also dependent upon internal motivations which 'develop from attitudes and values, such as feelings about the legitimacy of group authorities or about people commitment to the group'.[22]

However, the use of tax incentives, assuming economic-rational behaviour, stimulates taxpayers to adopt a dominant economic rationality in their fiscal decision-making process. Consequently, the dominance of the economic-rational perspective may crowd out important legal-ethical principles in taxpayers' decision-making process, such as the principle of equality and the ability-to-pay principle, as will be argued more extensively below.

This preoccupation with the economic-rational framework may even become more pregnant, because tax incentives and repair or refinement of these incentives have a rule-based character, with many technical details to fulfil their goal of stimulating a specific activity and exclude an unintended broad scope of application. Such rule-based regulations often come with a lot of supervisory power and bureaucratic controls and thus create a legal 'command-and-control' environment.[23] In such an environment, it is easy to lose sight of important legal-ethical principles enshrined in the law, both for

---

19 Grant R W (2002) The Ethics of Incentives: Historical Origins and Contemporary Understandings. 18 *Economics and Philosophy* 1: 111.
20 Sedlacek T (2011) *Economics of Good and Evil: The Quest for Economic Meaning from Gilgamesh to Wall Street*. Oxford: Oxford University Press: 14.
21 Kirchler E (2007) *The Economic Psychology of Tax Behaviour*. Cambridge: Cambridge University Press.
22 Tyler T R (2011) *Why People Cooperate: The Role of Social Motivations*. Princeton: Princeton University Press: 26.
23 Braithwaite J (2005) *Markets in Vice: Markets in Virtue*. Oxford [etc.]: Oxford University Press: 145-149.

the legislator and the taxpayer. Tax statutes establish a rule-based context to control the behaviour of the taxpayer and the taxpayers will play with the rules. The focus of both legislator and taxpayer is on rules, not on ethical behaviour. As a result, a dominantly rule-bound regulatory and compliance focus is likely to undermine a more principle-based ethical thinking. This may cause both actors to not consider tougher issues that a more ethics-focused approach might demand.[24] Moreover, and analogous to empirical economic-psychological research, it can be argued that in a 'command-and-control' environment of coercive tax legislation where people feel they have very little influence, a crowding-out effect of intrinsic motivations – such as ethical considerations – to comply with the law, may occur.[25] In that case, not only actual ethical thinking is undermined, but even the motivation to do so.

Another negative repercussion of fiscal instrumentalism, and changes and refinement of rules, is, as shown in section 2.1, that it adds to the complexity and lack of transparency of the law. This leads in turn to increased uncertainty for taxpayers about their legal rights and responsibilities and again incites taxpayers to carefully study the rules to improve certainty of their tax position. This reinforces a tendency of using tax incentives in a mechanistic, rule-based way. Indeed, empirical research has found that continuous changes and complexity in tax law have a negative effect on the level of compliance.[26]

4 Rule based tax planning

4.1 Corporate tax planning: playing the rules

The tax legislator often introduces tax incentives to steer taxpayers' behaviour to achieve all kinds of policy goals. For taxpayers this is an opportunity for tax planning, which is exploited by some taxpayers. They find ways to use these rules to their advantage; they turn around the rules. The tax legislator, with his rule focus, usually reacts with refined or new rules which add to the existing complexity of tax law, which accounts for lack of transparency and opens up new tax-planning opportunities. The exclusively rule-based focus of high-tech tax structures crowds out attention to the ethical rationale behind the rules.

---

24   Berenbeim R E & Kaplan J M (2007) The Convergence of Principle- and Rule-Based Ethics Programs: An Emerging Trend. *The Conference Board*, Executive Actions Series March 2007. No. 231: 2.
25   Frey B S & Jegen R (2002) Motivation Crowding Theory. *Journal of Economic Surveys* Vol. 15, No. 5: 594-595.
26   Kirchler (2007): 39.

Businesses engaging in tax planning play an important part in this rule-based interplay between tax legislators and taxpayers. For businesses, taxation is part of their cost-calculation, tax planning being a means of saving in expenses.[27] Again, it will be seen that the interplay of tax legislator and (corporate) taxpayers increases the complexity and lack of clarity of tax rules – rules being the main focus in the mindset of both legislator and businesses. Complex and unclear rules are carefully studied to be played with by businesses, and, in turn, the legislator supplements the existing body of rules with even more rules to curb this game playing.

It was shown above how the different treatment of debt and equity instruments in corporate income tax laws is a driver for tax planning. In fact, all tax planning can be traced back to a different treatment of income or any other relevant criterion defining the tax base. Tax planning entails nothing more than shifting profits to low(er)-tax bases. In a basic scenario, only the effective tax rates of a parent company and the subsidiary in need of funding are taken into account. To further reduce the tax base, the financing may be structured through a group financing a company resident in a tax haven.[28] Another possibility would be using a financial instrument – in the tax practice called a hybrid loan – that qualifies as debt for the debtor (leading to tax deductible interest expenses), and as equity for the creditor (leading to tax exempt dividend receipts). A quite similar example would be the lease of an asset under such conditions that both the lessor and the lessee are regarded as owner of the asset for national tax purposes in their country of residence. Consequently, the asset is depreciated at the expense of two tax bases. Of course, different and more complex solutions for exploiting disparities between domestic tax laws are possible – e.g. the use of hybrid entities, permanent establishments, tax grouping facilities etc. – to achieve a disparate treatment of income in two countries, leading to a tax benefit.[29]

Thus, multinational companies seek to eliminate or reduce their tax liabilities. They exploit 'areas where several tax systems must interact and the scope for tax arbitrage, playing the rules of one system off against another,

---

27 Scholes M S, Wolfson M A, Erickson M, Maydew E L & Shevlin T (2002) *Taxes and Business Strategy: A Planning Approach*. New Jersey: Prentice Hall (Second edition): 3.
28 For incentives and disincentives for transfer pricing manipulations and the use of tax havens, see, for example, Muchlinsky P T (2007) *Multinational Enterprises and the Law*. Oxford [etc.]: Oxford University Press (Second edition): 269-305.
29 For an overview of basic tax planning techniques and its legal limitations, see Russo R (ed.) (2007) *Fundamentals of International Tax Planning*. Amsterdam: IBFD; for a description of the five major stages of international tax planning, see Kessler W and Eicke R (2007) Back to BASIC – The Stages of International Tax Planning or: Getting the Grip on a Rocky Road. 35 *Intertax*: 373-377.

is considerable.'[30] Complexity and avoidance can go hand in hand. Tax authorities often face difficulties in constructing adequate countermeasures. Detailed rules, targeting relatively specific acts may lead to creative tax compliance. Taxpayers who engage in such behaviour make use of the many loopholes inevitably present in very specific tax laws. Complex business structures in the global market are put in place and these are extremely difficult to monitor and control by tax administrations. Avoidance is often difficult to distinguish from illegal evasion.[31] According to Braithwaite, '[a] smorgasbord of rules engenders a cat-and-mouse legal drafting culture – of loophole closing and reopening by creative compliance.'[32]

4.2 No rule-following without ethics

As shown above, tax planning is pervasive and actively stimulated by tax legislation. Therefore, every engagement in tax planning cannot be dismissed as unethical. Consequently, the ethical assessment of tax planning needs careful evaluation. This is a matter of degree.

The result of the foregoing is twofold. At the one hand, tax legislators and taxpayers share a focus on rules. Tax statutes establish a rule-based context to control the behaviour of taxpayers and taxpayers will play with the rules. On the other hand, these tax rules are often muddled, complex and inconsistent. That may render compliance with the rules more difficult. Moreover, businesses may maintain that bending the rules may qualify as compliance, be it creative compliance with the letter of the law. Even taxpayers who engage in aggressive tax planning may think they honestly subscribe to the viewpoint that 'everybody should pay their taxes.' Apparently, this view can be taken in a seemingly very formalistic way by bending the rules in order to minimize tax liability. Here, complying with the rules is taken in the sense of complying with the letter of the law.

However, the letter of the law is often a poor instrument for guiding taxpayer behaviour, e.g., because it is often unclear how the letter of the law should be interpreted. Moreover, as we have seen taxpayers may comply with the law, and still pay no tax at all. Also, tax behaviour may be within the letter of the law, but take the form of creative compliance. The essence of creative compliance is that it escapes the intended impact of the substantive law. Creative compliance is not a tax issue but a much more general law issue. Law is treated as a formal, self-contained system of norms that 'is

---

30 Shaw J, Slemrod J & Whiting J (2010) Administration and Compliance. In: *Dimensions of Tax Design: The Mirrlees Review*. edited by Institute for Fiscal Studies (IFS). Oxford: Oxford University Press: 1151.
31 Shaw, Slemrod & Whiting J (2010): 1150.
32 Braithwaite (2005): 147.

"there", identifiable without any reference to content, aim and development of the rules that compose it, is the very essence of formalism'.[33] Nonetheless, this formalism does not deny the importance of ethical considerations. Moral convictions are only put outside the legal system in order to keep it pure. Consequently, formalism as a way of compliance, itself reflects a moral stance. Thus, creative compliance uses formalism to avoid legal control, for example, a tax liability. Taxpayers may comply with the letter of the law, while totally undermining the rationale behind the words.[34] They evade the spirit of the law through loopholes or creatively interpreting its requirements to avoid substantive compliance.

In my view, compliance with tax law, often cannot, therefore, simply be a matter of rule-following. The ethical stance involved in the interpretation and use of legal rules should be less formalistic. Ethical behaviour cannot be reduced to rule following. Rules demand for interpretation which, in turn, should be guided by some ethical view. But even if clear cut rules are available, complying with the rules of two or more different tax jurisdictions may result in the payment of nil corporate tax in each of these countries. Perfectly legal and compliant behaviour, therefore, may lead to a result which might be deemed unethical.

A pitfall for the described rule based behaviour of both companies and the legislator may thus be that they are so preoccupied with the technicalities and complexities of tax law, that they do not pay enough attention to the bigger picture and leave out other than technical tax considerations in their choices.[35] Turning to this broader perspective and focusing on businesses rather than the legislator, the question is whether companies ought to include ethical considerations in their tax decision-making framework. In recent years this has become quite an urgent issue, an important reason being the increasingly ingenious and aggressive corporate tax planning. Therefore, the question to be addressed is whether the legal system contains specific guidelines for ethical conduct which go beyond the (letter of the) law.

---

33 Shklar J N (1964) *Legalism: Law, Morals, and Political Trials*. Cambridge (Mass.) / London: Harvard University Press: 33-34.
34 McBarnet D (2003) When Compliance is not the Solution but the Problem: From Changes in Law to Changes in Attitude. In: V Braithwaite (ed.), *Taxing Democracy: Understanding Tax Avoidance and Evasion*. Aldershot: Ashgate Publishing: 229-230.
35 This pitfall is described in KPMG's 2004 discussion report 'Tax in the Boardroom', where the view is advocated that the tax function should be a board responsibility, which probably would partly solve the problem of taking a too narrow perspective in the fiscal decision-making process, as board members may, in general, be expected to have a broader perspective than experts in a certain field, such as taxation.

5   CSR: Legal and Ethical Responsibilities

Should ethical considerations determine a corporation's compliance with tax rules? Are there ethical boundaries to tax planning? Corporate taxpayers who engage in CSR would be expected to clearly answer this question in the affirmative.[36] Carroll's well-known view on CSR advocates ethical obligations on top of the obligations to comply with the law for (corporate) taxpayers (see below). Creative compliance, therefore, may pass the test of legality, but generally fails on the test of CSR.[37]

Interestingly, CSR (as represented by Carroll) views ethical considerations as 'beyond compliance'; businesses have to go beyond what is required by the law. Therefore, I will now explore this notion of 'beyond compliance.'[38] CSR regards business community's concern for society. What exactly is CSR? The EU Commission gives a very brief definition: 'the responsibility of enterprises for their impact on society.'[39] For the purpose of this chapter the definition given by David F. Williams suffices:

CSR [Corporate Social Responsibility] is defined for this purpose as a manner of doing business that takes into account the economic, social and environmental impact of the company's actions (the so-called 'triple bottom line'). A company's approach to this issue will reflect its chosen ethical stance; i.e., the set of values or rules of conduct that govern its interactions with other parties.[40]

Interestingly, Carroll's view on CSR emphasizes obligations for businesses that go beyond what is required by the law and the quest for greater

---

36 For a discussion of three different theories of the corporation, which may account for different views on CSR and the obligation to pay taxes, see Avi-Yonah R (2008) Corporate Social Responsibility and Strategic Tax Behaviour. In: W Schön (ed.), *Tax and Corporate Governance*. Berlin / Heidelberg: Springer-Verlag: 183-198.

37 Sikka P (2010) Smoke and Mirrors: Corporate Social Responsibility and Tax Avoidance. *Accounting Forum* 34: 153-168 is very skeptical. This paper provides examples to show how corporations talk about social responsibility, but 'indulge in tax avoidance and evasion.' Hasseldine J & Morris G (2013) Corporate social responsibility and tax avoidance: A comment and reflection. *Accounting Forum* 37: 1-14, is a critical response to Sikka.

38 For a business case to include tax as a corporate responsibility issue, see: Eijsden, van A (2013) The Relationship between Corporate Responsibility and Tax: Unknown and Unloved. *EC Tax Review* 2013-1. Lanis & Richardson's (2012) analysis of a sample of 408 publicly listed Australian corporations indicates that the higher the level of CSR disclosure of a corporation, the lower is the level of tax aggressiveness.

39 European Commission (2011), *A Renewed EU Strategy 2011-14 for Corporate Social Responsibility*. COM(2011) 681 final: 6.

40 Williams D F, *Tax and Corporate Social Responsibility*, <http://www.kpmg.co.uk/pubs/Tax_and_CSR_Final.pdf> (Sept.2007: 1.) In his view, CSR is distinguished from corporate philanthropy (which relates to the distribution of profits rather than to the manner in which they are earned).

profits.⁴¹ Carroll captures these beyond-compliance social responsibilities in his famous pyramid of corporate social responsibility. He makes an analytical distinction between a company's economic, legal, ethical and philanthropic responsibilities, which are not mutually exclusive. The total social responsibility of business entails the concurrent fulfilment of these four responsibilities, ethical and philanthropic responsibilities positioned on top of legal (and economic) responsibilities. In this respect, CSR companies have a certain view of legal responsibilities. At first glance, it is clear that these companies do not have a narrow view on legal responsibilities, for they strive for more than fulfilling their legal obligations. This should translate to their tax planning strategy. Of course, taxpayers may arrange their tax affairs as they wish. They may plan and structure their affairs to achieve a favourable tax treatment within the limits set by law. But CSR companies are not looking for the most favourable tax treatment which does not overstep the boundaries of the tax law.

Carroll elucidates businesses' legal responsibilities: society expects business to obey the law. The framework of legal requirements set forth by a society's legal system represents the basic 'rules of the game' by which business is expected to function.⁴² The firm's legal responsibilities reflect a view of 'codified ethics' in the sense that they embody basic notions of fair practices as established by lawmakers.⁴³ Thus, the legal system is distinguished from ethics. Ethical responsibilities are not codified in the law. Therefore, law is one thing, and ethics is another thing.⁴⁴ In my view, the relationship between law and morality is a more complicated one (see, section 7).

However, as Carroll points out, laws are essential but not always adequate. First, laws present the picture at a given moment. New topics and issues continuously emerge. As a result, the legal rules cannot possibly address

---

41 Carroll, A B (1991). The Pyramid of Corporate Social Responsibility: Toward the Moral Management of Organizational Stakeholders. *Business Horizons*, July-August 1991: 39-48.
42 This legal framework is extending, fostering CSR, e.g. through indirect legislation, using disclosure as a tool, or private law used by private parties. See McBarnet D (2007) Corporate Social Responsibility beyond Law, through Law, for Law: The New Corporate Accountability. In: D McBarnet et al (eds.), *The New Corporate Accountability: Corporate Social Responsibility and the Law*. Cambridge: Cambridge University Press: 31 ff and Lambooy T (2010) *Corporate Social Responsibility: Legal and Semi-Legal Frameworks Supporting CSR*. Deventer: Kluwer.
43 Buchholtz A K & Carroll A B (2008) *Business & Society*. Seventh edition. South-Western: 39-48.
44 On the other hand the law is often the referent around which ethical decisions are made, therefore, not only a boundary of constraint on decisions; see Christensen S L (2008) The Role of Law in Models of Ethical Behavior. *Journal of Business Ethics*. 77: 451-461.

all the issues that business may face. As shown above, even with the very frequent changing tax legislation will lag behind because of sophisticated tax advisers. Secondly, the law often lags behind evolving ethical values and norms. Thirdly, legislative rules may lack integrity, because they are made by lawmakers and 'may reflect the personal interests and political motivations of legislators rather than appropriate ethical justifications'.[45] Here, ethical responsibilities come in. They are needed 'to embrace those activities and practices that are expected or prohibited by society even though they are not codified by law'.[46] Ethical social responsibilities exceed the legal (and economic) ones in exceptional cases, or so it seems.

Thus, according to Carroll, if the body of rules has shortcomings we need to fall back on ethical considerations. However, which kind of ethical considerations offer taxpayers guidance when their behaviour is not regulated by rules? Are they by definition to be looked for outside the legal system?

6 Taxation: fair play and fair share

As shown above, Carroll's CSR pyramid distinguishes legal responsibilities from other responsibilities. Paying taxes is one of these legal responsibilities. It is a moral obligation 'fixed by an institutional decision, by law.' Why is paying taxes a moral obligation? Taxes are seemingly payments to the state. These payments are payments to society, taxes are contributions to society viewed as 'a cooperative venture for mutual advantage', in the wording of John Rawls.[47] In taxes the legitimacy of the state and the level of trust of citizens in each other's contribution to the co-operative venture and in the state find expression.[48] The state facilitates and supports this co-operative venture by all kind of public goods paid for by taxes, which account for a sense of indebtedness to the state and to the society one lives in. Rawls argues that this co-operative venture implies a duty of fair play This duty of fair play binds citizens to pay their taxes since they benefit from the fiscal system. This duty of fair play is reasonable, because 'the system of cooperation consistently followed by everyone itself produces the advantages generally enjoyed'.[49]

---

45 Buchholtz & Carroll (2008): 41.
46 Buchholtz & Carroll (2008): 41.
47 Rawls J (1999a) A Theory of Justice (revised edition). Oxford: Oxford University Press: 4.
48 Hence, the German philosopher Sloterdijk recently labelled taxation 'the central moral phenomenon of our civilization; Sloterdijk P (2010) Steuern sind das zentrale moralische Phänomen unserer Zivilisation. In: P Sloterdijk, *Die nehmende Hand und die gebende Seite*. Berlin: Suhrkamp Verlag: 141-145.
49 Rawls J (1999b) Legal Obligation and the Duty of Fair Play. In: J Rawls, *Collected*

According to Rawls, usually acting unfairly is not so much the breaking of any particular rule, but taking advantage or exploiting often inevitable loopholes or ambiguities in the rules, 'availing oneself of unexpected or special circumstance which make it impossible to enforce them (...) acting contrary to the intention of the practice'.[50] Acting fairly, therefore, requires more than simply following the rules, in the sense of keeping to the letter of the law. The duty of fair play demands citizens to accept the inevitable imperfections of the legal system and to exercise a certain restraint in taking advantage of them. As Rawls states, '[w]ithout some recognition of this duty mutual trust and confidence is liable to break down.'[51] The principle of fair play demands that taxpayers pay their fair share of taxes.

To conclude, contributing to society understood as a co-operative venture demands fair play, and within the context of this chapter, fair play with regard to legal obligations, including taxes. Fair play in contributing to society as a co-operative venture demands paying a fair share of taxes. This obligation cannot be reduced to rule-following, in the sense of keeping to the letter of the law. This would amount to acting against the spirit of a societal co-operation – itself demanding a reciprocal commitment to fair play.

7 CSR and tax planning: guided by legal principles

As shown above, corporations, which accept CSR as a guideline for their actions, impliedly take into account ethical considerations when using and applying legal rules. They admit the law should be handled prudently. To my mind, they have all the more reason to do so because legal rules themselves necessarily have a basis in morality, viz. the moral core of law which is made up by legal principles.

It may be tempting to view rules as the only behavioural norms of a legal system by which a business is expected to function. It may be rewarding to have a closer look at this idea - may a legal system really be reduced to a body of rules? Dworkin famously argued that law itself is more than a body of rules. Legal rules are not free-floating but are embedded in legal principles. Dworkin defines a principle as a standard which is to be observed because it is 'a requirement of justice or fairness or some other dimension of morality.'[52] Legal principles embody Fuller's internal morality of law

---

Papers. Cambridge (Mass.)/London: Harvard University Press: 127.
50 Rawls J (1999c) Justice as Reciprocity. In: J Rawls, *Collected Papers*: 20-211. Rawls admits that to refer to the principle of 'fair play', 'in this way, is, perhaps, to extend the notion of fairness.'
51 Rawls J (1999a): 312.
52 Dworkin R (1977) Taking Rights Seriously. London: Duckworth: 22.

par excellence.⁵³ Therefore, a legal principle is to be observed as a standard because it is a requirement of the internal morality of law - not so much of the external, non-legal, dimension of morality. As such, legal principles are the basis of rules. Compliance with the law, therefore, cannot be restricted to (strict) rule abidance.

Principles are the normative core of the legal system and the basis of legal rules. Legal rules, therefore, should be the result of a process of weighing and balancing colliding principles. Rules may be seen as the operationalisation of principles which in their turn constitute the normative basis for the creation, interpretation, and application of rules. Consequently, rules have a more concrete and 'technical' character than principles and are normally less value laden.

Legal principles act as potential constraints on government's production and use of legal rules. They act as restraints on the legislator's conduct, for they constitute a moral code which governs lawgiving.⁵⁴ Moreover, the interpretation and application of rules by the tax administration should be guided by principles - in The Netherlands, for example, these are the principles of proper administrative behaviour.

However, is it possible that the internal morality of law, made up by legal principles, somehow restrains the actions of citizens? Could legal principles offer guidance to taxpayers who want to exercise self-restraint when engaging in tax planning? I would suggest that they may do so. According to Dworkin, citizens can only identify with (the binding force of) law if it satisfies the model of principle. Then, they 'accept that they are governed by common principles, not just by rules hammered out in political compromise'⁵⁵. Thus, legal rules should be in conformity with the fundamental principles of the legal system. This way, principles justify and determine our (legal) obligations towards each other, paying taxes included, laid down in rules.

The point is that rules as the operationalisation of legal principles are never exhaustive of the law. There always is a normative residue which is embodied by legal principles. Thus, a corporation's obligations to society

---

53 Fuller L L (1977) *The Morality of Law* [1964]. New Haven/London: Yale University Press: 200-224.
54 Luban D (2001) Natural Law as Professional Ethics: A Reading of Fuller. 18 *Social Philosophy and Policy*: 180. These principles may be labeled principles of proper lawmaking; Popelier P (2000) Legal Certainty and Principles of Proper Law Making. 2 *European Journal of Law Reform*: 325. Note the difference with the use of the principles in the context of 'principles-based legislation' which is not intended to imply 'any introduction of morality into tax law'; Freedman J (2010) Improving (Not Perfecting) Tax Legislation: Rules and Principles Revisited. 6 *British Tax Review*: 729-730.
55 Dworkin R (1986) *Law's Empire*. Cambridge (Mass.) / London: Harvard University Press: 211.

are not exhausted by rules. Of course, rules are of vital importance to a legal system, and therefore to a system of tax law. It is the responsibility of states to determine a fair share and lay it down in legal rules. Established rules provide taxpayers with legal certainty – a fundamental, though not absolute, legal value.[56] However, this, inevitably, imperfect body of rules is but the surface of the legal system, one's obligations towards community cannot be reduced to a body of rules. The same goes for tax obligations, as argued above, for taxes are indirect payments to society. Principles determine these obligations, especially in hard cases, e.g. when rules are unclear or when there seems to be no rule applicable (cf. Hobbes' silence of the law[57]). Tax planning should not only be legal, i.e. in conformity with legal rules, but also in conformity with principles, at least for companies engaging in CSR. (Again, they are not required when facing different options to choose for a business transaction that involves paying the highest amount of tax.) The fair share principle, a principle of distributive justice, is of special importance with regard to tax planning. Thus, compliance with tax laws often cannot simply be a matter of following rules, especially in matters of ambiguity, gaps etc. which allow for a use of rules which does by no manner of means result in paying a fair share of taxes.

Principles should be fleshed out in more concrete principles or rules for they are often too abstract to provide guidance for human conduct.[58] Moreover, as shown above, principles may compete. One such context is taxation, and even more specific international income taxation. Principles have to be fleshed out in this specific context to have guiding power for conduct in this field of taxation. Certainly, principles do not provide clear-cut answers; they are not comparable to hard and fast rules in this respect. One possible specification of 'fair play' in international income taxation, for example is the single tax principle, as advocated by Avi-Yonah.[59] Of course, there may be other possible specifications; agreement on the best specification may be reached after the arguments pro and contra different specifications have been widely discussed. Compliance with ethical

---

56 Tipke K (2010) Steuerrecht als Wissenschaft. In: *Gestaltung der Steuerrechtsordnung: Festschrift für Joachim Lang*. Cologne: Verlag Dr. Otto Schmidt: 27-28 and Gribnau H (2013) Legal Certainty: A Matter of Principle. In Gribnau H & Pauwels M (eds.), *Retroactivity of Tax Legislation* (2010 EATLP Congress Leuven). Amsterdam: EATLP: 69-93.
57 Hobbes Th (1991) *Leviathan. Or the Matter, Forme, & Power of a Common-Wealth Ecclesiastical and Civill*. (R. Tuck, ed.) Cambridge: Cambridge University Press [1651]: 148, 152.
58 Gribnau H (2014) Not Argued from but Prayed to. Who's Afraid of Legal Principles? 12 *eJournal of Tax Research* 1: 185-217.
59 Avi-Yonah (2006-2007) 8-10. He proposes that the resulting revenues should be divided among taxing jurisdictions according to the benefits principle (11-13).

obligations, then, should focus on clarifying and fostering principles – and not focus (exclusively) on conformity to rules – be it rules-based legislation or rule based treaties.

Under the rule of law, fleshing out abstract principles in concrete rules is primarily the task of the legislator. The legislator clearly has the responsibility to carefully devise and put in place a body of precise rules, but in my view there remains some moral responsibility for the taxpayer. As Dworkin argues a member of a community of principles cannot allow himself 'a permissive, self-interested attitude', but should reflect on the community scheme of principles if 'explicit rules are unclear or incomplete or because the abstract rights it deploys conflict in some way.'[60] Law as integrity demands 'a reciprocal interplay between law and morals in ordinary practical life, even when no lawsuit is in prospect and each citizen is judge for and of himself.'[61] Tax law should not be seen as an exception to the ideal of law as integrity, for 'cases for legitimacy and integrity are at least as strong in tax's empire as they are in law's'[62].

This is a view that CSR corporations should endorse. Of course, they may arrange their tax affairs as they wish within the boundaries of the legal rules. However, these companies accept ethical obligations beyond (strict) compliance with the law. Legal obligations, therefore, should not be narrowed down to the letter of the law nor should they use and manipulate the tax rules in order to minimize their tax liability. They should fall back on the scheme of principles underlying the tax system in hard cases when possible use of the rules evidently does not remotely result in paying a fair share of taxes. Principles then should guide – and if necessary correct – the use of rules. This way, CSR companies see legal responsibilities in conformity with the internal morality of tax law. They do not need to appeal to confessed ethical responsibilities on top of their legal responsibilities, for these legal responsibilities cannot be separated from their moral dimension. Admittedly, it is a thin line to draw, ethical responsibilities on top of their legal responsibilities and ethical responsibilities within legal responsibilities, but it does away with the idea of silence of the law in hard cases

---

60 Dworkin (1986): 300.
61 Dworkin (1986): 301.
62 McCaffery E J (1996) Tax's Empire. 85 *The Georgetown Law Journal*: 107.

8 Conclusion

Due to the excessive complexity of tax law businesses are almost forced to engage in tax planning. Tax planning is nowadays all the more important because the tax legislator often tries to steer citizens' behaviour to achieve all kind of policy goals. This way the tax legislator stimulates taxpayers to adopt a calculating attitude towards the tax system and sometimes consciously disregards the internal morality of law by violating fundamental legal principles. In practice, the tax legislator by using tax incentives to affect taxpayers' behaviour breeds a rule-based mindset focused on tax planning.

Taxpayers engaging in aggressive tax planning manipulate the legal system in order to minimize their tax liability. They are bending the rules. However, rules established by the tax legislator are inevitably imperfect. These imperfectly drafted rules account for loopholes (gaps in the law) and ambiguities in the rules which demand interpretation when applying the rules. The Rawlsian duty of fair play demands citizens exercise a certain restraint in taking advantage of these inevitable imperfections of the tax system; all the more because it regards the provision of public goods and the distribution of tax burden.

Should companies include ethical considerations in their tax decision-making framework? The answer to this question is twofold. Taxpayers may arrange their tax affairs as they wish. However, companies endorsing CSR accept ethical obligations beyond compliance with the law. In my view, they should certainly accept ethical obligations embedded in the law – conceived of as not just a body of rules. Therefore, CSR companies should take seriously the principles, the internal morality of law, underlying the body of rules. This is the answer to the question whether the legal system contains specific guidelines for ethical conduct which go beyond the (letter of the) law.

Bibliography

Avi-Jonah R S (2006-2007) The Three Goals of Taxation. *Tax Law Review* 60: 1-28.

Avi-Yonah R (2008) Corporate Social Responsibility and Strategic Tax Behaviour. In: W Schön (ed.), *Tax and Corporate Governance*. Berlin / Heidelberg: Springer-Verlag: 183-198.

Berenbeim R E & Kaplan J M (2007) *The Convergence of Principle- and Rule-Based Ethics Programs: An Emerging Trend*. The Conference Board, Executive Actions Series March 2007. No. 231.

Braithwaite J (2005) *Markets in Vice: Markets in Virtue*. Oxford [etc.]: Oxford University Press: 145-149.

Buchholtz A K & Carroll A B (2008) *Business & Society*. Seventh edition. South-Western.

Bundesministerium der Finanzen (2010) Die gefühlte Steuerbelastung. In: Idem, *Monatsbericht* Februar 2010.

Campbell A L (2012) America the Undertaxed: U.S. Fiscal Policy in Perspective. *Foreign Affairs* 91: 99-112.

Carroll A B (1991) The Pyramid of Corporate Social Responsibility: Toward the Moral Management of Organizational Stakeholders. *Business Horizons* July-August 1991: 39-48.

Christensen S L (2008) The Role of Law in Models of Ethical Behavior. *Journal of Business Ethics*. 77: 451-461.

Dworkin R (1977) *Taking Rights Seriously*. London: Duckworth.

Dworkin R (1986) *Law's Empire*. Cambridge (Mass.) / London: Harvard University Press.

Eijsden, van A (2013) The Relationship between Corporate Responsibility and Tax: Unknown and Unloved. *EC Tax Review* 2013-1.

European Commission (2012) *Action Plan to Strengthen the Fight Against Tax Fraud and Tax Evasion*. COM (2012) 722 final. 6 December 2012.

European Commission (2011), A Renewed EU Strategy 2011-14 for Corporate Social Responsibility. COM(2011) 681 final, <http://ec.europa.eu/enterprise/newsroom/cf/_getdocument.cfm?doc_id=7010>

Freedman J (2010) Improving (Not Perfecting) Tax Legislation: Rules and Principles Revisited. *British Tax Review*. 6: 717–736.

Frey B S & Jegen R (2002) Motivation Crowding Theory. *Journal of Economic Surveys* Vol. 15, No. 5: 594-595.

Fuller L L (1977) *The Morality of Law* [1964]. New Haven/London: Yale University Press.

Goldberg D S (2013) *The Death of the Income Tax: A Progressive Consumption Tax and the Path to Fiscal Reform*. New York: Oxford University Press

Grant R W (2002) The Ethics of Incentives: Historical Origins and Contemporary Understandings. 18 *Economics and Philosophy* 1: 111-139

Greider W (2006) The Future is Now. *The Nation* 26th June. <http://www.thenation.com/article/future-now >.

Gribnau J L M (2003) Equality, Consistency, and Impartiality. In: Tax Legislation. in H Gribnau (ed.), *Legal Protection against Discriminatory Tax Legislation*. The Hague, London, Boston: Kluwer Law International: 7-32.

Gribnau H (2013) Legal Certainty: A Matter of Principle. In Gribnau H & Pauwels M (eds.), *Retroactivity of Tax Legislation* (2010 EATLP Congress Leuven). Amsterdam: EATLP: 69-93

Gribnau J L M (2013) Legislative Instrumentalism vs. Legal Principles in Tax Law. *Coventry Law Journal* (special issue) 18: 89-109.

Gribnau H (2014) Not Argued from but Prayed to. Who's Afraid of Legal Principles? 12 *eJournal of Tax Research* 1: 185-217.

Gribnau H (2015) Corporate Social Responsibility and Tax Planning: Not by Rules Alone. 24 *Social & Legal Studies* 2: 225–250

Hasseldine J & Morris G (2013) Corporate social responsibility and tax avoidance: A comment and reflection. *Accounting Forum* 37: 1-14.

Hobbes Th (1991) *Leviathan. Or the Matter, Forme, & Power of a Common-Wealth Ecclesiastical and Civill.* (R. Tuck, ed.) Cambridge: Cambridge University Press [1651].

Kessler W and Eicke R (2007) Back to BASIC – The Stages of International Tax Planning or: Getting the Grip on a Rocky Road. 35 *Intertax*: 373-377.

Kirchler E (2007) *The Economic Psychology of Tax Behaviour.* Cambridge: Cambridge University Press.

KPMG (2004) *Tax in the Boardroom.* www.kpmg.com/Global/IssuesAndInsights/ ArticlesAndPublications/Pages/TaxInTheBoardroom.aspx.

Lambooy T (2010) Corporate Social Responsibility: Legal and Semi-Legal Frameworks Supporting CSR. Deventer: Kluwer.

Lanis R & Richardson G (2013) Corporate Social Responsibility and Tax Aggressiveness: An Empirical Analysis. *Journal of Accounting and Public Policy* 32: 68-88.

Luban D (2001) Natural Law as Professional Ethics: A Reading of Fuller. *Social Philosophy and Policy* 18: 176-205.

McBarnet D (2003) When Compliance is not the Solution but the Problem: From Changes in Law to Changes in Attitude. In: V Braithwaite (ed.), *Taxing Democracy: Understanding Tax Avoidance and Evasion.* Aldershot: Ashgate Publishing: 229-243.

McBarnet D (2007) Corporate Social Responsibility beyond Law, through Law, for Law: The New Corporate Accountability. In: D McBarnet et al (eds.), *The New Corporate Accountability: Corporate Social Responsibility and the Law.* Cambridge: Cambridge University Press: 9-56.

McCaffery E J (1996) Tax's Empire. *The Georgetown Law Journal* 85: 71–154.

Muchlinsky P T (2007) *Multinational Enterprises and the Law.* Oxford [etc.]: Oxford University Press: 269-305.

Perrini F, Pogutz S & Tencati A (2006) *Developing Corporate Social Responsibility: A European Perspective.* Cheltenham: Edward Elgar.

Peters C (2014) *On the Legitimacy of International Tax Law.* Amsterdam: IBFD.

Pinto C (2003) *Tax Competition and EU Law.* The Hague/London/New York: Kluwer Law International.

Popelier P (2000) Legal Certainty and Principles of Proper Law Making. 2 *European Journal of Law Reform*: 321-342.

Rawls J (1999a) *A Theory of Justice* (rev. ed.). Oxford: Oxford University Press

Rawls J (1999b) Legal Obligation and the Duty of Fair Play. In: J. Rawls, *Collected Papers.* Cambridge (Mass.)/London: Harvard University Press: 117-129.

Rawls J (1999c) Justice as Reciprocity. In: J. Rawls, *Collected Papers*, Cambridge (Mass.)/London: Harvard University Press: 190-224.

Russo R (ed.) (2007) *Fundamentals of International Tax Planning*. Amsterdam: IBFD.

Scholes M S, Wolfson M A, Erickson M, Maydew E L & Shevlin T (2002) *Taxes and Business Strategy: A Planning Approach*. New Jersey: Prentice Hall. Second edition.

Sedlacek T (2011) *Economics of Good and Evil: The Quest for Economic Meaning from Gilgamesh to Wall Street*. Oxford: Oxford University Press.

Shaw J, Slemrod J and Whiting J (2010) Administration and Compliance. In: *Dimensions of Tax Design: The Mirrlees Review*. edited by Institute for Fiscal Studies (IFS). Oxford: Oxford University Press: 1100-1162.

Shklar J N (1964) *Legalism: Law, Morals, and Political Trials*. Cambridge (Mass.) / London: Harvard University Press.

Sikka P (2010) *Smoke and Mirrors: Corporate Social Responsibility and Tax Avoidance*. Accounting Forum 34: 153-168.

Sloterdijk P (2010) Steuern sind das zentrale moralische Phänomen unserer Zivilisation. In: P Sloterdijk, *Die nehmende Hand und die gebende Seite*. Berlin: Suhrkamp Verlag: 141-145.

Snape J (2007) Corporation Tax Reform – Politics and Public Law. 103 *British Tax Review* 4: 374-405.

The European Commission (2011) *A Renewed EU Strategy 2011-14 for Corporate Social Responsibility*. (COM(2011) 681 final). <http://ec.europa.eu/enterprise/newsroom/cf/_getdocument.cfm?doc_id=7010>.

Tipke K (2010) Steuerrecht als Wissenschaft. In: *Gestaltung der Steuerrechtsordnung: Festschrift für Joachim Lang*. Cologne: Verlag Dr. Otto Schmidt: 21-56.

Tyler T R (2011) *Why People Cooperate: The Role of Social Motivations*. Princeton: Princeton University Press.

Vording H (2013) The Concept of Instrumentalism in Tax Law. 18 *Coventry Law Journal* (special issue): 41-60.

Williams D F, *Tax and Corporate Social Responsibility*, <http://www.kpmg.co.uk/pubs/Tax_and_CSR_Final.pdf> (Sept.2007).

8 Tax Risk Management and Tax Compliance Behaviour: Findings from a study of large Australian companies

Catriona Lavermicocca and Margaret McKerchar

Abstract

This chapter presents the research findings from a study investigating the impact of the identification and management of tax risk on the tax compliance behaviour of large Australian companies (both listed and unlisted with turnover exceeding AUD$250 million). The main research question concerns the impact of the identification and management of tax risk on the income tax compliance behaviour of large Australian companies. The findings in respect of each of the specific research questions when applied to answer the main research question indicate that the comprehensive identification and management of tax risk leads to an improvement in the level of tax compliance by large Australian companies.

1 Introduction

In recent years, an increased emphasis on the need for large companies to have in place frameworks and management processes to meet reporting obligations and satisfy local income tax authorities that tax risk has been addressed has been evident in many countries, including Australia.[1] This increased emphasis reflects the risk to revenue collection that large companies pose.[2] In the Australian context, large companies, defined herein as a company with an annual turnover in excess of AUD250 million, represent 0.1 per cent of total companies but contribute 58 per cent of company tax

---

1 C Millett and C McKenna, 'Managing Communications and Tax Risk in a Corporate Tax Group: An Internal View; Commonwealth Bank of Australia' (Paper presented at the Annual Corporate Tax Intensive, Taxation Institute of Australia, Hunter Valley, Australia, 26–27 October 2006).
2 J Black, 'The Emergence of Risk Based Regulation and the New Public Management in the United Kingdom' [2005] *Public Law* 512.

revenue.[3] In response to the increased emphasis by the Australian Taxation Office (ATO) and revenue authorities in other jurisdictions, the large international chartered accounting firms have targeted tax risk management as an area in which they can provide services to large business and have become actively engaged including publishing guidance materials and surveying tax executives.[4] Indeed, these survey findings report that there is increasing pressure on tax departments in large companies to manage tax risk within a corporate governance framework.[5] However, whilst tax executives reported that tax risk management was an important aspect of risk management practices, its importance was not reflected in either the documented tax risk management procedures of these large companies or in the amount of time tax departments devote to tax risk management.[6]

In recent years, the ATO has increasingly emphasised that large companies need to have good tax governance procedures in place, including a comprehensive tax risk management system, and that directors need to be aware of the material tax positions relating to their company and determine its acceptable risk profile. More importantly, large companies that do not have a comprehensive and documented tax risk management system will be considered a greater risk to the revenue and, as a result, will be subject to closer review.[7] Similarly, there is evidence of other jurisdictions introducing measures to hold an individual or individuals accountable for tax decision-making in large companies.[8] It appears that revenue authorities anticipate

---

3   Australian Taxation Statistics 2009–2010, p39; available at ato.gov.au.
4   C Jackson, F Moore and T Dalton, 'Managing Dealings within the Corporate Tax Group and with the ATO — An External View' (Paper presented at the Annual Corporate Tax Intensive, Taxation Institute of Australia, Hunter Valley, Australia, 26–27 October 2006); PricewaterhouseCoopers, 'Tax Risk Management' (2004); PricewaterhouseCoopers, 'The ATO and Large Business — The Way Forward' (2006); Ernst and Young, Tax Risk Management (LexisNexis Butterworths, 2007).
5   'Ernst and Young, Global Tax Risk Survey' (2008) <http://www.ey.com/GL/en/Services/Tax/Business-Tax/Tax-Accounting-and-Risk-Advisory/Tax_2008_Ernst-Young_tax_risk_survey>; Ernst and Young, 'Steady Course, Unchartered Waters — The Australian Perspective from the Third Ernst and Young Global Tax Risk Survey 2008'; KPMG, 'Tax Department Survey' (2006) <http://www.amr.kpmg.com/aci/docs/surveys/KPMG_Tax_Survey.pdf
6   KPMG, 'The Rising Tide — Regulation and Stakeholder Pressure on Tax Departments Worldwide', < http://www.kpmg.com/ES/es/ActualidadyNovedades/ArticulosyPublicaciones/Documents/TheRisingTide.pdf >.
7   OECD Forum on Taxation Information Note 'General Administrative Principles: Corporate Governance and Tax Risk Management' (2009) <http://www.oecd.org/tax/taxadministration/43239887.pdf>; M D'Ascenzo, 'Individual Interests and Community Needs — Focus on Legal Professional Privilege' (Speech delivered at The Australian Italian Lawyers Association Tax Seminar, Melbourne, 18 September 2003) 2.
8   For example, HMRC, 'HMRC Approach to Compliance Risk Management for Large

that shifting the responsibility for the development of a large company's tax strategy from the internal tax department to the board should discourage aggressive tax planning as directors will be held directly accountable for the tax risk.[9]

Against this background, this chapter reports on research that investigates the relationship between tax risk management practices and income tax compliance behaviour of large Australian companies. Revenue authorities expect an improvement in income tax compliance by large companies as a consequence of the existence of a tax risk management system and the identification of directors as accountable for tax decision-making.[10] However, the extent to which this expectation is realised is unknown particularly given that the literature on the impact of tax risk management practices on company tax compliance behaviour is limited.[11] The definition of a tax risk management system for the purposes of this research is having in place documented and operationalised systems and procedures to identify and manage tax risk.

The main research question addressed in this chapter concerns the impact of the identification and management of tax risk on the income tax compliance behaviour of large Australian companies. Firstly, this chapter introduces the concept and context of tax risk management in large companies in Australia

---

Business' (March 2007) <http://www.hmrc.gov.uk/lbo/risk-update.pdf>; D Butler, 'Corporate Insolvency — Tax Risk Management' (Speech delivered at the New Zealand Law Society Taxation Conference, September 2006); D Shulman, 'Speech delivered at the National Association of Corporate Directors Governance Conference' (Washington, 19 October 2009, IRS News Release IR-220-95) <http://www.irs.gov/newsroom/article/0,,id=214451,00.html>; Ireland Revenue Authority, 'The Co-Operative Approach to Tax Compliance' (September 2005) <http://www.revenue.ie/en/business/running/large-businesses.html>; section 93 and schedule 46 to the Finance Act 2009 (UK); Netherlands Tax and Customs Administration Co-ordination Group 2008, 'Tax Control Framework' (March 2008) <http://ec.europa.eu/taxation_customs/resources/documents/taxation/vat/vat_conferences/tax_control_framework_en.pdf>.

9 OECD Forum on Tax Administration, 'Seoul Declaration' (2006) <http://www.oecd.org/tax/taxadministration/37415572.pdf>; OECD Forum on Tax Administration, 'Good Corporate Governance: The Tax Dimension' (2006) <http://www.oecd.org/site/ctpfta/37207911.pdf>.

10 OECD, 'Study of the Role of Tax Intermediaries' (2008) <http://www.oecd.org/tax/taxadministration/39882938.pdf>; See also HMRC, 'Tax in the Boardroom' <http://www.hmrc.gov.uk/lbo/tax-in-the-boardroom.htm>.

11 G Richardson, G Taylor and R Lanis, 'The Impact of Risk Management and Audit Characteristics on Corporate Tax Aggressiveness: An Empirical Analysis' (Conference paper presented at the Journal of Accounting and Public Policy Conference at the London School of Economics, 25 May 2012, Session 1). This paper identified that the higher the firm's level of tax risk management and internal control effectiveness, the lower the level of tax aggressiveness.

followed by an analysis of existing research looking at large company tax compliance behaviour. The methodology is then outlined prior to setting out the findings and application of the findings to the main research question. Finally conclusions reached as a consequence of this research are proposed, limitations addressed and future directions for research identified.

2   Managing Tax Risk

Managing tax risk entails identifying and managing the inevitable tax uncertainties that arise in carrying on the company business and is mainly focused on, but not limited to, income tax. Despite the fact that tax risk management is identified as an essential part of a large company's internal controls, no universal definition of tax risk exists. This may be because the type of tax risk that a business faces is, to a large extent, a result of a particular jurisdiction's regulatory and compliance systems, and will vary according to industry, the size of the taxpayer, the level of government and over time. Further, tax risk has many dimensions including transactional risk, operational risk and reputational risk.[12] A broad definition of tax risk is used in this research, namely:

> [A]ny event, action, or inaction in tax strategy, operations, financial reporting, or compliance that adversely affects either the company's tax or business operations or results in an unanticipated or unacceptable level of monetary, financial statement or reputational exposure. [13]

An understanding of income tax compliance behaviour requires a consideration of the tax risk profile of a taxpayer, that is, the extent to which a company is prepared to accept uncertainty in the tax position it adopts. Because tax legislation is complex and its application at times unclear, a taxpayer may have to take a position where the ultimate tax treatment is uncertain. The position a taxpayer adopts can range from conservative to aggressive. A taxpayer may comply with the literal words in the tax legislation but not its intended application. One tax expert may consider certain actions and decisions to comply with the income tax law while another may have a different opinion. This conflict is seen in the degree to which the tax laws are the subject of litigation and dispute. Unintended systematic errors by the taxpayer and errors that relate to the uncertainty or lack of agreement in the application of the tax laws tend to be the focus of adjustments and disagreement between the revenue authority and large

---

12   T Elgood, I Paroissien, and L Quimby, 'Managing Global Risk for Multinationals' (2005) 16(5) *Journal of International Taxation* 22; H F Wunder, 'Tax Risk Management and the Multinational Enterprise' (2009) 18 *Journal of International Accounting, Auditing and Taxation* 14.
13   Ernst and Young, above n 5, 5.

company taxpayers.[14]

This uncertainty and complexity enables taxpayers to take positions that are considered aggressive or risky but reduce their ultimate tax liability. Similarly, a taxpayer may choose to invest in a tax shelter that complies with the letter of the law but has as its primary motivation a reduction in income tax. It is anticipated that a company's position in terms of tax aggressiveness is reflected in the level of tax risk acceptable or tax risk profile. The more aggressive the taxpayer's behaviour with respect to tax risk, the higher the tax risk profile. The less aggressive the taxpayer's behaviour with respect to tax risk, the lower the tax risk profile. A comprehensive tax risk management system should identify a company's agreed tax risk profile and ensure that it is applied across company decision making. However, in the next section of this chapter it will become apparent that the extant literature does not sufficiently explain the likely impact of a tax risk management system on large company tax compliance behaviour. That is, it may be that the revenue authorities (and in particular, the ATO) have not yet fully understood the drivers of compliance behaviour for these taxpayers.

3   Compliance behaviour of large corporate taxpayers

The relationship between tax decisions and tax outcomes in large companies is complex, mainly because the tax compliance decision-makers are not necessarily the same individuals that hold shares in the company.[15] That is, the decision-maker acts as an agent of the company,[16] with the company being recognised as a legal entity separate from its shareholders, directors and other officers or employees, and one that can own assets and sue or be sued.[17] A 'corporate veil' separates the company and its shareholders and a shareholder's financial exposure is limited to the contributed share capital.[18]

---

14   J Freedman, 'Tax Risk Management and Corporate Taxpayers — International Tax Administration Developments' Chapter 4 in A Bakker and S Kloosterhof (eds), *Tax Risk Management: From Risk to Opportunity* (IBFD, 2010).

15   C Lavermicocca, 'Managing Tax Risk and Compliance' (2009) 13(2) The Tax Specialist 66.

16   A Friese, S Link and S Mayer, 'Taxation and Corporate Governance' (Working Paper Max Planck Institute for Intellectual Property, Competition and Tax Law, Munich, Germany, 19 Jan 2006) 68; C Lavermicocca, 'Impact of the Corporate Structure on an Understanding of Taxpayer Compliance Behaviour' in C Evans and M Walpole (eds), *Tax Administration: Safe Harbours and New Horizons* (Fiscal Publications, 2008) 200.

17   L Oats, 'Taxing Companies and Their Shareholders: Design Issues', in A Lymer and J Hasseldine, (eds) *The International Tax System* (Kluwer, 2002).

18   *Salomon v Salomon and Co Ltd* (1897) AC 22 recognises the legal concept of a 'corporate veil' in which the personality of a company is distinguished from the personalities of its shareholders and protects shareholders from being held personally liable for the company's debts and obligations.

The Australian courts have been reluctant to lift this corporate veil because the benefits it conveys (i.e. limited liability and separate existence) are thought to encourage investment and entrepreneurial activity and thereby ensure a successful economy.[19]

In terms of legal obligations, directors and managers in Australia have a number of duties imposed on them by the common law and the *Corporations Act 2001* (Cth) (*'Corporations Act'*) in respect of corporate governance - or the internal operation of the company – which implicitly include tax risk management.[20] The common law duties require a director to act as a fiduciary with respect to the company and include a requirement to act in good faith and in the best interests of the company as a whole. The common law duties to a large extent overlap with the director's duties under the *Corporations Act*. Importantly, a statutory duty of care is set out in section 180 of the *Corporations Act*. It applies to both directors and officers of a company.

Whether a person has breached the common law or statutory duty of care is determined by considering the circumstances of the company and also the individual's position and responsibilities within the company. There are no universal benchmarks, however general principles require that the directors and officers ensure they are in a position to guide and monitor the management of the company. Whilst the ATO has advised that directors and company officers must ensure that they are informed in relation to their company's material tax risk and that they will be held accountable for the ultimate tax position that the company takes in relation to a transaction,[21] the extent of this obligation remains untested in Australia.[22]

---

19 D Parker, 'Piercing the Veil of Incorporation: Company Law for a Modern Era' (2006) 19 *Australian Journal of Corporations Law* 35.

20 In accordance with section 252 of the Income Tax Assessment Act ITAA 1936 (Cth) (ITAA 1936) the public officer of a company can be held personally liable for any penalty arising from a failure by the company to comply with its obligations under the tax legislation. Section 252 of the ITAA 1936 is limited in its application to the public officer and does not make the public officer personally liable for the company's income tax.

21 M Carmody, 'Large Business and Tax Compliance — A Corporate Governance Issue' (Speech delivered at the Leaders' Luncheon, Sydney, 10 June 2003). Note further reforms imposing personal criminal liability on corporate officers see, D Bradbury, 'Press Release with Exposure Draft of the Personal Liability for Corporate Fault Reform Bill 2012' (Press Release, 27 January 2012).

22 In the US, section 404 of the Sarbanes-Oxley Act of 2002 (US) (SOX) includes a formal requirement to report material weaknesses which has resulted in increased focus on internal control systems in relation to tax risk and accounting for income taxes. Similarly, the UK government introduced section 93 and schedule 46 to the Finance Act 2009 (UK). These require senior accounting officers of certain qualifying UK companies to take reasonable steps to ensure that they establish and maintain appropriate tax accounting arrangements; For the level of diligence required of directors see, 'The Centro Decision' *Australian Securities and Investments Commission v Healey and Others* (2011) 196 FCR 291.

Turning now to the compliance literature more generally, it is important to explain first what is meant by compliance. In this context, a compliant company taxpayer can be described as one that files all required income tax returns accurately and at the proper time, pays any outstanding taxes as they fall due and maintains all required records in accordance with the prevailing legislation (both tax and otherwise), rulings, return instructions and court decisions.[23] However, due to the complexity and uncertainty of the income tax laws, whether or not a taxpayer is compliant (intentionally or otherwise) can be difficult to determine, and taxpayers may adopt a tax position (from conservative to aggressive) according to their risk appetite.[24]

The body of compliance literature, particularly in respect of individual taxpayers is quite vast and has been extensively reviewed by many[25] and is beyond the scope of this chapter. The intention herein is to limit the review to the literature that relates only to the influences on the compliance behaviour of company taxpayers, from which five main themes have emerged, namely corporate governance (including corporate social responsibility), executive remuneration, decision-making and codes of conduct; board composition; and financial disclosure requirements.[26]

In respect of the impact of corporate governance practices on tax decision making, there is evidence from the United States (US) to suggest that companies with good governance practices usually have a high level of transparency (and a commitment to being a responsible corporate citizen), and that this, in turn, would prevent managers from engaging in tax avoidance or aggressive tax planning.[27] No contrary evidence was

---

23   M McKerchar, The Impact of Complexity Upon Compliance: A Study of Australian Personal Taxpayers (Australian Tax Research Foundation, Research Study No 39, 2003), 34.
24   D Weisbach, 'Corporate Tax Avoidance' (Published in the proceedings of the National Tax Association 96th Annual Conference, 2003).
25   For example, see, M McKerchar, 'Why Do Taxpayers Comply? Past Lessons and Future Directions in Developing a Model of Compliance Behaviour' (2001) 16(1) *Australian Tax Forum* 99; M Richardson and AJ Sawyer, (2001) A Taxonomy of the Tax Compliance Literature: Further Findings, Problems and Prospects' (2001) 16(2) *Australian Tax Forum* 137; and L Book, 'Freakonomics and the Tax Gap: An Applied Perspective' (2007) 56(5) *American University Law Review* 1163.
26   There are other likely influences that are evident in the literature including the size and type of company, organisational goals, shareholder composition, the role of external tax advisors; profitability, multinational characteristics and industry; differences between book and tax income; effective tax rate; and level of debt and cash. However, given the scope of this chapter, the focus has been narrowed to what appear to be the main influences.
27   M Desai and D Dharmapala, 'Corporate Tax Avoidance and High Powered Incentives' (2006) 79 *Journal of Financial Economics* 145; K Minnick and T Noga, 'Do Corporate Governance Characteristics Influence Tax Management?' (2010) 16 *Journal of Corporate Finance* 703.

found in respect of the effect of standards of corporate governance on tax decision making. However, it is recognised that statements about corporate social responsibility may be merely symbolic and aimed at satisfying critical external stakeholders.[28]

Turning to the second theme, there is evidence of a link between the form of an executive's remuneration and the likelihood of accounting manipulation and fraud,[29] though this may in part be attributed to the way the remuneration contract is structured (i.e. rewards based on taxable income or book profit).[30] Whilst it has not yet been demonstrated that incentivising executive remuneration results in false tax reporting (i.e. noncompliance),[31] a compelling argument exists that such incentives (including equity-based) could result in the taking of more aggressive tax decisions by managers.[32]

The third theme that emerges from the literature concerns the individual decision maker within the company. Research has shown that this person's assessment of the legality of a transaction moderates the effects of the high expected value of a transaction.[33] That is, individuals bring their own preferences to the decisions they make. Directors and managers who make tax decisions, as well as their external tax advisors, are usually members of a professional association, such as the Institute of Chartered Accountants in Australia (ICAA) or CPA Australia, which apply professional codes of conduct to their members. The application of these codes could be expected to guide the decisions made and, thereby, impact (positively) on the company's income tax compliance behaviour.[34] Similarly, registered tax

---

28 P Sikka, 'Smoke and Mirrors: Corporate Social Responsibility and Tax Avoidance' (2010) 34 *Accounting Forum* 153, 156.
29 B Ke, 'Why Do CEO's of Publicly Traded Corporations Prefer Reporting Small Increases in Earnings and Long Duration of Consecutive Earnings Increases' (Pennsylvania State University Working Paper. University Park, PA: Pennsylvania State University, 2001); M Erickson, M Hanlon and E Maydew, 'Is There a Link Between Executive Compensation and Accounting Fraud?' (University of Chicago, University of North Carolina, and University of Michigan Working Paper 2004).
30 L Goerke, 'Tax Overpayments, Tax Evasion and Book-Tax Differences' (2008) 10(4) *Journal of Public Economic Theory* 643.
31 J Slemrod, 'The Economics of Corporate Selfishness' (2004) Dec *National Tax Journal* 877.
32 S Rego and R Wilson, 'Equity Risk Incentives and Corporate Tax Aggressiveness' (2012) 50(3) *Journal of Accounting Research* 775.
33 A Downs and B Stetson, 'Economic Versus Non-Economic Factors: An Analysis of Corporate Tax Compliance' (Paper presented at the 2011 American Accounting Association Annual Meeting — Tax Concurrent Sessions, Denver, Colorado US, August 2011).
34 APES110 Code of Ethics for Professional Accountants, issued by the Accounting Professional and Ethical Standards Board (APESB) is binding on members of CPA Australia and the Institute of Chartered Accountants in Australia. APES110 is principles-based rather than rules-based and identifies fundamental principles that a

agents in Australia must also comply with the Code of Professional Conduct ('the Code') as set out in part 3, division 30 of the *Tax Agents Services Act 2009* (Cth). The Code sets out the professional and ethical standards required of registered tax agents including the core obligations of honesty and integrity, independence, confidentiality, competence and other responsibilities. Other responsibilities include the requirement that a registered tax agent must not knowingly obstruct the proper administration of the taxation laws. A tax decision-maker within a large company who is a registered tax agent is bound by these core principles.

The effectiveness of codes of professional conduct in guiding decision-making, focusing on auditors, has been the subject of some research in the US and Canada[35] in which it was found that an auditor's ethical judgment was most influenced by rule-based reasoning that focused on compliance with standards. That is, rule-based standards of professional conduct for tax professionals appear to be more influential than ethics or conventional moral reasoning.[36]

Regarding the fourth theme of board composition, Lanis and Richardson analysed 32 Australian companies, including 16 accused by the ATO of undertaking tax aggressive activities. They found that having a higher proportion of independent members on a company's board of directors reduced the likelihood of the company being tax aggressive.[37] These results were then validated against data from a cross section of 401 publicly listed Australian companies from which it was concluded that the composition of the board of directors may have an impact on a public company's tax risk profile.[38]

Whilst there is evidence from a large scale US study that boards that are more independent tend to focus more on foreign tax management, and that larger boards tend to focus more on management of domestic taxes,[39] ultimately boards are comprised of individuals who bring their own preferences and concerns to a determination of the appropriate tax strategy for a particular company. Further, it is not only boards that make decisions

---

professional accountant must not compromise in carrying out their work. APES220 'Taxation Services' also sets out standards for members in the provision of quality and ethical taxation services.

35 L Ponemon and D Gabhert, *Ethical Reasoning and Accounting in Auditing* (1993) CGA Canada Research Foundation Vancouver.
36 J Flanagan, 'Values, Codes of Ethics and the Law' The Institute of Chartered Accountants in Australia — Discussion Paper June 2006.
37 R Lanis and G Richardson, 'The Effect of Board of Director Composition on Corporate Tax Aggressiveness' (2011) 30(1) *Journal of Accounting and Public Policy* 50.
38 Lanis and Richardson, above n 37.
39 K Minnick and T Noga, 'Do Corporate Governance Characteristics Influence Tax Management?' (2010) 16 *Journal of Corporate Finance* 703.

about the tax position of a company, in practice there are a multiplicity of people involved in the decision-making process,[40] and holding them individually accountable (by the imposition of penalties and sanctions) remains a significant challenge for the tax administrator.

Finally, there is evidence from both the US and the United Kingdom (UK) that increased regulation in terms of tax reporting (requiring greater transparency and accuracy) can have a positive impact on company tax compliance.[41] That is, companies value their reputation and want to be seen as a good corporate citizen. They do not want to attract negative media attention and will weigh up the potential impact on their reputation when considering whether to take a tax aggressive position.[42]

Based on the literature reviewed, it is clear that the income tax compliance behaviour of large companies is influenced by a number of often interrelated factors, and that the compliance literature on individual taxpayers, particularly in respect of the application of economic deterrence models, is not always directly relevant. Whilst unintentional non-compliance does not appear to be specifically addressed in the corporate compliance literature, there is a clear reference to uncertainty and complexity in the tax laws and the problems that they create in attempting to be tax compliant.[43]

Uncertainty and complexity in the law brings its own risks and opportunities to both companies and the tax administrator. Companies may not want to be seen to be 'too aggressive', but they are still accountable to shareholders who will generally expect maximum returns. That is, while companies may be concerned about the cost of non-compliance, the benefits may be judged to outweigh the cost. Tax administrators in many OECD countries (including Australia and the UK) are increasingly

---

40 K Chen and C Chu, 'Internal Control Verses External Manipulation: A Model of Corporate Income Tax Evasion' (2005) 36(1) *RAND Journal of Economics* 151.
41 K Epps and C Cleaveland, 'Insiders' Perspectives of the Effects of Recent Regulation on Corporate Taxation' (2009) 21 *Research in Accounting Regulation* 34; G Frow, 'Corporate Tax Professionals Need Better Tools to Manage Data in Post-Sarbanes Environments' (2005) 57(September) *The Tax Executive* 460; E Rice, 'The Corporate Tax Gap: Evidence on Tax Compliance by Small Corporations' in J Slemrod (ed), *Why People Pay Taxes: Tax Compliance and Enforcement* (Ann Arbor: University of Michigan Press, 1992) 125.
42 Hanlon, M and Slemrod, J, 'What Does Tax Aggressiveness Signal? Evidence from Stock Price Reactions to News about Tax Shelter Involvement' (2009) 93 *Journal of Public Economics* 126; FDS International, 'Large Groups' Tax Departments: Factors that Influence Tax Management — A Qualitative Study' (Prepared for HMRC (UK), September 2006); A Christians, 'How Starbucks Lost its Social License – and Paid £20 million to Get it Back' *Tax Notes International* (2013) 71(7) 637.
43 G A Plesko, 'Multidisciplinary Issues in Corporate Tax Policy' (2006) 59 *National Tax Journal* 599.

using risk rating measures to signal to companies their assessment of their compliance behaviour, and this may well be an effective deterrence tool.[44] That is, there is pressure on large companies to have in place comprehensive tax management systems to ensure that directors and tax managers make informed decisions on the level of tax risk faced. This then leads to the overarching research question to be addressed - what impact does the existence of a comprehensive tax risk management system have on income tax compliance of large Australian companies?

4 Methodology

This research uses an exploratory sequential mixed methods design in that the results of the first qualitative method were used to develop and inform the second quantitative method and demonstrates face validity.[45] This type of exploratory design is one that Creswell and Plano Clark refer to as the 'Exploratory Design: Taxonomy Development Model' in which the 'initial qualitative phase is conducted to identify important variables, develop a taxonomy or classification system, or develop an emergent theory, and the secondary quantitative phase tests or studies these results in more detail.'[46]

In-depth interviews with tax managers from large Australian companies were conducted during the first qualitative research phase. The purpose of Phase One was to gain an understanding of tax risk management practices and the tax managers' views as to the impact of those practices on tax decision-making and tax compliance behaviour. A total of 15 in-depth semi-structured interviews were carried out in which 19 open-ended questions relating to tax risk management practices and income tax compliance behaviour (questions listed in Appendix 1) were asked relating to tax risk and tax decision-making.

The interviews provided insights into what motivates large companies to consider and evaluate tax risk; the factors that affect the level of tax risk that a large company faces; the factors that limit the ability of a large company to identify and manage tax risk; the acceptable levels of tax risk in large Australian companies; the nature of tax risk management practices in large Australian companies; as well as the participants' views as to the impact of

---

44 ATO, 'Risk Differentiation Framework', http://www.ato.gov.au/corporate/content.aspx?menuid=0&doc=/content/33802.htm&page=49&H49; R Bayer and F Cowell, 'Tax Compliance and Firms' Strategic Interdependence' (2009) 93 *Journal of Public Economics* 1131; OECD, 'Tackling Aggressive Tax Planning Through Improved Transparency and Disclosure', (Centre for Tax Policy and Administration, 2011) http://www.oecd.org/ctp/exchangeofinformation/48322860.pdf.
45 J Creswell and V Plano Clark, *Designing and Conducting Mixed Research Methods* (Sage Publications, 2007).
46 Creswell and Plano Clark, above n 45.

tax risk management practices. Whilst not all interviewees attested to having a formalised tax risk management system in place, they did believe that they had systems in place that worked for them. However, even where there were formalised tax risk management systems in place, it appeared that 'gut instinct' and the 'smell test' were still relied on in evaluating transactions and arrangements. Data collected via the in-depth interviews were analysed thematically and the following themes and relationships were identified from the responses to the in-depth interviews:

1. A reduction in the level of tax risk acceptable to a large company is not a consequence of the existence of a tax risk management system.

2. The tax manager, tax department and directors within a large company are more informed concerning potential tax risk as a result of the existence of a tax risk management system.

3. A tax risk management system will ensure that the tax manager, tax department and directors are informed of the large company's tax risk profile.

4. A tax risk management system results in greater awareness by staff outside the tax portfolio of the tax risk that the large company is exposed to in carrying on its business.

5. A number of factors affect level of tax risk to which a large company is exposed.

6. A number of factors limit the ability of a tax risk management system to identify and manage all tax risk of a large company.

7. Large companies seek to comply with the income tax laws.

8. Large companies seek to take advantage of tax provisions that would reduce income tax payable.

9. Most large companies do not have a clear definition of what constitutes a tax risk.

10. The level of acceptable tax risk is ultimately determined by the board of directors.

11. Tax risk management systems in large Australian companies include a variety of procedures and practices that include both formal and informal components.

12. Tax managers, the CFO and directors in a large Australian company are interested in tax risk.

13. A tax risk management system is an essential part of good business practice.

14 Some large companies in Australia are still in the process of implementing and/or documenting their tax risk management system.

15 Directors accept that good corporate governance requires them to be informed about tax risk and to be involved in tax decision-making.

16 Factors that affect the level of tax risk that a large company is exposed to include uncertainty/complexity of tax laws, staffing, demand for franking credits, level of concern for reputation, complexity of business transactions, limited information provided to tax staff by other divisions, size of the transaction, change in ATO interpretation/approach to a tax issue, growth of the business, global nature of the business, staff not following guidelines and the economic environment.

17 Factors that limit the ability of a tax risk management system to identify and manage all tax risks of a large company include limitations of ATO staff, limited information provided to tax staff by other divisions, time/cost/staff constraints, countries where the company carries on business, uncertainty/complexity of tax laws, complexity of business transactions, commercial pressure and staff turnover.

18 Large companies in Australia tend to adopt a low tax risk profile.

19 A public company is more likely than a private company to have a formalised and documented tax risk management system.

20 ATO announcements and statements concerning tax risk management best practice have influenced the formalised tax risk management procedures put in place by large companies.

The themes and relationships identified above guided the development of 10 research questions which formed the basis of the survey instrument used during Phase Two. The survey is set out at Appendix 2 and the link between themes and relationships and research questions is set out at Appendix 3. The ten research questions are as follows:

1 Does the adoption of a tax risk management system by a large company reduce the level of tax risk that is acceptable to a large company?

2 Does the adoption of a tax risk management system ensure that directors and tax decision-makers in a large company are informed concerning the tax risk to which a company is exposed?

3 Does the adoption of a tax risk management system by a large company result in the identification of potential non-compliance with the income tax laws that would not otherwise be identified?

4 Does the adoption of a tax risk management system by a large company result in the identification of opportunities to minimise its

income tax liability that would not otherwise be identified?

5   Does a large company act to ensure potential non-compliance with the income tax laws, as identified by its tax risk management system, if any, does not occur?

6   Does a large company act to ensure opportunities to minimise its income tax liability identified by its tax risk management system, if any, are realised?

7   How do large company taxpayers define tax risk?

8   What factors affect the level of tax risk to which a large company in Australia is exposed?

9   What factors limit the ability of a large company in Australia to identify and manage tax risk?

10 What is the nature of tax risk management practices in large companies in Australia?

The survey itself was an anonymous mail survey sent in late 2011 to the Chief Financial Officer (CFO) of all large companies in Australia using contact details downloaded from the Dunn and Bradstreet Company 360 database. The survey instrument contained both closed and open questions. In total 123 usable responses were received, giving an overall response rate of 13.3 per cent (n = 983). Both descriptive and inferential statistical techniques (using SPSS software) were used in analysing the survey data and testing hypotheses.

It is acknowledged that the usual limitations arising from the use of the chosen methods apply to this research. In spite of the modest response rate to the survey, it was conducted using as close as possible to the total population of Australian large companies, and with no evidence of non-response bias, the results are believed to be reasonably generalisable to this population.

5   Findings

Before detailing the results that relate to the specific research questions some of the descriptive statistics derived are particularly relevant and inform subsequent discussion. Firstly, while the survey was addressed to the CFO, it was not always completed by the CFO. The three main groups who completed the survey were CFOs (38.2 per cent, n=123), tax managers (22.7 per cent, n=123) and tax directors (18.7 per cent, n=123). Almost all respondents (98.3 per cent, n=123) confirmed that the CFO was a very influential person in determining the acceptable level of tax risk to the company, followed by the Board (82.2 per cent, n=123). Whilst Boards were found to be involved few respondents (16.3 per cent, n=123) indicated that their board was involved to a great extent. In 96.8 per cent of cases (n=123) it was the CFO who made the final determination of the level of acceptable tax risk.

Secondly, whilst 84.2 per cent (n=123) of respondents indicated that their company had documented systems and/or procedures in place to manage tax risk, only 76.8% (n=123) had systems and/or procedures that were operationalised. Further, only 45.5 per cent (n =123) had statements or guidelines in place on what constituted a tax risk. Just a small majority (56.9 per cent, n=123) of respondents indicated that their company had a fully documented and operationalised tax risk management in place, with 60.3 per cent of these having been introduced prior to 2008. At the outset it does appear that the persuasive communications employed by the ATO since 2003 have not been as effective as anticipated.

The approach taken in the following section of this chapter is to detail the survey results that relate to each of the 10 research questions identified and what they indicate in answering the particular research question, followed by the drawing of overall conclusions.

Research Question 1

Does the adoption of a tax risk management system by a large company reduce the level of tax risk that is acceptable to a large company?

The results indicate that in a majority of large Australian companies a tax risk management system results in a reduction in the level of tax risk acceptable to a large company.

Basis of finding

- Of respondents that have a tax risk management system, 82.4 per cent agree or strongly agree that it has an effect on the level of tax risk considered acceptable. The responses to the open-ended component of the relevant survey question indicate that the tax risk management system results in a reduction in the level of acceptable tax risk.

- Reasons for the reduction in the level of acceptable tax risk as a result of the tax risk management system include a greater awareness of tax risks and their ramifications; an increasingly global approach to tax risk; the increased involvement of external tax specialists in the determination of the correct income tax treatment; and that the tax risk management system puts tax at the front of mind of the company's directors and managers. The tax risk management system is a means by which the acceptable level of tax risk is enforced and this results in more transparent tax decision-making in a large company.

- 73.5 per cent of respondents that have a tax risk management system indicate that it results in the lowest level of tax risk.
- Statistical analysis indicates that there is a relationship between the existence of a tax risk management system and a company's tax risk profile specifically companies that have a tax risk management system have a lower tax risk profile.

Research Question 2

Does the adoption of a tax risk management system ensure that directors and tax decision-makers in a large company are informed concerning the tax risk to which a company is exposed?

The results indicate that in almost all large Australian companies the adoption of a tax risk management system ensures that directors and tax decision-makers are informed concerning the tax risk to which a company is exposed.

Basis of finding
- Directors (92.6 per cent), tax decision-makers (98.5 per cent), CFOs (98.5 per cent), CEOs (89.7 per cent) and chairperson of the board (82.4 per cent) are, as a result of a tax risk management system, informed concerning the tax risk to which the company is exposed.
- 95.5 per cent of respondents feel that a tax risk management system results in more informed decision-making.

Research Question 3

Does the adoption of a tax risk management system by a large company result in the identification of potential non-compliance with the income tax laws that would not otherwise be identified?

The results indicate that in almost all large Australian companies the adoption of a tax risk management system results in the identification of potential non-compliance with the income tax laws that would not otherwise be identified.

Basis of finding
- 86.7 per cent of respondents agree that the tax risk management system ensures compliance with the income tax laws and open-ended responses also support this result. The tax risk management system identifies potential non-compliance as a result of the elevation of the importance of income tax compliance, the increased investment in training tax staff and the increased use of private ruling requests from the ATO.

- 72.1 per cent agree that the tax risk management system does identify potential non-compliance with the income tax laws that would not otherwise be identified. Respondents in open-ended responses feel that a documented and operationalised tax risk management system is more effective in identifying non-compliance compared to an arbitrary system. The strong lines of communication ensure that non-compliance is identified.

- Some respondents that have a tax risk management system still had an adjustment to taxable income in the last 3 financial years (11.8 per cent) and/or a tax position adopted by the company that was subsequently found to be incorrect (19.1 per cent).

- 98.6 per cent of respondents indicate that a tax risk management system results in better documented tax risk.

- 92.7 per cent of respondents indicate that a tax risk management system results in an improvement in compliance with the tax laws.

- 97 per cent of respondents indicate that a tax risk management system results in an improvement in the management of tax risk.

- 86.7 per cent of respondents indicate that a tax risk management system results in a greater range of tax risks identified.

Research Question 4

Does the adoption of a tax risk management system by a large company result in the identification of opportunities to minimise its income tax liability that would not otherwise be identified?

The results indicate that in the majority of large Australian companies (61.8 per cent) the adoption of a tax risk management system results in the identification of opportunities to minimise the income tax liability that would not otherwise be identified.

Research Question 5

Does a large company act to ensure potential non-compliance with the income tax laws, as identified by its tax risk management system, if any, does not occur?

The results indicate that the majority of large Australian companies (61.8 per cent) that have a tax risk management system act to ensure that potential non-compliance with the income tax laws, as identified by the tax risk management system, does not occur.

Research Question 6

Does a large company act to ensure opportunities to minimise its income tax liability identified by its tax risk management system, if any, are realised?

The results indicate that a minority of large Australian companies (47.1 per cent) that have a tax risk management system act to ensure opportunities to minimise their income tax liability identified by its tax risk management system are put in place.

Research Question 7

How do large company taxpayers define tax risk?

The results indicate that only 45.5 per cent of large Australian companies have statements and/or guidelines on what constitutes a tax risk. Of those companies that have statements and/or guidelines on what constitutes tax risk the focus is on transaction, compliance and financial accounting risk.

Basis of findings

- 45.5 per cent of respondent companies have statements and guidelines on what constitutes a tax risk.

- Statistical analysis indicates that there is a relationship between the existence of a tax risk management system and the existence of statements and guidelines on what constitutes a tax risk. Specifically, companies that have a tax risk management system are more likely to place greater emphasis on the need for a clear definition of what constitutes a tax risk.

- Statistical analysis indicates that there is a relationship between the existence of statements and guidelines on what constitutes a tax risk and the importance of income tax compliance. Specifically, companies that have a clear definition of what constitutes a tax risk place greater importance on income tax compliance.

Research Question 8

What factors affect the level of tax risk to which a large company in Australia is exposed?

The results indicate that a number of factors determine the level of tax risk that a large Australian company is exposed to. The factors most identified by large Australian companies are the uncertainty and complexity of the income tax laws, reputational concerns, and the complexity and size of business transactions.

Basis of findings

- Uncertainty in the application of the income tax laws increases the level of tax risk (82.9 per cent).
- Complexity in the application of the income tax laws increases the level of tax risk (88.6 per cent).
- Complexity of business transactions increases the level of tax risk (77.3 per cent).
- Size of business transactions increases the level of tax risk (71.6 per cent).
- Business growth increases the level of tax risk (69.1 per cent).
- Global nature of the business increases the level of tax risk (56.9 per cent).
- Economic environment increases the level of tax risk (47.9 per cent).
- Staff turnover increases the level of tax risk (33.4 per cent).
- Staff not following guidelines increases the level of tax risk (50.4 per cent).
- Time and/or cost constraints increase the level of tax risk (46.4 per cent).
- Limited information provided to tax staff increases the level of tax risk (52.1 per cent).
- Reputational concerns increase the level of tax risk (73.2 per cent).

Research Question 9

What factors limit the ability of a large company in Australia to identify and manage tax risk?

The results indicate that a number of factors limit the ability of a large company in Australia to identify and manage tax risk. The factors most identified by large Australian companies are the uncertainty and complexity of the income tax laws and the complexity of business transactions.

Basis of findings

- Uncertainty in the application of the income tax laws limits the ability to identify and manage tax risk (70.6 per cent).
- Complexity of the income tax laws limits the ability to identify and manage tax risk (72.6 per cent).
- Complexity of business transactions limits the ability to identify and

manage tax risk (62.1 per cent).

- Staff turnover limits the ability to identify and manage tax risk (27.4 per cent).
- Staff not following guidelines limits the ability to identify and manage tax risk (47.3 per cent).
- Time and/or cost constraints limit the ability to identify and manage tax risk (41 per cent).
- Limited information provided to tax staff limits the ability to identify and manage tax risk (54.8 per cent).
- Commercial pressure from other divisions limits the ability to identify and manage tax risk (43.3 per cent).
- Foreign operations limit the ability to identify and manage tax risk (36.8 per cent).
- Limitations of ATO staff limit the ability to identify and manage tax risk (46.3 per cent).
- Statistical analysis indicates that listed public companies are more likely to consider the limitations of ATO staff as impacting their ability to identify and manage tax risk compared to unlisted public and private companies.

Research Question 10

What is the nature of tax risk management practices in large companies in Australia?

The results indicate that the tax risk management practices in large Australian companies are varied and reflect the company's characteristics. A large proportion of large Australian companies do not have a tax risk management system and of those companies that do a majority introduced it prior to 2008.

The individuals most involved in the determination of acceptable tax risk are the CFO and the tax manager of a large Australian company whilst the tax manager is more involved in the determination of acceptable tax risk in public companies (listed and unlisted) than in private companies. Company group policy is more likely to play a part in the determination of acceptable tax risk in public companies (listed and unlisted) than in private companies and shareholders are identified as having very little or no involvement in the determination of acceptable tax risk.

Listed public company shareholders are less involved in the determination of acceptable tax risk as compared to shareholders in private and unlisted public companies and companies that have a tax risk management system place greater importance on income tax compliance than companies that do not have a tax risk management system. Public companies (listed and unlisted) are more likely to have a very low or low tax risk profile than private companies whilst private companies are more likely to have a moderate to very high tax risk profile than public companies (listed and unlisted). Listed public companies are more likely to have experienced a change in their tax risk profile in the last three years compared to unlisted public or private companies.

Basis of findings

- 77.2 per cent of respondents have some system and/or procedure to identify and manage tax risk while only 56.9 per cent have a documented and operationalised tax risk management system.

- Those companies that have some system and/or procedure but not a documented and operationalised tax risk management system indicate in open-ended responses that the systems and procedures largely include checks and balances incorporated into the financial accounting system.

- Those companies that have a documented and operationalised tax risk management system indicate in open-ended responses that the systems and procedures are particular to the individual company's requirements. Accordingly, a variety of systems and procedures are identified.

- 75 per cent of those respondents that have a documented and operationalised tax risk management system had it in place by the end of the 2008 financial year and the remaining respondents introduced their tax risk management system between January 2009 and December 2011.

- The individuals most involved and who ultimately make the final decision on the acceptable level of tax risk are the CFO and the tax manager. The board of directors, the CEO and company group policy also have a significant role.

- Statistical analysis indicates that the tax manager in a public company (both listed and unlisted) is more involved in the determination of acceptable tax risk than in a private company.

- Statistical analysis indicates that company group policy in a public company (both listed and unlisted) is more likely to play a part in the decision concerning acceptable tax risk as compared to a private company.

- Shareholders are identified in only a few instances as having a significant role in the determination of acceptable tax risk (17.1 per cent) and the majority of respondents felt that the shareholders have very little or no involvement in the determination of acceptable tax risk (84%).
- Statistical analysis indicates that a listed public company's shareholders are the least involved in the determination of acceptable tax risk as compared to private and unlisted public companies.
- Statistical analysis indicates that companies that have a tax risk management system place greater importance on income tax compliance compared to companies that do not have a tax risk management system.
- Statistical analysis indicates that public companies (listed and unlisted) are more likely to have a very low or low tax risk profile and private companies are more likely to have a moderate to very high tax risk profile.
- Statistical analysis indicates that a listed public company is more likely to have experienced a change in their tax risk profile in the last three years as compared to an unlisted public or private company. Internal and external factors including the nature of the company's business, ownership structure, economic environment and ATO activity affect a company's tax risk profile as indicated in responses to open-ended Survey Question 10.

6 Application to the Main Research Question

The main research question concerns the impact of the identification and management of tax risk on the income tax compliance behaviour of large Australian companies. The findings in respect of each of the specific research questions when applied to answer the main research question indicate that the comprehensive identification and management of tax risk leads to an improvement in the level of income tax compliance by large Australian companies. That is, 82.4 per cent of large Australian companies consider the tax risk management system reduces the acceptable level of tax risk, and 73.5 per cent indicate that a tax risk management system results in the lowest level of tax risk.

In addition, a relationship exists between a company's tax risk management system and its tax risk profile: a company that does have a comprehensive tax risk management system is likely to have a lower tax risk profile than those companies that do not. Companies that have a tax risk management system were found to place greater importance on income tax compliance and it is anticipated that this finding will further drive improvements in the management of tax risks and ultimately improvements in the level of income tax compliance by large companies.

Further support for the conclusion that the comprehensive identification and management of tax risk leads to an improvement in the level of income tax compliance by large Australian companies is reflected in the view of the majority of respondents that a tax risk management system leads to more informed tax decision-making, the identification of potential non-compliance with the income tax laws and the identification of opportunities, to a certain extent, to minimise income tax. Companies act on the issues identified by the tax risk management system and the tax risk management system has a substantial role in ensuring tax compliant behaviour. The introduction of a comprehensive tax risk management system results in an improvement in income tax compliance by a large company because it identifies potential non-compliance as well as opportunities to minimise tax, companies act on the tax compliance issues identified by the tax risk management system and, ultimately, place greater importance on income tax compliance. In addition, this research highlights that companies with a tax risk management system accept a lower level of tax risk than companies who do not have a tax risk management system as it ensures the lowest level of tax risk arises. Tax decision makers within a company are more informed concerning the tax implications of their decisions and as a consequence fewer surprises in relation to a company's final tax position arise.

This research highlights the fact that many large Australian companies have not put in place a tax risk management system and, as a result, the improvements in income tax compliance identified will not be reflected in a substantial number of large companies. In addition, large Australian companies face a variety of limitations in identifying and managing tax risk, and the findings demonstrate that some of the limitations are external to the company while others relate to internal factors. These limitations need to be addressed to maximise the income tax compliance benefits of a tax risk management system. Some differences are identified in the tax risk management practices of public and private companies and in the individuals within the company that are responsible for the company's tax risk profile. Consistently, the board is involved in setting a company's tax risk profile while shareholders play a minor role in setting the tax risk agenda.

7 Conclusion

The results of this research support the efforts of revenue authorities around the world to increase large company tax compliance via the communication to large companies that they need to identify and manage tax risk and to include the board in the group of appropriate tax decision makers. Large companies view the tax risk management system as a mechanism that ensures more informed tax decision making and, ultimately, a lower tax risk profile. Documented and operationalised systems and procedures to identify and manage tax risk do identify potential non-compliance with the income tax laws and large companies act on the issues identified. Although tax risk management systems also identify opportunities to minimise income tax these opportunities take a back seat to efforts aimed at ensuring non-compliance is minimised.

As is the case with all research, this research does have a number of limitations. In relation to Phase One, the concern is that the small number of in-depth interviews, at 14, may not capture all of the relevant issues relating to tax risk management by large companies. However, the additional in-depth interview with a tax partner from a 'Big 4' professional accounting firm did act as a confirmation of the views of the in-depth interview participants.

With respect to the mail survey in Phase Two, there is the potential for non-response bias and also the possibility that respondents to the survey did not interpret the questions in the manner intended. An analysis of non-response bias did not highlight non-response bias as an area of major concern. Survey respondents did not indicate confusion or identify issues in understanding the questions or response options.

In addition, while the survey responses are based on a specific definition of what constitutes a tax risk management system, a different definition may have been more appropriate in capturing information on a large company's tax risk management system. Importantly, survey respondents did not indicate any confusion with the definition of a comprehensive tax risk management system as set out in the survey.

Some limitations in the survey results should be borne in mind. Specifically during both research phases, the opinion of the individual employed by the large company is the source of the data concerning a large company's tax risk management system and tax compliance behaviour. There is a risk that the individual's opinion, as expressed in the in-depth interviews and survey responses, is different to the actual company facts. This risk is minimised as the participants remain anonymous and can speak and write in an open and frank manner. A mismatch between opinion and fact could still occur.

8   Future Directions for this Research

This study indicates that the existence of a tax risk management system does have an effect on a company's tax risk profile, resulting in a lower acceptable tax risk and more informed tax decision making, however, further research is required to understand the specifics of this relationship and how it applies to different types of taxes. Ultimately, a large company's decision to put in place a system to identify and manage tax risks and the form that the system takes would be based on a cost benefit analysis to the company. Whilst the research data relates to Australian companies with a turnover exceeding AUD250 million the applicability of the findings to other companies in Australia, and to large companies in other tax jurisdictions, requires further research.

Appendix 1

Interviewer: Catriona Lavermicocca, PhD student, UNSW

Project description: In-depth interviews

This research project forms part of the data collection for the purposes of completion of a PhD in Taxation at the Australian School of Taxation (ATAX) at UNSW. The title of the PhD thesis is 'Tax Risk Management as a Corporate Governance Issue in Australia and the Impact on Income Tax Compliance by Large Company Taxpayers'.

Proposed questions for in-depth interviews concerning tax risk management

1. To what extent does your organisation consider/evaluate tax risk?

2. Does your organisation have clear statements/guidelines on what constitutes a tax risk?

3. Who (not by name but by title) in the organisation determines the acceptable level of tax risk?

4. Do the organisation's corporate governance guidelines require tax risk to be managed?

5. Does your organisation have a tax risk management system?

6. What systems/procedures does your organisation have in place to ensure that tax risk is managed? To what extent are those systems/procedures documented and reviewed for compliance?

7. Have there been any recent changes in the approach the organisation takes to tax risk management?

8. What criteria are used to determine the acceptable level of tax risk in your organisation?

9. What factors do you consider have an impact on the level of tax risk that the organisation faces?

10 What limitations, if any, does the organisation face in managing tax risk?

11 What pressures do you believe have had an impact on the organisation's decision to adopt/not adopt a tax risk management system?

12 To what extent have the following had an impact on the organisation's decision to adopt/not adopt a tax risk management system?

- ATO;
- Shareholders;
- Customers;
- Stock market/listing rules;
- Directors; and
- SOX legislation.

13 What influence have the ATO announcements had on your organisation's tax risk management practices?

14 Have you received any correspondence from or entered into discussions with the ATO concerning tax risk management and tax decision-making practices?

15 Who (not by name but by title) are the key tax decision-makers in your organisation? Is there any board/director involvement in tax decision-making and, if any, what is the level of that involvement?

16 What are the performance measures in respect of the key tax decision-makers in your organisation?

17 What do you consider to be the impact of tax risk management systems on the determination of the acceptable level of tax risk?

18 Is the organisation more or less tax risk averse (or has there been no change) after the introduction of a tax risk management system?

19 To what extent does the organisation consider corporate social responsibility issues and if it does, does that include a consideration of the organisation's tax compliance profile?

Appendix 2

Survey of Tax Risk Management Practices of Large Australian Companies

Completing the Survey

You can answer most questions by ticking the appropriate box. In some instances further detail is requested. Please return your completed survey form in the reply paid envelope provided.

Definitions of some terms used in the survey

Compliance with the income tax laws — the taxpayer files all required income tax returns accurately and at the proper time, pays all outstanding taxes as they fall due and maintains all required records. The accuracy of the return and the records required are determined in accordance with the prevailing income tax laws, rulings, return instructions and court decisions.

Income tax liability — net income tax payable by a taxpayer in respect of a particular year of income

Large company — gross turnover exceeds AUD250 million

Non-compliance with the income tax laws — the taxpayer does not file all required income tax returns accurately and at the proper time, and/or does not pay all outstanding taxes as they fall due and/or does not maintain all required records and/or the accuracy of the return and the records required are not in all instances determined in accordance with the prevailing income tax laws, rulings, return instructions and court decisions.

Operationalised — put in place and acted upon by decision-makers as part of the ongoing and active business systems used by the organisation.

Tax risk — any event, action, or inaction in tax strategy, operations, financial reporting, or compliance that adversely affects either the company's tax or business operations or results in an unanticipated or unacceptable level of monetary, financial statement or reputational exposure.

Tax risk management system — documented and operationalised systems and procedures to identify and manage tax risk.

Tax risk profile — reflects the behaviour of a taxpayer towards tax risk. The more aggressive the taxpayer's position with respect to tax risk, the higher the tax risk profile. The less aggressive the taxpayer's position with respect to tax risk, the lower the tax risk profile.

Please turn the page to commence the survey

Survey questions

1) **Please indicate your company type**

Public company ☐   Private company ☐
If your company is a public company is it listed on the Australian Securities Exchange? Yes ☐ No ☐

2) **In which of the following industries does the company carry on business? If your company operates in more than one industry please indicate the industry that best describes the industry in which the company carries on business**

Agriculture, forestry and fishing ☐
Mining ☐
Manufacturing ☐
Electricity, gas, water and waste services ☐
Construction ☐
Wholesale trade ☐
Retail trade ☐
Accommodation and food services ☐
Transport, postal and warehousing ☐
Information media and telecommunications ☐
Financial and insurance services ☐
Rental, hiring and real estate services ☐
Professional, scientific and technical services ☐
Administrative and support services ☐
Public administration and safety ☐
Education and training ☐
Health care and social assistance ☐
Arts and recreation services ☐
Other services ☐
Other ☐
Please specify..

3) **What is your position in the company?**

Chief Financial Officer ☐
Tax Director ☐
Chief Executive Officer ☐
Tax Manager ☐
Assistant Tax Manager ☐
Other ☐
Please specify ....

4)   To what extent are the following persons <u>involved in the determination</u> of the acceptable level of tax risk with respect to a transaction or series of transactions?

Tax risk — *any event, action, or inaction in tax strategy, operations, financial reporting, or compliance that adversely affects either the company's tax or business operations or results in an unanticipated or unacceptable level of monetary, financial statement or reputational exposure.*

a)	CFO
	To a great extent ☐ To some extent ☐ Very little ☐ Not at all ☐
b)	CEO
	To a great extent ☐ To some extent ☐ Very little ☐ Not at all ☐
c)	Board of Directors
	To a great extent ☐ To some extent ☐ Very little ☐ Not at all ☐
d)	Tax manager
	To a great extent ☐ To some extent ☐ Very little ☐ Not at all ☐
e)	Shareholders
	To a great extent ☐ To some extent ☐ Very little ☐ Not at all ☐
f)	Corporate group policy
	To a great extent ☐ To some extent ☐ Very little ☐ Not at all ☐
g)	Other ☐ Please provide detail
	....
	....
	....
	....

5)   To what extent are the following persons in your company <u>ultimately make the final decision</u> on the acceptable level of tax risk with respect to a transaction or series of transactions?

a)	CFO
	To a great extent ☐ To some extent ☐ Very little ☐ Not at all ☐
b)	CEO
	To a great extent ☐ To some extent ☐ Very little ☐ Not at all ☐
c)	Board of Directors
	To a great extent ☐ To some extent ☐ Very little ☐ Not at all ☐
d)	Tax manager
	To a great extent ☐ To some extent ☐ Very little ☐ Not at all ☐
e)	Shareholders
	To a great extent ☐ To some extent ☐ Very little ☐ Not at all ☐
f)	Corporate group policy
	To a great extent ☐ To some extent ☐ Very little ☐ Not at all ☐
g)	Other ☐ Please provide detail
	....
	....

6)   Does your company have <u>statements and/or guidelines</u> on what constitutes a tax risk?

Yes ☐ No ☐
If yes, what constitutes a tax risk according to your company's statements and/or guidelines?...
....
....
....
....

7) Please indicate the extent to which each of the following factors <u>increase the level of tax risk</u> your company is exposed to in carrying on its business activities.

a)	Uncertainty in the application of the income tax law To a great extent ☐ To some extent ☐ Very little ☐ Not at all ☐
b)	Complexity of the income tax law To a great extent ☐ To some extent ☐ Very little ☐ Not at all ☐
c)	Complexity of business transactions To a great extent ☐ To some extent ☐ Very little ☐ Not at all ☐
d)	Staff turnover To a great extent ☐ To some extent ☐ Very little ☐ Not at all ☐
e)	Staff not following guidelines To a great extent ☐ To some extent ☐ Very little ☐ Not at all ☐
f)	Time and/or cost constraints To a great extent ☐ To some extent ☐ Very little ☐ Not at all ☐
g)	Limited information provided to tax staff by other divisions within the company To a great extent ☐ To some extent ☐ Very little ☐ Not at all ☐
h)	Level of concern for reputation To a great extent ☐ To some extent ☐ Very little ☐ Not at all ☐
i)	Size of the transaction To a great extent ☐ To some extent ☐ Very little ☐ Not at all ☐
j)	Growth of the business To a great extent ☐ To some extent ☐ Very little ☐ Not at all ☐
k)	Global nature of the business To a great extent ☐ To some extent ☐ Very little ☐ Not at all ☐
l)	Economic environment To a great extent ☐ To some extent ☐ Very little ☐ Not at all ☐
m)	Other ☐ Please provide detail ....

8) How important is <u>compliance with the income tax laws</u> to your company?

Compliance with the income tax laws - the taxpayer does file all required income tax returns accurately and at the proper time, pays all outstanding taxes as they fall due and maintains all required records. The accuracy of the return and the records required are determined in accordance with the prevailing income tax laws, rulings, return instructions and court decisions.

Very important ☐
Important ☐
Moderately important ☐
Of little importance ☐
Unimportant ☐

9) **Which of the following best describes the <u>tax risk profile</u> of your company?**

Tax risk profile – *reflects the behaviour of a taxpayer towards tax risk. The more aggressive the taxpayer's position with respect to tax risk, the higher the tax risk profile. The less aggressive the taxpayer's position with respect to tax risk, the lower the tax risk profile.*

> Very high ☐ High ☐ Moderate ☐ Low ☐ Very low ☐

10) **Has there been a change in the <u>tax risk profile</u> of your company in the last three financial years?**

> Yes ☐ No ☐
>
> If yes what is the nature of the change and what do you believe to be the reason for it?
> ....
> ....
> ....
> ....
> ....
> ....
> ....
> ....
> ....
> ....
> ....
> ....

11) **Does your company have <u>systems and/or procedures</u> in place to identify and manage tax risk**

> Yes ☐ No ☐
>
> If yes describe the systems and/or procedures in place to identify and manage tax risk and continue on to question 12)
> ....
> ....
> ....
> ....
> ....
> ....
> ....
> ....
> ....
> ....
> ....
> ....

If you answered NO to question 11) the survey is now complete. Thank you.
If you answered YES to question 11) please turn the page and continue this survey.

12) Considering the following factors please indicate the extent to which they <u>limit the ability of your company</u> to identify and manage the tax risk to which the company is exposed.

a)	Uncertainty in the application of the income tax laws To a great extent ☐ To some extent ☐ Very little ☐ Not at all ☐
b)	Complexity of the income tax laws To a great extent ☐ To some extent ☐ Very little ☐ Not at all ☐
c)	Complexity of business transactions To a great extent ☐ To some extent ☐ Very little ☐ Not at all ☐
d)	Staff turnover To a great extent ☐ To some extent ☐ Very little ☐ Not at all ☐
e)	Staff not following guidelines To a great extent ☐ To some extent ☐ Very little ☐ Not at all ☐
f)	Time and/or cost constraints To a great extent ☐ To some extent ☐ Very little ☐ Not at all ☐
g)	Limited information provided to tax staff by other divisions within the company To a great extent ☐ To some extent ☐ Very little ☐ Not at all ☐
h)	Commercial pressure outside your tax department To a great extent ☐ To some extent ☐ Very little ☐ Not at all ☐
i)	Limitations of ATO staff To a great extent ☐ To some extent ☐ Very little ☐ Not at all ☐
j)	Country or countries where the company carries on business To a great extent ☐ To some extent ☐ Very little ☐ Not at all ☐
k)	Other ☐ Please provide detail ....

13) Are the current systems and/or procedures used by your company to identify and manage tax risk <u>documented</u>?

To a great extent ☐   To some extent ☐   Very little ☐   Not at all ☐

14) Are the current systems and/or procedures used by your company to identify and manage tax risk <u>operationalised</u> in the company's business systems?

Operationalised - *put in place and acted upon by decision makers as part of the ongoing and active business systems used by the organisation*

> To a great extent ☐   To some extent ☐   Very little ☐   Not at all ☐

The following questions should only be answered if your company has systems and/or procedures in place to identify and manage tax risk that are to some extent documented and operationalised. If that is the case please continue.

If your company <u>DOES NOT</u> have systems and/or procedures in place to identify and manage tax risk that are to some extent documented and operationalised the survey is now complete.

Thank you

For the purposes of this survey systems and/or procedures that identify and manage tax risk that are to some extent documented and operationalised constitute a tax risk management system (TRMS).

15) When was the company's <u>current tax risk management system</u> introduced?

Tax risk management system – *documented and operationalised systems and procedures to identify and manage tax risk*

In the 2012 financial year? ☐
In the 2011 financial year? ☐
In the 2010 financial year? ☐
In the 2009 financial year? ☐
In the 2008 financial year? ☐
Prior to the 2008 financial year? ☐
Progressively over a number of years ☐   If so please specify the relevant years   ....

16) **The current tax risk management system does have an effect on the <u>level of tax risk considered acceptable</u> by your company.**

Strongly agree ☐ Agree ☐ Undecided ☐ Disagree ☐ Strongly disagree ☐

If you agree, describe ways in which the current tax risk management system has an effect on the level of tax risk considered acceptable by your company.
....
....
....
....
....
....
....

If you disagree, why do you believe the current tax risk management system does not have an effect on the level of tax risk considered acceptable to your company?
....
....
....
....
....
....
....

---

17) **The current tax risk management system ensures <u>compliance with the income tax laws</u> by your company.**

Strongly agree ☐ Agree ☐ Undecided ☐ Disagree ☐ Strongly disagree ☐

If you agree, describe ways in which the current tax risk management system ensures compliance with the income tax laws by your company.
....
....
....
....
....
....
....

If you disagree, why do you believe the current tax risk management system does not ensure compliance with the income tax laws by your company?
....
....
....
....
....
....
....
....
...

18) **The current tax risk management system results in <u>the identification of potential non-compliance with the income tax laws</u> that would not otherwise be identified by your company.**

> Strongly agree ☐ Agree ☐ Undecided ☐ Disagree ☐ Strongly disagree ☐
>
> If you agree, describe ways in which the current tax risk management system identifies potential non-compliance with the income tax laws that would not otherwise be identified by your company.
> ....
> ....
> ....
> ....
> ....
> ....
> ....
>
> If you disagree, why do you believe the current tax risk management system does not identify non-compliance with the income tax laws that would not otherwise be identified by your company?
> ....
> ....
> ....
> ....
> ....
> ....
> ....
> ....

19) If you disagree with the statement at 18) above you can continue to 20).

If you agree with the statement at 18) above, does your company act to ensure potential non-compliance with the income tax laws <u>identified by your current tax risk management system do not occur?</u>

> To a great extent ☐   To some extent ☐   Very little ☐   Not at all ☐

20) The current tax risk management system results in the identification of opportunities to minimise your company's income tax liability that would not otherwise be identified.

Strongly agree ☐ Agree ☐ Undecided ☐ Disagree ☐ Strongly disagree ☐

If you agree, in what way does the current tax risk management system result in the identification of opportunities to minimise your company's income tax liability that would not otherwise be identified?

....
....
....
....
....
....
....

If you disagree, why do you believe the current tax risk management system does not result in the identification opportunities to minimise your company's income tax liability that would not otherwise be identified?

....
....
....
....
....
....
....
....

If you disagree with the statement at 20) above you can continue to 22)

If you agree with the statement at 20) above, does your company act to ensure opportunities to minimise the company's income tax liability identified by your current tax risk management system are put in place?

To a great extent ☐ To some extent ☐ Very little ☐ Not at all ☐

21) The current tax risk management system **ensures that the following persons** are informed concerning the tax risk that your company is exposed to

a) Directors
Strongly agree ☐ Agree ☐ Undecided ☐ Disagree ☐ Strongly disagree ☐
b) Tax decision makers
Strongly agree ☐ Agree ☐ Undecided ☐ Disagree ☐ Strongly disagree ☐
c) Chief Financial Officer
Strongly agree ☐ Agree ☐ Undecided ☐ Disagree ☐ Strongly disagree ☐
d) Chief Executive Officer
Strongly agree ☐ Agree ☐ Undecided ☐ Disagree ☐ Strongly disagree ☐
e) Chairman of the Board
Strongly agree ☐ Agree ☐ Undecided ☐ Disagree ☐ Strongly disagree ☐
f) Other person Please specify ....

22) The current tax risk management system **results in**:

a) Better documented tax risk
Strongly agree ☐ Agree ☐ Undecided ☐ Disagree ☐ Strongly disagree ☐
b) More informed tax decision making
Strongly agree ☐ Agree ☐ Undecided ☐ Disagree ☐ Strongly disagree ☐
c) Greater range of tax risk identified
Strongly agree ☐ Agree ☐ Undecided ☐ Disagree ☐ Strongly disagree ☐
d) Improvement in the management of tax risk
Strongly agree ☐ Agree ☐ Undecided ☐ Disagree ☐ Strongly disagree ☐
e) The lowest level of tax risk
Strongly agree ☐ Agree ☐ Undecided ☐ Disagree ☐ Strongly disagree ☐
f) Improvement in compliance with the income tax laws
Strongly agree ☐ Agree ☐ Undecided ☐ Disagree ☐ Strongly disagree ☐
g) Other benefits Please specify ....

23) Has your company been the subject of an <u>adjustment to taxable income</u> as a consequence of audit by the ATO relating to any of the last three financial years?

Yes ☐ No ☐
If yes, was the company aware of a tax risk associated with the issue that gave rise to the adjustment by the ATO before the audit commenced?   …………………………………………………………………………………………   …………………………………………………………………………………………   …………………………………………………………………………………………   …………………………………………………………………………………………   …………………………………………………………………………………………   …………………………………………………………………………………………   …………………………………………………………………………………………   …………………………………………………………………………………………

24) Are you aware of a transaction or series of transactions in respect of which the income tax treatment adopted by the company was <u>subsequently found to be incorrect</u> relating to any of the last three financial years?

Yes ☐ No ☐
If yes, were you aware of any tax risk associated with that transaction or series of transactions when the transaction or series of transactions was entered into?   …………………………………………………………………………………………   …………………………………………………………………………………………   …………………………………………………………………………………………   …………………………………………………………………………………………   …………………………………………………………………………………………   …………………………………………………………………………………………   …………………………………………………………………………………………

The survey is now complete.

Thank you for participating.

Appendix 3

Themes and Relationships Identified from the Responses to the In-depth Interviews Linked to the Specific Research Questions (RQs)

1. A reduction in the level of tax risk acceptable to a large company is not a consequence of a tax risk management system. RQ1.

2. The tax manager, tax department and directors within a large company are more informed concerning potential tax risk as a result of the existence of a tax risk management system. RQ2.

3. A tax risk management system will ensure that the tax manager, tax department and directors are informed of the large company's tax risk profile. RQ2.

4. A tax risk management system results in greater awareness by staff outside the tax portfolio of the tax risk that the large company is exposed to in carrying on its business RQ2.

5. A number of factors affect level of tax risk that a large company is exposed to. RQ8.

6. A number of factors limit the ability of a tax risk management system to identify and manage all tax risk of a large company. RQ9.

7. Large companies seek to comply with the income tax laws RQ3 and 5.

8. Large companies seek to take advantage of a tax provision that would reduce income tax payable RQ4 and 6.

9. Most large companies do not have a clear definition of what constitutes a tax risk. RQ7.

10. The level of acceptable tax risk is ultimately determined by the board of directors. RQ11.

11. Tax risk management systems in large Australian companies include a variety of procedures and practices including both formal and informal components. RQ10.

12. Tax managers, the CFO and directors in a large Australian company are interested in tax risk. RQ2.

13. A tax risk management system is an essential part of good business practice. RQ10.

14. Some large companies in Australia are still in the process of implementing and/or documenting their tax risk management system. RQ10.

15 Directors accept that good corporate governance requires them to be informed about tax risk and to be involved in tax decision-making. RQ2.

16 Factors that affect the level of tax risk that a large company is exposed to include uncertainty/complexity of tax laws, staffing, demand for franking credits, level of concern for reputation, complexity of business transactions, limited information provided to tax staff by other divisions, size of the transaction, change in ATO interpretation/approach to a tax issue, growth of the business, global nature of the business, staff not following guidelines and the economic environment. RQ8.

17 Factors that limit the ability of a tax risk management system to identify and manage all tax risk of a large company include limitations of ATO staff, limited information provided to tax staff by other divisions, time/cost/staff constraints, countries where the company carries on business, uncertainty/complexity of tax laws, complexity of business transaction, commercial pressure and staff turnover. RQ9.

18 Large companies in Australia tend to adopt a low tax risk profile. RQ1.

19 A public company is more likely than a private company to have a formalised and documented tax risk management system. RQ11.

20 ATO announcements and statements concerning tax risk management best practice have influenced the formalised tax risk management procedures put in place by large companies. RQ10.

Bibliography

ATO, 'Risk Differentiation Framework', <http://www.ato.gov.au/corporate/content.aspx?menuid=0&doc=/content/33802.htm&page=49&H49>.

Australian Taxation Statistics 2009–2010.

Bayer, R and F Cowell, 'Tax Compliance and Firms' Strategic Interdependence' (2009) 93 *Journal of Public Economics* 1131.

Black, J, 'The Emergence of Risk Based Regulation and the New Public Management in the United Kingdom' [2005] *Public Law* 512.

Book, L, 'Freakonomics and the Tax Gap: An Applied Perspective' (2007) 56(5) *American University Law Review* 1163.

Bradbury, D, 'Press Release with Exposure Draft of the Personal Liability for Corporate Fault Reform Bill 2012' (Press Release, 27 January 2012).

Butler, D, 'Corporate Insolvency — Tax Risk Management' (Speech delivered at the New Zealand Law Society Taxation Conference, September 2006).

Carmody, M, 'Large Business and Tax Compliance — A Corporate Governance Issue' (Speech delivered at the Leaders' Luncheon, Sydney, 10 June 2003).

Chen, K and C Chu, 'Internal Control Verses External Manipulation: A Model of Corporate Income Tax Evasion' (2005) 36(1) *RAND Journal of Economics* 151.

Christians, A, 'How Starbucks Lost its Social License – and Paid £20 million to Get it Back' *Tax Notes International* (2013) 71(7) 637.

Creswell, J and V Plano Clark, *Designing and Conducting Mixed Research Methods* (Sage Publications, 2007).

D'Ascenzo, M, 'Individual Interests and Community Needs — Focus on Legal Professional Privilege' (Speech delivered at The Australian Italian Lawyers Association Tax Seminar, Melbourne, 18 September 2003) 2.

Desai, M and D Dharmapala, 'Corporate Tax Avoidance and High Powered Incentives' (2006) 79 *Journal of Financial Economics* 145.

Downs, A and B Stetson, 'Economic Versus Non-Economic Factors: An Analysis of Corporate Tax Compliance' (Paper presented at the 2011 American Accounting Association Annual Meeting — Tax Concurrent Sessions, Denver, Colorado US, August 2011).

Elgood, T, I Paroissien, and L Quimby, 'Managing Global Risk for Multinationals' (2005) 16(5) *Journal of International Taxation* 22.

Epps, K and C Cleaveland, 'Insiders' Perspectives of the Effects of Recent Regulation on Corporate Taxation' (2009) 21 *Research in Accounting Regulation* 34.

Erickson, M, M Hanlon and E Maydew, 'Is There a Link Between Executive Compensation and Accounting Fraud?' (University of Chicago, University of North Carolina, and University of Michigan Working Paper 2004).

Ernst and Young, 'Global Tax Risk Survey' (2008) http://www.ey.com/GL/en/Services/Tax/Business-Tax/Tax-Accounting-and-Risk-Advisory/Tax_2008_Ernst-Young_tax_risk_survey.

Ernst and Young, 'Steady Course, Uncharted Waters — The Australian Perspective from the Third Ernst and Young Global Tax Risk Survey 2008'.

Ernst and Young, Tax Risk Management (LexisNexis Butterworths, 2007).

FDS International, 'Large Groups' Tax Departments: Factors that Influence Tax Management — A Qualitative Study' (Prepared for HMRC (UK), September 2006).

Flanagan, J, 'Values, Codes of Ethics and the Law' The Institute of Chartered Accountants in Australia — Discussion Paper June 2006.

Freedman, J, 'Tax Risk Management and Corporate Taxpayers — International Tax Administration Developments' Chapter 4 in A Bakker and S Kloosterhof (eds), *Tax Risk Management: From Risk to Opportunity* (IBDF, 2010).

Friese, A, S Link and S Mayer, 'Taxation and Corporate Governance' (Working Paper Max Planck Institute for Intellectual Property, Competition and Tax Law, Munich, Germany, 19 January 2006) 68.

Goerke, L, 'Tax Overpayments, Tax Evasion and Book-Tax Differences' (2008) 10(4) *Journal of Public Economic Theory* 643.

Hanlon, M and Slemrod, J, 'What Does Tax Aggressiveness Signal? Evidence from Stock Price Reactions to News about Tax Shelter Involvement' (2009) 93 *Journal of Public Economics* 126.

HMRC, 'HMRC Approach to Compliance Risk Management for Large Business' (March 2007) <http://www.hmrc.gov.uk/lbo/risk-update.pdf>.

HMRC, 'Tax in the Boardroom' <http://www.hmrc.gov.uk/lbo/tax-in-the-boardroom.htm>.

Ireland Revenue Authority, 'The Co-Operative Approach to Tax Compliance' (September 2005) <http://www.revenue.ie/en/business/running/large-businesses.html>.

Jackson, C, F Moore and T Dalton, 'Managing Dealings within the Corporate Tax Group and with the ATO — An External View' (Paper presented at the Annual Corporate Tax Intensive, Taxation Institute of Australia, Hunter Valley, Australia, 26–27 October 2006).

Ke, B, 'Why Do CEO's of Publicly Traded Corporations Prefer Reporting Small Increases in Earnings and Long Duration of Consecutive Earnings Increases' (Pennsylvania State University Working Paper. University Park, PA: Pennsylvania State University, 2001).

KPMG, 'The Rising Tide — Regulation and Stakeholder Pressure on Tax Departments Worldwide', <http://www.kpmg.com/ES/es/ActualidadyNovedades/ArticulosyPublicaciones/Documents/TheRisingTide.pdf>.

KPMG, 'Tax Department Survey' (2006) <http://www.amr.kpmg.com/aci/docs/surveys/KPMG_Tax_Survey.pdf.

Lanis, R and G Richardson, 'The Effect of Board of Director Composition on Corporate Tax Aggressiveness' (2011) 30(1) *Journal of Accounting and Public Policy* 50.

Lavermicocca, C, 'Managing Tax Risk and Compliance' (2009) 13(2) *The Tax Specialist* 66.

Lavermicocca, C, 'Impact of the Corporate Structure on an Understanding of Taxpayer Compliance Behaviour' in C Evans and M Walpole (eds), *Tax Administration: Safe Harbours and New Horizons* (Fiscal Publications, 2008) 200.

McKerchar, M, 'Why Do Taxpayers Comply? Past Lessons and Future Directions in Developing a Model of Compliance Behaviour' (2001) 16(1) *Australian Tax Forum* 99.

McKerchar, M, The Impact of Complexity Upon Compliance: A Study of Australian Personal Taxpayers (Australian Tax Research Foundation, Research Study No 39, 2003), 34.

Millett, C and C McKenna, 'Managing Communications and Tax Risk in a Corporate Tax Group: An Internal View; Commonwealth Bank of Australia' (Paper presented at the Annual Corporate Tax Intensive, Taxation Institute of Australia, Hunter Valley, Australia, 26–27 October 2006)

Minnick K and T Noga, 'Do Corporate Governance Characteristics Influence Tax Management?' (2010) 16 *Journal of Corporate Finance* 703.

Netherlands Tax and Customs Administration Co-ordination Group 2008, 'Tax Control Framework' (March 2008) <http://ec.europa.eu/taxation_customs/resources/documents/taxation/vat/vat_conferences/tax_control_framework_en.pdf>.

Oats, L, 'Taxing Companies and Their Shareholders: Design Issues', in A Lymer and J Hasseldine, (eds) *The International Tax System* (Kluwer, 2002).

OECD, 'Tackling Aggressive Tax Planning Through Improved Transparency and Disclosure', (Centre for Tax Policy and Administration, 2011) <http://www.oecd.org/ctp/exchangeofinformation/48322860.pdf>.

OECD Forum on Taxation Information Note 'General Administrative Principles: Corporate Governance and Tax Risk Management' (2009) <http://www.oecd.org/tax/taxadministration/43239887.pdf>.

OECD, 'Study of the Role of Tax Intermediaries' (2008) <http://www.oecd.org/tax/taxadministration/39882938.pdf>.

OECD Forum on Tax Administration, 'Good Corporate Governance: The Tax Dimension' (2006) <http://www.oecd.org/site/ctpfta/37207911.pdf>.

OECD Forum on Tax Administration, 'Seoul Declaration' (2006) <http://www.oecd.org/tax/taxadministration/37415572.pdf>.

Parker, D, 'Piercing the Veil of Incorporation: Company Law for a Modern Era' (2006) 19 *Australian Journal of Corporations Law* 35.

Plesko, G A, 'Multidisciplinary Issues in Corporate Tax Policy' (2006) 59 *National Tax Journal* 599.

Ponemon, L and D Gabhert, 'Ethical Reasoning and Accounting in Auditing' (1993) CGA Canada Research Foundation Vancouver.

PricewaterhouseCoopers, 'The ATO and Large Business — The Way Forward' (2006).

PricewaterhouseCoopers, 'Tax Risk Management' (2004)

Prow, G, 'Corporate Tax Professionals Need Better Tools to Manage Data in Post-Sarbanes Environments' (2005) 57(September) *The Tax Executive* 460.

Rego, S and R Wilson, 'Equity Risk Incentives and Corporate Tax Aggressiveness' (2012) 50(3) *Journal of Accounting Research* 775.

Rice, E, 'The Corporate Tax Gap: Evidence on Tax Compliance by Small Corporations' in J Slemrod (ed), *Why People Pay Taxes. Tax Compliance and Enforcement* (Ann Arbor: University of Michigan Press, 1992) 125.

Richardson, G, G Taylor and R Lanis, 'The Impact of Risk Management and Audit Characteristics on Corporate Tax Aggressiveness: An Empirical Analysis' (Conference paper presented at the Journal of Accounting and Public Policy Conference at the London School of Economics, 25 May 2012, Session 1).

Richardson, M and A J Sawyer, (2001) A Taxonomy of the Tax Compliance Literature: Further Findings, Problems and Prospects' (2001) 16(2) *Australian Tax Forum* 137.

Shulman, D, 'Speech delivered at the National Association of Corporate Directors Governance Conference' (Washington, 19 October 2009, IRS News Release IR–220–95) <http://www.irs.gov/newsroom/article/0,,id=214451,00.html>.

Sikka, P, 'Smoke and Mirrors: Corporate Social Responsibility and Tax Avoidance' (2010) 34 *Accounting Forum* 153.

Slemrod, J, 'The Economics of Corporate Selfishness' (2004) Dec *National Tax Journal* 877.

Weisbach, D, 'Corporate Tax Avoidance' (Published in the proceedings of the National Tax Association 96th Annual Conference, 2003).

Wunder, H F, 'Tax Risk Management and the Multinational Enterprise' (2009) 18 *Journal of International Accounting, Auditing and Taxation* 14.

9 Taxation and Trade: Examining the Relationship Between SADC Trade Agreements and Tax Agreements

Puseletso Letete

Abstract

The increasing integration of the world economies has revived interest in regional integration schemes which may be regarded as a first step in the process of globalisation. Africa has not been left behind in this process. More particularly, countries in southern Africa have also shown a keen appreciation of the significance of regional integration. This chapter focuses on the Southern African Development Community (SADC) which is a free trade area. Taxation is central to economic development in African countries and there is no doubt that taxation shapes the environment in which international and regional trade and investment occur. On the other hand, taxes in the form of tariffs can be used by a government to hinder imports. Therefore, there is a case to be made for the examination of the relationship between regional trade agreements and tax agreements entered into by SADC Member States.

1 Introduction

The Southern African Development Community[1] (SADC) was formed as an international regional organisation established in terms of a treaty and declaration referred to as the "Treaty of Southern African Development Community". This Treaty was signed by the heads of state and government of the signatory Member States in Namibia on 17 August 1992 with a focus

---

1   Hereafter, the SADC. The SADC is a regional organisation which has 15 member countries. These are:- Angola, Botswana, Democratic Republic of Congo (hereafter referred to as Congo DR), Lesotho, Madagascar, Malawi, Mauritius, Mozambique, Namibia, Seychelles, South Africa, Swaziland, Tanzania, Zambia and Zimbabwe. The SADC was established in 1980 as SADCC (Southern African Development Coordination Conference) and it was transformed to the SADC (Southern African Development Community) in 1992. For the historical background see www.sadc.int (Accessed 6 August 2013). See also, Annex 1 for a map that identifies SADC countries.

on both socio-economic co-operation and political-security.[2]

The SADC Treaty provides the legal framework of the organisation by setting out the status, principles and objectives, obligations of Member States, membership, institutions, procedural matters relating to areas of co-operation among Member States, co-operation with other international organisations, financial issues, dispute settlement and, lastly, sanctions, withdrawal and dissolution.[3] The SADC Treaty makes provision for the formulation of subsidiary legal instruments such as protocols, memoranda of understanding, charters, regulations and guidelines giving specific mandate to various SADC institutions. A total of twenty three protocols have so far been formulated. Apart from these fundamental instruments, the SADC has also adopted three major strategic documents.[4]

This chapter examines what effect, if any, trade agreements (including trade in goods and services) which are entered into to achieve free movement of goods, labour and capital have on the members' tax agreements? It looks into how tax and trade agreements interact in the wider context of achieving free trade. The question which is to be asked is what kind of relationship should exist between tax agreements and trade agreements? These questions are examined in the context of the legal instruments which govern issues of trade amongst SADC Member States as well as in the context of the Free Trade Area agreement which was concluded in 2011 between the SADC, the Common Market for Eastern and Southern Africa (COMESA)[5] and the East African Community (EAC).[6] It also considers the relationship between the SADC tax instruments and regional free trade agreements.

The chapter commences with a reflective literature review on the legal regime in SADC Member States and the status of trade agreements. It critically examines the relationship between these trade agreements and tax issues and the relevance of tax issues vis-a-vis trade agreements. It is also argued that taxation should form part of trade issues and agreements, particularly in the present developing economic situation. As regional integration deepens and trade barriers are being lifted, it is apposite that taxation should be at the centre of such developments. The chapter examines whether SADC trade agreements take cognisance of tax issues and how these can impact on trade and regional integration. Finally, the chapter draws conclusions on the main themes extrapolated from these areas of inquiry.

---

2 Saurombe A 'The SADC trade agenda, a tool to facilitate regional commercial law: An analysis' (2009) 21 *South African Mercantile Law Journal* 697.
3 See, the SADC Declaration and Treaty of 1992.
4 The Regional Indicative Strategic Development Plan, the blueprint for development, and the Strategic Indicative Plan for the Organ on Politics, Defence and Security Co-operation.
5 Hereafter, the COMESA.
6 Hereafter, the EAC.

2 The SADC Legal Regime

The SADC institutional and legal framework is enshrined in a Treaty[7] and a wide range of protocols, memoranda of understanding, charters, declarations, regulations and guidelines. The legal framework relevant for both trade and taxation matters has been developed in accordance with Articles 21 and 22 of the SADC Treaty which is the supreme law of the organisation. These two provisions encourage Member States to co-operate in all areas which will foster regional development and integration and to conclude protocols in each area of co-operation. As a result, the SADC has adopted a number of protocols on trade and taxation respectively.

3 The SADC Protocol on Trade

The SADC Protocol on Trade (the Protocol on Trade) was adopted in 1996 and it was implemented in 2000. It provides a framework for SADC's trade integration programme. This Protocol on Trade sets out the basis for regional economic integration, which is a key objective of economic liberation as set out in the first statement of the Preamble to the Treaty.

The main objective of the Protocol on Trade is to further liberalize intra-regional trade in goods and services in fair, mutually equitable and beneficial trade arrangements.[8] The Protocol on Trade also aims to contribute towards the improvement of the climate for domestic, cross-border and foreign investment.[9] Member States, therefore, intended to create a conducive climate for investment not only for their own investors but also for investors from the African region and international investors.

Furthermore, the Protocol aims to enhance the economic development, diversification and industrialisation of the region.[10] It is, however, noteworthy for its objective to establish a free trade area in the SADC region. This has been achieved and a Free Trade Area (FTA)[11] has been established in accordance with Article 2(5) of the Protocol. The FTA enables SADC Member States to eliminate tariffs and other restrictive regulations of commerce (see further below, p. 174).

The main principles which are at the centre of achieving the Protocol on Trade's objectives are elimination of barriers to intra-SADC trade[12],

---

7   The SADC Treaty was adopted in 1992.
8   Article 2 (1) of the Protocol on Trade. See also Saurombe op cit note 2 at 700.
9   Article 2 (3) of the Protocol on Trade.
10 Article 2 (4) of the Protocol on Trade.
11 Hereafter, the FTA.
12 Article 3 of the Protocol on Trade.

elimination of import duties[13], and elimination of export duties.[14] Article 6 emphasises that, in relation to intra-SADC trade, Members States shall adopt policies and implement measures to eliminate all existing forms of non-tariff barriers and refrain from imposing any new non-tariff barriers. The Protocol is, therefore, a significant development within this region in the area of trade. Its overriding purpose is to regulate trade among SADC Member States, as well as with third party states at both bilateral and multilateral levels. Article 9 provides for general exceptions which are acceptable under the Protocol. Such exceptions refer to the adoption of measures by a Member State necessary, for example, to protect public order; to protect human life; to secure compliance with laws and regulations which are consistent with World Trade Organisation (WTO) obligations. Annex VI to the Protocol on Trade establishes a trade dispute settlement mechanism for SADC Member States which is modelled on the WTO dispute settlement mechanism.[15]

4 The SADC Protocol on Trade in Services

The SADC Protocol on Trade in Services (the Protocol on Trade in Services) was adopted in 2012. This Protocol aims to achieve deeper regional integration and sustainable economic growth through the creation of an integrated regional market for services. Its objectives are to progressively liberalise intra-regional trade in services on the basis of equity, balance and mutual benefit with the objective of achieving the elimination of discrimination between Member States as well as achieving a liberal trading framework for trade in services with a view to creating a single market for trade in services, to promote sustainable economic growth and development, to ensure consistency between liberalization of trade in services and to pursue services trade liberalization.[16]

Under this Protocol, Member States undertake to uphold consistency between liberalization in the region and WTO obligations and, therefore, they undertake to take into account the disciplines developed under the General Agreement on Trade in Services (GATS) regime. Article 11 deals with subsidies. Paragraph 1 provides that nothing shall be construed to prevent Member States from using subsidies in relation to their development programmes. The Committee of Ministers is given a mandate to review all subsidies related to trade in services that Member States provide to their domestic service suppliers and it will negotiate disciplines to avoid any trade-distortive effects of subsidies.

---

13 Article 4 of the Protocol on Trade.
14 Article 5 of the Protocol on Trade.
15 Letete P & Saurombe A 'Analysing the role of the MOU on Cooperation in Taxation and Related Matters as an instrument for coordination and integration in SADC' (2012) in Kierkegaard S (ed) *Law, Governance and World Order* 527-636 at 629.
16 See, Article 2 of the Protocol on Trade in Services.

Article 4 adopts the 'most favoured nation treatment' principle. Member States have a general obligation to accord most-favoured nation treatment to services and service suppliers of any Member that it accords to like services and services suppliers of any other Member or third country.[17] This means that a Member State cannot treat the services and service suppliers of one Member State less favourably than those from another Member State or non-Member State. However, Member States are permitted to deviate from this general obligation in certain circumstances. According to Cronje`, "any two or more Member States may negotiate the liberalization of specific sectors or sub-sectors provided they afford the other Members a reasonable opportunity to negotiate the preferences granted therein on a reciprocal basis."[18] At the international level, as already seen, WTO Member States have concluded the GATS to cover trade in the service sectors. Therefore, since all the SADC Member States are Members of the WTO, they are committed to observe the obligations under the GATS. This is seen in the importation of the principles contained in the GATS in the Protocol on Trade in Services.[19]

5 The SADC Free Trade Area (FTA)

The FTA was established in 2000 by 12 Member States[20] but it was only launched in 2008.[21] The FTA is established under the Protocol on Trade (as amended in 2005). With the creation of a FTA (and the consequent freeing of trade), the ultimate intention is to create a larger market, releasing the potential for trade, economic growth and employment creation.

A free trade area constitutes a group of countries in which tariffs and non-tariff barriers are eliminated on substantially all trade between them. Each Member State maintains its own tariffs on non-members.[22] Cnossen, for example, has described an FTA as existing where Member States agree to eliminate tariffs, quotas and preferences on most goods and services which

---

17 Section 4 (1) of the Protocol on Trade in Services.
18 Cronje` J.B 'The SADC Protocol on Trade in Services: What is necessary to support the establishment of an integrated market?' (2014) Tralac working paper S14WP05/2014 9.
19 This chapter does not deal with the provisions of the GATS in detail. For a detailed discussion on the GATS, see Brown C 'Tax Discrimination in the NAFTA Bloc: The Impact of Tax and Trade Agreements On the Cross-Border Trade in Services' (2005) *The Dalhousie Law Journal* Issue 28, pp. 99-139.
20 These are Botswana, Lesotho, Madagascar, Malawi, Mauritius, Mozambique, Namibia, South Africa, Swaziland, Tanzania, Zambia and Zimbabwe. Angola, Congo DR and Seychelles remain outside of the FTA. For a detailed analysis of the FTA, see Sandrey R 'An analysis of the SADC Free Trade Area' (2013) Trade Brief Stellenbosch: Tralac.
21 See, http://www.sadc.int/about-sadc/integration-milestone/free-trade-area/ (Accessed 4 June 2015).
22 See, Evans D 'Options for Regional Integration in Southern Africa' (2000) SAJE 68 3 pp664-693 for a detailed discussion on the various options of regional integration.

are traded between them.²³

The perceived advantages of the FTA include the following: to facilitate trade by reducing red tape and paperwork at the borders and to provide a framework for improving the movement of goods throughout the region.²⁴ Furthermore, some of the potential benefits of the FTA, particularly for the smaller countries of SADC, include the following - access to an enlarged market within the region which can contribute to economic growth of those smaller economies, and increased investment opportunities which will be available to all the countries within the FTA. This will be a particular advantage to the smaller countries as they will be able to invest in South Africa which is a bigger economy and benefit from its advanced technological knowledge. As one study has noted, increased intra-regional trade along with inflows of foreign capital can be one of the benefits.²⁵

Prior to the implementation of the FTA, a survey of over 600 businesses and other State actors was undertaken in 2008 throughout the region. The survey identified the following barriers: time consuming customs procedures, substantial paperwork and bureaucracy, import duties and taxes to be paid in cash, current customs tariffs as a trade barrier, export/import licensing and permits, high transport costs, poor transport infrastructure, and high communication costs.²⁶ It was expected, therefore, that the FTA would address some of the key barriers to trade in SADC that had been identified by the survey. Since the implementation of the FTA, Member States have been engaged in harmonising customs procedures and customs classifications at different border posts and there is an increased customs co-operation between Member States. Furthermore, Member States have established "one stop" border posts to reduce the time which businesses spend at borders. Currently, there are pilot programmes at the border between Mozambique and Zimbabwe, South Africa and Mozambique, and Zimbabwe and Zambia.²⁷ Member States have also introduced a single declaration and a single bond to be used when transporting goods across several borders within the Community. This contributes towards making the transhipment across Member States easier and facilitates the movement of goods.²⁸

---

23 Cnossen S 'Coordination of Indirect Taxes in the Southern African Development Community (SADC): Lessons from European Experience' 2011 61 *Tax Notes International* 943.
24 SADC Free Trade Area Handbook, 2008 Gaborone, Botswana: SADC at 2.
25 Chauvin S & Gaulier G 'Prospects for Increasing Trade among SADC Countries' (2002) Trade and Industrial Policy Strategies Annual Forum Muldersdrift South Africa at 4.
26 SADC FTA Handbook (2008) at 6, available at www.sadc.int (Accessed 4 June 2015).
27 See, www.sadc.int (Accessed 4 June 2015).
28 Ibid.

However, despite the positive aspects of the FTA, there are still some challenges which remain. The continuing delays and difficulties at the border remain one of the key barriers to doing business in the region and Member States will have to develop strategies to reduce the delays. The other challenge is that many SADC Member States are landlocked, with imports and exports having to cross several borders. This makes trade facilitation a key factor in their economic competitiveness. The introduction of rules which are intended to facilitate the movement of goods will lessen the impact of this challenge.

Furthermore, Member States have also agreed to eliminate all non-tariff barriers[29] and not to impose any new ones, except where it would be necessary to do so, on the grounds of health and safety, public morals or national security.[30] It has been noted by the SADC Secretariat that the removal of import and export restrictions has proved to be challenging, and this is complicated by the fact that often non-tariff barriers result from policies that are not intended to restrict imports. It is clear from this analysis that though SADC achieved the implementation of the FTA in 2008 there is still a long road ahead to realise the success of the FTA. This is compounded by the fact that Angola, Congo DR and Seychelles have not yet joined the FTA.

6 The Tripartite Free Trade Agreement between COMESA,[31] EAC[32] and SADC

The COMESA-EAC-SADC Tripartite Free Trade Agreement was entered into in 2006[33] with a view to harmonising programmes and policies within and between the three regional economic communities of COMESA, EAC and SADC and to advance the establishment of the African Economic

---

29 A non-tariff barrier is any measure that obstructs international trade and its measures other than tariffs.
30 SADC Free Trade Area Handbook, op cit note 24 at 8.
31 The Common Market for Eastern and Southern Africa (COMESA) is a preferential trade area and its main objective is to forge economic integration with the establishment of a Common Market and the consolidation of economic co-operation through the implementation of common policies and programmes aimed at achieving sustainable growth and development. COMESA has nineteen members. They are Burundi, Comoros, Congo DR, Djibouti, Egypt, Eritrea, Ethiopia, Kenya, Libya, Madagascar, Malawi, Mauritius, Rwanda, Seychelles, Sudan, Swaziland, Uganda, Zambia and Zimbabwe.
32 The East African Community (EAC) is a customs union which aims to achieve free trade amongst Member States and a common external tariff with third states. The EAC has five members. They are Burundi, Kenya, Rwanda, Tanzania and Uganda.
33 The Tripartite FTA was endorsed in 2008 at the Tripartite Summit which was held in Kampala, Uganda in 2008. It was launched on 12 June 2011.

Community (see further below).³⁴ These regional integration programmes focus on expanding and integrating trade and include the establishment of free trade areas, customs unions, monetary unions and common markets.³⁵ The Tripartite FTA is based on three key issues which are market integration, infrastructure development and industrial development.³⁶ Its objectives are to facilitate trade and to make provision for non-tariff barrier programmes and so it aims to reduce tariffs imposed on goods originating in the region and traded in the region. An important aspect of the Tripartite FTA is the design and implementation of a programme that is aimed at improving trade and transport measures and reducing non-tariff barriers to trade.³⁷

The Member States of these three regional economic communities have recognized the fact that non-tariff barriers constitute a major obstacle to the expansion of intra-regional trade. This has led to the identification of the elimination of non-tariff barriers as one of the key objectives of the Tripartite FTA.³⁸ Non-tariff barriers include export taxes, import bans, government monopolies, burdensome administrative requirements and a lack of physical infrastructure.³⁹

The Tripartite FTA makes no provision for issues of taxation and related matters. It leaves out crucial issues of taxation which underlie the facilitation of trade or how such issues, if they arise, should be dealt with within the existing economic climate at the regional level. It is widely accepted that tariffs are not the only type of taxes that can impact trade. For example, the extent to which producers are asked to pay taxes that support government services can also affect trade. The Tripartite FTA does make provision for the co-operation of Member States in other areas such, industrial policy, financial and payment systems, development of capital markets and commodity exchanges (see, Article 35). It can, therefore, be argued by analogy, that co-ordination and incorporation of tax related issues in the Tripartite FTA in future could be covered by this provision. However, on the other hand, it might be argued that since tax issues are excluded by this provision, then they cannot be covered by it, and rather that a separate agreement would need to be drawn up or the Tripartite FTA suitably amended to provide, specifically, for tax related issues.

---

34 Pearson M 'Trade facilitation in the COMESA-EAC-SADC Tripartite Free Trade Area' (2012) in *Tralac The Tripartite Free Trade Area: Towards a new African integration paradigm?* at 142-179 at 143.
35 See, www.eac.int. (Accessed on 14th February 2015).
36 Pearson M op cit note 34 at 144. See also, the Tripartite Vision and Strategy document, June 2011.
37 Ibid at 144.
38 Viljoen W 'Non-tariff barriers affecting trade in the COMESA-EAC-SADC Tripartite Free Trade Agreement' (2011) Stellenbosch: Tralac at 1.
39 Ibid at 1.

The Tripartite FTA is a starting point for collaboration between these regional organisations and it is of major importance to the harmonisation and strengthening of new trade facilitation measures within that area. The completion of the Tripartite FTA simplifies the complicated aspect of the various regional integration schemes as they currently exist.

The Tripartite FTA is not an attempt to merge COMESA, the EAC and SADC. It is about bringing together the existing FTAs in COMESA, EAC and SADC into a single wider FTA within the context of intra-regional liberalisation. Therefore, it is not a regional economic community negotiation process, but a process driven by Member States, as customs territories, within the regional economic communities. It will be interesting to see how these negotiations develop considering that Member States of these regional economic communities are also pursuing other agenda at the continental level, for example, in relation to the African Economic Community, which is created under the Constitutive Act that establishes the African Union, through which African countries have concluded a continental free trade area agreement (CFTA) which is intended to commence in 2017.[40]

7 The SADC Protocol on Finance and Investment

The SADC tax agenda is reflected in the SADC Protocol on Finance and Investment of 2006 (the Protocol on Finance and Investment) and in the Memorandum of Understanding on Co-operation in Taxation and Related Matters of 2002 (the MOU on Taxation). These instruments deal with issues such as the establishment of a SADC data base, personal capacity building, the application and treatment of tax incentives for income tax purposes, tax treaties, indirect taxes, and review and dispute settlement arrangements. In the preamble to the MOU on Taxation, Member States recognise that the MOU on Taxation is intended to pursue and attain the objectives of SADC as an organisation. These objectives include, among other things, development and economic growth, to achieve complementarity between national and regional strategies, to harmonise political and socio-economic policies and plans, and to improve economic management and performance through regional cooperation and reduce economic imbalances.[41] The MOU is reproduced in Annex 3 of the Protocol on Finance and Investment.[42]

Article 2 of the Protocol on Finance and Investment recognises the need to have a comprehensive database which is publicly accessible. Member

---

40 The Organization of African Union Charter and the Constitutive Act establishing the African Union call for the creation of an African Economic Community (EAC) the membership of which will include all countries within the African continent.
41 The Preamble to the MOU in Taxation, adopted in 2002 by SADC Member States.
42 Reference to the various provisions in this chapter relate to the provisions as they appear in Annex 3 of the Protocol on Finance and Investment.

States are required to take the necessary steps to develop a SADC tax database which will include detailed information regarding all direct and indirect taxes and other levies for each Member State. In order to keep the tax database up to date, Member States undertake to provide, on an annual basis or when significant changes occur, the relevant information to the relevant body. However, it remains to be determined who will host this database as well as deal with issues pertaining to accessibility for Member States that struggle with their ICT capabilities. The question is who can compete with the South African Tax system that is so complex and advanced and one which meets global standards. SADC has established an online tax database for all the Member States. This is accessible on the website of SADC. However, at present, the database is under review, and, therefore, it is not available at all times.

Article 3 deals with capacity building. This article recognises the need to develop the expertise of tax officials and to develop training initiatives to develop professionalism in tax. Member States also recognise the importance of information technology and the challenges which they face in this area. They have undertaken to work together in responding to such challenges, including the review of issues relating to E-Commerce, E-Billing or E-Customs clearance and the impact they may have on tax revenue collection and on the flow of goods and services. In order to achieve this collaboration between Member States there must be rules, not simply a loose agreement or memorandum. There has not been any significant development in this area since the Protocol on Finance and Investment came into force, and SADC Member States have not developed any rules in this area.

Article 4 deals with the application and treatment of tax incentives. In this provision, Member States agree to achieve a common approach to the treatment of tax incentives. This will ensure a more co-ordinated approach to tax incentives in order to avoid tax competition which is likely to arise in Member States from the different treatment and application of tax incentives. The issue of tax competition is a serious issue in taxation and needs to be discouraged as it can distort trade practices. SADC has established a tax sub-committee which is tasked with the implementation of Annex 3 of the Protocol on Finance and Investment. In turn, this sub-committee has set up technical working groups to facilitate the implementation of various technical areas of tax co-ordination which are identified in the Protocol. In view of this, a tax incentives working group has been established to focus, primarily, on the application and treatment of tax incentives by Member States in a co-ordinated approach.

Article 5 deals with tax treaties. Member States have recognised the importance of developing a common policy for the negotiation of tax treaties either between themselves and other countries outside the Community or amongst themselves. The Member States agreed to develop a model tax treaty for the SADC, which takes account of the particular socio-economic development needs of Member States. This approach will be enhanced by Member States drawing up guidelines for the effective exchange of information and the implementation of mutual assistance and co-operation procedures. The implementation of this provision has resulted in the adoption of two important tax agreements by Member States, namely the SADC Model Tax Agreement[43] and the SADC Agreement on Assistance in Tax Matters.[44]

The SADC Model Tax Agreement has been developed pursuant to Article 5 (4) thereof in order to establish a common policy for Member States for the negotiation of tax agreements between or amongst themselves or with countries outside the region, and which takes account of the particular socio-economic development needs of each Member State. The main objective of this Agreement is to encourage exchange of tax information amongst states. Broadly, Article 26 of the Model Tax Agreement provides for the exchange of tax information that is foreseeably relevant to the administration or enforcement of domestic taxes of every kind and description.

Furthermore, the SADC Agreement on Assistance in Tax Matters has been adopted in terms of Article 5 (5) thereof which requires Member States to draw up guidelines for the effective exchange of tax information and implementation of a mutual agreement procedure. This Agreement is intended to ensure that parties to the Agreement assist each other in relation to various tax matters, particularly those which concern the exchange of information, carrying out of joint tax examinations, and assistance in the collection of taxes.

Article 6 recognises that Member States will, in line with the WTO Agreements, gradually substitute taxes on internationally traded goods and services with broad-based taxes on consumption. This indicates that the SADC Member States have recognised to some extent the overlap between trade and taxes on consumption. This is an important development as it does envisage the need for overlap between the two notions. SADC Member States also need to take steps to achieve effective co-ordination and harmonisation in the administration of indirect taxes. At the centre of this harmonisation will be the possible co-ordination of excise duties, value added tax (VAT) and sales tax. This Article also provides for the establishment of a SADC forum for dealing with VAT matters by Member States at the regional level. The establishment of a SADC forum has not yet occurred. However, this will be a development which will be welcomed and beneficial to the Member States when it is established.

---

43 Adopted 2009, updated in 2010 and in 2011.
44 Concluded in 2009 and signed in 2012.

Both the MOU and the Protocol are relevant to the SADC's policies and are intended to pursue the objectives set out in the SADC Treaty with the intention of the SADC becoming a customs union (and later a common market). This requires discriminatory border taxes to be abolished and the adoption of uniform and common tax systems. Therefore, the implementation of the provisions of these tax instruments will be the first step towards achieving a co-ordinated and harmonised indirect tax system within the SADC.

8 The relationship between trade and tax agreements
8.1 Trade Agreements

Trade agreements are multilateral in nature, but, generally, are limited to trade-in-goods issues, exclude investment issues and also, in some cases, trade in services.[45] Since trade agreements (such as the WTO Agreements, SADC's Free Trade Agreements, economic partnership agreements, and international investment agreements) address trade measures, references in these documents to taxation often do not specify what aspects of taxation and tax measures are to be regulated. However, it has become globally recognised that trade agreements have an important regulatory impact on taxation. According to Slemrod and Avi-Yonah, "it is widely accepted that a multilateral agreement covering only tariffs would not be sufficient to achieve free trade".[46]

Trade agreements are also significant in addressing how to reduce or remove barriers to trade (tariffs, quotas, technical barriers voluntary import and export restraints, import expansions and export subsidies).[47] Most importantly, trade agreements provide for the principle of 'national treatment' which deals with the notion of non-discrimination between domestic and foreign producers.[48] This means that producers in a state will be treated the same, be afforded similar opportunities and should be taxed in the same way whether they are based domestically or in a foreign country.

Trade agreements also make provision for the principle of 'most favoured nation' which entitles all parties to a trade agreement to the benefits offered by one signatory to any of the others.[49] This principle is one of the main pillars of trade agreements either at multilateral or regional level. As far as the WTO is concerned, prior to 1985, the General Agreement on Tariffs and

---

45 Slemrod J & Avi-Yonah R '(How) Should Trade Agreements deal with Income Tax issues?'(2001-2002) 55 *N.Y.U. Tax Law Review* 533-544 at 534.
46 Ibid at 534.
47 McDaniel P R 'The impact of trade agreements on tax systems' (2002) in *International and comparative taxation: essays in honour of Klaus Vogel* 151-162 at 152.
48 Ibid at 153.
49 Ibid at 153.

Trade (GATT) procedures rarely applied to tax expenditure provisions that could distort free movement of goods, capital and labour as envisioned by the GATT.[50] The Uruguay Round on the GATT increased, significantly, the likelihood that tax expenditures would be subject to review by the WTO. This has been the case, to some extent, in the Agreement on Subsidies and Countervailing Measures.[51] The WTO has treaty powers which are likely to increase its involvement in examining a given country's tax expenditures which one or more other Member States allege violate the GATT as 'prohibited subsidies'.[52] According to McDaniel, the first step in the analytical process is to establish that a challenged provision is a 'subsidy'.

Of utmost importance among non-tariff barriers to trade are subsidies, including both production and export subsidies, and taxes, indirect and direct. Article XVI of the GATT treats subsidies, in principle, as undesirable interferences with the flow of goods.[53] The term 'subsidy' is understood differently by many people. The GATT Treaty does not provide a definition of the word subsidy. According to Perry, it seems, "the closest statement is in Article XVI of GATT, which implies that any form of income or price support that affects trade could be considered a subsidy".[54] In the 1993 GATT Agreement,[55] subsidies exist if a government provides income or confers other beneficial financial contributions. These financial contributions would cover, for example, situations where government revenue that is due is foregone or not collected, or where a government provides goods or services other than general infrastructure.[56]

Thus, greater integration in these areas allows virtual freedom of trade and factor movements among the members of a customs union or of an FTA and this should increase economic efficiency among members, for example, through economies of scale and specialisation.[57]

8.2 Tax Agreements

In contrast to trade agreements, a tax system has to address issues of the tax base, tax rates, the taxable unit, accounting principles, application of tax

---

50 Ibid at 154.
51 General Agreement on Tariffs and Trade, 1994, Agreement on Subsidies and Countervailing Measures April 15 1994.
52 See, Slemrod J & Avi-Yonah R op cit note 45 at 534-537.
53 Ibid at 535.
54 Perry GM 'Taxes Tax Subsidies and the Impact of Trade Agreements'(1995) *Review of Marketing and Agricultural Economics* Vol 63 (1) 155-163 at 156.
55 See, Agreement on Subsidies and Countervailing Measures in the 1993 GATT Agreement.
56 See, Perry GM op cit note 54 at 157.
57 Laird S 'Regional Trade Agreements: Dangerous Liaisons?' (1999) *The World Economy* Vol 22 (9) 1179-1200 at 1181.

to cross-border transactions, and administrative rules. These are important considerations for business and investment.[58] In view of these issues, it is necessary to examine whether trade agreements within the SADC do in anyway affect the tax issues which underlie the tax system of a Member State. The importance of the relationship between trade agreements and taxation becomes evident when a trade agreement is objectively interpreted by a third party, for example, where there is a concern whether specific trade incentives accorded to investors are acceptable or accord with the tax system of a Member State.

Tax agreements, on the other hand, deal with tax issues related to trade in goods and services and investment issues.[59] Tax agreements transcend what exists within tax systems (tax policies) of Member States. This means that, the tax agreements will deal with issues referred to above, namely the tax base, tax rates, the taxable unit, accounting principles, application of the tax to cross-border transactions, and administrative rules.

Taxation is central to the current SADC's development agenda.[60] It provides a stable flow of revenue to finance development priorities. Tax policy shapes the environment in which international trade and investment take place. Certainty and consistency of tax treatment, the avoidance of double taxation and efficient tax administration are all important considerations for business.

9 Summary and Conclusions

This chapter considers the view that both trade and tax agreements can impact the extent to which the goal of free trade is achieved. In this respect, it is clear that trade agreements need to take cognisance of tax issues arising at a regional or multilateral level. A multilateral agreement covering only tariffs is not sufficient to achieve free trade.

It can also be argued that subsidies provided through a tax system should be the subject of inquiry under trade agreements – they should not be removed from scrutiny under trade agreements simply because they are drafted as 'tax' rules. Further, tax and trade agreements acknowledge the principles of non-discrimination and national treatment. Such similar concerns indicate that there is an interrelationship between these agreements.

This chapter recommends that the SADC should take note of any such interrelationship between trade and tax issues within Member States.

---

58 McDaniel op cit note 47 at 153.
59 Slemrod J & Avi-Yonah R op cit note 45 at 534.
60 Letete P 'Between tax competition and tax harmonisation Coordination of value added taxes in SADC member states' (2012) *Law, Democracy & Development* Vol 16 119-138 at 120.

Therefore, trade agreements, which are negotiated in future, should take this issue into consideration to ensure that there are no conflicts between such agreements and tax agreements concluded multilaterally or bilaterally between Member States. This view is supported by Brown who suggests that, 'the role of taxation in trade agreements is likely to become a compelling issue among nations when negotiating Free Trade Agreements".[61]

10 Bibliography

Constitutive Act of the African Union, 11 July 2000 Togo: Organization of African Unity Draft Agreement establishing the COMESA, EAC and SADC Tripartite Free Trade Area, 2010 COMESA, EAC & SADC.

Brown C., 'Tax Discrimination in the NAFTA Bloc: The Impact of Tax and Trade Agreements On the Cross-Border Trade in Services' (2005) *The Dalhousie Law Journal* Issue 28, 99-139.

Chauvin S. & Gaulier G., 'Prospects for Increasing Trade among SADC countries' (2002) Trade and Industrial Policy Strategies Annual Forum Muldersdrift South Africa, 4.

Clough M. & Ravenhill J., 'Regionalism in Southern Africa: the SADCC' in Clough M. (ed) *Political Change in Southern Africa* (1982), 1-3.

Cronje JB., 'The SADC Protocol on Trade in Services: What is necessary to support the establishment of an integrated market?' (2014) Tralac Working Paper S14WP05/2014, 9.

Cnossen S., 'Coordination of Indirect Taxes in the Southern African Development Community (SADC): Lessons from European Experience' (2011) 61 *Tax Notes International* 943.

Evans D., 'Options for Regional Integration in South Africa' (2000) SAJE 68 3 664-693.

Hartzenberg T., 'Regional Integration in Africa' Trade Law Centre for Southern Africa (2011) available at http://www.tralac.org/cg bin/giga.cgi?cmd=cause_dir_news_item&news_id=45318&cause_id=1694

Kalenga P., 'Implementation of the SADC Trade Protocol: Some Reflections' (2011) SADC Annual Conference 7-9 September. Cape Town Available at: www.tralac.org [Accessed on 10 October 2014].

Laird S., 'Regional Trade Agreements: Dangerous Liaisons?' (1999) *The World Economy* Vol 22 (9), 1179-1200

Letete P., 'Between tax competition and tax harmonisation: Coordination of value added taxes in SADC member states' (2012) *Law, Democracy & Development* Vol 16, 119-138.

Letete P. & Saurombe A., 'Analysing the role of the MOU on Cooperation in Taxation and Related Matters as an instrument for coordination and integration in SADC' in Kierkegaard S. (ed) *Law, Governance and World Order*

---

61 Brown C op cit note 19 at 99.

(2012), 627-636.

McDaniel P.R., 'The impact of trade agreements on tax systems' in *International and Comparative Taxation: Essays in Honour of Klaus Vogel* (2002),151-162.

Pearson M., 'Trade Facilitation in the COMESA-EAC-SDAC Tripartite Free Trade Area' (2011) Tralac Working Paper No. SIIWPII,'2011

Perry GM., 'Taxes, Tax Subsidies and the Impact of Trade Agreements' (1995) Review of Marketing and Agricultural Economics Vol. 63(1), 155-163

Pfister M., 'Taxation for Investment and Development: An overview of policy challenges in Africa' (2009) Ministerial Meeting and Expert Roundtable NEPAD-OECD Africa Investment Initiative; available at www.oecd.org/dataoecd/44/43/43966821.pdf

SADC Free Trade Area Handbook, 2008 Gaborone, Botswana: SADC.

SADC Protocol on Finance and Investment, 2006 signed in Maseru, Lesotho: SADC.

SADC Memorandum of Understanding on Co-operation in Taxation and Related Matters, 2002 signed in Pretoria, South Africa: SADC.

SADC Protocol on Trade, 1996 signed in Maseru, Lesotho: SADC.

SADC Protocol on Trade in Services, 2012 signed in Maputo, Mozambique: SADC.

SADC Treaty signed at Windhoek, Namibia on 17 August 1992, entering into force on 30 September 1993. The Treaty was amended at Blantyre, Malawi in August 2001.

SADC website www.sadc.int

Sandrey R., 'An analysis of the SADC Free Trade Area' (2013) tralac Trade Brief Stellenbosch: tralac www.tralac.org

Saurombe A., 'The SADC trade agenda, a tool to facilitate regional commercial law: An analysis' (2009) *SA Mercantile Law Journal* Vol 21 (5) pp. 695-709.

Saurombe A., 'Regional Integration Agenda for SADC 'Caught in the winds of change: Problems and Prospects' (2009) *Journal of International Commercial Law and Technology* Vol 4 (2),100-106.

Saurombe A., 'The Sadc Trade agenda, a tool to facilitate regional commercial law: an analysis' in Dimande A.C, Cistac G. & Minega C.E. eds, *Regional Integration, Rule of Law and Development: Lessons from SADC Experiences* (2012) Vol. 1, 321 -338.

Slemrod J. & Avi-Yonah R., '(How) Should Trade Agreements deal with Income Tax issues?' (2001-2002) 55 *N.Y.U. Tax Law Review*, 533-544.

Tsikata Y., 'Southern Africa: Trade, Liberalisation and Implications for a Free Trade Area' (2000) Trade & Industry Monitor Vol 13,14

Understanding on rules and Procedures Governing the settlement of Disputes", 15 April 1994, Marrakesh Agreement Establishing the World Trade Organisation Geneva: WTO

Viljoen W., 'Non-tariff barriers affecting trade in the COMESA-EAC-SADC Tripartite Free Trade Agreement' (2011) Tralac Trade Brief Stellenbosch: Tralac. www.tralac.org

World Trade Organisation, Agreement on Subsidies and Countervailing Measures, 1994 15 April 1994 Marrakesh: WTO www.wto.org/ english/ docs_e/legal_e/legal_e.htm

World Trade Organisation, *Final Act Embodying the results of the Uruguay Round on Multilateral Trade Negotiations* 15 April 1994 (WTO Agreement) Marrakesh: WTO www.wto.org/english/docs_e/legal_e/legal_e.htm

World Trade Organisation, General Agreement on Tariffs and Trade (GATTS), 1994 Marrakesh: WTO www.wto.org/ english/docs_e/legal_e/legal_e.htm

World Trade Organisation, General Agreement on Trade in Services (GATS) 15 April 1994 Marrakesh: WTO www.wto.org/ english/docs_e/legal_e/legal_e. htm

11   Annex 1 – Map of SADC countries

10 Developing a Customs Agents Compliance Behaviour Model in relation to Import Tax in Malaysia: A Study inspired by the Theory of Planned Behaviour

Mirza Mohamed, Andrew Grainger and Jane Guinery

Abstract

This chapter extends tax compliance literature with a view to understanding the determinant factors in the prediction of compliance behaviour of customs agents (tax preparers), focusing on import declaration in the context of import tax. The main objective of this chapter is to present the first part of the two phases of exploratory sequential mixed method research design applied in designing a compliance behaviour model (CBM) that is developed within the framework of the Theory of Planned Behaviour (TPB). The first phase of this chapter focuses on the development of a CBM through an incremental study which was grounded in both tax compliance and related literature and a qualitative approach using the interview method. Eight customs agents and three head of customs and logistics associations took part in the interviews with the aim at identifying additional factors that could be incorporated into the CBM. The findings of the interviews identified 3 additional factors: (i) complexity of procedure (ii) quality of service (iii) fair share in paying taxes. These were incorporated into the existing compliance model to predict compliance behaviour. The finding of the first phase (qualitative phase) of this research shows that there is an alternative approach that is useful in identifying additional determinants factors in tax compliance studies for the purpose of developing a compliance model other than one which purely literature grounded. The detailed findings and implications of this research are considered in this chapter.

1 Introduction

Import tax is one indirect tax regime which is imposed on the importation of goods from other countries. On average, indirect tax (value added tax, sales tax and import tax account for 30% of all revenue collected by governments (OECD, 2012). In the Malaysian context, Royal Malaysian Customs Department (RMCD) is the second most important tax collection agency after the Malaysian Inland Revenue Board (IRB). Indirect tax collected by RMCD represents an average of 30% of revenue, or RM28 billion (GBP5 billion) a year (using a 10 years average from 2003 to 2012) collected from duty and taxes. This revenue is important to the government in funding government administrative and operating expenditure.

Administering a tax system is a challenging task for any tax administration, especially when it faces the issue of non-compliance which is commonly associated with the tax gap[1] (James & Alley, 2002). Although non-compliance is sometimes an intentional act which deliberately understates tax, in many cases, it is unintentional due to lack of knowledge, ignorance, mistake in tax reporting or complexity in the tax system itself (Brand, 1996). According to RMCD, the non-compliance associated with under-declaration of import taxes has resulted in losses of revenue amounting to RM8bil (GBP1.4 billion) in uncollected duties and taxes yearly (The Star, 2012). Studies and reports have indicated that non-compliance, such as indirect tax evasion, is prominent in developing countries and leads to significant revenue losses. Studies also suggest that, currently, about 50% of income tax and 23% of indirect taxes are evaded in developing countries, which shows a significant percentage of tax gap (Engel, Galetovic, & Raddatz, 2001).

Published studies and reports indicated that tax non-compliance such as tax evasions are prominent in developing countries and involves significant revenue losses. Studies suggest that about 50% of the income tax and 23% of indirect taxes are evaded, which is significantly high at about 6% of GDP, compared to tax revenues at 18% of GDP in developing countries (Engel, Galetovic, & Raddatz, 2001).

Evidence shows that an individual case may involve over USD50 million of import tax losses due to acts of non-compliance, such as an incorrect declaration, in order to reduce tax liability (Johnson, 2011). Other factors that may affect import taxes are misclassifications of customs tariff codes, under-declarations of value, under-declarations of goods and falsifying documents (Johnson, 2011; Chia, 2010; Uzzaman and Yusuf, 2010). Cases of this nature are reported almost monthly in the relevant trade press with

---

1 The tax gap is the difference between the amounts of tax that should be legally reported against the actual tax reported to the authority (James & Alley, 2002).

the latest case involving an import scam in the UK, which amounted to GBP 1.3million, involving an Irish garlic importer. In this case, garlic was labelled, incorrectly, as apple in order to avoid the higher duty of up to 232% which might be imposed on garlic (BBC News, 2012). Such acts of non-compliance affect revenue collection, a country's image and reputation, hinder foreign direct investment (FDI) and pose a threat to social justice {Formatting Citation}{Formatting Citation}{Formatting Citation}(Torgler, 2003; Wenzel, 2007). They may also interfere with a tax administration's ability to meet its objectives (Andreoni et al., 1998; Murphy, 2005; Wenzel, 2007) and may lead, ultimately, to the paralysis or ineffectiveness of a tax system (Silver, 1995).

An initial investigation with Malaysian Customs officials, showed that customs agents are, on occasions, responsible for losses in revenue collection due to the deliberate act of understating tax. A Customs agent is an important intermediary between importers and government agencies, such as a customs department. In a developed country, such as the United States, more than 58% of clearance of import cargo was outsourced to a third party logistic provider i.e. to a customs broker or customs agent to handle clearance of cargo (Lieb & Bentz, 2005). In Malaysia, the interviews that were conducted revealed that 90% of cargo clearance was contracted out to customs agents. However, according to Malaysian customs officials, the causes and reasons underlying non-compliance, whether intentional or unintentional, are still unknown to RMCD despite the introduction of measures such as increased penalties and improved enforcement.

To address the challenges of non-compliance, it is necessary to identify factors that influence the decision to comply, or otherwise, with tax laws. The research undertaken, therefore, sought to understand the phenomenon of non-compliance in import tax declarations among customs agents. It aimed to do so in three ways: (1) by exploring the factors associated with compliance through an examination of relevant tax literature; (2) by conducting interviews with customs agents and the heads of state associations with a view to identifying new dimensions of tax compliance; (3) by applying the Theory of Planned Behaviour (TPB) in understanding the factors discovered in (1) and (2) with import tax compliance behaviour.

This chapter is structured as follows. The next section provides an introduction to import tax and the role of customs agents in its collection. It also briefly discusses tax compliance determinants in an indirect tax environment and the underlying theory that was selected for this research. The following sections cover, respectively, the development of a model development grounded in the literature, the exploratory sequential mixed method and first phase of a qualitative approach, and the findings of the interviews together with an analysis of the incorporation of various identified constructs within the TPB model. Finally, some brief conclusions are offered.

2 Literature Review

2.1 Import Tax and the Role of Customs Agents

What is import tax? Generally, import tax refers to taxes charged or levied when importers bring goods into a customs territory ("Malaysian Customs Act," 1967; WCO, 2006). It is categorised as an indirect tax in the same way as VAT (Value Added Tax) or GST (Goods and Services Tax).

Import tax may consist of import duty, excise duty and/or sales tax/VAT. Depending on the type of product, not all products attract these three elements of tax. For instance, for tobacco, the duty rate is 350% in the United States whereas, in Malaysia, there are three elements of duty which consist of import duty (30%), excise duty (90%) and sales tax (10%). Duty rates are determined by the type of product and its classification under under the customs tariff. In total, there are 21 sections, which consist of 99 chapters under the standard customs tariff classification. This tariff classification is the standard classification, which is commonly referred to as the Harmonised System Customs Tariff Nomenclature Classification , and is applied by customs administrations throughout the world. For instance, excise duty is levied on selected products namely cigarettes, tobacco products, alcoholic beverages, playing cards, mah jong tiles and motor vehicles. Such duty is imposed on imported products. It has to be paid in advance and before goods can be released. (RMCD, 2011

Customs clearance procedure at a border involves several processes such as physical inspection, classification of goods according to the customs tariff code, verification of country of origin and valuation of goods. Two international bodies administer these rules: (1) the World Customs Organization (WCO) on customs tariff classification; and (2) the World Trade Organization (WTO) on country of origin (C.O.O) and valuation of goods. From a commercial perspective, dealing with border agencies, such as customs departments, often involves extensive customs regulations and time-consuming border checks which persuade businesses to outsource the task of clearance to specialists or agents, such as customs agents or freight forwarders (Appeals & Swielande, 1998; Sawhney & Sumukadas, 2005).

Agents, as portrayed in Diagram 10.1, act as intermediaries who receive documentation from their client (the importer), lodge a declaration in terms of the value of the goods, describe the goods, and, finally a make a payment on behalf of their client to the customs department. Based on this declaration, a customs official will verify the tariff classification of the imported goods and calculate the duty that is to be paid (the assessment). This calculation is based on the tariff classification of the product. Once the duty has been calculated and paid by the importer (through the agents) the goods will be released from customs control.

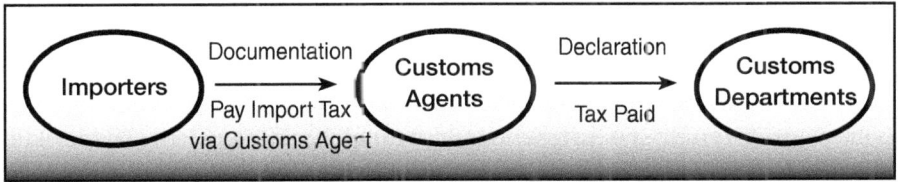

Diagram 10.1: process flow and import tax payment process

Source: (RMCD, 2012)

2.2 Tax compliance determinants

Previous research has identified several factors that are associated with tax compliance some of which are associated with the economic and non-economic determinants of tax compliance. Although there is no specific compliance behaviour study conducted in the field of import tax, lessons may be learned from tax compliance studies conducted in direct tax and other indirect tax fields.

Alm identified twelve factors that are associated with tax compliance determinants (Alm, 1991). These included audit, deterrence, taxpayers' education and service, change in tax law and positive incentives, such as material rewards, as well as factors that reinforced or increased the satisfaction of taxpayers such as pride, attitude, and identification with recognition by valuing others. Subsequently, others have suggested further factors. Wallschutzky (1993) added ignorance of the law, poor advice given by tax agents/revenue authorities, uncertainty or ambiguity of tax law, unfairness of the tax system and increases in tax rates. More recently, researchers have drawn attention to tax morale, knowledge, taxpayers' communication and cultural factors (Chan, Troutman, & O'Bryan, 2000; Chau, 2009; Palil, 2010; Torgler, 2003).

The focus of the above studies was mainly on direct tax where business income and individual income are a concern in relation to the reporting and payment of tax to revenue authorities. However, there is a lack of empirical evidence indicating to what extent the factors identified in relation to compliance influence customs agents' decisions to comply, or otherwise, with import tax laws. However, such factors have been tested in the indirect tax environment of VAT/GST and Sales Tax. In a study of indirect taxation, Adams and Webley, (2001) have demonstrated that tax compliance determinants such as penalties, sanctions, morale and perception of the tax authority are relevant to compliance in an indirect tax environment. Therefore, as relevant factors have been tested in relation to both direct and indirect tax compliance studies, it is submitted that they may also be tested and extended to compliance with import tax.

In researching import tax compliance, this research used the TPB the model. This was done because (1) it offers an alternative solution in understanding the determinants of tax compliance that include psychological and sociological dimension (2) it offers a more accurate prediction of actual behaviour through the prediction of behavioural intention (3) the TPB is open to any variables and can be expanded to best explain a particular situation. In tax compliance studies, the TPB has also been adopted by other tax compliance researchers, namely Bobek (1997), Bobek, Hatfield, et al., (2007) and Trivedi et al. (2005).

2.3 The Theory of Planned Behaviour

The TPB is a theory within social psychology. It is an extension of the Theory of Reason Actions (TRA) that was introduced by Ajzen, (1985), which is a well-known theory and one that has often been applied to explain various behavioural situations. It also incorporates a third construct, namely perceived behavioural control (PBC), to account for situations where an individual lacks substantial control over the target behaviour.

According to the TPB, an individual's behaviour is determined by an intention (I) to perform the behaviour. Intention is determined by a person's attitude (A), subjective norms (SNs) and perceived behavioural control (PBC). Behavioural intention refers to an individual's willingness to carry out a particular behaviour, and is an antecedent of behaviour. Ajzen, (2005) defines attitude towards behaviour as the degree to which an individual has a favourable or unfavourable evaluation of the behaviour in question. SNs are the influence of social pressure on the individual, and they operate as a function of beliefs i.e. normative beliefs. Finally, PBC reflects the perceived ability to execute the target behaviour (Ajzen, 2005).

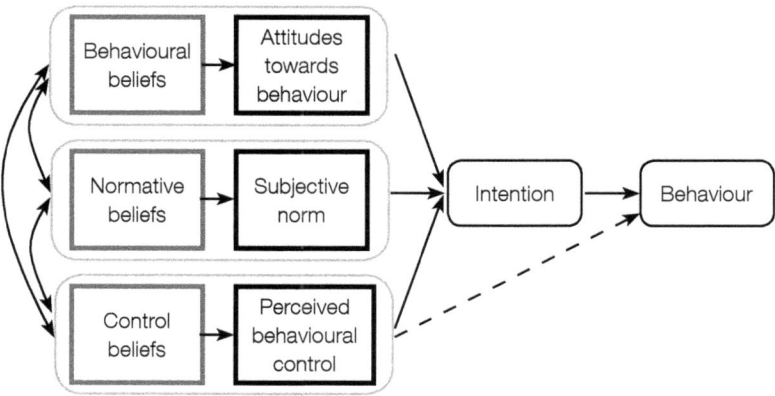

Diagram 10.2: The Theory of Planned Behaviour (TPB). From Attitudes, personality and behaviour, Ajzen, I., 2005, Open University Press, NY, USA, pg. 126.

The TPB model has also been applied in various non-tax fields such as the compliance of drivers with speed limits (Elliott, Armitage, & Baughan, 2003; Poulter, Chapman, Bibby, Clarke, & Crundall, 2008), tourist behaviour (Lee, 2011) and IT adoption (Huang & Chuang, 2007; Taylor & Todd, 1995).

3 Research Model Development

The research model developed in this chapter (see Diagram 10.4 below) includes the hypotheses to be tested. It is grounded in the relevant literature and interview findings. These hypotheses, which are examined in the next section, are based on the proposition that attitudes, SNs, perceived behavioural control and the other determinants of import tax compliance behavior, i.e. influence of the importer, influence of other agents, ethics, knowledge, law, law enforcement, service quality, fair share in paying taxes and complexity of procedure influence the customs agents' intention to comply (or not to comply) with import tax law.

4 Theory of Planned Behaviour Constructs

4.1 Intention and Import Tax Compliance

Ajzen and Fishbein, (1980) define intention as a description of cognitive readiness to perform a behaviour. Intention is a willingness to try to do something (Ajzen, 1991). The TPB clarifies that intention is the most influential factor on behaviour and posits that it is the intermediary (mediator) between attitude and the SN in relation to behaviour. Baron and Kenny, (1986) define a mediator as "The generative mechanism through which the focal independent variable is able to influence the dependent variable of interest...(and)...Mediation is best done in the case of a strong relation between the predictor and criterion variable". The mediator, according to Sekaran & Bougie, (2011) is a variable that appears between the time when independent variables operate to influence the dependent variable and, moreover, it affects the dependent variable. This means that the influence of attitudes and SNs on behaviour depends on the intention of a person to perform a behaviour.

The Literature shows that intention is an immediate antecedent and the mediator of attitudes and social influences on behaviour (Ajzen, 2005). Studies by Bagozzi and Warshaw, (1990), and Schifter and Ajzen, (1985) support the existence of a positive relationship between intention and behaviour. A report by Sheppard, Hartwick, and Warshaw, (1988) showed that a total of 87 studies using the TRA as a framework had found that intention has a significant relationship with behaviour. Studies related specifically to non-tax behaviour also support the influence of intention on behaviour. These include the behaviour in relation to condom use (Godin and Kok, 1996), compliance with speed limits (Elliott et al., 2003), blood donations (Giles and Cairns, 1995), engaging in leisure activities (Ajzen and Driver, 1992), the use of information technology (Taylor and Todd, 1995), consumption of soy product (Rah et al., 2004), and the purchase of electronic goods (Pavlou and Fygenson, 2006). In this research, it was anticipated that intention would be the most appropriate measure for determining the customs agents' compliance behaviour, and that intention would also act as a mediator between attitudes, SNs, and perceived behaviour control. Consequently, the following hypotheses are proposed:

H1 : Customs agents' behavioural intention to comply will influence their tax compliance behaviour

Influence Of Attitude

Attitude as suggested by Ajzen, (2005) fulfils an important role in influencing human behaviour. Attitude comprises the elements of cognitive, affective and behaviour each of which are bound together and inseparable as an object of attitude (see, Aronson and Pratkanis, 1993). Attitude is also believed to have a direct impact on behaviour intentions. This is because attitude is a key element in making a decision (Ajzen, 2005). Compliance behaviour in relation to import tax depends on a positive attitude among members of the public to tax and legal institutions concerned with the tax. The positive attitude based on feelings, civic duty and moral obligation or referred to as tax morale has a significant influence on tax compliance behaviour (Cummings et al., 2009; Hanno and Violette, 1996; Kirchler, 2007; Torgler, 2011).

Attitude towards tax compliance also relates to the individual assessment of whether to comply (or not comply) with a tax obligation. This assessment is based on the perception that a behavioural outcome would be favourable (or not) and improve emotional belief in relation to compliance with a tax obligation. Thus, the attitude of customs agents covers their assessment based on feelings, civic duty and moral obligation of whether to comply or not to comply with tax law would be perceived as beneficial or disadvantageous.

The significant role of attitude on behavioural intention is explained by studies in various disciplines (see, for example, Bobek and Hatfield, 2003; Ross, Kohler, Grimley, and Anderson-Lewis, 2007; Taylor and Todd, 1995; Trivedi et al., 2005). Studies in the area of tax compliance have shown that an important variable in influencing behaviour is the attitude towards tax compliance, for example attitude towards intention to comply with sales tax payment (Bidin, et al., 2011) and attitude towards tax reporting (Trivedi et al., 2005). Thus, attitudes towards compliance with import tax are expected to have a significant positive relationship with the intention to comply or not comply with tax law. In this respect, the following hypotheses will be tested:

H2 : Attitude of customs agents towards tax compliance will significantly influence their tax compliance intention

4.2 Influence of Subjective Norms (SNs)

A subjective norm may be defined as the influence of a third party on others or commonly refers to the influence of close referent groups such as family, friends, colleagues and business acquaintances Ajzen, (1991). The referent group plays a significant role in determining and influencing intention and the performance of specific behaviour. The stance adopted by a reference group may vary depending on the situation and its particular position.

Previous studies have supported the view that subjective norms have a positive and significant impact on behavioural intentions. Direct tax literature demonstrates that SNs play an important role in influencing behavioural intention (see, Bobek and Hatfield, (2003). Further, Hanno and Violette (1996); and Trivedi et al., (2005) have also reported that SNs positively and significantly influence behavioural intentions in relation to tax compliance. Meanwhile, Bobek et al. (2005) have demonstrated that SNs affect the behaviour intention of taxpayers with regard to tax refunds or overpaid tax. In other disciplines, such as information technology and marketing, the positive and significant influence of SNs on behavioural intentions has also been recognized (Bonne, Vermeir, Bergeaud-Blackler. and Verbeke, 2007; Pavlou and Fygenson, 2006; Taylor and Todd, 1995).

The influence of referent groups may not only have a significant impact on behavioural intention but also on ethics (Cindy Blanthorne & Kaplan, 2008; Chau, 2009; Wenzel, 2005). Different referent groups and ethical values will form a different level of motivation towards tax compliance (Chau, 2009). Taxpayers' ethical values which be influenced by the close referent groups and this may deter taxpayers from engaging in tax evasion (Cindy Blanthorne & Kaplan, 2008). In the context of import tax, the influence of reference groups is expected to have a strong influence on importer's behavioural intention and their ethical stance towards tax compliance. Researchers (see, for example, Ajzen & Fishbein, 1980) have also measured the subjective norm within various referent groups. This research has indicated that a decomposition must be made within referent groups because the views or opinions of individuals within the referent group may vary. Moreover, some researchers have divided referent groups into two groups based on a distinction drawn between primary and secondary normative beliefs respectively (see, for example, Bidin et al, 2011; Chu and Wu, 2004). This approach was followed by Chu and Wu (2004); Taylor and Todd (1995) in their studies of local sales tax. Moreover, this division into two categories was justified by Bidin et al., (2011) in the context of taxation on the ground that there may be distinctive actors within a referent group, for example, tax agents as representatives of primary normative belief and collegues in other companies, who are responsible for managing sales tax affairs, influential within the context of secondary normative belief. Finally, it has been demonstrated that the role of a third party in a primary referrent group, for example, tax preparers and account preparers may be particularly influencial in a taxpayer's decision about compliance/non-compliance (see, Hai and See, 2011a, 2011b; Klepper, Mazur, and Nagin, 1991).

In the import tax environment, the role of customs agents as the interface between importers and a customs administration is apparent. The often complex customs and port procedures relating to the clearance of goods at borders necessitate the use of the expertise and advice afforded to importers by customs agents. In this respect, it is also possible that the importer's attitude will, in turn, influence the decisions about compliance/non-compliance made by the customs agents.

In the light of the above observations about the influence of referent groups and/or SNs on behaviour intentions, the following proposed initial hypotheses may be tested (with, as will be seen, some subsequent redefinition when interview findings are taken into account, see, p.211):

H3a : Customs agents' primary referent group will positively influence their tax compliance intention

H3b : Customs agents' primary referent group will positively influence their ethical belief towards tax compliance intention

H4a : Customs agents' secondary referent group will positively influence their tax compliance intention

H4b : Customs agents' secondary referent group will positively influence their ethical belief towards tax compliance intention

4.3 Influence Of Perceived Behaviour Control

Perceived behavioural control (PBC) is defined as the perceived ability to execute target behaviour (Ajzen, 2005). PBC variables play an important role in influencing behavioural intentions as recognised in the theory of TPB. In the area of tax compliance, PBC not only refers to the factors that encourage or hinder compliance with tax obligation in general, but also to whether an individual believes he or she is able to control a specific behaviour (Bobek and Hatfield, 2003). These two aspects: the encouragement (or hindrance factor) and the control factor in performing a particular behaviour (often referred to as self-efficacy and controllability respectively) (Ajzen, 2002; Francis, Eccles, & Johnston, 2004; Kraft, Rise, Sutton, & Roysamb, 2005).

The terms 'self-efficacy' and 'controllability' are also, in turn, known as 'perceived difficulty' which refers to the extent to which behaviour is perceived to be easy or difficult for an individual to perform and 'perceived control' which refers to the extent to which the behaviour is perceived to be under an individual's voluntary control (Sparks, 1997; Trafimow, Sheeran, Conner, & Finlay, 2002). The controllability or 'perceived control' aspect of PBC relates to factors such as the constraints, opportunity, resources and finance which determine the desired behaviour (Carrington, Neville, & Whitwell, 2010; Chang, 1998; Sideridis, Kaissidis, & Padeliadu, 1998).

In the context of import tax, PBC relates to the ease or difficulty of complying with import declaration under the controllability factor and takes into account the opportunity to evade import tax payment and the financial situation. Here, if the customs agents perceive that there are opportunities to evade tax they may understate tax in the import declaration. On the other hand, if the customs agents perceive that there are few opportunities to evade tax they are more likely to comply to complete the import declaration accurately. Thus, the PBC of customs agents toward import tax can be expected to have a significant positive relationship with the intention to comply with tax law and their related behaviour. In the light of this, the following hypotheses will be tested

H5a : Customs agents' perceived behavioural control will significantly influence their tax compliance intention

H5b : Customs agents' perceived behavioural control will significantly influence their tax compliance behaviour

5 Additional Constructs To The Model

5.1 Law and enforcement

One of the factors that may affect the intention to comply is the perception of law and enforcement undertaken by RMCD. The law is an instrument to control and draw the power of an institution. Law should be administered and enforced by the governing institutions such as a customs administration in the context of indirect taxation. The Customs Act 1967 indicates that penalties and fines will be imposed for those who fail to pay or avoid paying taxes. If there is failure in payment the penalties and duties in section 123 of this Act could lead to imprisonment. Such punishment is seen as a lesson to the public about the effects and consequences that will follow if an offence is committed. This can also ensure that people perform their duties according to law (Devos, 2007; Langham, Paulsen, & Hartel, 2012). The effect of enforcement on compliance is such that increased enforcement efforts will increase compliance levels (Davis, Hecht, & Perkins, 2003; Hanno & Violette, 1996).

Several studies in taxation have investigated the relationship between the perception of law and enforcement of compliance behaviour. Among the early researchers to explore the variables of law enforcement are Allingham and Sandmo, (1972), who used economic crime to explain and predict the taxpayer behaviour. According to them, in the case of a tax evader if the fine imposed is heavy, this will increase tax compliance. This view is supported by (Murphy, 2005; Virmani, 1989) whose research findings indicate that penalty rates and action to impose financial penalties on those who evade tax may be the best way to prevent evasion from recurring. This statement is consistent with deterrence theory, which indicates that individuals will try to avoid doing an act which is wrong if a valid sentence (legal punishment) is heavy and swiftly executed (Sutinen & Kuperan, 1999). In contrast, there are also studies that have indicated that penalty rates have a negative association with tax evasion (Marrelli & Martina, 1988; Marrelli, 1984).

Meanwhile, a study conducted by Trivedi et al., (2005) found that increasing audit rates increase tax compliance in declarations. This finding is supported by Alm et al., (1995) who found that the number of audits and the fine imposed is closely related to compliance behaviour - the higher the level of audit carried out the greater is taxpayer compliance. However, Ho and Wong (2006) found high levels of non-compliance when rates low penalties are imposed. This is because the low penalty is not seen as a burden to taxpayers involved in tax evasion. A study conducted by Wenzel (2007) found that detection and punishment imposed on those who avoid paying taxes is not influential and can be doubted because individual social factors also influence behaviour. Bobek and Hatfield (2003) found that individuals who do not comply tend to have a negative attitude towards the penalty imposed and to the legality or otherwise of the conduct.

Based on these previous studies, law enforcement has been found to influence intentions and the behaviour of individuals in relation to tax compliance. However, the majority of these studies related to direct rather than indirect taxation. Accordingly, this chapter expects that the customs law and customs enforcement will affect import tax compliance intentions in line with the TPB, with intention as an intermediary factor. Therefore, the following hypotheses will be tested:

H6a : Perception of law will positively influence the customs agents' tax compliance intention

H6b : Perception of law will positively influence the customs agents' tax compliance behaviour

H7a : Perception of law enforcement will positively influence the customs agents' tax compliance intention

H7b : Perception of law enforcement will positively influence the customs agents' tax compliance behaviour

5.2 Knowledge

Knowledge is expected to influence the behaviour of customs agents with regard to import tax compliance. According to Eriksen and Fallan, (1996), the level of knowledge of tax laws is important as a source of reference for the existing tax system and it can influence the attitude of a taxpayer towards tax compliance. Early tax compliance studies found a positive relationship between knowledge of the legal system relating to taxation and tax compliance behaviour (Palil, 2010; Nor Aziah, 2004; Eriksen and Fallan, 1996). These studies also found that an understanding of tax legislation influenced compliance attitudes. Accordingly, individuals will be more compliant with knowledge and act in accordance with legal requirements relating to tax declarations (Palil, 2010; Nor Aziah, 2004).

The influence of knowledge on behavior, as reported in the tax field, is also evident in other research areas such as insurance (Lin and Chen, 2006), online banking (Karjaluto et al., 2002) and information behaviour (Brucks, 1985). Based on such previous studies, it can be stated that knowledge of behavioural intentions and of behaviour influence the adherence of individuals in matters such as taxes. However, previous studies in tax have only focused on the behaviour not on behavioural intention. Consistent with the TPB, which emphasizes the role of intention, appropriate variables are tested for knowledge of intention to see the impact on import tax compliance. Therefore, the following hypothesis will be tested:

H8 : Customs agents' level of knowledge will significantly influence their tax compliance intention.

5.3 Ethics

Ethical is defined as the normative rules which give guidance on social environment and relationships between individuals in society (Recker et al., 1994). Past studies have evidenced that ethics is an important determinant of tax compliance (Bobek, 1997; Henderson and Kaplan, 2005; Jackson and Milliron, 1986; Wenzel, 2007) rather than, for example, financial self-interest (Roth et al., 1989). Conventional tax compliance models of taxpayer behaviour largely overlook the ethical aspect of tax compliance (Eisenhauer, 2008). Some researchers emphasize individual internal factors (such as moral factors) in their studies because these factors can affect compliance (Hanno and Violette, 1996).

Based on the findings of previous studies, ethics have a significant impact on improving tax compliance (Alm & Torgler, 2011; Blanthorne, 2013; Bobek,

1997; Jackson and Milliron, 1986; Wenzel, 2007). This is because taxpayers may feel that tax evasion is immoral behaviour. Bobek (1997) found a consistent moral obligation influenced taxpayer compliance. He found that the stronger the moral obligation not to cheat, the greater was the individual's intention to comply. Wenzel (2007) found that taxpayers who define themselves as having high ethical values (tax favourable ethics) would feel culpable if they were to be involved in evading tax and apprehended by the tax authorities. This statement is supported by Henderson and Kaplan (2005) who found that an individual's ethical evaluation communicated directly with tax compliance. A study by Recker et al., (1994) also indicated that individual moral beliefs significantly influence tax compliance. In a study of indirect tax, Bidin et al., (2011) demonstrated that ethics have a strong influence on the intention to comply with a local sales tax.

There is also empirical evidence which suggests that ethical values may play a significant role in the compliance attitudes of taxpayers. So, individuals with high ethical values may have a positive compliance attitude because they will assume that compliance with tax law is a moral obligation (Ho and Wong, 2008). Similarly, a study conducted in three European multicultural countries indicated a strong relationship between moral obligations or tax ethics and the attitude of taxpayers towards compliance with tax law (Torgler and Schneider, 2007). This finding has support the finding of a further study which indicated that the level of tax compliance is higher when there is a stronger belief that tax evasion is unethical (Reckers et al., 1994). Indeed, ethical belief may the best means of improving tax compliance (Bobek and Hatfield, 2003).

In summary and based on these previous studies, the ethics of an individual plays an important role in influencing attitude and behavioural intentions. However, in the context of indirect taxes, notwithstanding the work of researchers such as Bidin et al., (2011), the influence of ethics is still under-explored. Consequently, this variable is tested to understand the influence of ethics on attitudes towards tax compliance. Therefore, the following hypotheses will be tested:

H9a : The ethical belief of customs agents towards tax compliance will significantly influence their tax compliance intention

H9b : The ethical belief of customs agents towards tax compliance will significantly influence their attitude and tax compliance intention

6 Method

6.1 Exploratory Sequential Mixed Methods Research Design

The research design applied for the purposes of this chapter is the two-phase exploratory mixed methods sequential design (Creswell, 2009). The first sequence is the qualitative approach was conducted through interviews in phase one. The second sequence is the quantitative approach that was conducted through a survey questionnaire in phase two. This chapter will concentrate on the first sequence of the mixed method research design.

Phase one was an exploratory qualitative study conducted with eight customs forwarding agents and three head of customs and logistics associations. The objective of this phase was to define and ascertain the dimensions of import tax compliance and to use the TPB as the model in understanding compliance behaviour. This was accomplished within the constructs identified in the literature review and then corroborated through interviews wherein customs forwarding agents were asked to describe their experiences and perceptions of import tax compliance.

Phase one was a design exploration phase. Its purpose was to explore in depth a topic or phenomeron through qualitative methods and then to generalize the result through a larger sample of quantitative designs. Such design exploration is essential due to the lack of empirical work that is needed to identify the dimensions of tax compliance from the perspectives of customs agents in their role as indirect tax agents/tax preparers. For the purposes of this chapter, variance associated with the design of sequential exploration was used to help with model development and improvement to instruments within the theory development framework

In this regard, Creswell, (2009) defined the collecting, analyzing, and incorporating of both qualitative and quantitative data in a series of research studies. As indicated above, the research underlying this chapter combined two research methods using both qualitative and quantitative data. However, the type of mixed design method used for this study is exploration. This design was chosen because the initial phase involving qualitative data collection and analysis was followed by a quantitative data collection phase and analysis (Bryman, 2006). Greater emphasis or weight was placed on the quantitative methods in Phase Two. The findings of the qualitative phase helped develop and inform the quantitative phase.

In other areas such as sociology, communications and the medical field, the use of mixed methods is a long-standing. However, using mixed-method research within a tax compliance study is a relatively new paradigm. Traditionally, research in relation to tax compliance has followed the primary route of survey method, laboratory experiments and economic analysis (Cummings et al., 2009; Torgler, 2003). Diagram 10.3 illustrates the steps that are followed in sequential research design.

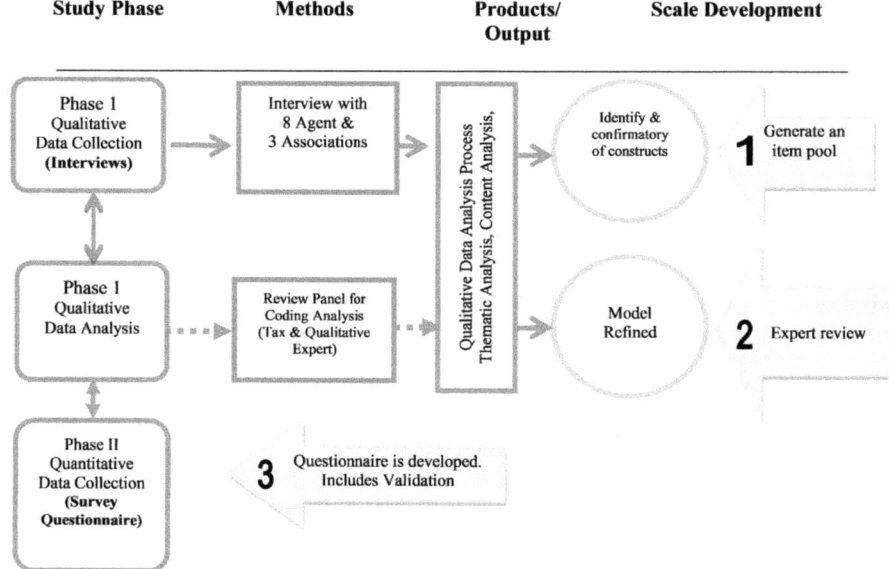

Diagram 10.3: Visualization of steps of the sequential research design. Source: Author

6.2 Qualitative Phase (Phase 1)

6.2.1 Interviews

The collection of qualitative data is part of the exploratory sequential mixed method. This qualitative data in understanding the phenomenon was obtained through semi-structured interviews (Bryman, 1989). The interviews were part of the mixed–method phase as the issues are extremely difficult to investigate solely through questionnaires (Vanderstoep & Johnston, 2009). The interviews provided the opportunity to ascertain the respondents' views on and thoughts on import tax compliance.

Potential interviewees were sourced from the database of forwarding agents held by RMCD. A total of eight interviews were conducted with customs agents and three were held with the respective heads of customs forwarding agents and logistics associations. Initially, the Respondents were sent an email advising them of the survey and seeking their support and willingness to participate. The email was followed with a telephone call seeking a suitable time for an interview. Prior to the interview, a questionnaire was emailed to each interviewee to aid the understanding of questions and to allow interviewees time to think about their responses prior to the interview.

The interviews started by establishing a rapport between the interviewer and interviewee and with a view to putting interviewees at ease. The interview then continued with investigating interviewees' views on improper customs declaration by customs agents. Reference was made to the open-ended questionnaire which had been developed to focus discussion on salient issues during interviews, whilst at the same time encouraging the interviewees to talk freely and to include other aspects that they felt were important.

6.2.2 Analysis of interviews

The data analysis was carried out by content analysis through drawing up a list of coded categories and 'cutting and pasting' each segment of the transcribed data into one of these categories. In view of the small number of interviewees, this was done manually. This approach for small cohorts with limited data has been supported by Welsh (2002).

Further reading and analysis of the transcripts of the interviews and the identification of emergent themes allowed the categories identified in the coding process to be collapsed yielding broader, more inclusive themes. Clear and repetitive patterns became evident in the data suggesting that the objective of the research had been achieved. Following this analysis, an expert panel assessed the process used and verified the subsequent themes and categories identified from coding, comparing, and analyzing the interview data. The experts were tax academics and academic experts in qualitative methods.

7 Findings

Generally from the interview findings, the views of the interviewees on tax compliance could be subdivided into three categories: the customs agents, their clients and the institutional issues that influence compliance. Most of the interviewees described customs agents as falling into two groups: a compliant group and an ignorant group. The first group viewed import tax as important and supported the payment of import tax. The second group were risk-takers who regarded tax as a burden. Thus, this group sought to avoid tax and to pay as little tax as possible often through improper declarations. According to the interviewees, the RMCD should focus on this latter group. This group should be penalised heavily as the avoidance of tax was intentional. Licences to act as customs agents could be revoked thereby highlighting the consequences of their actions. Here, it is interesting to see that there are similarities with deterrence theory where an increase in punishment increases compliance.

7.1 Influence of importer (client) and other customs agents

The interviewees were also asked for their views about whether they were influenced by importers and other agents when completing their import declarations. The reaction to this question was mixed. However, it was acknowledged that importers have a strong influence on the customs agents' approach to the completion of import declarations. Among the responses were;

'We're being paid by the importer and as our client we normally try to meet our client need to be honest. I believe it goes the same with most agents.' (Interviewee 2)

'There are cases where the importer does not agree with the amount of tax calculated and if we can help them to reduce it.' (Interviewee 7)

'It's common in business, we try to save every penny and it (the?) same goes with the importer, always asking...can we pay slightly less tax? (Interviewee 5)

Some of the interviewees also mentioned that there is a possibility that customs agents might be influenced by each other leading to declarations to pay less tax.

'We operate in a community where almost everyone knows each other quite well. There is a possibility that they under-declare the tax amount because of competition and seeing other agents which did the same thing.' (Interviewee 1)

The interviewees also mentioned the role that institutions could play in making compliance easier. In this respect, their views could be related to three factors; (1) perception of front line service quality, (2) perception of fairness of tax contribution, and (3) complexity of procedure. Each of these factors is now considered.

7.2 Quality of service

Interviewees indicated that RMCD should look into its daily operations to improve the quality of front line services with a view to improving compliance among customs agents. It was felt that front line staff who assess customs import declarations are often incompetent, inefficient, lack knowledge and are too slow in processing customs import declarations.

The following responses are indicative;

'There are a lot of new officers who have lack of experience and don't even know how to classify goods according to customs tariff classifications.' (Interviewee 11)

'If customs want agents to comply with their requirement, customs must also comply with the client charter. If they promise the assessment process is 30mins please deliver within the time frame set.' (Interviewee 4)

'The same product that we declared being valued differently by different officers.' (Interviewee 6)

7.3 Fair share in paying taxes

When asked for their views on customs agents who under-declare tax, the interviewees mentioned that there are customs agents who under-declare tax. This could be solely for their own financial gain. It could also be due to deteriorating trust in the government as to how tax revenue is being spent. However, there was some recognition that there was a direct impact of government spending on development purposes. In this respect, the following responses are in point;

'I just wonder how the government spent all the tax that we have paid because there haven't been any upgraded work to this two-lane road that linked to the ..... port.' (Interviewee 7)

'I'm sure all the tax paid will be spent mostly for this coming election.' (Interviewee 10)

The interviewees' responses also indicated that there was a negative perception of where tax paid would be spent by government, especially in the context of a general election. The issue of tax was also regarded as a sensitive topic. However, there were also positive views about tax when the issue of under-declaration was raised:

'We must have the patriotism spirit for the government. Those who try to evade tax have no patriotism spirit and show no sign of care about our country.' (Interviewee 1)

'There are some out there who do not have the awareness about the important of tax for development. These are the ignorant category who just thinks about themselves.' (Interviewee 11)

7.4 Complexity of procedure

Interviewees also commented upon the import declaration procedure and the difficulties it creates for compliance. The import declaration procedure was viewed as being too rigid, difficult to adhere to, changed too frequently, without flexibility, requiring excessive documentation and imposing too many requirements.

The following are illustrative of some of the responses:

'Customs procedure is making us difficult to understand. The requirements are changing constantly.' (Interviewee 9)

'There's no uniformity in procedure between ports within the same states of .....' (Interviewee 8)

'Import declarations are now paperless but customs still require us to produce paper invois, bill of lading, packing list and so on.' (Interviewee 3)

The framework developed in Diagram 10.4 is the framework that builds upon the two stages that have been discussed in this chapter, namely the literature review and the qualitative findings of the research that was undertaken.

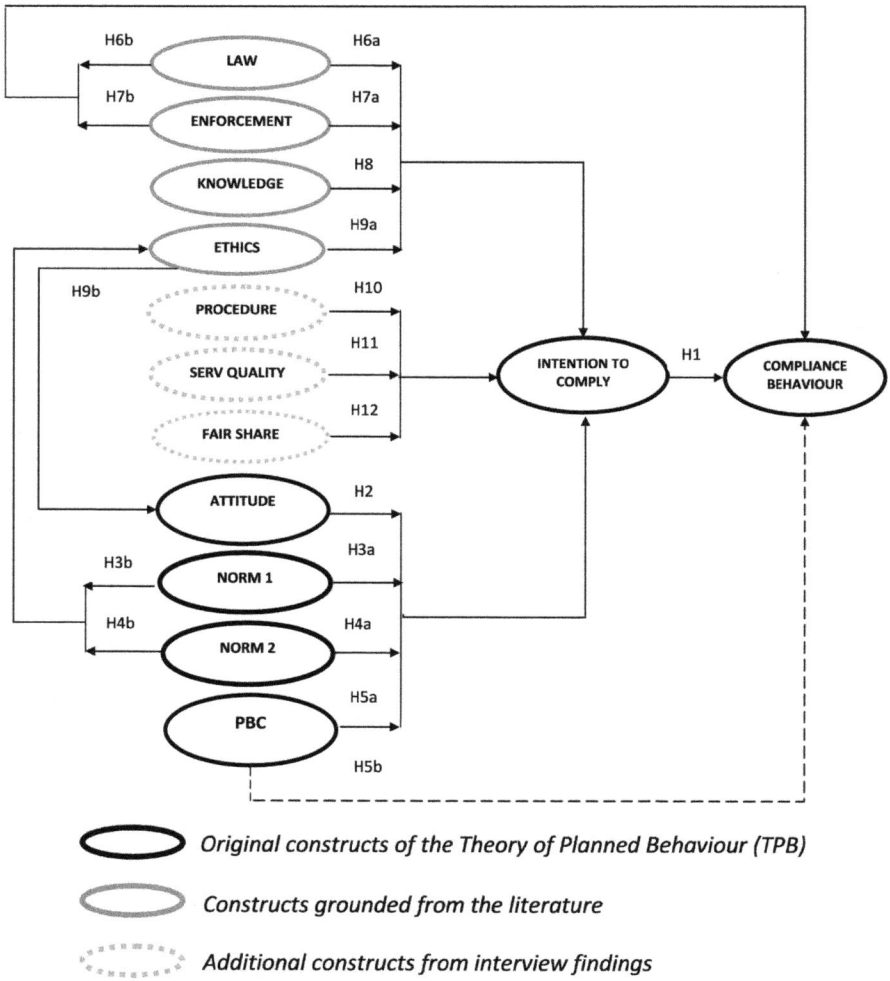

Diagram 10.4: Import Tax Compliance Behaviour Model (Decomposed TPB Model), adapted from the Theory of Planned Behaviour (TPB), Ajzen (1991).

As asserted by Ajzen, (2005), TPB can be decomposed and opened up to in order to include other variables. This enhances the understanding of the research. Hence, three factors, namely perception of service quality, perception of fairness of tax contribution and complexity of procedure may be added as PBC is constructed. The influence of the importer (client) and the influence of other customs agents may be identified as characteristics of a subjective norm within the primary and secondary referent group. Therefore, the following additional hypotheses may be tested:

H10 : Perception of procedure complexity will positively influence the customs agents' tax compliance intention

H11 : Perception of quality of service will positively influence the customs agents' tax compliance intention

H12 : Perception of exchange fairness will positively influence the customs agents' tax compliance intention

8 Conclusion

Despite the growing research interest in tax compliance behaviour, little attention has been devoted to understanding the compliance determinants in the area of import tax. Since most importers outsource the goods clearance process to customs agents relying on them to deal with customs clearance and tax payments, the behaviour of customs agents has been examined. This study sought to understand the compliance determinants of customs agents (tax preparers) in relation to customs import declarations.

Therefore, the purpose of this chapter was, first, to introduce import tax as a topic in indirect tax compliance to tax compliance literature and, secondly, to explore this topic through the two phases of exploratory sequential mixed method design and to identify new determinants factors that could be incorporated into an existing CBM that was developed within the framework of the TPB. This CBM was developed with reference to an extensive literature review in the field of tax compliance and relevant interdisciplinary literature. Qualitative research was also undertaken through interviews that were conducted with 8 customs agents and 3 heads of customs and logistics associations.

The findings of this qualitative study identified additional dimensions which may be predictors of the customs agents' compliance behaviour. These are (1) perception of quality of service; (2) perception of fairness of tax contribution; and (3) complexity of procedure.

Consequently, this chapter makes five main contributions:

1 Extending tax compliance literature in the relative *new research area of import tax* in indirect tax studies.

2   Understanding tax compliance behaviour from the perspective of *customs agents who adopt a dual role* as tax preparers as well as tax collectors/payers (intermediaries to the client/importer).

3   Adopting a *psychological and behavioural research approach* in tax compliance studies with the application of the behavioral theory of TPB.

4   Understanding the *determinants of compliance behaviour through qualitative interpretation*. Here, the findings of the first phase of this study show that there is an alternative approach that is useful in discovering additional determinant factors in tax compliance studies for the purpose of a developing compliance model that is other than purely literature grounded.

5   The *exploratory sequential mixed method research design* used in this study could be useful to other researchers in tax compliance studies and other disciplines.

Future researchers could attempt to adapt and test the model in other areas of indirect tax, such as value added tax (VAT) which is another under-explored area. This study could also be extended to cover the perspectives of importers within a specific sector, such as tobacco, cigarettes and liquor with a view to understanding the relationship between these sectors and tax compliance. Commonly, these sectors are among the high dutiable products in many countries and require additional documentation to comply with regulatory requirements, such as permits. The methodology adopted in this study could also be used to complement other studies with a view to providing a more holistic compliance behaviour model.

Bibliography

Adams, C., & Webley, P. (2001). Small business owners' attitudes on VAT compliance in the UK. *Journal of Economic Psychology, 22*, 195–216.

Accountant General of Malaysia. (2013). Federal government financial statements 2012. Kuala Lumpur: Ministry of Finance and Accountant General of Malaysia.

Andreoni, J., Erard, B., & Feinstein, J. (1998). Tax compliance. *Journal of Economic Literature, 36*(2), 818-860.

Ajzen, I. & Fishbein, M. 1980. *Understanding attitudes and predicting social behaviour.* New Jersey: Prentice-Hall.

Ajzen, I. (1991). The theory of planned behavior. *Organizational behavior and human decision processes, 50*(2), 179–211.

Ajzen, I. (2002). Perceived Behavioral Control, Self-Efficacy, Locus of Control, and the Theory of Planned Behavior. *Journal of Applied Social Psychology,* 665–683.

Ajzen, I. (2005). *Attitudes, personality and behavior* (2nd ed.). New York: Open University Press.

Allingham, M. G., & Sandmo, A. (1972). Income tax evasion: A theoretical analysis. *Journal of public economics*, 1(3-4), 323–338. Retrieved from http://darp.lse.ac.uk/papersdb/Allingham-Sandmo_(JPubE72).pdf

Alm, J.(1991) A Perspectives on the experimental analysis of taxpayer reporting. *The Accounting Review*, vol.2: 577-593.

Alm, J., & Torgler, B. (2011). Do ethics matter? Tax compliance and morality. *Journal of Business Ethics*, 101(4), 635–651.

Amin, M. A. M. (2010). Measuring the performance of Customs Information Systems (CIS) in Malaysia. *World Customs Journal*, 4(2), 89–104. Retrieved from http://www.worldcustomsjournal.org/media/wcj/-2010/2/WCJ_Volume_4_Number_2.pdf

Appeals, T., & Swielande, H. S. De. (1998). Rolling Back the Frontiers: The Customs Clearance Revolution. *The International Journal of Logistics Management*, 9(1), 111–118.

Aronson, E. and A. R. Pratkanis (1993). What is Social Psychology? *Social Psychology*. Vol. 1, Edward Elgar Publishing, UK.

Baker, E. W., Al-Gahtani, S. S., & Hubona, G. S. (2007). The effects of gender and age on new technology implementation in a developing country: Testing the theory of planned behavior (TPB). *Information Technology & People*, 20(4), 352–375.

Bandura, A. (1986). *Social foundations of thought and action*. Englewood Cliffs, NJ: Prentice-Hall.

Bandura, A. (1992). On rectifying the comparative anatomy of perceived control: Comments on 'Cognates of personal control'. *Applied and Preventive Psychology*, 1, 121–126.

Bandura, A. (1997). *Self-efficacy in changing societies*. Cambridge University Press.

Bandura, a, Caprara, G. V., Barbaranelli, C., Pastorelli, C., & Regalia, C. (2001). Sociocognitive self-regulatory mechanisms governing transgressive behaviour. *Journal of personality and social psychology*, 80(1), 125-35.

Barjoyai, B. (1987). Taxation: Principle and Practice in Malaysia (Pencukaian Prinsip dan Amalan di Malaysia. Kuala Lumpur: Dewan Bahasa dan Pustaka.

Baron, R. M., & Kenny, D. a. (1986). The moderator-mediator variable distinction in social psychological research: conceptual, strategic, and statistical considerations. *Journal of personality and social psychology*, 51(6), 1173–82.

BBC News. (2012, March 9). Ireland garlic scam : Paul Begley jailed for six years. Retrieved from http://www.bbc.co.uk/news/world-europe-17320460

Bidin, Z., Faridahwati, M. S., Mohd Salleh, S., & Othman, M. Z. (2011). Factors Influencing Intention To Comply with Local sales Tax In Malaysia. *Social Science Research Network*.

Blanthorne, C., & Kaplan, S. (2008). An egocentric model of the relations among the opportunity to underreport, social norms, ethical beliefs, and underreporting behavior. *Accounting, Organizations and Society, 33*(7-8), 684–703.

Blanthorne, C. (2013). The aggressiveness of tax professional reporting: Examining the influence of moral reasoning. *Advances in Accounting Behavioural Research, 16,* 149–181.

Bobek, D. D. (1997). *Tax Fairness: How Do Individuals Judges Fairness And What Effects Does It Have On Their Behaviour,* University of Florida, Gainesville.

Bobek, D. D., & Hatfield, R. (2003). An investigation of the theory of planned behaviour and the role of moral obligation in tax compliance. *Behavioral Research in Accounting, 15,* 13.

Bobek, D. D., Hatfield, R. C., & Wentzel, K. (2007). An Investigation of Why Taxpayers Prefer Refunds: A Theory of Planned Behavior Approach. *Journal of the American Taxation Association, 29*(1), 93–111.

Bond, M. J. (2002). The roles of self-efficacy, outcome expectancies and social support in the self-care behaviours of diabetics. *Psychology, Health & Medicine, 7,* 127-141.

Brand, P. (1996). Compliance: A 21st century approach. *National Tax Journal, 49*(3), 413–419.

Bryman, a. (2006). Integrating quantitative and qualitative research: how is it done? *Qualitative Research, 6*(1), 97–113.

Bryman, A. (1989). *Research Methods and Organization Studies* (p. 235). Routledge, Taylor & Francis Group.

Carrington, M., Neville, B., & Whitwell, G. (2010). Why ethical consumers don't walk their talk: Towards a framework for understanding the gap between the ethical purchase intentions and actual buying behaviour of ethically minded consumers. *Journal of Business Ethics, 97*(1), 139–158.

Chan, C. W., Troutman, C. S., & O'Bryan, D. (2000). An expanded model of taxpayer compliance: Empirical evidence from the United States and Hong Kong. *Journal of International Accounting, Auditing and Taxation, 9*(2),

Chang, M. (1998). Predicting unethical behavior: a comparison of the theory of reasoned action and the theory of planned behavior. *Journal of Business Ethics,* 1825–1834.

Chau, G. (2009). A critical review of Fischer tax compliance model: A research synthesis. *Journal of Accounting and Taxation, 1*(2), 034–040.

Chia, SY 2010, 'Accelerating ASEAN trade and investment cooperation and integration: progress and challenges', in P Gugler & J Chaisse (eds), *Competitiveness of the ASEAN countries: corporate and regulatory drivers,* Edward Elgar, UK, pp. 103-129.

Chu, P., & Wu, T. (2004). Factors influencing tax-payer information usage behavior: Test of an integrated model. *The Eight Pacific-Asia Conference on Information Systems, Shanghai, China, proceedings.*

Creswell, J. W. (2002). *Research Design: Qualitative, Quantitative, and mixed methods approaches* (2nd ed., Vol. 33, p. 252). SAGE Publication Inc, Thousand Oaks, California 91320.

Cummings, R. G., Martinez-Vazquez, J., McKee, M., & Torgler, B. (2009). Tax morale affects tax compliance: Evidence from surveys and an artefactual field experiment. *Journal of Economic Behavior & Organization, 70*(3), 447–457.

Dzewaltowski, D. A., Noble, J. M., & Shaw, J. M. (1990). Physical activity participation—social cognitive theory versus the theories of reasoned action and planned behaviour. *Journal of Sport and Exercise Psychology, 12*, 388–405.

Devos, K. (2007). Measuring and analysing deterrence in taxpayer compliance research. *Journal of Australian Taxation*, 182–219.

Eisenhauer, J. (2008). Ethical preferences, risk aversion, and taxpayer behavior. *Journal of Socio-Economics, 37*(1), 45–63.

Elliott, M. a, Armitage, C. J., & Baughan, C. J. (2003). Drivers' compliance with speed limits: an application of the theory of planned behavior. *The Journal of applied psychology, 88*(5), 964–72.

Engel, E. M. R. ., Galetovic, A., & Raddatz, C. E. (2001). A note on enforcement spending and VAT revenues. *Review of Economics, 83*(2), 384–387.

Eriksen, K., & Fallan, L. (1996). Tax knowledge and attitudes towards taxation; A report on a quasi-experiment. *Journal of Economic Psychology, 17*(3), 387–402.

Feld, L. P., & Frey, B. S. (2007). Tax compliance as the result of a psychological tax contract: The role of incentives and responsive regulation. *Law & Policy, 29*(1), 102–120.

Francis, J., Eccles, M., & Johnston, M. (2004). *Constructing Questionnaires Based on the Theory of Planned Behaviour: A Manual for Health Services Researchers*. Centre for Health Service Research, University of Newcastle, UK

Hai, O. T., & See, L. M. (2011a). Intention of Tax Non-Compliance-Examine the Gaps. *International Journal of Business and Social Science, 2*(7), 79–83.

Hai, O. T., & See, L. M. (2011b). Behavioral Intention of Tax Non-Compliance among Sole-Proprietors in Malaysia. *International Journal of Business adn Social Science, 2*(6), 142–152

Hanno, D. M. & Violette, G. R. 1996. An analysis of moral and social influences on taxpayer behaviour, *Behavioural Research in Accounting* 8: 57-75.

Henderson, B. C., & Kaplan, S. (2005). An examination of the role of ethics in tax compliance decisions. *Journal of the American Taxation Association, 27*, 39-72.

Ho, D., & Wong, B. (2008). Issues on compliance and ethics in taxation: what do we know? *Journal of Financial Crime, 15*(4), 369–382.

Huang, E., & Chuang, M. H. (2007). Extending the theory of planned behaviour as a model to explain post-merger employee behaviour of IS use. *Computers in Human Behavior, 23*(1), 240–257.

Jackson, B.R. and V.C. Milliron, (1986). Tax compliance research: Findings, problems, and prospects. *Journal of Accounting Literature*, 5: 125-65.

James, S., & Alley, C. (2002). Tax compliance, self-assessment and tax administration. *Journal of Finance and Management in Public Services*, 2(2), 27–42.

Jenkins, AL (1994). The role of managerial self-efficacy in corporate compliance with the law. *Law & Human Behavior*, 18, 71-88.

Johnson, C. (2011). *Enforcing America's Trade Laws in the Face of Customs Fraud and Duty Evasion*. National Council of Textile Organizations, Washington DC.

Kidwell, B., & Jewell, R. (2003). An examination of perceived behavioral control: Internal and external influences on intention. *Psychology and Marketing*, 20(7), 625-642.

Kirchler, E. (2007). *The Economic Psychology of Tax Behaviour*. Cambridge, UK: Cambridge University Press.

Kraft, P., Rise, J., Sutton, S., & Roysamb, E. (2005). Perceived difficulty in the theory of planned behaviour: Perceived behavioural control or affective attitude? *British Journal of Social Psychology*, 44(3), 479-496.

Klepper, S., Mazur, M., & Nagin, D. S. (1991). Expert Intermediaries And Legal Compliance: The Case of Tax Preparers. *Journal of Law and Economics*, 34, 205-229

Langham, J., Paulsen, N., & Hartel, C. (2012). Improving tax compliance strategies: Can the theory of planned behaviour predict business compliance? *eJournal of Tax Research*, 10(2). 364–402.

Lee, S. J., Mcgehee, N. G., Mills, B. F., & Perdue, R. R. (2011). Volunteer Tourists ' Intended Participation : Using the Revised Theory of Planned Behavior Volunteer Tourists ' Intended Participation : Using the Revised Theory of Planned Behavior.

Lieb, R., & Bentz, B. (2005). The use of third-party logistics services by large American manufacturers: the 2004 survey. *Transportation Journal*.

Malaysian Customs Act (1967). The Government of Malaysia.

Marrelli, M., & Martina, R. (1988). Tax evasion and strategic behaviour of the firms. *Journal of Public Economics*, 37, 55–69.

Marrelli, Massimo. (1984). On Indirect Tax Evasion. *Journal of Public Economics*, 25, 181–196.

Murphy, K. (2005). Regulating more effectively: the relationship between procedural justice, legitimacy, and tax non-compliance. *Journal of Law and Society*, 32(4), 562-589.

Nor Aziah, M. (2004). *Land tax administration and compliance attitude in Malaysia*, unpublished doctoral disertation. University of Nottingham, UK.

OECD. (2006). *Consumption Tax Trends: VAT/GST and Excise Rates, Trends and Administration Issues*. OECD Publishing.

Palil, R. (2010). Tax Knowledge And Tax Compliance Determinants In Self Assessment System In Malaysia. *PhD Thesis, University of Birmingham, UK.*

Pavlou, P. A., & Fygenson, M. (2006). Understanding and predicting electronic commerce adoption: An extension of the theory of planned behaviour. *MIS Quarterly*, 30(1): 115-143.

Poulter, D. R., Chapman, P., Bibby, P. a, Clarke, D. D., & Crundall, D. (2008). An application of the theory of planned behaviour to truck driving behaviour and compliance with regulations. *Accident; analysis and prevention*, 40(6), 2058–64.

Reckers, P., Sanders, D., & Roark, S. (1994). The influence of ethical attitudes on taxpayer compliance. *National Tax Journal*, 47, 825- 825.

RMCD (2011). *Import Declaration Process, in MS ISO 9001:2000 Quality Manual*, Royal Malaysian Customs

Ross, L., Kohler, C., Grimley, D , & Anderson-Lewis, C. (2007). The theory of reasoned action and intention to seek cancer information. *American Journal of Health Behavior*, 31(2), 123-134.

Roth, J.A, Scholz, J.T., and Witte. A.D. (1989). *Taxpayer Compliance: An Agenda for Research*. Philadelphia: University of Pennsylvania Press.

Saad, N. (2011). Fairness Perceptions and Compliance Behaviour: Taxpayers' Judgements in Self-Assessment Environments. *Doctoral Thesis, University of Canterbury, New Zealand.*

Sawhney, R., & Sumukadas, N. (2005). Coping with customs clearance uncertainties in global sourcing. *International Journal of Physical Distribution & Logistics Management*, 35(4), 278–295.

Schwarzer, R., & Kwiatek, P. (1997). The Assessment of Optimistic Self-beliefs: Comparison of the German, Spanish, and Chinese Versions of the General Self-efficacy Scale. *Applied*, 46(We 10), 69–88.

Sekaran, U., & Bougie, R. (2011). *Research methods for business: A skill building approach* (5th ed.). Padstow, Cornwall, Great Britain: TJ International Ltd.

Sheppard, B. H., Hartwick, J., & Warshaw, P. R. (1988). The theory of reasoned action: A meta-analysis of past research with recommendations for modifications and future research. *Journal of consumer research*, 15(December), 325–343.

Sideridis, G. D., Kaissidis, A., & Padeliadu, S. (1998). Comparison of the theories of reasoned action and planned behaviour. *British Journal of Educational Psychology*, 68(4), 563–580.

Silver, D. (1995). Tax Compliance and Taxpayer Attitude. *National Public Accountant*, 40(11), 32–34.

Sparks, P. (1997). The Dimensional Structure of the Perceived Behavioral Control Construct. *Journal of Applied Social Psychology.* 418–438.

Taylor, S., & Todd, P. A. (1995) Understanding Information Technology Usage: A Test of Competing Models. *Information Systems Research*, 6(2).

Terry, D. J. (1993). Self-efficacy expectancies and the theory of reasoned action. In D. J. Terry, C. Gallois, & M. McCamish (Eds.), *The theory of reasoned action: Its application to AIDs-preventive behaviour* (pp. 135–151). Oxford: Pergamon.

The Star. (2012). Customs dept losing RM8bil in taxes yearly. *The Star Publication*, pp. 8–9. Putrajaya, 27 June 2012. Retrieved from http://www.thestar.com.my/news/story.asp?file=/2012/6/27/nation/11554167

Torgler, B. (2003). Tax morale: theory and empirical analysis of tax compliance. Retrieved from http://edoc.unibas.ch/56/

Torgler, B., & Schneider, F. (2007). What Shapes Attitudes Toward Paying Taxes? Evidence from Multicultural European Countries*. *Social Science Quarterly*, (2117).

Torgler, B. (2011). Tax Morale and Compliance Review of Evidence and Case Studies for Europe (No. WPS5922). Policy Research Working Paper. The World Bank, Europe and Central Asia Region.

Trafimow, D., Sheeran, P., Conner, M., & Finlay, K. (2002). Evidence that perceived behavioural control is a multidimensional construct: Perceived control and perceived difficulty. *British Journal of Social Psychology, 41*(1), 101-121.

Trivedi, V. U., Shehata, M., & Mestelman, S. (2005). Attitudes, Incentives, and Tax Compliance. *Managerial and Decision Economics, 53*.

Uzzaman, M. A., & Yusuf, M. A. (2010). The role of Customs and other agencies in trade facilitation in Bangladesh : hindrances and ways forward. *World Customs Journal, 5*(1), 29–42.

Vanderstoep, S., & Johnston, D. D. (2009). *Research Methods for Everyday Life: Blending Qualitative and Quntitative Approaches* (p. 315). John Wiley & Sons

Virmani, A. (1989). Indirect tax evasion and production efficiency. *Journal of Public Economics, 39*(2), 223–237.

Wallschutzky, I.G. & B. Gibson, (1993), Small Business Cost of Compliance, *Australian Tax Forum, 10(4) 527*

WCO. (2006). Revised KYOTO Convention. World Customs Organization, 3 February 2006, Brussel, Belgium.

Wenzel, M. (2005). Motivation or rationalisation? Causal relations between ethics, norms and tax compliance. *Journal of Economic Psychology, 26*(4), 491–508.

Wenzel, M. (2007). The multiplicity of taxpayer identities and their implications for tax ethics. *Law & Policy, 29*(1), 31-50.

Welsh, E. (2002). Dealing with data: Using NVivo in the qualitative data analysis process. Forum: Qualitative Social Research, 3 (2). Retrieved March 11, 2011, from www.qualitative-research.net/fqs-texte/2-02/2-02welsh-e.htm.

Workman, M. (2007). Punishment and ethics deterrents: A study of insider security contravention. *Journal of the American Society for, 58*(c), 212–222.

Zainol, B. (2008). Faktor-Faktor Penentu Niat Gelagat Kepatuhan Zakat Pendapatan Gaji. Retrieved from http://etd.uum.edu.my/2106/

11 Alignment of Tax Planning Functions and Activities with Corporate Strategy in Multinational Corporations

Emer Mulligan, James Gawley, and James Cunningham

Abstract

The central focus of this chapter is to examine how multinational corporations (MNCs) organise their tax department and to what extent tax planning is aligned with corporate strategy. It addresses the alignment of tax strategy and corporate strategy, an area that has received little attention in the strategy and tax literatures. The chapter also examines what factors influence the degree of this alignment.

Using an interpretative inductive methodology this study draws on interviews with tax executives from a sample of ICT firms based in the USA, post interview notes, email correspondence with interviewees, and recent 10ks of the participating MNCs. With respect to the organisation of the MNC tax function various department profiles were found. In addition, size, organisation position and reporting levels were found to be important factors in determining the influence of the tax department. We also found that the 'customer focus' of the in house tax department was primarily internal. In terms of tax planning and corporate strategy alignment, we found the focus of tax missions was primarily on compliance and that the value of tax strategies and mission was narrowly understood by tax professionals.

We found the importance of tax in a company to be influenced by eight factors, the most important of these being the Chief Financial Officer. The practical implications of these findings include the need for tax departments to develop a greater understanding of the business activities and strategy of the MNC, in order for it to transform to a strategic support role.

1 Introduction

Since the Lehmans collapse in August 2008 most European nations have suffered from slowing economic growth, fiscal austerity and a need to increase the overall taxation (The Economist, 2001). The need to raise taxes has resulted in increasing scrutiny of MNCs and their tax affairs. In December 2012, this led to the UK's Parliamentary Public Accounts Committee (PAC) publishing a report ("Tax avoidance by multinational companies," 2012) looking at the UK subsidiaries of Starbucks, Google and Amazon, and exploring how, while in 2011-12 total UK tax revenues increased by £4.5 billion, corporation tax revenue declined by £6.3 billion. Looking more broadly, the UK was instrumental in making taxation a key focus of the recent G8 Lough Erne summit and subsequent declaration ("G8 Lough Erne Declaration," 2013). In July 2013, the reason for this focus was highlighted by Reuters in a special report (Reuters, 2013), which detailed an "average 2012 tax charge of 6.8% on non-US earnings published by 37 of the top 50 U.S. tech firms whose PE (permanent establishment) structures help avoid tax". Again in July 2013, the international nature of MNC tax affairs resulted in the OECD publishing a report (OECD, 2013) which argued that global integration has facilitated MNC tax planners identifying and exploiting legal arbitrage opportunities that are at "the boundaries of acceptable tax planning". The resulting minimization of MNC's tax burden has created "a tense situation in which citizens have become more sensitive to tax fairness issues". The OECD report goes on to claim that action is needed to prevent harm to G20 governments, citizens and businesses.

Against this backdrop, a greater understanding of the extent to which taxation is aligned with the strategy of a business is important. This alignment question is addressed here by drawing on literatures from strategy management, organisational structures and taxation. This chapter examines how MNCs organize their tax departments and how this influences the degree of alignment between tax planning and corporate strategy. Following a review of the literature, section 3 outlines the methodology employed in this study. The findings are presented in section 4, and this is followed by discussion and conclusions in section 5.

2 Literature Review

2.1 Tax and Strategy

Given the global nature and complexity of MNCs they must be looked at as a 'Heterarchy' (a series of nodes), that are, as Hedlund (1986) notes "actively seeking advantages originating in the global spread of the firm". The MNC as a Heterarchy (rather than a hierarchy) has a number of key features such as centers with different attributes, loose coupling between units, and normative control systems. The corporate parent and subsidiary relationship, issues of fit and parenting style have been the focus of some debate within the strategy field. Usually the role of the corporate parent includes corporate strategy and planning, investments and divestments, providing centralized services to business units (See Ginsberg, 1990; (van Oijen and Douma, 2000). Some MNCs structure their subsidiary business around product families and geographic arenas, while basing their locational decisions on a variety of factors including incentives. Subsidiaries are in competition with each other to appropriate resources and services from the corporate parent and to enhance their own mandate. Subsidiaries need to develop their own competencies and organization characteristics (Manolopoulos, 2008; Scott, Gibbons and Coughlan, 2010). Traditional mechanisms of strict control were placed on the subsidiary by the corporate parent through hierarchical organizational structures. Corporate strategy, policies and procedures were developed by the corporate parent who assigned roles to the subsidiaries (Delany, 2000; Hansen, Petersen and Wad, 2011; Schollhammer, 1971). The corporate parenting style adopted influences value creation capability in the business (Goold and Campbell, 2002). The structure of the organization matters but the reality is that value adding corporate parenting is dependent on complex interdependent structures. The challenge for the corporate parent is to manage and co-ordinate these complexities to achieve some form of organization uniformity and consistency. Parental fit is assessed through mental maps, systems, process and structures, central functions as well as the resources and experience and skills of the corporate parent's management (Goold and Campbell, 2002). A danger for corporate parents is that they destroy rather than create value in managing and co-ordinating such complexities. In doing so MNCs have taken different organisational approaches such as portfolio management and have adopted different diversification strategies (backward, forward or horizontal).

In a legal context at the subsidiary level, Hu (1992) explains that MNCs are global concerns using subsidiaries and entities to hide behind the legal principles of separate personalities. From a tax perspective, nations that adopt a worldwide taxation principle (US, Britain and most of the OECD) can tax the home-based MNC on its worldwide operations by virtue of the international subsidiaries earnings accruing to the parent's home jurisdiction. Scholes, Wolfson, Erickson, Maydew and Shevlin (2008) explain that where a US MNC has a subsidiary operating under a foreign jurisdiction for tax purposes, bilateral tax agreements[1] prevent double taxation by (generally)

---

1   Bilateral tax agreements can either (1) require tax be paid in the country of residence (home country) and be exempt in the country in which it arises (host country) or (2) in others cases it can allow for the country where the gain arises (host country) to deduct taxation at source (withholding tax) while the taxpayer receives a compensating (foreign tax credit) in the domestic or home country thereby accounting for the fact that tax has already been paid.

only making income from that subsidiary taxable to the domestic parent when it is repatriated to the parent. Hu (1992) sets this in context when he explains that the primary source of competitive advantage lies in the home nation, supported by a tapestry of international advantages, including lower corporation tax rates acting as supplements but not substitutes.

The alignment of tax strategy with overall business strategy is one that has received little attention in the literature. There is no overall consensus on how important tax actually is in organisations. For instance, Porter (1999, p. 36) reported that just over 50 per cent of tax managers surveyed 'believe their company's directors accord "considerable" or "very great" importance to minimising tax liabilities'. There is some debate in the literature about the role of tax in business decisions, the extent to which tax personnel should be consulted when business decisions are being made and what types of business decisions merit a tax input. Wilson (1995) goes on to question whether an in-house tax professional is perceived as a 'tax policeman', 'service provider' or 'business partner'.

2.2 Strategic Importance of Tax

As noted by Skaerback and Tryggestas (2010, p. 108) 'over the last 40 years or so, accounting research has enquired into the relationship between accounting and strategy', and, importantly, the tax literature is not short of advocates as to the strategic importance of tax. Valente (2002) posits the 'strategic alignment of the taxation variable with the goals pursued by top management' as representing 'the most forward-looking approach within the multinational entrepreneurial scenario'. He notes that globalisation has tax implications from both the perspective of states and enterprises. It presents the former with obstacles and challenges but the latter with new opportunities. He sees the strategic vision for taxation policy within multinational groups as taking place on a global scale and is 'consequently implemented (on a corporate level) in a transnational spirit, to the primary benefit of the country in which the top holding resides'. Tax regulations in different countries can influence individual and corporate behaviours as well as influencing the choices firms make (Hines, 1999). MNCs need to consider the tax implications of their transaction activities and how to optimize their tax structure Picciotto (1995, p. 25). Karayan and Swenson (2007, p. 63) argue that 'good decision makers generally seek to manage taxes on every major transaction' and that tax management should 'work to enhance the firm's strategy and should not cause the firm to engage in tax-minimising transactions'. This perspective is further reaffirmed by Yancey and Cravens (1998) who note the importance of a company's tax strategy complementing and thereby having a role to play in implementing a company's overall business strategy. Scholes et al. (2008) advocate a strategic approach to tax planning through consideration of all parties, all taxes and all costs and engaging in income shifting.

When companies make strategic decisions with respect to strategy and its implementation there are taxation implications in terms of transactions. This is something that is neglected in the strategy literature and textbooks (James, 2005). Moreover, Glaister and Frecknall-Hughes (2008, p. 34) point out that 'in general, models which set out the prescriptive approach to strategic management make no reference to tax implications of strategic decisions.' The dearth of consideration of tax issues in the strategy and management literature contributes to the 'black box' status of tax. Similarly, Holzman (2001) believes that most management decisions have tax consequences which should be addressed, and the management group must 'know enough about taxation to solve the organizational, commercial and financial problems that have to be met.' The latter emphasises the importance of effective communication and relationships skills, which are at the core of Wilson's (1995) efforts to find ways to have senior management and in-house tax personnel work together towards optimisation of after-tax profits.

The limited evidence from practice indicates a mixed approach taken by companies. Internal marketing of the tax function to colleagues in other functions is an important task in the context of the tax function helping to implement an organisation's corporate strategy (PWC, 2001). These colleagues are like customers and should be supported through seminars, training and road shows. At Board level studies have shown the increasing interest among members in tax and how it can support corporate strategy, whilst tax directors' focus is on the larger strategic plan (PWC, 2001). As noted by Glaister and Frecknall- Hughes (2007, p. 34), there are some unanswered questions including 'how within the firm strategic decision-makers interface with tax decision-makers'.

The extent to which tax is embedded strategically in organisations could also be a function of the size of the organisation, as Rego (2003, p. 812) notes 'large firms generally engage in more business activities and more financial transactions than small firms do, thereby providing more opportunities to avoid income taxes'. There is a counter argument however, as also acknowledged by Rego (2003, p. 812), 'proponents of the political cost hypothesis argue that larger firms are likely to pay more income taxes than smaller firms do, as a result of increased visibility and government scrutiny and expropriation of resources'[2].

While there is some consensus in the literature that tax should be strategically important, it sometimes struggles to really matter greatly in

---

2   Zimmerman (1983) discusses the 'political cost hypothesis' in detail.

practice. None of the research has gained a real understanding of how a strategic role for the tax function is defined, mapped out, implemented, managed and monitored on an ongoing basis in complex, ever-changing organisations. Also this literature fails to examine the formalisation (or not) of an overall tax strategy/mission within MNCs, and the factors which establish the importance of tax (tax embeddedness) within these organisations. This includes, for example, the role of key players such as the CFO, the extent to which tax is integral to the way business is done within MNCs, and the extent to which tax personnel understand and/or are enabled to understand the business within which they are operating.

2.3 Organisation of the Tax Function

The issue of strategy and structure is one that has been debated at length in the strategy literature. Chandler (1962) argued that structure followed strategy whereas Mintzberg (1994) argued the logic of strategy following structure. Behaviours, strategic initiatives, managerial talent and other factors ultimately shape strategy and structure (Burgelman, 1983; Miles, Snow and Pfeffer, 1974). MNCs have adopted different organizational structures for their subsidiaries/single business units, including function, multidivisional, matrix and networked. All these organization structures come with strengths and weaknesses and create challenges for corporate parents in optimizing the organizational position of key services such as taxation, finance etc. Goold and Campbell (2002) suggest organizations create a 'working' organizational structure and analyse optimal fit of functions and business units based on several tests including parenting and market advantage, people, feasibility, and accountability and specialist tests. In essence as Kaplan and Norton (2006, p. 102) note, organizations do not need to find the perfect structure for their strategy, but create one that 'works without major conflicts and then design a customized strategic system to align that structure with strategy.' The specificity of the rationale of organization structure does not matter, what matters is the simplicity of structure to implement corporate and business strategy (Nohria, Joyce and Roberson, 2003, p. 49).

A key question for all organisations, particularly large organisations, is how best to organise the tax function. The tax function comprises compliance and planning, both of which are referred to in this context. The decisions to have an in-house tax department, or to outsource some or all of the tax function and the extent to which external advisors should be consulted are among the key considerations addressed in the literature. As complexity increases, tax directors must establish clear responsibility for direct and indirect tax compliance and support in overseas territories as well as ensure those reporting lines are briefed on tax issues (PWC, 2001). According to

Levine and Lerner (1993) the in-house tax executive must be able to combine technical competence with 'an understanding of the corporation's goals… ongoing experience with the myriad personalities involved…knowledge of the company's practices…and appreciation of the corporate culture that enable the tax executive to bring more to the table than the outside consultants'. For in house tax functions to create more added value more time should be spent by the function on tax planning and advisory work (Porter, 1999). This adding value can be done through improving the human capital of tax professionals business knowledge, tax expertise and relationship skills (Wilson, 1995).

One of the main themes that has received empirical and practice attention concerns outsourcing. Given the complexities involved, companies need to consider the implications, benefits and impacts of outsourcing the tax function. Key considerations are the value added aspects of outsourcing for the company and the impact on communications between tax executives, auditors and the management team (Levine and Lerner, 1993). In the context of outsourcing, tax executives have to balance compliance with more strategic support in optimizing the overall organizational unit. In essence, Levine and Lerner (1993) suggest that the corporate tax executive should try to 'transform the tax department from simply a service department into a strategic resource for management'. This means outsourcing compliance activities and focusing on the value adding activities. A study by Dunbar and Phillips (2001) provided further insights into the relationships between a number of organisational and environmental factors, including the organisation of the tax function in terms of being outsourced or managed in-house. They found that tax is not outsourced when top management perceives the interaction between tax professionals and operating managers to be important[3] or if the company generates proprietary technology[4]. Furthermore while larger firms tend to outsource less than smaller firms, the evidence did not support the idea that companies with a wide range of activities are more likely to outsource the tax function. And while growth firms outsource more, where the companies' tax professionals are of a high status it is less likely to outsource the tax function.

With increasing complexity and compliance pressures companies use external advisors to various degrees. They are typically employed to help out with excess workloads and/or, generate, confirm, provide, comfort, reassure, or consult on tax planning ideas or proposed transactions, specialist knowledge (technically/territorially), and compliance. External tax advisors

---

3 High importance was deemed in evidence where operating managers were assessed on an after-tax basis.
4 Measured by investment in research and development.

are important actors in the tax organisational field and are typically placed in accountancy or legal firms. Picciotto (1995, p. 26) argues that 'lawyers have greater independence and can offer a more creative approach…Lawyers can also offer client confidentiality'. According to PWC (2001), 'most interviewees consider the Big Five advisers "essential" for management of international tax profiles because of their extensive international networks'.[5] In order to ensure consistent quality throughout the group, responsibility for appointing external advisors should be centralised.

3 Methodology

3.1 Research Design

An interpretative inductive methodological approach was adopted to move from generalizations to specific facts and thereby gain an insight into the data, with the study focusing on tax strategy and its integration with overall corporate strategy. The primary research method was semi-structured face-to-face interviews, with heads of tax and/or senior managers within fifteen US MNCs operating in the ICT sector and headquartered in Silicon Valley (SV) California. The companies that our research focused on all operated in a rapidly changing business environment. The interpretive methodology used allowed us to move from generalizations to specific facts, and thereby gain unique insights into the actual practices of the interviewees, which arguably could not be obtained through other methods such as questionnaires.

3.2 Data Collection

After selecting the MNCs, interviews were secured with the respective heads of tax using two primary sources of contact. Obtaining access in this way, resulted in a quicker route to interviews with the MNC tax 'elites' (Odendahl & Shaw, 2001) that are both difficult to identify and challenging to access. Interviews were secured with 26 tax executives (TE[6]) in 15 MNCs in total. Many interviewees headed the tax function, or were in senior management positions reporting directly to the head of tax. Care was taken to select the right individuals for interview, ensuring they were capable of answering the questions posed. In addition three tax advisers to these US MNCs were interviewed at an earlier stage in the research process. Two of these advisers were senior tax partners with two of the 'big four' accountancy practices

---

5   The 'Big Five' providers of accountancy and taxation services worldwide at the time, consisted of Price Waterhouse (now PricewaterhouseCoopers), Ernst and Young, Deloitte, KPMG and Arthur Anderson. Since the demise of Arthur Anderson, the other advisers are now referred to as the 'Big Four'.

6   TE denotes in-house tax executive. Both male and female tax executives were interviewed. However to protect anonymity, all of the interviewees are referred to as he/his/him etc. as the context requires.

in Dublin, Ireland. The third adviser was a SV-based tax adviser to these companies and was a partner with a large US legal firm.

Secondary research data came from the selected companies' 10Ks, websites, press releases, press comments as well as any internet-accessible executive biographies for the interviewees. Material from recent legislation was also considered. The 10k reports filed by each company include financial statements, and provided important contextual documentary information on the nature of the company's business, the countries in which it had a physical presence, the identity of its auditors and so on.

3.3 Data Analysis

All interviews were taped and written up immediately afterwards, noting the tone of the interview, overall impression formed, and any other significant observations.[7] The interview transcripts, post-interview notes and email correspondence from interviewees before and after the interview amounted to a significant amount of data for analysis. We used QSR NVivo to assist our data management and data interrogation and analysis, and it also provided a form of 'audit trail' (Bringer, Halley Johnston and Brackenridge, 2006).

3.4 Limitations

The research methodology has three main weaknesses. The first of these is quantitative verification; although the approach allows for an enhanced understanding of tax planning and strategy in practice, by adopting a qualitative approach requiring interviews of tax executives from fifteen companies, the result is findings that are not statistically verifiable. The second is physical concentration of the sample; as all of the MNCs were (apart from the tax advisors) based in SV California, it is arguable that some of the findings are limited to SV based companies. The third weakness is judgement and subjectivity; as with all qualitative research, including this one, this weakness must be acknowledged. However this subjectivity was not at the expense of rigour.

4 Findings

The research focus of this chapter is twofold, first, to examine the functional organization and activities of the tax department, and, second, to examine the alignment of the tax function with strategy, and the factors that influence the extent of that alignment.

---

[7] For example, some individuals were keen to distinguish his/her company from others in SV using phrases like: 'we are different', 'maybe other companies don't do it this way', 'SOX may have changed things for other companies, but not for us'.

4.1 Tax Department - Functional Organisation and Activities

4.1.1 Profiles of Tax Departments

The profiles of the tax departments of the companies in this study are quite diverse in terms of number of personnel, and their location as summarized in Table 11.1 below. These facts provide an important context within which to explore and understand the workings of the various in-house tax departments. The number of tax employees as represented refers to employees who work exclusively in the tax department. Interestingly, while these companies are all MNCs trading internationally with a number of foreign operations, with the exception of companies Five and Six, the tax personnel are substantially physically located in the US. For the most part, these employees are all involved in tax planning[8] and compliance work. Exceptionally, Company One had some staff engaged in compliance work only.

Table 11.1: Profiles of Tax Department

Company	No. Tax Employees	US-Based	Non-US Based
Company 1	17	17	
Company 2		2+ ?	3
Company 3	1		
Company 4	11	?	?
Company 5	135	< 68	>68
Company 6	c. 160	110	50
Company 7	3	3	
Company 8	2	2	
Company 9	57	?	?
Company 10	9	8	1
Company 11	40	33	7
Company 12	19	18	1
Company 13	10	8	2
Company 14	4	4	0
Company 15	14	13	1

Many of the companies also have some non-tax specific personnel based

---

8 While tax *planning* refers to any activity or process concerning the consideration of the tax aspects/implications of any business activity/transaction, and *compliance* is largely understood to refer to administration incorporating, for example, data collection and completion and filing of tax returns, most interviewees agreed tax planning and compliance are inextricably linked.

in foreign operations, typically a 'finance' person, 'managing a compliance process as distinct from necessarily having a material role in the decision making as to what is going on' (Advisor 1).[9] Based on the above facts and other findings, tax planning in these companies tends to be US-centric, where the tone is set and the real tax planning decisions are made: 'the fundamental tax decisions are made in the US' (TE 25) and are thereby 'centralised' (TE 12). The tax executives interviewed were almost all heading up the worldwide, US, or international tax function in their respective organisations from the US, and the three tax advisors were partners in large tax advisory firms with a US MNC client base. Notably, three of the interviewees hold senior VP positions, which according to Advisor Three is very unusual for tax executives.

The higher the level/position held in an organisation by the head of tax, the more embedded the tax function is likely to be. Job titles held by the tax executives included: Senior Director of Taxes, VP Tax and Trade, VP Tax, VP Tax, Licensing and Customs, International Tax Director, Director, US International Tax and Audits, and Senior VP Taxation. The minor variations in title reflect different organisational structures and cultures. As can be seen from some titles, a number of the interviewees are responsible for more than tax, which may be of some significance in the context of making tax important within an organization.

4.1.2 Reporting Lines

Another source of 'power' for tax stems from reporting lines. In most of these companies, the head of tax reports directly to the CFO, and this was seen as important. In one company, the VP Tax reports to the VP Finance who in turn reports to the CFO. In another company the tax director reports to the VP Accounting who importantly was the tax director previously (which means he is sympathetic to and supportive of the tax function). TE 8 emphasised the importance of having non-US-based tax employees reporting directly to the head of tax based in US. He argued that having them report locally does not always serve to encourage them or indeed reward them for coming up with tax solutions outside of their own country or region (for example, Europe). He similarly accuses tax advisors of the same parochial type thinking. One company has a very strong dotted or matrix' (TE 11) reporting line between the international tax managers (non-US) and the International Tax Director (US based). Arguably, from a country manager's perspective, having a direct or 'dotted' reporting line to the US elevates his/her status within the organisation also.

---

9   In addition to interviewing in-house tax executives in MNCs, three tax advisors to such companies were interviewed, hereafter denoted as Advisor One, Advisor Two and Advisor Three.

4.1.3 Size

The size of an in-house tax department (in terms of staff and other resources) is dependent on both internal and external factors, but size and complexity of the company and the amount of resources a company is willing to put into tax, and the increasing demands on tax departments arising from the changing regulatory environment, were the recurring determinants referred to by the interviewees. TE 14 (one of two tax employees in his company) was hired because the company: 'Had crossed through the two hundred to three hundred million dollars and they were beginning to get complex enough that their accountants were saying, you know if you don't bring in help it's going to become more expensive and you are going to be missing things, you don't want to rely on Ernst & Young or whomever to be managing the tax function.'

4.1.4 Customers of In-House Tax Departments

We found that there was a strong internal customer focus in our study. There certainly was some consensus on who the internal customers are, although as was noted, 'customers is always a hard word in tax' (TE 9).[10] TE 19 thought customer was an 'interesting' word particularly when he spoke of their relationship with their accounting department which she described as 'a very close relationship and interdependency'. Many companies prioritised the operations groups, sometimes referred to as business units (BUs) as being a very important and sometimes the most important internal customer.

Other customers identified in our study include the CFO; country directors; payroll; stock services; financial reporting; human resources; the rest of the finance group; the executive office/management team; sales personnel (reviewing customer contracts etc); legal department; treasury; business development group (responsible in one company for acquisition and licensing activity); the technology and manufacturing group (specific to one company in which this group determines plant location and expansion decisions and where tax feeds into the cost analysis).

Only a limited number of responses dealt with external customers. Arguably, however, most of the interviewees do not perceive themselves as having external customers or at least they are not as important (or as clearly defined) as the internal ones. 'I don't know that we have any external customers' (TE 24). Three interviewees (from Companies Six, Eight and Eleven) did however state that ultimately the shareholders are their customers also.

Based on the range of internal customers which tax has, it is quite clear

---

10 Taxpayers are also referred to as customers now by the state in many countries which can be contentious. See Lamb, Tuck and Hoskin (2003) and Tuck (2004).

that tax crosses a lot of operational matters in any company in which the MNC operates, this clearly presents great challenges and opportunities for tax executives. Interpersonal and communication skills (Wilson, 1995) are of major importance to facilitate tax executives serving their internal customers well. External customers do not appear to be top of the tax executive's agenda which must cause some concern from a shareholder perspective.

4.2 Tax and Strategy

As noted previously, very little tax research to date has provided a real understanding of how a strategic role for the tax function is defined, mapped out, implemented, managed and monitored on an ongoing basis in complex ever-changing organisations like the MNCs of this study. Gaining this understanding, therefore, was a key objective when discussing tax strategy with the interviewees.

4.2.1 Alignment of Tax with Overall Business Strategy

There was general agreement that a tax strategy should not drive the business but on the contrary, 'the business should drive tax and company tax strategies' (TE 14). Similarly, TE 5 believes 'the tax tail shouldn't wag the operational dog'. It was clear that sales drives these companies and that tax strategies should not interfere with sales or the company's ability to sell products. Business decisions are generally made in principle, for example to set up a shared service centre for Europe or EMEA[11] and at that point the in-house tax department becomes involved to find the best tax-based structure that will also deliver on the business decision. Extending this further it is 'incumbent upon tax to understand management's overall objectives and to develop strategies that are in line with those objectives' (TE 14). In support of this, TE 15 stated 'it doesn't matter how great a tax planning idea you have if that doesn't align with the business interests then there's nothing really of value that we can add'. TE 10 was keen to point out 'we are not an Enron where we view tax as a standalone function that should be creating its own planning and savings, tax is an adjunct to the business'. One interviewee, TE 21, did hold the view that tax can change the way they do business, for example a new or changed tax treaty could lead to a change in the location of a sales operation and save significant money.

4.2.2 Tax Strategy/Mission

Within our study seven of the fifteen companies had a documented tax strategy or tax mission statement. These statements are similar to some extent but vary in length and emphasis. Most of the other companies do not have a formal documented tax strategy in place but may have monthly or

---

11 EMEA denotes Europe, Middle East and Africa.

quarterly objectives in relation to tax. While those interviewees did not see a real need for a documented strategy they did say that they understand what their own company's tax strategy is. TE 19 said he is 'more about making sure that it's clear to everybody as opposed to putting a document out there'.

It may be that having a documented tax strategy is more important for bigger companies with bigger tax departments so that 'the department people know what is going on…and it also helps the bigger broader management understand(ing).'(TE 14) In smaller companies, with say less than ten tax employees, they are typically in daily communication with each other, the CFO, and in some cases members of the wider company management team. For such smaller companies, a documented tax strategy may not add value. TE 12's view was 'it's in so few people's heads it could be construed…that we have a coherent strategy'.

There was no consensus as to the merits of having a formalised documented tax strategy in place. Tax strategy was frequently interpreted as meaning tax structure, and some interviewees were less than convinced that having a formalised documented tax strategy would add value. Unsurprisingly, those companies that have strategies firmly documented believe in their importance and role in tax.

4.2.3 Tax Mission Focus

The focus of the tax missions for firms within our study was compliance and shareholder value. For TE 24, tax mission incorporates four distinct elements and distinguishes itself somewhat from others through its emphasis on recognising tax personnel as business partners, 'we are excellent partners who proactively identify tax opportunities, minimise risk and efficiently fulfill regulatory requirements'. In TE 10's case the mission has a strong focus on compliance but since 'the beginning of time' its overriding philosophy is 'cash is king', so from a tax perspective, 'tax just nests right under that, where our goal is to make sure that we save cash. Financial statements are nice but secondary to cash'. This company is very process-driven and sets annual objectives, sets out and deals with 'quarterly hots' (items which they expect to happen in the quarter), and detailed monthly progress reports. The senior tax team also meets every month for a Project Status Review Meeting to deal with and update each other on 'big ticket items' in order to ensure 'everyone's on the same page'. Company Ten, whose strategy incorporates minimising cash taxes, also incorporates maximising EPS which are sometimes in conflict with each other. The CFO becomes involved in deciding which of these strategies wins out in any particular situation. Interestingly, TE 8's first strategy is to measure performance throughout the company on a post-tax basis. It is the only company out of the fifteen in this study that does this very detailed documented tax mission/strategy statement and it was presented by TE 8 as follows:

Increase shareholder value:

1   After tax management reporting
2   Attract and develop and retain high quality people who think globally
3   Excellent working relationship and credibility with governmental authorities
4   Long-term tax rulings and other agreements with governmental authorities
5   Develop, acquire and implement integrated tax planning opportunities relevant to [the company's] global tax profile
6   High quality in all we do
7   Strong relationship with the business and global operations
8   Proactive representation of [the company's] interests before legislative and regulatory bodies

These eight objectives are prefaced by the overriding objective of seeking to increase shareholder value. Importantly, in seeking to recruit the global thinker, it is concerned about its 'relationship' with governmental authorities and significantly and possibly relatedly, it is proactive in its representation before legislative and regulatory bodies. This mission statement is according to the VP for US tax in this company, 'the most articulated and best crafted one' he has ever seen. It is driven by a 'strong leader' in the Sr. VP for tax who frequently reminds staff of the above objectives. Essentially these things matter 'because he makes them matter'. The latter emphasises the power of this Sr. VP in this organisation (Perrow, 1985). This tax strategy had obtained Board approval which in itself may indicate an elevated position for tax within this particular company. The Sr. VP stated clearly that this company wants to be 'squeaky clean' and has an overall strategy of 'uncompromising integrity'. In relation to tax planning, he spoke very openly about their strategy of developing (coming up with ideas internally), acquiring (buy and steal) and implementing (completed internally and can be a very under-rated function) tax plans. Other mission focuses reported by others included managing world-wide tax risk and providing strategic support to business units.

One company's tax mission clearly incorporates the economic-based objective, seeking international competitive advantage through its tax mission. It does also reflect however the company's desire to foster and encourage a particular type of working environment. It states, 'to give [the company] an international competitive advantage, by minimizing taxes, thereby maximizing worldwide cash and earnings per share'. The intention is 'to maintain an energetic working environment, where initiative, creativity, continuing education and knowledge sharing are highly valued'.

4.2.4 Value of Tax Strategies/Missions

Many interviewees described the company's tax strategy in terms of overall goals and objectives. Common goals and objectives filtering through many companies include legally minimising the effective tax rate,[12] looking for opportunities to lower taxes further, tax law compliance worldwide, keeping out of trouble (with Revenue Authorities), and being responsive to internal customers. For example, TE 5 said his objectives include keeping, 'our effective tax rate below a certain percentage of pre-tax income and…it's certainly to minimise our worldwide tax burden consistent with complying to all laws and regulations'. One large company's senior VP for taxes (TE 15) admitted to having a tax mission statement for the company but rather jokingly said 'I haven't seen it for a long time. It exists somewhere'. In addition to referring to tax compliance, this company's mission statement specifically emphasises optimisation, 'it is never minimisation; it has to be optimisation with acceptable risk'. Importantly, this mission statement recognises there is some degree of risk taking within tax management.

For a minority of companies the idea of having a formalised tax strategy/mission appeared to be irrelevant. They were not concerned about it and establishing one was not high on their agenda. Surprisingly, one VP (TE 18) stated: 'There is a mission statement but I couldn't tell you what it was you know…I haven't updated it'. This individual however had difficulty in getting the CFO to believe the tax function could add value. TE 26 was of the view that 'strategy-wise there isn't a whole lot of attention given to actually documenting planning out and I haven't experienced to what merit it is'. This company does identify key projects for the year which gives some strategic direction (tactics?). He did acknowledge however that 'there is the usual departmental mission statement and vision of how you operate…and that's just fairly nice and woolly and contributing to the greater good etc'.

4.2.5 Adding Value

Our findings show the importance of reporting lines, where in the organizational structure the head of tax operates and having processes in place contributes to the strategic alignment of tax.

Reporting lines and the level at which the head of tax operates in the organisation was strongly emphasised in this context by TE 15: 'A tax person

---

12 We recognise the term 'legally minimising' is not necessarily a simple one in this context.

should always report to the CFO, not to anybody else. I get equal time at our Audit Committee. I'm on our Disclosure Committee. I go to the governance meetings. I have to sign off on the 10K, I have to sign off on the Rep letters. You know all of those things, those are all critical because if tax isn't seen at that level, forget it.' This company's tax department recently enjoyed increased visibility throughout the entire organisation through an acquisition project whereby the tax department decreed what could and couldn't happen on a country-by-country basis and those at the highest level had to listen and obey with 'the threat of a $10 billion capital gain across the board' (TE 15).

Processes that involves regular meetings and updates from the BUs were also identified and do take place in these companies. Some companies have quarterly meetings, and others have them less frequently.[13] Company Five rather uniquely enhances strategic alignment by having a single point of contact between the tax department and each line of business. This facilitates what they see as the continuing need for tax and business to talk to each other.[14] TE 8 spoke of the importance of having a legal structure that is cross-functional and a strong VP for international tax. This interviewee also thought the company deals with international tax issues better than tax advisors as its tax personnel have more cross-border interaction than the advisors do. Specifically, he feels that some European-based tax advisors cannot think of solutions outside of Europe whereas a strong VP for international taxes will look for a solution anywhere in the world. All of these processes/mechanisms facilitate the early consideration of the tax ramifications of any business plan, which would be deemed good practice.

In line with the tax planning literature, there was significant support for the idea that tax should not drive business decisions (J. E. Karayan and C. W. Swenson, 2007; P. Valente, 2002; Yancey and Cravens, 1998). Our findings suggest that in-house tax executives work towards strategic alignment of tax through reporting directly to the CFO, having as senior a title as possible in the organisation, and regular meetings and updates with BUs. All of the latter should enhance the prospect of tax being consulted as early as possible on the time line of any business transaction as advocated by R. S. Holzman (1965), James (2005) and Karayan and Swenson (2007).

---

13   For example, Company Twelve has an annual meeting called 'Focus' where the President, CEO, Finance etc, meet and the objectives for the year are set out and discussed. The tax department like all other departments are then expected to ensure its work throughout the year doesn't conflict with these overall business objectives but complements them instead.
14   This works well in this company of course as this idea is inextricably linked with its philosophy of assessing business units on a post-tax basis.

4.2.6 Importance of Tax in the MNC

The literature provides some mixed findings on how important tax actually is in MNCs and on how its level of importance could be improved upon (Porter, 1999; PWC, 2001). The main objective therefore was to establish how important tax is perceived within these companies, how well embedded tax is in the organisations and to establish, in particular, the extent to which tax executives are consulted and brought in sufficiently early on in transactions. This all helps explain to what extent tax can, and does, play a strategic role in business. Our study also shows mixed findings on the importance of tax and the internal supports for tax and points to the need for tax personnel to 'sell' the importance of tax and to thereby become more visible in the organization.

While all interviewees felt tax is important to the company (often subject to some caveats) the findings here demonstrate different degrees of importance and internal supports for tax (Wilson, 1995). The level of tax awareness among non-tax executives (as perceived by the interviewees) was quite mixed throughout the companies. TE 4 felt strongly that what tax executives do is not appreciated, it is important but 'they (the non-tax executives) don't know it'. However, they did refer to a growth in awareness but only because 'over the last number of years we've raised the profile'. TE 2 also spoke of a positive change. 'I would have to say that over the last five years we have become much more strategic in our role' (although he did acknowledge that there are still instances when he is consulted after something has happened). This trend towards involvement of tax executives upfront is partly driven by the tax personnel pushing themselves forward over time and becoming as engaged as possible with the business. It is also driven by the fact that these companies are operating in so many different countries so the tax risks are greater:

> I do think that the message is getting loud and clear that tax is a key player and especially as we expand internationally, there is a lot of concern about taxes, there is a lot of concern about the structure that we have and so the groups tend to involve me a lot more early on. (TE 2)

There was general consensus that the earlier on in a business transaction that tax gets involved the better. As described by TE 24, 'if you're not in on the very beginning you often miss a lot by the time you get to it'. TE 5 did refer to tax planning however as frequently being a case of 'damage control', where tax is consulted far too late in the process.

Four companies stood out in terms of the very high regard for tax which they perceived as existing within their respective organisations. Perhaps unsurprisingly, three of these were the biggest companies in terms of turnover, number of employees, and number of tax employees. TE 11 spoke of tax being given a great deal of respect in the company both from a 'keeping [the company] legal' standpoint and from having 'a seat at the table before transactions are completed' standpoint. This company's tax function appears to be very visible and the country managers regularly approach them for their tax input. TE 24 attributes its tax function's high degree of integration with the business in part to the fact that his boss is one of the five leading executives in the company and has great admiration for the tax department. The latter again emphasising the importance of having an admirer of tax at a high level within the organisational structure. He lets TE 24 know about things before anybody else 'just in case'. This tax department does not have to 'go begging' to be involved. The latter, of course, supports the view that the function must be supported from the top down. TE 23 viewed tax as being important to the organisation because 'it's a very material part of our external financial reporting'. TE 18, despite having lots of problems internally selling the idea that tax can add value, is of the view that within the organisation tax is seen as very important due to its impact on EPS. It's a 'huge driver' in EPS and is, therefore, very important.

Other interviewees were not so convinced that the tax function was highly valued in-house. TE 25 thought it would be viewed as 'being slightly academic and technical and something that happens in the background' and in relation to that company's 'tax structure' he was not convinced that a lot of people in the company understand it, nor that 'the tax people have ever gone out of their way to explain it, it's sort of on a need-to-know basis almost'. Interestingly, this interviewee works in the company's shared service centre (located outside of the US) with some responsibility for EMEA tax compliance, with little opportunity to participate in tax planning. His view does contrast somewhat with that of the Director of Taxes of this company based in the US. This interviewee showed significant frustration at the fact that the sales people did not (in his view) understand and appreciate the tax structure. There is a clear need for the tax department to communicate outwardly also however.

4.2.7 Factors Influencing the Importance of Tax

We found seven factors impacting on the importance of tax within an organisation. These are:

CFO

For all of the companies involved in the study the tax function sits in the finance side of the business and almost all of the tax directors and VPs for tax report to the CFO. There was strong evidence to suggest that tax is more likely to be integral to business decisions if the CFO highly regards the tax function. The CFO, therefore, is in quite a powerful position in relation to tax. The concern raised by some interviewees around a change of CFO and the impact of this change on tax within the organisation provides more support for the view that the CFO's attitude to tax is extremely influential. Interviewees felt the tax function has to be sold again to the new CFO and this may create uncertainty. 'You don't know what he's coming in with, how he has done business before, what his expectations are of the tax department... we'll see how he pounces on me as to why our rate is what it is.' (TE 15) TE 22 refers to 'educating him on the issues that we have and how they differ from the issues that he may be used to seeing in his previous employment.' TE 3 expressed the view that the tone of the Board and the CFO sets the tax culture in an organisation. TE 14 referred to his 'uphill battle to make tax more visible' as his current CFO does not have high regard for the possible contributions the tax function can make to the business. He went on to say that tax, 'can be so much more effective with management that appreciate the value that can be added rather than seeing tax as just another cost centre'. This level of importance attached to tax by the CFO may be very difficult to change over time as it becomes 'embedded' in the organisation. A change to this level of importance may only come about through a change in CFO (the controller of resources), pressure from the peer group (organisational field), and changes in tax legislation or economic climate (economic and political level).

We also found that he background of the CFO may well influence his/her perception of the tax function and the length of time a CFO is with an organisation seems to matter also, particularly where the VP for tax and the CFO have been working together within the one organisation for a long time. The power of the CFO in terms of his lack of willingness to understand and engage with tax, and bring tax in at the early stages of business transactions was particularly evident in one company. Some interviewees also noted the need for CFOs to engage with and understand tax is driven to some extent by the necessity of dealing with analysts' questions on tax. Analysts, whose commentaries may have an impact on share price, are particularly interested in the company's effective tax rate (ETR). They also want to know what rate should they use for their modeling purposes and why? Why is it different to competitor tax rates? Whatever views the CFO has on tax, the nature of the relationship between tax and the CFO has to be right for everyone involved.

The CFO has emerged as one of the most powerful organisational actors in terms of tax being an integral part of how these companies do business. He/she appears to be very well positioned to engage in the necessary political processes associated with the institutionalisation (Covaleski, Dirsmith, & Weiss, 2007) of tax, and thereby is a key player in setting the tax culture of an organisation.

Length of Service to the Company

The length of time over which the tax personnel, in particular the VP for tax is in place is an important factor. One VP for tax who has been with the company for eighteen years has 'an institutional history, institutional connections...in the forefront with the senior management' so that 'we sort of are involved, you know, pretty early on in transactions' (TE 15). Relationships between the VP for tax and senior management are vital. This VP is on the Disclosure Committee, goes to governance meetings, signs off on the company's 10K and so forth.

Business Profitability and Diversity

We found some evidence to suggest that the importance of tax is driven by businesses becoming more profitable and diverse. Both of these changes can make senior executives more concerned about tax exposures and about minimising taxes. TE 25 summed this up: 'as the European operation expands and matures and makes more money, I think tax becomes more relevant'. The corollary of this which was also evident in the interviews, is that it is often very difficult for tax to be treated as important strategically when a company has significant net operating losses (NOLs). TE 12 actually described its NOLs as a 'safety drop'. Therefore, from a tax planning perspective, even if something goes wrong the company will not be paying taxes for a very long time and the reputation of the tax department is not at stake. It was clear that tax gets noticed and is appreciated much more for reducing ETR significantly than efficiently utilising NOLs. For a company with large NOLs it would appear that investment in tax planning is well down the chain of management's priorities. TE 25 spoke of ongoing tax planning opportunities being limited due to the company's loss making position. TE 18 agreed: 'people won't pay enough attention to the tax function because it's not a cash out'.

Major Tax Events

A major tax event or accomplishment brings tax upfront and to the notice of senior executives. Thereafter, tax can often be seen as highly strategic. Company Four managed to significantly drop the ETR from a high of 44% in a short timeframe. Another interviewee secured a very favourable outcome on a potential $140 million tax liability. Even after such events, however, tax must continue to lobby itself within the organisation or lose its 'lustre' (TE 7). TE 17 spoke of the value of having some 'proven accomplishments', related to the Board in terms of reducing cash taxes and ETR.

Resources

Resources available to the tax department are also indicative of the extent to which tax planning is integral to business transactions. Tax planning is sometimes seen 'as a luxury as opposed to a necessity...for most tax departments that are very leanly staffed, tax strategy and tax planning are the first things to go because people are just trying to comply' (TE 2).

Regulatory Changes

Recent changes in the regulatory environment generally, have put tax high on the Boardroom agenda. Complying with Sarbanes Oxley 2002[15] reporting requirements as they apply to tax has 'changed the world (TE 10) and who 'rules the roost' (TE 21). Changes in transfer pricing regulations and the post-Enron era generally have also elevated tax onto the Boardroom agenda.

Integration Processes

The extent to which integration processes are in place within an organisation facilitates tax interacting with others in the organisation (and thereby becoming integral to business transaction) whether it be the CFO or operations people. A limited number of the companies examined are process driven in this regard. Company Eight has regular meetings with the CFO, VP Controller, financial planning and analysis people and the attorneys (always involved in writing contracts which may need a tax executive's perusal). The bigger companies certainly have regular meetings, while for the smaller companies the need to formally set up regular meetings is not necessary as it may be easier to be in regular communication with colleagues across the company. Communication is paramount and providing sufficient opportunities on a formal regular basis for interaction might well be good practice, going some way to ensuring that tax is engaged with and on a timely basis.

Many of the factors identified here as influencing the extent to which tax is embedded in an organisation can also serve as catalysts for changing the role of tax within organisations. In any event, continually internally lobbying for tax and selling and educating on the role of tax, play a significant part in determining the extent to which tax is embedded within the organisation.

While there was evidence to suggest that tax tends to be more embedded in larger organisations (Rego, 2003), the degree of embeddedness depends

---

15 SOX established new/enhanced standards for all US public company boards, management, and public accounting firms. It also established a new 'quasi-public' agency, the Public Company Accounting Oversight Board (PCAOB), also referred to by many of the interviewees. This Board is charged with overseeing, regulating, inspecting, and disciplining accounting firms in their roles as auditors of public companies. Interviewees were particularly exercised about section 404 of SOX which requires management and the external auditor to report on the adequacy of the company's internal control over financial reporting. The latter, therefore, requires documenting and testing important manual and automated controls with respect to tax.

on a range of factors ranging from the attitude of the CFO, to a change in profitability levels, to increasing risk levels arising from international expansion, to a changing regulatory environment and the extent of integration processes in place. A recurring theme here, however, is the idea that tax integration and embeddedness is facilitated mostly through good communication and relationship skills (R. S. Holzman, 1965; Wilson, 1995). It is useful when the head of tax is also responsible for some other function (for example trade administration) which provides important 'pulse points'.

4.2.8 Tax Understanding the Business

The literature does allude to the importance of tax understanding the business (Scholes et al., 2008; Wilson, 1995). Such an understanding enhances the tax executives' abilities to become integral players in business transactions and to be strategically aligned with overall business strategy. This section provides the interviewees' views on the importance of having an understanding of the business, the extent to which they have this knowledge, and outlines what enables and prohibits in-house tax personnel from gaining relevant and, sometimes, necessary business knowledge.

Some interviewees felt very strongly about the need to understand the business. 'It's invaluable to understand what the business is about and how the business operates, absolutely essential to get any perspective on the tax analysis or the tax exposures or risks.' (TE 26) TE 14 said very firmly 'we better' understand the business because 'a head of a tax department that doesn't understand his business isn't any help to his company at all'. Despite this, many interviewees felt they did not have a thorough and complete knowledge of the business. However, there are a number of factors inhibiting this from happening. Firstly, tax executives are so busy with 'doing tax stuff', they have a very limited amount of time available for learning more about the exact nature of the business, its products, manufacturing processes and so forth. Secondly, the companies do not appear to require their tax executives to really know the business in detail. The tax executives are presumably, therefore, in no way directly measured on their business knowledge per se, so acquiring such knowledge may not therefore be a priority. What is not measured may not get done. Thirdly, the physical location of the tax personnel vis-à-vis the operations may be a factor. TE 11 spoke of being 'disconnected' from the business as his office is based at Corporate in the US. Generally, it is easier to understand the business when one is physically located in the countries and offices where opportunities exist for 'bumping into people in the halls' that are dealing with the operations on a daily basis. Fourthly, some interviewees felt the technology industry was a particularly difficult one to understand where business models are often complex, particularly if you have not worked in the IT sector before. TE 26 described his company's product as 'invisible largely' and it would be easier to understand if the end product was something 'you can touch, see and feel'.

Opportunities to learn about the business do exist, which are availed of to different degrees and engaging in such learning seems to be 'up to yourself' and largely a 'self-service' system and the expectation is that tax executives should be proactive in this context. The one referred to by many interviewees was the intranet. 'It's amazing how much I could learn, for example, about [the company's] organisation and business and products and people just on our intranet site, if I had the time.' (TE 9)

On-line training resources and education opportunities are made available by many of the companies. TE 9 has a lack of time but said he learns a lot from 'hallway conversations' which take place throughout the normal course of his required work. For senior tax executives overseeing the international tax function, they travel to the regions as much as possible and interact with the business people. TE 17 spoke of a previous SV company he worked for that would have twice yearly European finance team meetings at which business product and sales personnel present to the finance team (which includes tax) to update them on the business.

TE 8 is 'too far removed' to understand the company's businesses. However, he has assigned a tax department person to every business within the company. This contact person is thereby closer to the business and develops strong business and personal relationships in some cases with the business personnel (admittedly some better than others) and meet on a weekly, monthly or quarterly basis depending on the tax sensitivity of the different businesses. This facilitates tax staff being kept in touch with how the businesses operate and what developments are happening and being planned that may need a tax input. Similarly, TE 24 spoke of continuous education taking place through 'business partnering relationships' among the senior tax staff, meetings of trade managers from around the world (this VP is in charge of the trade group), and many employee meetings where there are communications directly from the CEO, chief operating officer and CFO. In Company Eleven, the tax staff meets regularly for a presentation by a guest speaker from the business such as the chief technology officer.

While there was a consensus that a tax executive's integration with the business would be enhanced through a sound knowledge of the business (Scholes et al., 2008; Wilson, 1995), but for the most part such business knowledge seems to be at a minimum among tax executives in SV companies. Such limited knowledge is obtained on a 'self-service' basis, and with time clearly at a premium, where tax personnel are mostly working physically at a distance from the BUs, they are not rewarded directly for their level of business knowledge per se. The IT sector is inherently multifaceted and difficult to understand and so perhaps this limited knowledge is to be expected. Only a small minority of companies have formalised business partnership relationships to facilitate tax executives understanding the true nature of the business. Does such business knowledge give these companies a competitive advantage? Or perhaps tax executives are not concerned because they know from each other that most executives in SV companies are in the same boat, which, may well reflect a 'cosiness' for tax executives operating within the 'black box' of tax. How can these executives aspire to being 'business partners' (Wilson, 1995) without understanding the business? Arguably, Wilson (1995) over-rates the importance of business knowledge in this context.

5 Discussion and Conclusions

Our findings highlight the significant variation in the organisation, location and focus of the tax functions in our study. This further confirms the argument of Nohria et al. (2003) about having in place an organisational structure that works. However, taking the feasibility test as part of the working organisation structure outlined by Goold and Campbell (2002) it is clear that it has created some constraints in the operations of some of the firms in the study. For future research this is worthy of further empirical investigation at business unit and corporate levels. However, the tax function organisational structure would pass the accountability test in the same working organisation structure, as it provided effective control when it came to compliance. We also found evidence of the importance of the relationship between senior tax experts and the firm's CFO. In firms where there was a strong reporting and working relationship taxation was more prominent in the corporate activities of that firm.

For the purposes of the study we were seeking evidence that would illustrate or point to the nature of the alignment between tax and firm strategy. Overall our assessment of the alignment was that it was weak and focused more on compliance than planning. Mission statements provide a guide to behaviours and decisions (Ledford, Wendenhof and Strahley, 1995) as well as assisting a firm in shaping their identity, purpose and direction (Leuthesser and Kohli, 1997). Moreover, Collins and Porras (1994) argue that mission statements are an important tool in communicating direction and purpose to internal and external audiences. More fundamentally a mission statement is an important tool in directing the formulation and implementation of strategic planning (Pearse and David, 1987). Mission statements also influence organizational behavior (Bart, 1996a, 1996b). Our study found that 7 out of 15 companies had documented a tax mission strategy. We found evidence that tax mission statements were being used to identify and reinforce purpose and direction as well as being used as a communications tool as posited in the strategy literature. Furthermore, various tax strategies/mission statements found to be in place reflect a mix of quantitative (Porter, 1999; Scholes et al., 2008) and qualitative goals, which collectively reflect the roles of policeman, service provider and business partner alike provided by tax executives (Wilson, 1995). Strategy and mission statements having quantitative measures components are rare (Bart, 1997), but having them as a component of a tax mission statement is aligned to the core purpose of a tax function.

We found variable practices among MNCs around the formalisation of tax strategy, and there is limited evidence of (tax) strategy needing or seeking Board approval. Some tax executives were not convinced that having a formalised documented tax strategy adds value. This might be explained by the monitoring and control processes that tax departments are involved in, one of the three strategy processes posited by Garvin (1998, p.45). We found little evidence of tax department involvement in the other two strategy processes – direction setting, negotiation and selling. Within the monitoring and control processes of the strategy process there was some evidence of frictions (Scholes et al., 2008) within a tax strategy, for example, where a company aspires to minimising cash taxes while maximising EPS. Whatever the degree of formalisation of a company's tax strategy, the tax executives strongly supported the idea that tax should not drive business decisions. Strategic alignment of tax is supported in practice through reporting directly to the CFO, having as senior a title as possible in the organisation (two internal sources of power identified above), and having regular meetings and updates with business units. Overall, the evidence of tax planning mirrored characteristics of emergent strategy formulation for future orientated tax planning. Compliance based tax planning was the focus of all tax departments in our study mirroring the core characteristics of deliberate strategy (Ansoff, 1991), with a separation of strategy formulation from implementation (Mintzberg, 1994).

Findings in relation to the relationship between tax and other departments and business units were mixed and insightful. Despite acknowledging the value of having a sound knowledge of the business (Wilson, 1995), tax executives have only limited business knowledge, frequently obtained on a 'self-service' basis. Only a small minority of companies have formalised business partnership relationships to facilitate tax executives understanding the true nature of the business. On the other hand, educating non-tax personnel on the role of tax and its value add capability, while recognised as important, tends to take place over time in a rather ad hoc reactive manner, achieving varying degrees of success. There are some natural tensions and exercises of power (Fligstein, 1991) between tax and accounting personnel. A smooth and effective working relationship between tax and accounting personnel demands empathy as well as good communication (PWC, 2001; Wilson, 1995). It is difficult to see how tax executives can operate as 'business partners' (Wilson, 1995) without being more formally integrated operationally into BUs and other departments. However, such integration may be more likely now, due to the increased attention in tax risk management by Management.

Bibliography

Ansoff, H. I. (1991). Critique Of Henry Mintzberg's 'The Design School: Reconsidering The Basic Premises Of Strategic Management'. *Strategic Management Journal, 12*(6), 449-461.

Bart, C. K. (1996a). High-tech firms: does mission matter. *Journal of High Technology Management Research, 7*(2), 209-226.

Bart, C. K. (1996b). The impact of mission on firm innovativeness. *International Journal of Technology Management, 11*(479-493).

Bart, C. K. (1997). Sex, lies and mission statements. *Business Horizons, 40*(6), 9-18.

Bringer, J. D., Halley Johnston, L., & & Brackenridge, C. H. (2006). Using Computer-Assisted Qualitative Data Analysis Software to Develop a Grounded Theory Project. *Fields Methods, 18*, 245-266.

Burgelman, R. A. (1983). A Model of the Interaction of Strategic Behavior, Corporate Context, and the Concept of Strategy. *Academy of Management Review, 8*(1), 61-70. doi: 10.5465/AMR.1983.4287661

Chandler, A. D. (1962). Strategy and Structure: Chapters in the History of the Industrial Enterprise. *MIT Press*.

Collins, J., & Porras, J. (1994). *Built to Last – Successful Habits of Visionary Companies*. Harper Collins, New York, NY.

Covaleski, M. A., Dirsmith, M. W., & Weiss, J. M. (2007). 'The Market-Based Delivery of Welfare: A Field Study of On-Going Institutional Processes. *University of Wisconsin Working Paper*.

Delany, E. (2000). Strategic development of the multinational subsidiary through subsidiary initiative-taking. *Long Range Planning, 33*(2), 220-244. doi: http://dx.doi.org/10.1016/S0024-6301(00)00029-7

Dunbar, A. E., & Phillips, J. D. (2001). The Outsourcing of Corporate Tax Function Activities. *Journal of American Taxation Association, 23*(2), 35-49.

Fligstein, N. (1991). 'The Structural Transformation of American Industry: An institutional account of the causes of diversification in the largest firms, 1919-1979', in DiMaggio, P. J. and Powell, W. W. (eds.) *The New Institutionalism in Organizational Analysis*. Chicago: University of Chicago Press.

G8 Lough Erne Declaration. (2013). 1.

Garvin, D. A. (1998). The processes of organization and management. *Sloan Management Review, 39*(4), 33-50.

Glaister, K. W., & Hughes, J. F. (2007). Corporate Strategy Formulation and Taxation: Evidence from UK Firms. *British Journal of Management*, 1-16.

Glaister, K. W., & Hughes, J. F. (2008). Corporate Strategy Formulation and Taxation: Evidence from UK Firms. *British Journal of Management*, 19(1), 33-48. doi: 10.1111/j.1467-8551.2007.00532.x

Goold, M., & Campbell, A. (2002). Parenting in Complex Structures. *Long Range Planning*, 35(3), 219-243. doi: http://dx.doi.org/10.1016/S0024-6301(02)00052-3

Hansen, W. M., Petersen, B., & Wad, P. (2011). Change of Subsidiary Mandates in Emerging Markets: The Case of Danish MNCs in India. *Transnational Corporations Review*, 3(2), 104-116.

Hedlund, G. (1986). The Hypermodern MNC - A Heterarchy. *Human Resource Management*, 25(1), 9-35. doi: 10.1002/hrm.3930250103

Hines, J. R. (1999). Lessons from Behavioral Responses to International Taxation. *National Tax Journal*, 52(2), 305-322.

Holzman, R. S. (1965). Tax Implications of Management Decisions. *Management Review*, 54(4), 4-16.

Holzman, R. S. (2001). Tax Implications of Management Decisions. *Management Review*, 4-16.

Hu, Y. S. (1992). Global or Stateless Corporations are National Firms with International Operations. *California Management Review*, 34(2), 107-126.

James, S. (2005). 'Taxation Research as Economic Research', in Lamb, M., Lymer, A., Freedman, J. and James, S. (eds.) *Taxation: An Interdisciplinary Approach to Research*. Oxford: Oxford University Press.

Kaplan, R. S., & Norton, D. P. (2006). How to Implement a New Strategy Without Disrupting Your Organization. *Harvard Business Review*, 84(3), 100-109.

Karayan, J. E., & Swenson, C. W. (2007). *Strategic Business Tax Planning* (2nd ed.): John Wiley & Sons, New Jersey.

Lamb, M., Tuck, P., & Hoskin, K. (2003). The Emergence of the Customer Concept in Inland Revenue Discourse and Practices: A Dilemma', paper presented at the 13th ICAEW sponsored Tax Research Network Conference. *Oxford University*.

Ledford, G. E., Wendenhof, J. R., & Strahley, J. T. (1995). Realizing a Corporate Philosophy. *Organizational Dynamics*, 23(3), 5-19.

Leuthesser, L. & Kohli, C. (1997). Corporate Identity: The role of Mission Statements. *Business Horizons*, 40 (3), 59-66.

Levine, M. A., & Lerner, H. J. (1993). Outsourcing: Opportunities and Challenges for the Corporate Tax Executive. *Tax Executive*, 45(5), Unpaginated.

Manolopoulos, D. (2008). A Systematic Review of the Literature and Theoretical Analysis of Subsidiary Roles. *Journal of Transnational Management*, 13(1).

Miles, W. E., Snow, C. C., & Pfeffer, J. (1974). Organization-Environment: Concepts and Issues. *Industrial Relations*, 13(3), 244-264.

Mintzberg, H. (1994). The Fall and Rise of Strategic Planning. *Harvard Business Review, 72*(1), 107-114.

Nohria, N., Joyce, W., & Roberson, B. (2003). What Really Works. *Harvard Business Review, 81*(7), 42-52.

Odendahl, T., & Shaw, A. (2001). 'Interviewing Elites', in Gubrium, F. G. and Holstein, J. A. (eds.) *Handbook of Interview Research: Context and Method.* California: Sage Publications.

OECD. (2013). *Action Plan on Base Erosion and Profit Shifting.* OECD Publishing.

Pearse, J.A. & David, F. (1987). Corportate Mission Statement: The Bottom Line. *Academy of Management Perspectives*, 1(2), 109-115.

Perrow, C. (1985). Review: Overboard with Myth and Symbols. *American Journal of Sociology, 91*(1), 151-155.

Picciotto. (1995). The Construction of International Taxation, in Dezalay, Y. and Sugarman, D. (eds.) *Professional Competition and Power* London: Routledge.

Porter, B. A. (1999). Survey of In---House Tax Departments in United Kingdom Corporates. *British Tax Review*(1), pp. 32-51.

PWC. (2001). *Tax Function 2001*. PricewaterhouseCoopers.

Rego, S. O. (2003). Tax-avoidance activities of US multinational corporations. *Contemporary Accounting Research, 20*(4), 805-833. doi: 10.1506/vann-b7ub-gmfa-9e6w

Reuters. (2013). Special Report - How Big Tech stays offline on tax.

Scholes, M. S., Wolfson, M. A., Erickson, M., Maydew, E. L., & & Shevlin, T. (2008). *Taxes and Business Strategy: A Planning Approach.* NJ: Prentice Hall.

Schollhammer, H. (1971). Organization Structures of Multinational Corporations. *Academy of Management Journal, 14*(3), 345-365. doi: 10.2307/255079

Scott, P., Gibbons, P., & Coughlan, J. (2010). Developing subsidiary contribution to the MNC—Subsidiary entrepreneurship and strategy creativity. *Journal of International Management, 16*(4), 328-339. doi: http://dx.doi.org/10.1016/j.intman.2010.09.004

Skaerback, P. & Tryggestas, K. (2010). The role of accounting devices in performing corporate strategy. *Accounting, Organizations and Society, 1*(35), 108-124.

The Economist (2011). *A Very Short History of the Crisis.*

Tax avoidance by multinational companies. (2012). UK Parliament. Available at: http://www.publications.parliament.uk/pa/cm201213/cmselect/cmpubacc/716/71605.htm

Tuck, P. (2004). No Accounting for Taste; Remaking the Large Corporate Taxpayer into a Visible Customer', paper presented at the European Accounting Association Conference, Prague.

Valente, P. (2002). Tax Planning in the Global Village. *International Tax Review, 13*(6), 47-50.

Valente, P. (2002). Tax Planning in the Global Village. *International Tax Review, 36*(6), Unpaginated.

van Oijen, A., & Douma, S. (2000). Diversification Strategy and the Roles of the Centre. *Long Range Planning, 33*(4), 560-578. doi: http://dx.doi.org/10.1016/S0024-6301(00)00063-7

Wilson, G. P. (1995). *Corporate Tax Effectiveness: Adding Value Through the Tax Function*. Harvard University Press.

Yancey, W. F., & Cravens, K. S. (1998). A Framework for International Tax Planning for Managers. *Journal of International Accounting, Auditing & Taxation, 7*(2), 251-272.

Zimmerman, J. L. (1983). Taxes and firm size. *Journal of Accounting and Economics, 5*, 119-149.

12 An Examination of Two Alternative Approaches to Corporate-Shareholder Taxation of Inbound Investment for Australia

C John Taylor

Abstract

This chapter considers the problem of attacting foreign investment to a small open economy while maintaining sufficient revenue from the perspective of an Australian academic tax lawyer. It begins by analysising the present Australian rules relating to direct and portfolio inbound investment. The chapter then examines and analyses two alternative approaches to inbound investment [an Allowance for Corporate Equity (ACE) or an Allowance for Corporate Capital (ACC) and franked debt] that Australia could consider. The analysis is confined to portfolio and non-portfolio investment in Australian companies. The highly complex nature of the present Australian rules will be evident from their exposition and analysis. A further aim of the analysis of alternative approaches is to identify those which result in significant simplification of Austrailan rules relating to inbound corporate investment. The conclusion of the chapter is that if Australia were to adopt an ACC system coupled with franked debt and a proportionate franking ordering rule the result would be a more attractive environment for inbound investment at a lower revenue cost than under an ACE system and would enable several complex divisions to be removed from Australian tax law. While implementation details would necessarily have to be varied due to historic features of particular national systems the proposed system would also merit consideration by similarly placed small to medium sized resource rich open economies.

1 Introduction

The global financial crisis and its aftermath placed governments throughout the western world under increasing budgetary pressure with revenues declining as a consequence of business failures and general reductions in economic activity. While smaller, resource rich, open economies like

Australia and Canada weathered the storm better than many concerns remain, in the Australian case at least, about the longer term sustainability of revenues the so called 'mining boom' coupled with ongoing declines in the local manufacturing sector. One of the challenges for Australia, and for small open economies more generally, is of encouraging the inbound investment perceived to be necessary for economic growth while maintaining sufficient revenue to fund public and social goods at levels to which their populations have become accustomed. While the problem has been apparent since the beginnings of the process of globalisation of the world economy it has been exacerbated by the global financial crisis and its aftermath. Falls in business activity and cross border investment meant falling revenues at a time when higher unemployment and the risk of business failures were leading to increased government expenditure on social security benefits and economic stimulus programs. More recently, in Australia, with the 2013 election of a Liberal-National Coalition Government, focus has shifted to possibly reducing the role of government, cutting certain expenditures and examining Federal – State relations with a further review of the taxation system scheduled for release in 2015.

This chapter aims to bring the perspective of an Australian academic tax lawyer to the problem of attacting foreign investment while maintaining sufficient revenue. As such it begins by analysising the present Australian rules relating to direct and portfolio inbound investment. Following that analsyis, the chapter examines and analyses two alternative approaches to inbound investment that Australia could consider. The analysis will be confined to portfolio and non-portfolio investment in Australian companies. The aim of the analysis will be to attempt to identify an approach which better meets the dual goals of encouraging inbound investment while maintaining revenue adequacy. The highly complex nature of the present Australian rules will be evident from their exposition and analysis. A further aim of the analysis of alternative approaches will be to identify those which result in significant simplification of Austrailan rules relating to inbound corporate investment.

1.1 Outline of Domestic Operation of Australian Dividend Imputation System

Australia currently operates a variable credit or shareholder credit account form of imputation system of corporate – shareholder taxation.[1] Australian

---

1 Space considerations have not permitted detailed reference to the statutory provisions supporting the statements in the text. For general discussions of the Australian dividend imputation system, see R H Woellner, S Barkoczy, S Murphy, C Evans and D Pinto, *Australian Taxation Law,* 24th edition, 2014, CCH (hereafter, 'Woellner et al') paragraphs 18-330 to 18-492 and F Gilders, J Taylor, M Walpole, M Burton and T

companies, and New Zealand companies that elect to join the Australian imputation system, are required to maintain a 'franking account' which tracks, among other things, Australian corporate tax paid or payable by the company. Payments of foreign corporate tax do not generate franking credits for Australian companies. To the extent that a dividend paid to an Australian resident shareholder has franking credits attached to it (conceptually, to the extent that the dividend is funded from profits that have been subject to Australian tax) the shareholder receives a gross up and credit for the franking credit. A resident shareholder then receives a tax offset (credit) equal to the franking credit on the dividend. The end effect of the tax offset is that a resident individaul shareholder only bears tax on the dividend at the excess of the shareholder's average rate over the corporate rate. If the shareholder's average rate is below the corporate rate the excess of the corporate rate over the shareholder's average rate is refundable to the shareholder. A resident company receiving a dividend with franking credits attached also includes both the dividend and the franking credit in its assessable income and is entitled to a tax offset. As discussed, above, the franking credit on the dividend also generates a franking credit in the recipient resident conpany's franking account. However, excess tax offsets generated by franking credits are not refundable to resident companies but are converted into tax losses which can be deducted in the following year. Importantly, Australian complying superannuation funds are currently taxed at 15% on their investment earnings and are entitled to refunds of excess franking credits.

Tax preferences received by Australian resident companies do not generate franking credits and are 'washed out' on distribution to Australian resident shareholders. Where a resident company either derives foreign income or receives foreign source dividends, to the extent that the Australian corporate tax paid is less than would otherwise be payable on an equivalent amount of Australian source income, then, assuming that the Australian resident company wishes to avoid a franking deficit tax liability, a redistribution of that foreign income or dividend to Australian resident shareholders can only be unfranked. This will mean that, except where the shareholder is tax exempt, the dividend will be fully taxable to the resident shareholder with the effect that the tax preference in relation to foreign source income at the recipient Australina company level will be washed out on a distribtuion of that foreign source income to resident shareholders. In these circumstances a lesser amount of Australian corporate tax will be payble because either: (a) the dividends or income are non-assessable non-exempt income; or (b)

Ciro, *Understanding Taxation Law* 2014, (hereafter, 'Gilders et al') Lexis Nexis, 2014, paragraphs 12.34 to 12.71 and at 13.4 to 13.56. All subsequent references to Woellner et al and to Gilders et al are to paragraph numbers.

because the company receives a foreign income tax offset for certain types of foreign tax paid on the foreign income or dividend.

1.2 Current Australian Treatment of Inbound Investment

Where a non-resident conducting busines in Australia through a permanent establishment receives a dividend or a non-share dividend that is attributable to the permanent establishment with Australian franking credits attached the amount of the dividend is included in the non-resident's assessable income and the non-resident is entitled to a gross up and tax offset equal to the amount of the franking credit. However, the non-resident is not entitled to a refund of any excess tax offset. The dividend attributable to the permanent establishment is not subject to Australian dividend withholding tax. [2]

To the extent that a dividend or a non-share dividend paid to a non-resident shareholder, other than one carrying on business in Australia through a permanent establishment to which the dividend or non-share dividend is attributable, has franking credits attached to it (conceptually, to the extent that it is funded from profits that have been subject to Australian tax) it is exempt from Australian withholding tax and is not taxed on an assessment basis. In the absence of a bilateral taxation treaty the unfranked portion of a dividend or non-share dividend paid to a non-resident is subject to dividend withholding tax of 30%. Australia's older bilateral taxation treaties reduced dividend withholding tax to 15% in nearly all cases, but more recent Australian treaties reduce dividend withholding tax on non-portfolio intercorporate dividends to 5% and, in the case of the Australia – United Kingdom and Australia – United States treaties reduce dividend withholding tax to zero in the case of dividends paid by an 80% or more Australian subsidiary to its United Kingdom or United States parent.[3] Differences in the treatment of dividends paid to non-residents as compared with those paid to residents have led to the development of further complex rules to prevent practices known as 'dividend streaming'[4] and 'franking credit trading'[5].

Interest incurred by Australian companies on money borrowed to fund income producing activities is generally deductible to the Australian

---

2   See the discussion in Woellner at al at 24-620 and in Gilders et al at 13.54 and at 18.39.
3   See the discussion in Woellner et al at 24-605 and 24-620 and in Gilders et al at 13.54, 18.39, 18.40 and 18.78.
4   See the discussion in Woellner et al at 18.350, 18.415 and 18.425 and in Gilders et al at 12.63 to 12.71.
5   See the discussion in Woellner et al at 18-415 and 18-420 and in Gilders et al at 12.72 to 12.73.

company.[6] Complex inbound thin capitalisation rules[7] apply to Australian companies controlled in a defined sense by foreign investors and to Australian branches of foreign entities.

Timing differences aside, the Australian dividend imputation system means that for domestic investors equivalent tax treatment is given to interest and dividend income. At the company level, however, the non-deductibility of dividends means that the normal rate of return on equity is taxed at the company level while the deductibility of interest means that the normal rate of return on debt is not. In a full imputation system, however, the gross up and credit at the shareholder level means that domestic shareholders can be provided with the same after tax return as domestic lenders at no higher cost to the paying company. That is a dividend of $70 with $30 of fully refundable franking credits attached has the same value to a resident shareholder as an interest receipt of $100 or a dividend of $100 with no franking credits attached. With some significant exceptions, interest paid to non-resident is subject to a 10% withholding tax[8] which is generally not reduced in Australia's bi-lateral taxation treaties except, in some treaties in the case of interest derived by financial institutions.[9] The differential treatment of returns on debt and equity investments accounts for the existence of complex inbound thin capitalisation rules accompanied by complex and somewhat indeterminate rules which aim to distinguish between debt and equity funding of Australian companies.[10]

1.3 Analysis of Outcomes under Current Australian Rules on Inbound Investment

Example 1.1.a [11]

Austco 1 Pty Ltd is an Australian resident company with $A1,000,000 of Australian source income on which it will pay $A300,000 of Australian Corporate Tax. When made this payment will generate $A300,000 of

---

6 See the discussion in Woellner et al at 10-460.
7 The rules are contained in ITAA 1997 Division 820 and are discussed in Woellner et al at 24-860 and in Gilders et al at 18.50 to 18.63.
8 See the discussion in Woellner et al at 24-610 and in Gilders et al at 18.41 to 18.45.
9 For example: Article 11(3) Australia – United Kingdom Taxation Treaty 2003; Article 11(3) Australia – United States Taxation Treaty 1982 as amended by 2002 Protocol; Australia – New Zealand Taxation Treaty 2009 Article 11(3); Australia – Japan Taxation Treaty 2008 Article 11(3); Australia – France Taxation Treaty 2006 Article 11(3).
10 The debt and equity rules are set out in ITAA 1997 Division 974. The key to characterisation of an interest in a company as a debt interest is the effectively non-contingent nature of the returns on the interest. The rules are discussed in Woellner et al at 22-010 to 22-020 and in Gilders et al at 12.25.
11 Tax rates used in this and subsequent examples are Australian rates for the 2013-2014 year. All currency refrences are to Australian dollars.

franking credits in Austco 1 Pty Ltd's franking account. Austco 1 Pty Ltd has only one shareholder which is a company resident in Euphoria. Assume that the dividend is not attributable to a permanent establishment of the parent company in Australia. Assume also that Euphoria exempts foreign non-portoflio dividends received by resident companies and operates a classical corporate-shareholder tax system.

Austco 1 Pty Ltd's Australian Corporate Tax Position
Assessable Income (assumed to be equal to distributable profit)	1,000,000
Deductions	0
Taxable Income	1,000,000
Australian corporate tax	300,000
Franking credits generated	300,000
After tax distributable profit	700,000

Australian Tax Treatment of Dividend
Dividend	700,000
Franking credit attached	300,000
Dividend exempt from dividend withholding tax via ITAA 1936 s.128B(3)(ga)	
Dividend not taxed on an asssessment basis because of s.128D	
Australian tax on dividend	0

Euphorian Tax Position at Company Level
Dividend	700,000
Exempt from Euphorian tax	
After tax dividend	700,000

The Euphorian parent company then distributes its after tax profit as a dividend of $100,000 to each of its seven shareholders. Assume that the Euphorian individual rate scale is identical to the Australian individual rate scale. The tax effects for each shareholder will be:

Dividend	100,000
Euphorian tax	26,447
After tax dividend	73,553

The Euphorian shareholders would be in the same after tax position as if they had invested in a Euphorian company that had derived $1,000,000 of income, paid Euphorian tax and distribtued all of its after tax income to them equally as dividends. The effective rate of tax for the Euphorian shareholder will be 48.51%. The critical assumption here is that the Euphorian corporate rate has been assumed to be the same as the Australian corporate rate i.e 30%

If, on the other hand, the Euphorian corporate rate were 20%, the effective tax rate for a Euphorian shareholder receiving the redistribution of the Australian source dividend from the Euphorian company would still be 48.51%. On the other hand, the effective tax rate for a Euphorian shareholder receiving a dividend representing 1/7th of a distribution of a pre tax Eurphorian source profit by a Euphorian company would be 42.34%.

Where the Euphorian rate is 20% capital export neutrality (CEN)[12] is not achieved at the Euphorian shareholder level. Rather the result is national neutrality (NN). The fact that the corporate rate is lower in Euphoria means that when the Euphorian participation exemption is combined with the Euphorian classical system the amount of the dividend paid by the Euphorian company to the underlying Euphorian shareholder is less. Algebraically, the difference in the amount of the dividend can be represented as (Y − Yc_2) − (Y − Yc_1) = Yc_1 − Yc_2 where c_1 is the host corporate rate and c_2 is the home corporate rate. This result, therefore, is not a product of the Australian dividend imputation system as such or of its treatment of dividends paid to non-residents but rather is a consequence of the difference in corporate rates and the use of a participation exemption in combination with a classical system in Euphoria.

Example 1.1.b.i

Assume the facts in Example 1.1.a with the variation that the shareholder is a company resident in Utopia. Assume that Utopia operates a foreign tax credit

---

12 Since the 1960s discussion of international tax policy issues has been dominated by two, usually conflicting, policy objectives. These are 'Capital Import Neutrality' (CIN) and 'Capital Export Neutrality' (CEN). These objectives have overwhelmingly been viewed from the perspective a of capital exporting (or residence) country. From that perspective the technical differences between the two objectives amount to differences about the type and extent of relief from international double taxation that a residence country offers. When applied to outbound investment a policy of CIN requires that the same rates of tax apply to all investments in a particular country regardless of the country of residence of the investor. The implication of pursuit of a policy of CIN for a residence country in relation to its outbound investment is that it would relieve international juridical double taxation by an exemption for taxed foreign source income. See the discussion of CIN in M J Graetz, Taxing International Income: Inadequate Principles, Outdated Concepts, and Unsatisfactory Policies (2001) 54 *Tax Law Review* 261, at 270-271 and in R S Avi-Yonah, Globalisation, Tax Competition and the Fiscal Crisis of the Welfare State (2000) 113 *Harvard Law Review* 1573, at 1604-1610. Conversely, as a policy of CEN requires that the same rates of tax apply to residents' income regardless of whether it has a domestic or foreign source, pursuit of that policy in relation to outbound investment is generally regarded as requiring that the residence country relieve international juridical double taxation by granting a foreign tax credit. See the discussion of CEN in Graetz, supra at 270 to 271 and in Avi-Yonah supra at 1604 to 1610. A further possible tax policy objective is sometimes proposed. This is the objective known as 'national neutrality'. Under this policy national welfare is only seen as being maximized when pre tax returns on domestic investments are equal to after tax returns on foreign investments. The rationale for this approach is that domestic taxes paid benefit the country of residence whereas foreign taxes paid benefit only the foreign country and are of no benefit to either the country of residence or the resident investing abroad. A country pursuing a policy of national neutrality in relation to outbound investment would only treat payments of foreign tax as a pre domestic tax expense (just as it would treat payments of foreign interest or foreign rents). The argument in favour of national neutrality was developed by Peggy Musgrave in *United States Taxation of Foreign Investment Income* (1969) at 134 and at 153-4.

system for non-portfolio dividends received by resident companies. Assume that the Utopian company does not have any excess foreign tax credits. Assume that the Utopian corporate rate is 40% and that Utopia operates a classical system of corporate – shareholder taxation with a progressive rate scale identical to the Australian progressive rate scale.

	$
Utopian Tax Position at Company Level	
Dividend	700,000
Grossed up for underlying foreign tax	300,000
Grossed up dividend	1,000,000
Utopian tax	400,000
Foreign tax credit	300,000
Net Utopian tax	100,000
After tax dividend	600,000

If the Utopian company distributes the $600,000 to each of its seven shareholders equally they will each receive a dividend of $85,714.29. The after tax position of each shareholder will be:

Dividend	85,714.29
Utopian shareholder tax	20,947.00
After tax dividend	64,767.29

Here the Utopian shareholders are in the same position that they would have been if they had invested in a Utopian company which had derived $1,000,000 of taxable income, paid Utopian tax and distributed all of its after tax income to them equally as dividends. The effective tax rate for the Utopian shareholders in both cases would have been 54.66%.

If the Utopian corporate rate had also been 30% then no net Utopian tax would have been payable at the Utopian company level and the after tax dividend ultimately received by the shareholder would have been the same as in Example 1.1.a. Similarly, if the Utopian company has excess foreign tax credits sufficient to absorb the Utopian tax on the grossed up dividend then, again, no net Utopian tax would have been payable at the Utopian company level and the after tax dividend ultimately received by the shareholder would have been the same as in Example 1.1.a. Where the Utopian company has excess foreign tax credits it might be expected to plan to decrease its Australian source tax to the point where any net home tax on repatriation of profits absorbs the excess foreign tax credits. Where the Utopian corporate tax rate is lower than the Australian corporate tax rate the result (all else being equal) will be that the payment of Australian tax will produce excess foreign tax credits for the Utopian company. The result will be equivalent to the national neutrality position in Example 1.1.a when the Euphorian tax rate was assumed to be lower than the Australian corporate tax rate.

Example 1.1.b.ii

Assume the facts in Example 1.1.b.i with the variation that the Utopian company has only portfolio shareholdings in Australian companies and receives total dividends on $700,000 which were exempt from dividend withholding tax under ITAA 1936 s.128B(3)(ga).

	$
Utopian Tax Position at Company Level	
Dividend	700,000
Utopian tax	280,000
After tax dividend	420,000

If the Utopian company distributes the $420,000 to each of its seven shareholders equally they will each receive a dividend of $60,000. The after tax position of each shareholder will be:

Dividend	60,000
Utopian shareholder tax	11,947
After tax dividend	48,053

The effective tax rate for the Utopian shareholders would have been 66.36%.

Here the fact that the foreign tax credit in Utopia does not extend to underlying Australian corporate tax means that corporate tax has cascaded through the chain of companies. The benefit of Australia not levying dividend withholding tax on the franked portion of the dividend paid has benefited the Utopian treasury not the Utopian shareholder. This is an example of the 'treasury effect'. The Utopian shareholders are in a poorer position than they would have been if they had invested in a Utopian company which had derived $1,000,000 of income, paid Utopian tax and distributed its after tax income to them equally as dividends. In that situation the effective tax rate for the Utopian shareholders would have been 54.66%.

If the Utopian shareholder had been a Utopian pension fund taxed at a rate of 15% in Utopia then the effective tax rate applying to the distribution would have been 64.30% whereas if the Utopian pension fund had invested in a Utopian company which derived $142,857.14 of Utopian source income, paid Utopian tax and distributed its after tax profit to the pension fund the effective tax rate for the pension fund would have been 49%. The result is again national neutrality but no 'treasury effect' has been produced.

If an individual Utopian shareholder had invested directly in an Australian company and had received a distribution franked to 100% then the effective tax rate on the distribution of the pre tax profit of $142,857.14 would have been 48.51%. If a Utopian company had derived $142,857.14 of Utopian source income, paid Utopian corporate tax and distributed all of its after tax income to a single Utopian individual then that effective tax rate on the pre tax profits of $142,857.14 would have been 57.18%. The effective tax rate for the Utopian shareholder would be 57.18%. The cross border result is somewhere between CEN and capital import neutrality (CIN) and is due to: (a) the sum of the Australian corporate and withholding rates being lower than the Utopian rate; and (b) the use of a classical system in Utopia. Here the Utopian shareholder has benefited from Australia not levying withholding tax on the franked portion of the dividend. The conclusion that can be drawn here is that an individual shareholder or a pension fund in a classical country will be in a more favourable position by making a portfolio equity investment in an Australian company as compared with making a portfolio investment in a company resident in their home coutnry where the sum of the Australian corporate and withholding tax rates is lower than the home country corporate rate. In this instance the individual or pension fund portfolio investors will benefit from Australia not levying withholding tax on the franked portion of a dividend paid to them.

Example 1.2

Assume the facts in Example 1.1.a.with the variation that Austco 1 Pty Ltd pays interest of $750,000 to its Euphorian parent company. Assume that both the amount of the debt and the interest rate are on arm's length terms.

	$
Australian Tax Position	
Austco 1 Pty Ltd's position	
Income	1,000,000
Interest paid	750,000
Taxable income	250,000
Australian corporate tax & franking credits	75,000
Dividend franked to 100%	175,000
Withholding tax on interest	75,000
Euphorian Tax Position	
Company level	
Dividend	175,000
Grossed up interest	750,000
Euphorian corporate tax	225,000
Foreign tax credit	75,000
Net Euphorian tax	150,000
After tax income	700,000
Shareholder's Position	
Dividend	100,000
Euphorian tax	26,447
After tax dividend	73,553

Both the Euphorian company and the Euphorian underlying shareholder are in the same position as they were in Example 1.1.a. If, however, the Euphorian corporate rate were 20% the effective tax rate for the underlying shareholder would be 43.9%. At that Euphorian corporate rate both the Euphorian company and the Euphorian underlying shareholder would be in a better position than they were when the investment was wholly funded by equity, but the underlying shareholder would be in a poorer position than they would have been if a Euphorian company, funded wholly by equity, had made a distribution from Euphorian source profits.

The advantages of related party debt funding can be magnified through planning strategies utlising related entities in low tax jurisdictions. The results that can be obtained through planning of this type are illustrated in Example 2.1.

Example 2.1

Assume the facts in Example 1.2 with the variation that the interest was loaned to Austco 1 Pty Ltd by a wholly owned subsidiary of the Euphorian company resident in Haven. There is no corpoate tax or withholding tax in Haven. The Haven subsidiary redistributes all its interest income as a dividend to the Euphorian parent. Assume that Euphoria has no CFC rules.

The Australian tax position will be identical to Example 1.2.

	$
The position in Haven will be:	
Interest received	675,000
Dividend paid	675,000
Euphorian Tax Position	
Dividend received from subsidiary in Haven	675,000
Dividend from Austco 1 Pty Ltd	175,000
Total dividends received	850,000
Euphorian corporate tax	0
Euphorian shareholder	
Dividend received	121,458.57
Euphorian shareholder tax	34,708.55
After tax dividend	86,750.02

Both the Euphorian company and the Euphorian shareholder are in a significantly better position than they were in Example 1.2. The effective tax rate for the shareholder will be 39.50%. It is possible that planning of this nature could be curtailed by an accruals tax regime in Euphoria, but the characteristics of such regimes vary considerably from jurisdiction to jurisdiction and the specific rules which delineate their operation can leave scope for planning that avoids their operation. Example 2.1 highlights what revenue authorities in a source country would perceive to be a clear threat to their corporate income tax base. From a revenue authority's perspective, therefore, the extent to which any alternative approach protects the source country corporate tax base from the threat of related party debt financing will be a key or even critical consideration.

1.4 Conclusion on Inbound Investment

While arguably technically not in breach of the non-discrimination article in several of Australia's bilateral taxation treaties, Australia's practice of not extending franking gross ups and credits to non-resident shareholders arguably inhibits some inbound investment and, in some cases, Austraila's practice of not levying dividend withholding tax on the franked portion of dividends can produce significant 'treasury effects' which benefit foreign governments rather than foreign investors. Treasury effects occur in the home country when it uses a foreign tax credit system and the level of tax in the home country is greater than the level of Australian tax credited under the home country's foreign tax credit system. It should be noted, however, that the analysis has identified some circumstances in which a foreign investor (typically, but not exclusively, a non-portfolio investor) benefits from Australia not levying dividend withholding tax on the franked portion of dividends.

2 Allowance for Corporate Equity as an Alternative

One of the alternative approaches to corporate-shareholder taxation that has recently been considered in Australia[13] is introducing an allowance for corporate equity (ACE) under which companies would receive a deduction for a deemed rate of return on equity with the consequence that the normal return on equity would not be taxed at the corporate level.[14] The likely high

---

13 *Australia, Review of Australia's Future Tax System: Report to the Treasurer, Part 2 – Detailed Analysis*, Canberra, 2009, Volume 1 of 2 at p.165 made a cautious recommendation that: 'a business level expenditure tax (such as ACE) could suit Australia in the future and is worthy of further consideration and public debate.' Subsequently The Federal Government appointed Business Tax Working Group considered that: 'an ACE should not be pursued in the short-to-medium term but may be worthy of further consideration and public debate in the longer term.' Australian Government, The Treasury, Business Tax Working Group, Discussion Paper (August 2012), pp5-6 and 44-49 http://www.treasury.gov.au/Policy-Topics/Taxation/BTWG (Accessed 22nd January 2013).
14 There is an extensive literature on the ACE proposal usually traced back to R Boadway and N Bruce, 'A General Proposition on the Design of a Neutral Business Tax' (1984) 24 *Journal of Public Economics* 231 and to the Institute for Fiscal Studies, Capital Taxes Group, *Equity for Companies: A Corporation Tax for the 1990s*, London, Institute for Fiscal Studies, 1991. The Boadway and Bruce proposal, however, is better described as an Allowance For Corporate Capital (ACC) discussed in Part 3 of this chapter.

revenue cost of that approach has been noted in previous analysis[15] as have difficulties associated with determining an appropriate deemed rate of return for all companies.[16] One of the arguments advanced in favour of an ACE is that it reduces the bias in favour of debt[17] and reduces the need for thin capitalisation rules.[18] The focus of the analysis in this section of this chapter will be on testing these claims and in identifying the extent to which such reductions are made.

One argument of ACE advocates is that, as imputation benefits are not extended to non-residents, the treatment of distributions at the investor level should be ignored in evaluating an ACE as it is assumed that, in a small open economy, the marginal investor is a foreign investor.[19] Part 1 of this chapter demonstrated that, in the case of the Australian dividend imputation system in any event, this assertion is only true in some cases. Where the foreign investor is a non-portfolio investor from a country with a corporate rate equal to or higher than the Australian corporate rate then the Australian policy of not levying dividend withholding tax on the franked portion of dividends paid to foreign residents benefits the foreign non-portfolio investor and underlying shareholders in the foreign investor's home country. In these instances, the combined operation of the two countries tax systems produces either capital import neutrality or capital export neutrality at both the foreign company and the foreign shareholder level. Only in those cases, identified in Part 1, where the treasury effect is produced (typically in the case of foreign portfolio investors in Australian companies) does the foreign investor not benefit from the Australian policy of not levying dividend withholding tax on the franked portion of dividends paid to non-residents. In those instances, it is worth noting that the result is the product of typical limitations on the foreign tax credit in the foreign investor's home country.

For the argument to stand the assumption must be refined so that the marginal investor is assumed to be a foreign portfolio investor. Typically, these would be expected to be foreign pension funds, insurance companies,

---

15 A point made by the Australian Business Tax Working Group, supra note 11. G S Cooper, 'Implementing an allowance for corporate equity' (2012) 27 *Australian Tax Forum* 241 at 242, by applying general estimates in prior literature, calculated that the Australian revenue cost would be $ 1.5 billion each year.
16 The difficulties associated with determining the ACE rate are discussed in Cooper, supra note 14 at pp 251 to 253.
17 The arguments are summarized and criticized in Cooper, supra note 15 at pp. 244 to 246.
18 See, for example, Australia, Review of Australia's Future Tax System, supra note 13 Appendix E.
19 See, for example, P B Sorensen and S M Johnson, 'Taxing Capital Income: Options for Reform in Australia', Melbourne Institute, Australia's Future Tax and Transfer Policy Conference, June 2009, at pp. 186 to 188 and at pp.191 to 193.

banks or private equity entities. It is also clear from Part 1 of this chapter that these entities and investors in them will typically obtain greater benefits from debt rather than equity benefits in Australian companies. In this context, the debt bias exists because the reduction in dividend withholding tax under the Australian dividend imputation system is usually not as valuable to the foreign portfolio investor as the elimination of Australian corporate tax that arises from interest deductibility. Viewed from this perspective, the logic underpinning the ACE allowance appears compelling. If the marginal investor is a foreign portfolio investor then a higher pre tax rate of return has to be generated on equity to produce the same after tax rate of return as a debt investment by foreign portfolio investors. Hence, as ACE allows a deduction for the risk free rate of return on equity it appears to be solving the problem by attacking its very source.

One objection to this aspect of the agument of ACE advocates is that it is in fact unlikely that the marginal investor for all Australian companies will be a foreign portfolio investor. Foreign portfolio investors in Australian companies, almost by definition, have done so via global equity and bond markets. Many Australian companies are unlisted, many of these are trustees of unit or discretionary trusts, and of those that are not it is likely that many of them either do not have access to global equity or bond markets while many of those that have theoretical access do not utilise it. For these companies the marginal investor is likely to be an Australian resident and, as was demonstrated in Part 1, timing differences aside the Australian dividend imputation system elminates a bias in favour of debt over equity. For nearly all resident investors a dividend of $70 with $30 of franking credit attached is equivalent to an interest receipt of $100.

A second objection to this aspect of the argument of ACE advocates is that ACE only eliminates the bias for debt over equity when the actual borrowing cost to companies corresponds with the risk free rate of return used in the ACE allowance. Where the actual cost of debt is higher than the ACE allowance then, depending to some extent on the dividend policy of the company, a bias in favour of debt over equity will remain internationally and, if a classical system is operating at the shareholder level, will be reintroduced domestically. This is because the element of the return on equity which is greater than the ACE allowance will be taxed at both the company level and at the shareholder level on distribution. Conversely, where the actual cost of debt is lower than the ACE allowance a bias in favour of equity over debt will be produced.[20]

---

20 Cooper, supra note 15 at 268 makes similar points in relation to cross border investment by related entities. M P Devereux, 'Issues in the Design of Taxes on Corporate Profit' (2012) 65 *National Tax Journal* 709 at 723 also makes equivalent points.

Example 3.1.a

Austco Pty Ltd has one shareholder, Ocker, who is an Australian resident. Assume that Austco Pty Ltd is wholly funded by equity of $2,000,000. Assume also that Austco Pty Ltd produces a profit of 5% on its capital. Assume that Austco Pty Ltd has no debt. Assume that the ACE allowance rate is 3%. Assume that Ocker has no other income or deductions. Assume that following the introduction of an ACE the dividend imputation system is abolished.

	$
Austco Pty Ltd's Australian tax position	
Assessable income	100,000
Less ACE allowance	60,000
Taxable income	40,000
Australian corporate tax @ 30%	12,000
After tax income	28,000
After tax profit	88,000
Dividend declared	88,000
Ocker's position	
Dividend included in assessable income via ITAA 1936 s44(1)(a)	88,000
Tax and Medicare levy at 2013-2014 rates	21,827
After tax dividend	66,173

Effective tax rate on pre tax income of $100,000 is 33.83%. After tax rate of return on investment of $2,000,000 is 3.31%.

If instead of contributing equity of $2,000,000 to Austco Pty Ltd, Ocker had made a loan of $2,000,000 at 5% then Austco Pty Ltd would have had no Australian income tax liability and Ocker's Australian tax position would have been as follows:

Ocker's position	
Interest included in assessable income	100,000
Tax and Medicare levy at 2013-2014 rates	26,44?
After tax interest	73,55?

Effective tax rate on pre tax income of $100,000 is 26.45%. After tax rate of return on loan of $2,000,000 is 3.67%.

That is where the ACE allowance is lower than both the actual interest rate and the profit percentage on the company's capital the introduction of an ACE with a classical system operating at the shareholder level re-introduces a domestic bias in favour of debt funding.

Example 3.1.b

Assume the facts in Example 3.1.a with the variation that the ACE allowance rate is 5%. Ocker's position remains the same where Austco Pty Ltd is funded by $2,000,000 of debt but where Austco Pty Ltd is funded by $2,000,000 of equity the effects are as follows:

	$
Austco Pty Ltd	
Assessable income	100,000
Less ACE allowance	100,000
Taxable income	0
After tax profit /income	100,000
Dividend declared	100,000
Ocker's position	
Dividend included in assessable income via ITAA 1936 s.44(1)(a)	100,000
Tax and Medicare levy at 2013-201 4rates	26,447
After tax dividend	73,553

Effective tax rate on pre tax income of $100,000 is 26.45%. After tax rate of return on loan of $2,000,000 is 3.67%.

On the other hand, if Austco Pty Ltd had been funded by $2,000,000 of equity but distributed a dividend of $70,000 rather than a dividend of $100,000 the effective tax rate on the pre tax income of $100,000 would be 14.297% and the after tax rate of return on investment would be 2.79%. That, is under an ACE system, all else being equal, retentions of profits produce a lower effective tax rate on the distribution and a lower after tax return on investment at the point of distribution (both as compared with a fully debt financed investment and a fully funded equity financed investement in which all after tax profits are distributed).

That is in the situation where the ACE allowance, the pre-tax return on capital and the interest rate are all equal and 100% of the after tax profit is distributed to shareholders, ACE produces neutrality between debt and equity financing for a domestic investor. When one of these features is not present ACE will not produce neutrality between these forms of financing and will favour one form of financing over another. That the same point holds when the company is funded by a mixture of debt and equity financing is illustrated by Example 3.2.

Example 3.2.a

Austco Ltd has capital of $100,000,000 made up by equity of $50,000,000 and debt of $50,000,000. Superfund 1 (a complying superannutation fund) has a 5% equity interest in Austco Ltd and Superfund 2 (another complying superannuation fund) holds 5% of the debt interests in Austco Ltd. Assume that the ACE allowance is 3% and that Austco Ltd's revenues represent a

5% return on its debt and equity capital. Assume that the interest rate on the debentures is 5%. Assume that the dividend imputation system was abolished on the introduction of the ACE system. The Australian tax position of Austco Ltd, Superfund 1 and Superfund 2 will be as follows:

	$
Austco Ltd	
Assessable income	5,000,000
Less ITAA 1997 s.8-1 deduction for interest	2,500,000
Less ACE allowance	1,500,000
Taxable income	1,000,000
Australian corporate tax @ 30%	300,000
After tax income	700,000
After tax profit	2,200,000
Dividend declared	2,200,000
Superfund 1	
Dividend included in assessable income via ITAA 1936 s.44(1)(a)	110,000
Tax at 15%	16,500
After tax dividend	93,500

Effective tax rate on pre tax profit of $125,000 is 25.20%. After tax rate of return on investment of $2,500,000 is 3.74%.

Superfund 2	
Interest included in assessable income via ITAA 1997 s.6-5	125,000
Tax at 15%	18,750
After tax interest	106,250

Effective tax rate on pre tax interest of $125,000 is 15%. After tax rate of return on investment of $2,500,000 is 4.25%.

Again, only if the ACE allowance, the interest rate, the revenue on capital are equal and if 100% of the after tax profits of the company are distributed will the ACE system produce neutrality between domestic debt and equity financing. This is shown in Example 3.2.b

Example 3.2.b

Assume the facts in Example 3.2.a with the variation that the ACE allowance is 5%. Superfund 2 position will be unchanged but the Australian tax positions of Austco Ltd and Superfund 1 will be as follows:

	$
Austco Ltd	
Assessable income	5,000,000
Less ITAA 1997 s.8-1 deduction for interest	2,500,000
Less ACE allowance	2,500,000
Taxable income	0
After tax profit	2,500,000
Dividend declared	2,500,000
Superfund 1	
Dividend included in assessable income via ITAA 1936 s.44(1)(a)	125,000
Interest included in assessable income via ITAA 1997 s.6-5	125,000
Tax at 15%	18,750
After tax interest	106,250

Effective tax rate on pre tax interest of $125,000 is 15%. After tax rate of return on investment of $2,500,000 is 4.25%.

3 Cross Border Investors and ACE

The examples to this point in this part have been confined to the operation of an ACE in relation to domestic investors in domestic companies. As was the case domestically, except where the ACE allowance, the pre-tax return on capital and the interest rate are all equal and 100% of the after tax profit is distributed to shareholders the ACE will not produce neutrality between different forms of funding and will favour one form over another.

The critical test for an ACE from a revenue authority's viewpoint will be how it deals with loans from related entities in low tax juridictions (the situation examined in Example 3.1). The following Examples examine issues with the cross border operation of an ACE where loans are made by a related entity in a low tax jurisdiction.

Example 4.1

Assume the facts in Example 1.1.a with the variation that Australia has replaced the dividend imputation system with an ACE and has repealed ITAA 1936 s.128B(3)(ga). Assume that all the shares in Austco 1 Pty Ltd are owned by Euphorian Co No.1, but that 50% of the capital of Austco 1 Pty Ltd was in the form of loans from Haven Co a company resident in a tax haven where there is a zero rate of corporate tax. The capital of Austco 1 Pty Ltd was $20,000,000. Interest at the rate of 5% was payable to Haven Co. The revenue of Austco 1 Pty Ltd represented 5% of its capital. The ACE allowance is 3%. Haven Co is a wholly owned subsidiary of Euphorian Co No.2 and redistributes interest received as dividends to Euphorian Co No.2. Assume that 10% withholding tax is payable on interest paid to non-residents and that 15% withholding tax is payable on dividends paid to residents of Euphoria.

	$
Austco 1 Pty Ltd's Australian Corporate Tax Position	
Assessable Income	1,000,000
Interest paid to Haven Co	500,000
ACE allowance	300,000
Taxable Income	200,000
Australian corporate tax	60,000
After tax income	140,000
After tax distributable profit	440,000
Dividend	440,000
Australian Tax Treatment of Dividend	
Dividend	440,000
Withholding tax	66,000
After tax dividend	374,000
Australian Tax Treatment of Interest	
Interest	500,000
Withholding tax	50,000
After tax interest	450,000
Haven tax position	
Interest	450,000
Tax paid	0
After tax profit	450,000
Dividend paid to Euphoria Co	450,000
Euphoria Co No.1's tax position	
Dividend from Austco 1 Pty Ltd exempt from Euphorian tax	374,000
After tax dividend	374,000

Effective tax rate on pre tax income of $500,000 25.5%. After tax return on investment of $10,000,000 3.74%.

Euphoria Co No.2's tax position	
Dividend from Haven exempt from Euphorian tax	450,000
After tax dividends	450,000

Effective tax rate on pre tax interest of $500,000 10%. After tax return on investment of $10,000,000 4.5%.

If, instead of exempting foreign non-portfolio dividends, Euphoria provided an indirect foreign tax credit for foreign underlying tax on non-portfolio shareholdings the Australian tax position would be unchanged, as would the tax position of Haven and Euphoria Co No. 2, but Euphoria Co No. 1 would pay net Euphorian tax of $24,000, its effective tax rate would be 30% and the after tax return on its investment of $10,000,000 would be 3.5%. The effective tax rate on the dividend when it left Australia was 25.5%. The foreign tax credit system in Euphoria would mean that part of the benefit of the ACE allowance would accrue to the Euphorian treasury.

The conclusion is that under an ACE system Australia would need to maintain thin capitalisation rules and would need to maintain some rules for distinguishing between debt and equity. The chapter also demonstrates that, if an ACE were accompanied by the abolition of the dividend imputation system, funding biases between debt and equity would be reintroduced for domestic shareholders. There is evidence that Australian shareholders value franking credits and hence abolishing the dividend imputation system in conjunction with the introduction of an ACE would encounter transitional and political difficulties.

4 Allowance for Corporate Capital and Franked Debt

The second alternative considered in this chapter is the adoption of an allowance for corporate capital (under which companies would be granted a deduction for a deemed rate of return on both their debt and equity capital but would be denied further deductions in relation to either interest or dividends paid)[21] married with an extension of the franking system to cover returns on debt interests.

The way in which such a system would operate domestically is shown in Example 5.1

Example 5.1

Assume that Australia adopts an ACC system but retains the dividend imputation system and extends the imputation system to returns on debt interests. Assume that Austco 1 Ltd has income of $10,000,000 and has equity of $100,000,000 which represents its total corporate capital. Assume that the ACC allowance is 5%. Assume that Superfund 1 (a complying Superannuation fund) has a 5% shareholding in Austco 1 Ltd. Assume that Austco 1 Ltd distributes all of its after tax profits as dividends. Austco 2 Ltd has total corporate capital of $100,000,001 represented by $1 of equity and $100,000,000 of widely issued debentures. Assume that Superfund 2

---

21 This is derived from the Boadway and Bruce proposal, supra note 13 and from R A De Mooij and M P Devereux, 'An applied analysis of ACE and CBIT reforms in the EU' (2011) 18(1) International Tax and Public Finance 93 who at 99 regard an ACC as replicating a combined ACE-CBIT (comprehensive business income tax). Proposals for an ACC and for a combined ACE-CBIT can and do differ according to the deemed rate of return allowed as a deduction but, it is submitted, that this difference is not significant in the context of the issues examined in this chapter. The more significant point is that both these systems allow a deemed rate of return deduction, and that only, on the cost of both debt and equity capital in a company.

(a complying Superannuation fund) owns 5% of the debentures issued by Austco 2 Ltd. Assume that the interest rate on the debentures is 10%. The tax effects will be as follows:

	$
Austco 1 Ltd	
Assessable income	10,000,000
ACC allowance	5,000,000
Taxable income	5,000,000
Corporate tax	1,500,000
Dividend	8,500,000
Franking credit attached	1,500,000

Effective corporate rate becomes 15%.

	$
Superfund 1	
Dividend	425,000
Gross up for franking credit	75,000
Grossed up dividend	500,000
Tax at 15%	75,000
Tax offset	75,000
Net tax	0
After tax dividend	425,000
Austco 2 Ltd	
Assessable income	10,000,000
ACC allowance	5,000,000
Taxable income	5,000,000
Corporate tax	1,500,0000
Interest payment*	8,500,000
Franking credit attached	1,500,000
Superfund 2	
Interest received	425,000
Gross up for franking credit	75,000
Grossed up interest	500,000
Tax on grossed up interest at 15%	75,000
Tax offset	75,000
Net tax	0
After tax dividend	425,000

*Terms of debenture issues and loan contracts would need to provide for the grossing up of interest payments by the franking credit attached to the payment. That is, legislation would need to provide that franking credits attached to a payment could be taken into account in determining whether the company had met its requirements to pay interest at a specified rate. Effectively, the corporate tax here is functioning like a withholding tax.

The effective tax rates for both Superfund 1 and Superfund 2 have been 15%. The effective tax rate is the same as it would have been under the present Australian dividend imputation system. The difference is that instead of a

30% tax rate applying at the Australian company level with a refund of tax at the rate of 15% applying at the Superannuation fund level, the effective rate of tax at the company level has been 15% while the effective rate at the Superannuation fund level has been 0%.

If an Australian resident individual with no other income held 1% of the shares in Austco 1 Ltd the individual's effective tax rate would have been 19.45%, which is the same as his effective rate would have been if the individual had derived $100,000 of income from other Australian sources. The effective tax rate is also the same as it would have been if the Australian dividend imputation system had been maintained. The difference again is that the effective Australian corporate tax rate has been reduced from 30% to 15% while instead of there being a refundable tax offset at the shareholder level there is an effective tax rate of 4.45% at the shareholder level.

If an Australian resident individual with no other income held 1% of the debentures issued by Austco 2 Ltd that individual's effective tax rate would have been 19.45%. This is also the same effective rate as would have applied if the individual had derived $100,000 of income from other Australian sources. The effective tax rate is also the same as it would have been if the Australian dividend imputation system had been maintained. The difference here is that instead of there being no corporate tax there has been corporate tax payable of 15% and, at the investor's level, instead of tax of 19.45% being payable only tax at the rate of 4.45% has been payable.

In Example 5.1 although the Australian corporate tax collected is less in both instances the combined effect of an ACC system and a dividend imputation system is that the overall Australian tax payable is the same as it would be under the dividend imputation system. There is no economic double taxation, no substantial discrimination against the corporate form, and equal treatment is given to debt and equity financing.

If exsting Australian withholding tax rules continued and were adapted to an ACC and franked debt system then the overall effect would be to reduce the effective rate of Australian corporate tax and to increase the amount of distributions to non residents that were subject to dividend or interest withholding tax. In those instances in Part 1 where the non-resident did not benefit from Australia not levying dividend withholding tax on the franked portion of a dividend it was noted that this effect arose because an indirect foreign tax credit was not available in the investor's home country. As the effect of the ACC and franked debt system would be to reduce the effective rate of Australian corporate tax while increasing the amount of Australian withholding tax the system should, depending on comparative rates between countries, eliminate or at least mitigate the Treasury effect. This is illustrated in Example 5.2.

Example 5.2

Assume the facts in Example 1 1.b.ii with the variation that Australia adopts an ACC/Franked Debt system. Assume that Austco Ltd is an aggregate of Australian companies in which the Utopian company has portfolio shareholdings. The aggregate corporate capital of these companies is represented by $10,000,000 of equity.

	$
Austco Ltd's Australian Tax Position	
Assessable income	1,000,000
ACC allowance	500,000
Deductions	$0
Taxable Income	500,000
Corporate tax	150,000
After tax distributable profit	850,000
Dividend	850,000

Dividend divides into $350,000 exempt from withholding tax and $500,000 subject to 15% withholding tax.

Utopian Tax Position at Company Level	
Dividend	775,000
Gross up for withholding tax	75,000
Grossed up dividend	850,000
Utopian corporate tax	255,000
Foreign tax credit	75,000
Net Utopian tax	180,000
After tax dividend	595,000

If the Utopian company distributes the $595,000 to each of its 7 Utopian shareholders equally they will each receive a divdend of $85,000. The after tax position of each shareholder will be:

Dividend	85,000
Utopian shareholder tax	20,672
After tax dividend	64,328

The effective tax rate for Utopian shareholders would be 54.9%. This compares with the effective rate of 66.36% in Example 1.1.b.ii and is almost the same as the effective rate of 54.66% which would have applied if the Utopian shareholders had invested in a Utopian company which had derived $1,000,000 or income, paid Utopian tax and distributed all of its after tax income equally as divider ds. The total Australian tax would be $225,000 as compared with $300,000 in Example 2.b.ii. The loss of Australian corporate tax would be partially offset by increased Australian tax in the situation where Austco Ltd was furded wholly by debt.

If the Utopian company had debt interests on which interest were payable at the rate of 10% instead of shares in Austco Ltd then both the Utopian company and the Utopian individual shareholder would be in the same position as they would be when the investment by the Utopian company was wholly funded by equity. The effective tax rate for underlying Utopian shareholders would again be 54.9%. Here the Australian tax is higher by $50,000 than it would be under the present Australian system and the ACC/franked debt system is neutral between debt and equity financing. The effective rate of tax at the underlying Utopian shareholder level under the present Australian system would have been 48.51%. The higher effective rate of tax under the ACC/Franked Debt system is due to the higher rate of Australian source country tax and the fact that a portion of the Australian tax is corporate tax, for which a foreign tax credit is not allowed in Utopia, rather than withholding tax for which a foreign tax credit is allowed in Utopia. Possible approaches which would reduce the overall effective rate of tax without reducing the amount of Australian tax are discussed in Part 5 of this chapter.

It is extremely unlikely that companies would be wholly funded by foreign portfolio debt but it is clear that difficulties arise when tax is imposed at the corporate level on returns on debt and where debt deductions are limited. Usuually a company will have a blend of debt and equity financing with the result that lenders will should still be able to receive their full nominal interest entitlement before any source country withholding tax.

On the other hand, in some situations identified in Part 1, although there was no treasury effect, the non-resident investor was worse off investing in Australia than investing at home because the overall rates of tax were higher in Australia than at home. In those situations where the home country granted exemption treatment to foreign source dividends but gave foreign tax credit treatment to foreign source interest the introduction of an ACC/franked debt system should not alter the present position significantly. The non-portfolio dividend portion would continue to be exempt while the interest portion would probably generate excess foreign tax credits. Despite the use of an ACC/Franked Debt system in Australia there would appear to be an equity bias in the non-portfolio investor situation where the Australian corporate rate is lower than the home country corporate rate when non-portfolio foreign source dividends are exempt from home country tax while foreign interest receives a foreign tax credit. Here the non-portfolio dividend will be exempt from home country tax while the interest income will be subject to it, with a smaller amount of withholding tax to credit against any home country tax liability.

Importantly, by treating debt and equity virtually equivalently for Australian tax purposes the ACC/Franked Debt system would eliminate the planning possiblities illustrated by Example 2.1 This is shown in Example 5.3.

Example 5.3

Assume the facts in Example 2.1 with the variation that Australia has adopted an ACC/Franked Debt system. Assume that the corporate capital of Austco Ltd is $10,000,000 and that the ACC allowance is 5%. Assume a 'proportionate franking' rule (discussed in Part 4) applies to all distributions.

Austco Ltd's Australian tax position will be:

Income	1,000,000
ACC allowance	500,000
Taxable income	500,000
Tax @ 30%	150,000
Interest paid	750,000
Dividend	100,000

Proportionate franking will mean that 150 x 750/850 franking credits are attached to the interest and 150 x 100/850 franking credits are attached to the dividend.

Dividend withholding tax ($100,000 - $41176.45) x 15%	8,823,53
Interest withholding tax ($750,000 - $108,823.44) x 10%	64,117.66
Haven Tax Position	
Interest received	685,882.34
Dividend paid	685,882.34
Euphorian Tax Position	
Dividend received from Austco 1 Pty Ltd	91,176.47
Dividend received from subsidiary in Haven	685,882.34
Euphorian tax	$0
Total dividend received	777,058.81
Euphorian shareholder	
Dividend received	111,008.40
Euphorian shareholder tax	30,685.13
After tax dividend	80,323.27

The effective tax rate for the Euphorian underlying shareholder has been 43.77% as compared with 42.34% (the effective tax rate which would have applied if a single Euphorian shareholder had received a redistribution of all the after Eurphorian tax profits of a Euphorian company with Euphorian source income of $1,000,000) and as compared with 39.50% in Example 2.1. The Euphorian company and its underlying shareholder have gained little advantage by lending to Austco 1 Pty Ltd via a Haven subsidiary. On the other hand, if the Euphorian company had invested entirely in $10,000,000 of debentures issued by the Australian company at an interest rate of 10% the after tax dividend for any one of seven underlying Euphorian shareholder would be $71,795.86 and the effective tax rate would be 49.74%. Part 4 of this chapter examines an approach for reducing this advantage.

These examples also demonstrate that, except for the differences noted, and differences in withholding taxes, the adoption of an ACC/franked debt system would neutralise the choice between debt and equity investments in Australian companies for foreign resident taxpayers. This would mean that there would be no need for thin capitalisation rules or for rules distinguishing between debt and equity. For portfolio investors in Australian equities the effective rate of Autralian corporate tax would be reduced although for foreign debt investors the effective rate of Australian corporate tax would be increased. The effects of the tax system on these forms of investment would be largely neutral and it would be expected that the choice between them would be determined by non-tax factors.

Limiting the deduction for all interest to the deemed rate of return should mean that this system would have a lower revenue cost than an ACE system. Combining an ACC system with an extended imputation system should also mean that any bias against the corporate form in an ACE system is eliminated and any retention bias is reduced. To the extent that it produces a lower effective rate of Australian corporate tax an ACC/Franked Debt system would be more attractive to foreign portfolio equity investors than the current Australian system. The narrower corporate tax base would reduce the amount of Australian corporate tax paid by non-resident equity investors and would increase the amount of payments that were subject to withholding tax when paid to non-residents. For portfolio equity investors this would be advantageous as many tax systems allow portfolio investors a foreign tax credit for withholding taxes but not for underlying corporate taxes.

The interaction between an ACC system, franked debt, and alternative treatments of foreign source of Australian companies is discussed in Part 5.

5 Adapting New Zealand's Foreign Investor Tax Credit Regime to reduce any bias against debt in an ACC/ Franked Debt System.

The most problematic situation discussed in Part 3 arose where foreign investors in Australian companies via debt interests were in a poorer position than they would have been if they had made debt investments in companies in their home country. This was because, under an ACC/franked debt system, not only was a greater amount of Australian tax payable but it was in the form of Australian corporate tax for which foreign lenders did not receive a foreign tax credit in their home country. This problem could be mitigated to some extent, but not eliminated, by adapting the New Zealand foreign investor tax credit system to an ACC/franked debt system. Example 6.1 illustrates the effects of such an approach.

Example 6.1

Austco Pty Ltd issues $10,000,000 of debentures with interest payable at 10% to a Euphorian company. The corporate tax rate in Euphoria is 20%. Euphoria applies a foreign tax credit to foreign interest receipts and has individual tax rates identical to Australian tax rates. Australia permits a supplementary interest/dividend payment to be made in these circumstances calculated using the formula of the franked portion of the payment multiplied by w/1-w where 'w' is the relevant withholding tax rate for the type of payment. A proportionate franking rule has been used in calculating the franked portion of the payment.

	$
Austco Ltd's Australian corporate and withholding tax position will be	
Assessable income	1,000,000
ACC allowance	500,000
Australian corporate tax	150,000
Interest paid	850,000

The franked portion of the interest paid will be $350,000. A supplementary interest payment of $350,000 x 10/90 = $38,888.89, funded from the Australian corporate tax payable, will be allowed making the total interest payment $888,888.89 which will be subject to withholding tax at the rate of 10%. The withholding tax payable will be $88,888.89. It can be seen that $50,000 of the withholding tax has been payable on the unfranked portion and $38,888,89 has been payable on the franked portion.

The Euphorian tax effects will be as follows:

Euphorian company level	
Interest	800,000
Gross up for withholding tax	88,888.89
Grossed up interest	888,888.89
Euphorian corporate tax	177,777.77
Foreign tax credit	88,888.89
Net Euphorian tax	88,888.89
After tax interest	711,111.11

Euphorian Shareholder Level

Dividend	101,587.30
Euphorian Shareholder Tax	27,058.11
After tax dividend	74,529.19

The effective tax rate on the underlying Euphorian shareholder has been 47.82% as compared with 49.74% in which would have applied if Australia had not permitted a supplementary interest payment which was subject to withholding tax. As the effective tax rate on a Euphorian shareholder who received a dividend from a Euphorian company that had derived $1,000,000 of pre tax interest (representing pre tax interest of $142,857.14 per shareholder) would have been 42.36% the use of the foreign investor tax credit has not produced CEN at the underlying Euphorian shareholder level in this situation. The result has been between CEN and national neutrality (NN).

An adaptation of the New Zealand foreign investor tax credit regime also produces a result closer to NN where a pension fund invests directly in Australian debentures. If the Euphorian pension fund (Euphosuper) held debentures in Australian companies as portfolio investments then the effective rate of tax on the Euphosuper would be 24.44%. If Euphosuper had invested in debentures issued by a Euphorian company then the effective tax rate would have been 15%. If an adaptation of the New Zealand foreign investor tax credit system had not been in place then the effective rate of tax on Euphosuper would have been 27.75%.

Example 6.1 shows that an adaptation of the New Zealand foreign investor tax credit system would provide little benefit to a foreign lender while Australian withholding tax rates on interest remained at 10%. Paradoxically, the New Zealand foreign investor tax credit system produces greater benefits for foreign investors the higher the rate of withholding tax. This is because it has the effect of converting a non creditable payment of underlying corporate tax to a payment of withholding tax for which the foreign investor receives a foreign tax credit. Hence, counter intuitively, if Australia were to adopt an ACC/franked debt system it could align its withholding tax rates on portfolio investments with the corporate rate and combine that alignment with an adaptation of the New Zealand foreign investor tax credit system. This would produce the same amount of Australian tax but would provide the foreign investor with a larger foreign tax credit. In a taxation treaty context this would be likely to produce an absence of reciprocity of withholding tax rates an issue which countries using split rate systems have found to be problematic in the past. The argument that could be envisaged in negotiations would be whether the receiprocity principle and maintaining residence country revenues were more important than providing benenfits to investors from residence countries. In tax policy terms the context would be between an approach closer to CEN as opposed to one closer to NN.

One issue merits further comment. As noted in Part 1, because franking credits are regarded as being more valuable to resident shareholder than they are to non-resident shareholders, Australian tax law currently contains several provisions designed to prevent dividend streaming. The examples above show that in some circumstances under an ACC/franked debt system there would be an issue of how many franking credit should be allocated to a particular interest and dividend distributions. Time and space do not permit a comprehensive analysis of this issue in this chapter, but the author's view is that the best option here is to adopt a proportionate franking rule under which franking credits are attached to distributions in the same proportions as the distribution represents of the after tax distributable profit of the company. Such an approach would remove the need for anti dividend streaming provisions.

6 Conclusion

While further work would need to be done by economists on likely revenue costs and on technical details (such as establishing an appropriate deemed rate of return) the conclusion of this chapter is that if Australia were to adopt an ACC system coupled with franked debt and a proportionate franking ordering rule the result would be a more attractive environment for inbound investment at a lower revenue cost than under an ACE system and would enable several complex divisions (such as those dealing with thin capitalisation, debt and equity and dividend streaming) to be removed from Australian tax law. While implementation details would necessarily have to be varied due to historic features of particular national systems the proposed system would also merit consideration by similarly placed small to medium sized resource rich open economies.

Bibliography

Australia, Review of Australia's Future Tax System: Report to the Treasurer, Part 2 –Detailed Analysis, Canberra, 2009, Volume 1 of 2

Australia, Department of the Treasury, Business Tax Working Group, Discussion Paper (August 2012), pp5-6 and 44-49 http://www.treasury.gov.au/Policy-Topics/Taxation/BTWG (Accessed 22nd January 2013)

R S Avi-Yonah, "Globalisation, Tax Competition and the Fiscal Crisis of the Welfare State' (2000) 113 *Harvard Law Review* 1573

R Boadway and N Bruce, 'A General Proposition on the Design of a Neutral Business Tax' (1984) 24 *Journal of Public Economics* 231

G S Cooper, 'Implementing an allowance for corporate equity' (2012) 27 *Australian Tax Forum* 241

R A De Mooij and M P Devereux, 'An applied analysis of ACE and CBIT reforms in the EU' (2011) 18(1) *International Tax and Public Finance* 93

M P Devereux, 'Issues in the Design of Taxes on Corporate Profit' (2012) 65 *National Tax Journal* 709

F Gilders, J Taylor, M Walpole, M Burton and T Ciro, *Understanding Taxation Law 2014*, Lexis Nexis, 2014

M J Graetz, "Taxing International Income: Inadequate Principles, Outdated Concepts, and Unsatisfactory Policies" (2001) 54 *Tax Law Review* 261

Institute for Fiscal Studies, Capital Taxes Group, *Equity for Companies: A Corporation Tax for the 1990s*, London, Institute for Fiscal Studies, 1991

Peggy B Musgrave, *United States Taxation of Foreign Investment Income: Issues and Arguments*, International Tax Program, Harvard Law School, Cambridge, Mass., 1969

Peggy Musgrave in *United States Taxation of Foreign Investment Income* (1969)

P B Sorensen and S M Johnson, 'Taxing Capital Income: Options for Reform in Australia', Melbourne Institute, Australia's Future Tax and Transfer Policy Conference, June 2009

R H Woellner, S Barkoczy, S Murphy, C Evans and D Pinto, *Australian Taxation Law*, 24th edition, 2014, CCH

Lightning Source UK Ltd.
Milton Keynes UK
UKHW021250190122
397396UK00006B/256